# SUPPORTING TEACHING & LEARNING
# IN SCHOOLS (Primary)

**Louise Burnham**

**Brenda Baker**

www.pearsonschoolsandfe.co.uk

✓ Free online support
✓ Useful weblinks
✓ 24 hour online ordering

0845 630 44 44

Part of Pearson

Heinemann is an imprint of Pearson Education Limited, Edinburgh Gate, Harlow, Essex, CM20 2JE.

www.pearsonschoolsandfecolleges.co.uk
Heinemann is a registered trademark of Pearson Education Limited.
Text © Louise Burnham, Brenda Baker 2010

Edited by Juliet Mozley
Designed by AM design
Typeset by Phoenix Photosetting, Chatham, Kent
Original illustrations © Pearson Education 2010
Illustrated by Phoenix Photosetting/Gemma Correll
Cover design by Wooden Ark
Picture research by Susie Prescott
Cover photo © Masterfile UK Ltd
Printed in Malaysia (CTP-PJB)

First published 2010

15
10 9 8

**British Library Cataloguing in Publication Data**
A catalogue record for this book is available from the British Library.

ISBN 978-0-435032-04-3

**Websites**
The websites used in this book were correct and up to date at the time of publication. Pearson Education Limited is not responsible for the content of any external Internet sites. It is essential for tutors to preview each website before using it in class so as to ensure that the URL is still accurate, relevant and appropriate. We suggest that tutors bookmark useful websites and consider enabling students to access them through the school/college intranet.

**Acknowledgements**
Pearson Education Ltd would like to thank Claire Dickinson for providing all information and features relating to Functional Skills in this book.

# Contents

# Acknowledgements

Louise Burnham would like to thank the following individuals for their help and advice during the writing of this book:

Sue Robertson and Unicorn Primary School in Beckenham for allowing me to reproduce excerpts from school policies; Val Hughes and Sandhurst Junior School in Catford for a copy of their feedback form; Graham Jameson and Edmund Waller School in New Cross for their example of a staffing structure; Downderry Primary School in Downham for their accident report form; Lewisham Local Authority for a copy of a teaching assistant's job description; Helen Collins for her literacy plan; Richard Rieser and Disability Equality in Education for their medical and social model of disability; Linda Mellor and Elizabeth Evans for their thorough proofreading; Virginia Carter, Juliet Mozley and Céline Clavel for all of their support during this project; and as always, Tom, Lucy and Richard for putting up with my unsociable working hours!

The publisher would like to thank the following organisations for permission to reproduce material: retributive and restorative justice table, Transforming Conflict, an organisation which supports schools wanting to develop a whole-school approach based on the principles of restorative justice, p.83; BSI, Kitemark logo, p.137; the British Toy & Hobby Association, Lion Mark logo, p.137; Health and Safety Checklist Rounders England 2010, p.303.

The publisher would like to thank the following for their kind permission to reproduce photographs: Alamy Images: Image Source p.89, Juice Images p.33, Keith Morris p.1, Myrleen Pearson p.64; Corbis: JLP/Jose L. Pelaez p.324, Ocean p.315; Education Photos: John Walmsley p.169; Getty Images: Bachrach/Archive photos p.157; Pearson Education Ltd: Gareth Boden p.32, Jules Selmes p.39, p.56, p.57, p.77, p.88, p.93, p.103, p.132, p.133, p.140, p.148, p.149, p.151, p.152, p.168, p.205, p.215, p.227, p.233, p.235, p.245, p.251, p.259, p.269, p.280, p.289, p.298, p.301, p.319; Tudor Photography p.182; Ian Wedgewood p.105, p.193, p.230; PhotoDisc: Kevin Peterson p.72, p.102; Photoshot Holdings Limited: p.329; Shutterstock.com: Andresr p.219, Arrow Studio LLC p.187, Imagery Majestic p.186, Photobank.ch p.114, VG Studio p.342; Thinkstock: Brand X Pictures p.311, Katy McDonnell/Digital Vision p.273.

Thank you to the staff and children of Madley Brook and Springfield Schools, Witney and St Barnabus School, Oxford.

All other images © Pearson Education

Every effort has been made to contact copyright holders of material reproduced in this book. Any omissions will be rectified in subsequent printings if notice is given to the publishers.

# Introduction

Welcome to this handbook for the Level 3 Diploma for Supporting Teaching and Learning in Schools (Primary edition). If you are using this book you will be setting out to be or already working in school as a teaching assistant.

You may find yourself referred to under the general title of 'teaching assistant' within your school, but you may also be called a classroom assistant, school assistant, individual support assistant, special needs assistant or learning support assistant. These different job titles have come into effect due to the different types of work which assistants are required to do within the classroom. In recent years the role of the teaching assistant has developed and become professionalised so that qualifications now exist at different levels. These reflect the diverse job roles which are now present in schools for learning support staff.

This book contains everything you need to complete your Level 3 Diploma in Specialist Support for Teaching and Learning in Schools.

As you work towards this qualification, you will be developing your skills and expertise in a number of areas and you will need to think about how the theory fits in with your experiences in the classroom. As you gain experience and expertise in your work with children and young people, you may also find it a useful reference, particularly for specific issues such as working with bilingual children.

Level 3 is made up of a number of different units of assessment which sit within the QCF (Qualifications and Credit Framework). When you complete a unit successfully you will gain a certain number of credits.

The credit value of each unit indicates the size of the unit and approximately how long it will take to achieve. Credit is based on how long an average learner would take to complete a unit, and 1 credit is roughly equal to 10 hours of learning, including time spent in the following ways:

- classes or group sessions
- tutorials
- practical work
- assessments.

It also includes any time you spend that is not supervised, for example doing homework, independent research or work experience.

## Units of assessment

The units that make up these qualifications have been developed by the Sector Skills Councils responsible for setting and monitoring standards for specific occupational groups. In the case of Supporting Teaching and Learning, this is the Training and Development Agency, known as TDA. You will see that the unit reference numbers (see table page vii) carry the prefix TDA, which shows that TDA is the Sector Skills Council who developed or owns the units. There are other Sector Skills Councils or awarding organisations that work closely with TDA, and you may come across these acronyms linked to other units that you study:

- SfCD – Skills for Care and Development
- CWDC – Children's Workforce Development Council
- ASDAN – Award Scheme Development and Accreditation Network.

## Level 3 overview

Although the units in the new qualification are not exactly the same as the National Occupational Standards that made up NVQs, the areas they cover are similar. Each unit has several learning outcomes and each of these is broken down into a number of assessment criteria. All the learning outcomes of the unit have to be assessed in order for you to complete the unit.

The Level 3 Diploma in Specialist Support for Teaching and Learning in Schools is made up of two groups of units:

- Mandatory units
- Optional Group A units.

Everyone taking this qualification needs to complete all 11 units in the Mandatory group (32 credits), and then choose additional units from the Optional Group to make the full credit total of 44. There are certain rules of combination that apply to the optional units, so check with your tutor or assessor to see which ones you can choose.

# List of units in this book

| Unit reference No. | Unit title | Credit value |
|---|---|---|
| **Mandatory units** | | |
| TDA 3.1 | Communication and professional relationships with children, young people and adults | 2 |
| TDA 3.2 | Schools as organisations | 3 |
| TDA 3.3 | Support learning activities | 4 |
| TDA 3.4 | Promote children and young people's positive behaviour | 3 |
| TDA 3.5 | Develop professional relationships with children, young people and adults | 2 |
| TDA 3.6 | Promote equality, diversity and inclusion in work with children and young people | 2 |
| TDA 3.7 | Support assessment for learning | 4 |
| SfCD SHC 32 | Engage in personal development | 3 |
| CYP 3.4 | Support children and young people's health and safety | 2 |
| CYP 3.1 | Understand child and young person development | 4 |
| CYP 3.3 | Understand how to safeguard the well-being of children and young people | 3 |
| **Optional units (Group A)** | | |
| TDA 3.10 | Plan and deliver learning activities under the direction of a teacher | 4 |
| TDA 3.11 | Support literacy development | 3 |
| TDA 3.12 | Support numeracy development | 3 |
| TDA 3.17 | Support bilingual learners | 4 |
| TDA 3.18 | Provide bilingual support for teaching and learning | 6 |
| TDA 3.19 | Support disabled children and young people and those with special educational needs | 5 |
| TDA 3.20 | Support children and young people with behaviour, emotional and social development needs | 4 |
| CYPOP 44 | Facilitate the learning and development of children and young people through mentoring | 4 |
| TDA 3.25 | Lead an extracurricular activity | 3 |
| LLUK | Engage parents in their children's early learning | 3 |
| ASDAN TW3 | Team working | 3 |

## Assessing your skills and knowledge

Your awarding organisation, such as Edexcel, CACHE or City & Guilds, will allow you to be assessed using a range of different methods, based on the learning outcomes and assessment criteria in the unit. Your assessor or tutor will provide you with help and support throughout the assessment process. Some common assessment methods are described below but others may be used as well:

- knowledge, understanding and skills competence that you demonstrate through your practice in a work setting and that are observed directly by your assessor

- evidence from an expert witness who may be an experienced practitioner who has worked alongside you, or others with suitable backgrounds who can vouch for your practice

- questions (oral and written) and professional discussion, usually with your assessor, which allows you to talk about what you know

- assignments and projects of different types

- assessment of your work products such as plans, displays, observations, materials you have made to support children

- recognised prior learning.

Sometimes your awarding organisation will insist on a specific method such as a test or an assignment. Again your tutor or assessor will provide you with help and support to decide the best approach.

## Units that must be assessed in the workplace

In this qualification, TDA require that the following assessment criteria **must** be assessed in an appropriate setting, for example a primary school or secondary school:

| | |
|---|---|
| **TDA 3.3** | Assessment criteria 1.3, 1.4, 1.5, 2.1, 2.2, 2.3, 3.1, 3.3, 3.4, 3.5, 4.1, 4.2, 4.3, 5.2 |
| **TDA 3.4** | Assessment criteria 2.2, 2.3, 2.4, 2.5, 3.1, 3.2, 3.3, 3.4, 4.1, 4.2, 4.3, 4.4, 4.5, 5.1, 5.2, 5.3, 5.4 |
| **TDA 3.6** | Assessment criteria 1.4, 1.5, 3.3 |
| **TDA 3.7** | Assessment criteria 2.1, 2.2, 2.3, 2.4, 2.5, 3.1, 3.2, 3.3, 3.4, 4.1, 4.2 |
| **TDA 3.10** | Assessment criteria 1.3, 1.4, 2.1, 2.2, 2.3, 2.4, 3.1, 3.2, 3.3, 3.4, 3.5 |
| **TDA 3.11** | Assessment criteria 2.1, 2.2, 3.1, 3.2, 3.3, 3.4, 3.5 |
| **TDA 3.12** | Assessment criteria 2.1, 2.2, 3.1, 3.2, 3.3 |
| **TDA 3.17** | Assessment criteria 1.1, 1.2, 2.3, 2.4, 3.1, 3.2, 3.3, 3.4, 3.5 |
| **TDA 3.18** | Assessment criteria 1.1, 1.2, 1.4, 1.5, 2.1, 2.2, 2.3, 2.4, 2.5, 2.6, 3.1, 3.2, 3.3, 3.4, 4.1, 4.2, 4.3, 4.4 |
| **TDA 3.19** | Assessment criteria 3.1, 3.3, 3.4, 3.5, 4.1, 4.2, 4.3, 5.1, 5.2, 5.3 |
| **TDA 3.20** | Assessment criteria 3.1, 3.3, 3.4, 3.5, 3.6, 4.1, 4.2, 4.3, 4.4, 4.5, 4.6, 5.1, 5.2, 5.3, 5.4 |
| **CYPOP 44** | Assessment criteria 2.1, 2.2, 2.3, 3.1, 3.2, 4.1, 4.2 |
| **TDA 3.25** | Assessment criteria 2.1, 2.2, 2.3, 2.4, 3.1, 3.2, 3.3, 3.4, 3.5, 4.1, 4.2, 4.3, 4.4, 4.5, 4.6, 5.1, 5.2 |

# How to use this book

All the units in this book are matched closely to the specifications of each unit in the syllabus and follow the unit learning outcomes and assessment criteria — making it easy for you to work through the criteria and be sure you are covering everything you need to know.

This book is accompanied by a DVD which contains short clips of teaching assistants carrying out a variety of activities in primary school settings. Look out for the 'DVD activity' boxes which indicate there is a clip you can view.

# Key features of the book

 An activity that brings learning to life and suggests how to introduce new ideas, activities or practice into your school or setting

 A real-life scenario exploring major issues to broaden your understanding of key topics; demonstrates how theory relates to everyday practice and poses reflective questions

 An activity that helps you to create or gather evidence for your portfolio

 An activity that encourages you to reflect on your own performance

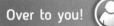 A short task to enhance your understanding of a piece of information (for example Internet research or a practical idea you could introduce in your school)

 A short activity linked thematically to the unit, specifically designed to develop your professional skills

 Highlights where content in the unit enables you to apply Functional Skills in the broad areas of English, ICT and Maths (matched to the FS Standards at Level 2). The tips and explanations given show how Functional Skills can be contextualised to work in early years and will be of particular benefit to learners on Apprenticeship programmes

 Several activities based on video footage showing other teaching assistants in everyday situations

**Key term** — Simple definitions of some of the more complex terms or pieces of jargon used in the book

**Link** — Highlights where text gives evidence for Assessment Criteria or where related information can be found in other units

**Getting ready for assessment** — An activity to help you generate evidence for assessment of the unit

**Check your knowledge** — At the end of each unit, questions to help you consolidate your understanding and ensure you are ready to move on to the next unit

**BEST PRACTICE CHECKLIST** — A checklist of key points to help you remember the main underpinning knowledge in a unit

**School Life** — Some units end with a full-page magazine-inspired feature covering a key issue or topic, with expert guidance relating to problems that may be encountered in your working life. It contains the following 'mini-features':

- **My Story** — a teaching assistant's personal account; sometimes inspirational or uplifting, other times sharing a problem
- **Ask the expert** — questions and answers relating to working practice
- **Viewpoint** — topical issues discussed around the wider issues of supporting teaching and learning.

# TDA 3.1 Communication & professional relationships with children, young people & adults

A central part of your role is to help children to develop positive relationships with others. Children will not only learn cognitive skills while at school: they need to learn how to work and play together co-operatively and to develop positive relationships with their peers and with adults from other backgrounds and cultures. You should demonstrate good relationships in your interactions to be an effective role model. You will need to demonstrate that you know and understand the boundaries of information which can be passed on, and the importance of observing school policies around confidentiality.

## By the end of this unit you will:

1. understand the principles of developing positive relationships with children, young people and adults

2. understand how to communicate with children, young people and adults

3. understand legislation, policies and procedures for confidentiality and sharing information, including data protection.

# Understand the principles of developing positive relationships with children, young people and adults

## Why effective communication is important

In order to contribute to **positive relationships**, you will need to demonstrate and model effective communication skills in your dealings with others. This means that you should consider both how you approach other people and how you respond to them. We are more likely to communicate information to one another if we have positive relationships. Parents and other adults who come into the school are more likely to give beneficial support if communication is strong and effective – this, in turn, benefits pupils. It is also important for pupils that we model effective communication skills. This means checking what we are saying sometimes in moments of stress or excitement, so that they can understand what our expectations are in school. If we ask pupils to behave in a particular way when communicating and then forget to do so ourselves, they will find it harder to understand the boundaries of what is acceptable.

Effective communication and positive relationships do not happen by chance. You should think about the way you relate to others and the messages that this sends out. In situations where communication breaks down, misunderstandings can lead to bad feeling.

### Key term

**Positive relationships** – relationships that benefit children and young people, and their ability to participate in and benefit from the setting

**CASE STUDY:** The importance of effective communication

Trudy is working as a teaching assistant in a small infant school. She usually 'floats' between classes and is asked to give support where it is needed. This morning she has been asked to work with an individual pupil in Year 2 where a teaching assistant is off sick. She works in the class until playtime, then goes on duty outside and afterwards takes her break for ten minutes in the staff room before going back into class. The teacher, who does not know that Trudy has been on playground duty, asks her where she has been for the last ten minutes. Trudy is upset at the way she has been spoken to and tells the teacher that she has been having her coffee. However, the teacher misunderstands her and thinks that she has taken a long time coming back after playtime. Both the teacher and Trudy are unhappy and hardly speak to one another until lunchtime.

- Who is in the wrong?
- Do you think that pupils in the class will have noticed this misunderstanding?
- How might this have been handled better by both the teacher and Trudy?

*How good are your relationships with other adults in your work environment?*

# The principles of relationship building

The principles of relationship building with children and adults in any context are that if others are comfortable in our company, they will be more likely to communicate effectively. Where people do not get along or are suspicious of one another, they are likely to avoid one another wherever possible. Positive relationships are not something which should be left to chance and it is important to consider the ways in which we can develop them.

We build relationships with others in school on a daily basis in a number of different ways. Although you may do some of these without necessarily thinking about it, it is worth taking time to consider whether you do all of the following.

---

### Functional skills

**English: Writing**
You could recall a time when communication has broken down with another adult in school and write a brief account of what happened. Using the points on the spidergram reflect on how you could have approached this situation differently. When you write your account, consider the layout and structure of the text.

---

- **Effective communication** — this is the key area for developing relationships with others and also covers many different forms of communication (see below).

- **Showing respect** — in order to develop positive relationships with others, it is very important to be courteous and respectful, and to listen to their points of view. Adults and pupils with whom you work may also be from different cultures and have different beliefs or values from your own. You should ensure that you acknowledge and respect the views of others at all times and take time to remember names and preferred forms of address.

- **Being considerate** — take the time to consider the positions of others. You may be working with a child or adult who is under particular pressure at a given time and need to understand why they may have behaved or reacted in a certain way or out of character.

- **Remembering issues which are personal to them** — it will always help to build positive relationships if you enquire after particular aspects of another person's life — for example, if you know that a colleague is concerned about their child getting into a particular secondary school, or if you are aware that it is a child's birthday.

- **Taking time to listen to others** — make sure that you take time to listen to other people, in particular if they are asking for advice or help, or if they need to confide in you. You should always show that you are interested in what they have to say and respond appropriately.

- **Being clear on key points** — when you have conversations with others in which you are giving them information, you should always ensure that

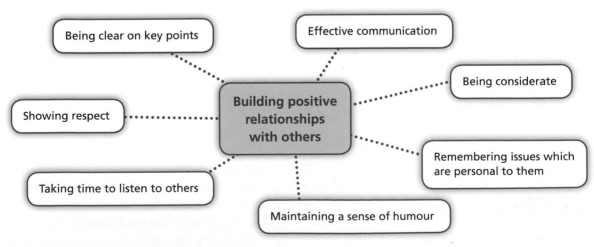

*Do you use all of these when building relationships with others?*

they are clear what you have said at the end of the discussion. This is because it can be easy to be distracted from the main point of the conversation. When talking to children, always ask them to repeat back to you what they need to do.

- **Maintaining a sense of humour** — although the nature of our work in school is important, we should also sometimes take time to see the funny side of different situations. Laughter can be a good icebreaker and is also a great way of relaxing and relieving stress.

## Social, professional and cultural contexts

When communicating with others, you will need to consider the context in which you are working. You will need to adapt the way you communicate in different situations. It is likely that you will do this automatically — for example, you should use more formal language and behaviour in a meeting. Your school will have a range of types of planned communication with other adults — when dealing with other professionals, there will be meetings and discussions as well as more informal communication at different times. However, the spoken word is not the only way in which we communicate — it happens through the way we respond to others, for example, how quickly we respond to an email or phone message, how attentive we are when speaking to someone, how we dress. You may find that the non-spoken forms of communication can be an issue if they are misread by others. You should also remember that different cultures will have their own norms of behaviour which will extend to gestures, body language and eye contact. In some cultures, for example, it is not polite to look another person in the eye when speaking to them.

### Reflect ?

Think about the ways in which your school passes information to adults outside school. They may be parents, carers or outside agencies. You may want to list the methods of communication under 'Formal' and 'Informal' headings.

# Understand how to communicate with children, young people and adults

## Skills needed to communicate with children and young people

You will need to demonstrate a number of skills in order to communicate effectively with children and young people. Although it is likely that you will do this every day without thinking, it is worth reflecting on the ways in which you do this — effective communication is a vital part of your role. Children learn to communicate through the responses of others: if they do not feel that their contribution is valued, they are less likely to initiate communication themselves. You will need to do the following.

- **Find opportunities to speak**. Make sure that pupils are given sufficient opportunities to talk. Some children have very little chance to put their own thoughts forward and express themselves with adults. They may lack confidence and need to be given a chance to 'warm up' first so that they feel able to do so.

- **Make eye contact and actively listen**. If you say that you are listening, but are looking away and are busy doing something else, this gives the child the message that you are not really interested in what they are saying. Make sure that if a pupil is talking, you are giving them your attention.

- **Use body language and facial expressions, and be approachable**. Make sure that you show your interest by the way in which you act when speaking to pupils. For example, with very young children, get down to their level. It can be very intimidating to have someone towering over them. Also make sure that you smile and react in a positive way to what they are saying.

- **React and comment on what they are saying**. You may need to repeat back to pupils to check on your understanding, particularly if they have used incorrect language: for example, 'I bringed my book in today.' 'You have brought your book in today? Oh good, that means we can change it.'

- **Be interested, responding and questioning to maintain conversation**. It is important to model and invite the 'norms' of conversation with children so that they build up an understanding about how it works. They will do this through experience, so show that you are interested and respond to their questions.

For children to be able to communicate effectively, you should encourage them to ask questions and put their ideas forward. Pupils should feel relaxed and confident enough in school to be able to do this, as it is by questioning and finding out that they learn. They should also be able to offer their own suggestions and ideas so that there is a two-way dialogue between adults and pupils rather than a one-way flow of instructions. This also encourages the formation of positive relationships.

---

### Reflect ❓

Think about those pupils with whom you work who are more quiet when communicating with adults. How can you encourage and develop their communication skills?

---

### Functional skills 💬

**ICT: Developing, presenting and communicating information**
You could produce an information leaflet on the computer that you could share with parent helpers or students that come into the setting. You could include some useful guidance and suggestions on how to communicate with the children.

---

## How to adapt communication with children or young people

In order to build relationships with children, you will need to adapt your behaviour and communication accordingly. Children of all ages, cultures and abilities need to feel secure and valued, and your interactions with them should demonstrate this. Through positively communicating with and being involved with children, you will show them that they are part of the school community. However, this is not the same as giving all children attention whenever they demand it!

- **The age of the child or young person** — children of different ages will require varying levels of attention. Younger children may need more reassurance, particularly when first starting school. They may also need to have more physical contact as a result. As children become more mature, they may need more help with talking through issues and reflecting on their thoughts. You will need to adapt your vocabulary and consider how you interact positively with pupils as you listen and respond to them.

- **Context of the communication** — you will be dealing with children in a variety of different situations. You will always need to be mindful of this and adapt your verbal communication accordingly. If you are working on a learning activity, it is important that the children are focused and that you deal with any distractions before they interrupt what you are doing. However, if talking to pupils in more social situations, such as the playground or dining hall, you should use this as an opportunity to develop positive relationships with pupils, although you should always speak to them in a way which maintains the relationship of professional carer to child. Pupils will often question you, for example, about how old you are or what your 'real name' is. It is sometimes best to answer these kinds of questions with humour — for example, 'But Miss Glenn **is** my real name!'

- **Communication differences** — you should ensure care and sensitivity with children who have communication differences, as they will need to take their time and feel unpressured when they are speaking. Some children may not have many opportunities to speak, or may be anxious or nervous. You should adapt the way in which you communicate according to their individual needs. If they have a speech disorder, such as a stammer, or conditions which make communication difficult for them, they should be allowed to take their time. Try not to fill in words for them or guess what they are going to say, as this may add to their distress.

You may need additional training — for example, in sign language — to be able to communi... effectively or know the most effective strate...

to use. In some cases where pupils have special educational needs, you may need to have additional equipment in order to communicate with one another.

## Main differences between communicating with adults and with children and young people

There are many similarities between communicating with adults and with children — always maintaining eye contact and interest, responding to what they are saying, and treating them with courtesy and respect. However, when communicating with children, we also need to think about how we maintain the relationship of carer to child and what this means in a school context. However well you get on with children, remember that they need to see you as a carer and that your relationships with them will always need to be formal when in school.

When communicating with children, we also need to be very clear and unambiguous in what we say. They need us to communicate what is expected of them so that they can learn to communicate well themselves. Sometimes we forget the importance of making sure that children understand what we mean and might ask them, 'What did I just ask you to do?' when they cannot answer the question! Make sure that the vocabulary and verbal expressions you use are at the right level for the children.

You also need to be aware that physical contact with children should not be encouraged when

communicating with them. It can be hard to avoid this with very young children, as they will often initiate hugs or want to hold hands. In this situation it would be inappropriate to tell them not to. However, you should not offer physical contact with children or be overly physical with them at any time.

## How to adapt communication to meet different communication needs of adults

It is important that we are sensitive to the needs of other adults, particularly if they have communication difficulties. It is possible that you will adapt the way you communicate with them without realising that you are doing it. We often change the way we react to others, depending on the way in which they react to us. For example, if you are speaking to a parent or carer who is hearing-impaired, you might make sure that you are facing them and making eye contact so that they can lip-read. However, if you have contact with adults who have other communication difficulties, you may need to reflect and make sure you adapt your means of communication.

Often, schools will send out or gather information in a particular way, for example, through letters or emails. Depending on their individual needs, the recipients may not be able to access this method of communication easily, and this will not always be clear. You may need to observe sensitivity, for example, if you need to ask a parent or carer why they have not responded to a note that was sent home.

If you need to communicate with other adults who speak English as an additional language, you may need to have a translator and meet together if the information you are communicating is complex or difficult to convey.

*In what ways can you show interest in what someone is saying?*

should be managed very carefully so that bad feeling does not persist afterwards. As adults we can sometimes misread or perceive information wrongly and may think that someone has communicated something to us when they have not. We will sometimes blame others for saying things that could be ambiguous or for having a different point of view from ourselves.

Where there are areas of conflict with other adults, you will need to show sensitivity and try to resolve the situation as soon as possible. The longer a problem is allowed to go on, the more difficult it will be to resolve it. You should not be drawn into a disagreement with a child and you will need to manage this sort of situation carefully and seek advice if necessary. (See also TDA 3.4 on promoting positive behaviour.)

### Poor communication

Often areas of conflict occur when communication has not been effective. This may be because:

- letters have not been passed on by parents or children
- there is a lack of time
- there has been a misunderstanding.

The best way to resolve areas of poor communication is to discuss them to establish a cause, and then find a way forward together. The important thing is not to ignore the problem or talk to everyone else about it except the individual concerned.

### Opposing expectations

Sometimes adults may not have the same ideas about the purpose of an activity or meeting, or come with a different idea in mind. You should always clarify exactly the aims of what you are there to do and why.

### Different values and ideas

Parents and schools may sometimes have different methods of dealing with situations. Whereas the school may request that children do things in a particular way, parental views may be very different. You may need to work alongside others to explain or clarify why things need to happen in a different way in school.

### External factors

You may be working with an individual who has considerable home pressures or other issues, which are affecting how they communicate. External professionals

---

**CASE STUDY:** Adapting communication to deal with the needs of adults

Yasser's mother has come up to the school because she is unhappy about the way in which an incident on the playground was dealt with. English is not her first language. She has an appointment to see the teacher and says to them that she is very angry that you spoke to Yasser and sent him to stand by the wall (which is your school's policy for managing negative playtime behaviour). You are upset as Yasser's behaviour was out of turn and you acted according to school policy. The class teacher has invited you to come in and speak to her, but you are reluctant to do so.

- Should you go and speak to Yasser's mother even if you do not want to?
- How might you reflect on the incident before going to meet with her?
- How might communication difficulties have influenced her reaction?
- What strategies can you think of to prevent this from happening again?

## How to manage disagreements

It is likely that at some point in your work you will have disagreements with others. In many cases, disagreements are down to lack of communication or miscommunication with others. However, they

or parents are likely to have time pressures and other pressures of which you are not aware. As we get to know people, we will be able to identify if they are behaving in an uncharacteristic way and be able to ask if there is anything wrong or if we can help.

## Lack of confidence

Sometimes adults can act in an aggressive way if they are not sure about what they are doing or if they lack confidence. This may come across in a personal way to others, but is more to do with how they perceive themselves and their own abilities. You may need to be sensitive to this and offer them encouragement and support.

---

## BEST PRACTICE CHECKLIST:
### Communicating with others

- Make sure you are friendly and approachable – smile!

- Speak clearly and give eye contact to the person with whom you are speaking.

- Ensure you use the correct form of address when speaking to others.

- Use an appropriate method of communication for the other person.

- Use positive body language and gestures.

- Be sympathetic to the needs of others.

- Acknowledge the help and support of others as much as you can.

- Do not interrupt or anticipate what others are going to say.

---

### Functional skills

**ICT: Developing, presenting and communicating information**
The checklist above provides you with an excellent opportunity to use and develop your ICT skills. You could transfer this information into a poster to display in your staff room.

---

# Understand legislation, policies and procedures for confidentiality and sharing information, including data protection

## Legislation and procedures covering confidentiality, data protection and the disclosure of information

Adults who work with children in any setting need to have some idea about current legislation, as this will affect their practice. There is an increased awareness of how important it is to recognise the uniqueness of each child and have respect for their human rights. Legislation is an area which is constantly under review and you will need to keep up to date through reading relevant publications.

### Every Child Matters (England 2003)/Help Children Achieve More

The Every Child Matters initiative came in to ensure more integrated services and information sharing between professionals. It followed the tragic case of Victoria Climbié and the terminology has since been amended by the coalition government although the emphasis is still on better outcomes for children.

### Data Protection Act 1998

In schools we ask parents and carers for a variety of information so that we are able to care for children as effectively as we can while they are with us. However, we can only ask for information which is directly relevant – for example:

- health or medical information

- records from previous schools

- records for children who have special educational needs.

This is **confidential information** and must be used only for the purpose for which it was gathered. If the

### Key term

**Confidential information** – information that should only be shared with people with a right to have it, for example, your teacher, your line manager or an external agency

*What damage do you think idle gossip about a child or parent could do?*

information needs to be passed on to others for any reason, parental consent will need to be given. This usually involves parents signing a consent form.

Under the Data Protection Act 1998, any organisation which holds information on individuals needs to be registered with the Information Commissioner. This is designed to ensure that confidential information cannot be passed on to others without the individual's consent. There are eight principles of practice which govern the use of personal information. Information must be:

- processed fairly and lawfully
- used only for the purpose for which it was gathered
- adequate, relevant and not excessive
- accurate and kept up to date where necessary
- kept for no longer than necessary
- processed in line with the individual's rights
- kept secure
- not transferred outside the European Union without adequate protection.

You will need to be aware of a range of information in your role as a teaching assistant, from issues around the school to the individual needs of the children with whom you work. You should know how and when

to share any information you have access to. If you are at all concerned or unclear about whom you can speak to, your first point of contact should be your line manager, or in the case of children with special educational needs (SEN), the SENCO. Many teaching assistants working in schools are also parents of children at the same school, and other parents may sometimes put pressure on them to disclose information. You should not pass on any information about the school or the children before being certain that this is the correct thing to do. If you pass on information without following the correct channels, you will be abusing your position of professional trust and this can be very damaging.

You should also be very careful if taking photographs for displays or if filming children for any purpose; again, parental permission will need to be given for this. You should not take pictures of children for your portfolio!

You should not pass on information to:

- other children in the school
- other parents
- other professionals unless parents have been consulted
- visitors.

## Reassuring children, young people and adults of the confidentiality of shared information

When you are party to gathering information, whatever this is, you may sometimes be in a position where you need to reassure others about the fact that it is confidential. If you attend meetings or need to be told about confidential items, you should make sure that you let others know your obligations. In most cases, parental consent would need to be given before any information about children can be shared with other professionals. However, if there are any issues to indicate that the child is at risk from harm or abuse, or if there is a legal obligation placed on the school to disclose information, this can be done (see the following case study). There may also be cases where information on pupils needs to be accessible to all staff, for example, where pupils have specific medial conditions such as asthma or epilepsy. In this case there should be an agreed system within the school for making sure that all staff are aware of these pupils. Some schools may display photographs of them in staffrooms or dining areas, for example, and remove them if the premises are used by others during the evening.

### CASE STUDY: Keeping information confidential

You are working in a Year 1 class. You have a new child who is on the **autistic spectrum**, and he is being monitored by all staff during his settling in. You have been asked to support him and have been given information on his background and access to reports from other professionals. At present his behaviour can be unpredictable and one of the mums who comes into school to hear readers has witnessed this. She has then spoken about it to other parents. A few days later, another parent asks you about the child when you are outside school with your own daughter. She wants to know where he has come from and why he is in a mainstream school. She says it is 'not the right place for him'.

- What would you say to her?
- What would you do if other parents continued to ask you about the child and voice their opinions?

## Situations when confidentiality protocols must be breached

If you find yourself in a position where another individual confides in you, it is important to remember that there are some situations in which you will need to tell others. This is particularly true in cases of suspected child abuse or when a child or young person is at risk. You should at all times tell the individual that you will not be able to keep confidentiality if they disclose something to you which you cannot keep to yourself for these reasons.

### CASE STUDY: Procedures for sharing information

Kit works in an infants' school where he supports in the Nursery and Reception classes. He has been given some information by a parent which has caused him concern regarding another child in Reception, who is being cared for by her mother but is the subject of a custody battle. He has also noticed that the child seems very quiet lately and is not eating much at lunchtimes. The parent asks Kit not to tell anyone else but says that she is very concerned about this child and is asking for his advice.

- What should Kit say to the parent?
- Why should Kit act immediately in this instance?

### Functional skills

**English: Speaking, listening and communication**
When holding a professional discussion, it is important always to think about using appropriate language and to keep the discussion moving.

### Key term

**Autistic spectrum** – a spectrum of psychological conditions characterised by widespread abnormalities of social interactions and communication, as well as severely restricted interests and highly repetitive behaviour

## Getting ready for assessment

Your school has an open-door policy, and parents and other adults are always welcome. Recently there has been an incident where a parent has complained to you at hometime that the open-door policy is not a reality. She has said that teachers are always too busy to speak to her, and anyway it is so difficult to get into the school because of security measures that she does not feel the description of 'open door' to be particularly accurate. She says that she has already mentioned it to the Head Teacher some time ago, but nothing seems to have been done about it.

- What would be your first reaction in this situation?
- What else could you do or say in order to support the parent?
- Can you think of any other strategies which would help to deal with the complaint?
- Why is it important that you and the school act to resolve this matter?

In this unit you will need to show that you know what to do in sensitive situations such as the above, where there are communication issues or relationships between adults or children have broken down. You may or may not have had to deal with them.

- If you have not, you can use the portfolio activities and case studies in this unit so you can show that you know what procedures you would follow.
- If you have been involved in a situation where communication has broken down, and do not want to write a reflective account about it, you can tell your assessor about it during a professional discussion. They can then record that you have told them and whether you have acted appropriately. The actual incident and individuals involved will not need to be named. This will avoid recording any sensitive information in your portfolio.

## Check your knowledge

1. What key things should you remember in order to communicate effectively with others?

2. How can you develop positive relationships with children as well as adults?

3. What kinds of contexts may affect relationships and how you communicate with others?

4. In which of these situations might you need to adapt the way in which you communicate with others?

    a) if the individual has communication difficulties

    b) if you do not have time to speak to them properly

    c) if the child is very young

    d) if they have not understood what you are saying.

5. Give two differences you may need to consider between communicating with children and communicating with adults.

6. How can you make sure that you do not have disagreements with others? (For example, what kinds of strategies could you use?)

7. What should you do if you have concerns about a child who has confided in you, but the child has asked you not to tell anyone?

---

### Websites

**www.atl.org.uk** – Association of Teachers and Lecturers

**www.education.gov.uk** – put 'Information sharing' into search engine (as well as SEN Code of Practice)

**www.education.gov.uk** – Department for Education (SENCode of Practice England and Wales)

**www.dcsf.gov.uk/everychildmatters** – Every Child Matters (DCSF)

**www.direct.gov.uk** – for information about the Data Protection Act 1998

**www.restorativejustice.org.uk** – Restorative Justice Consortium

**www.transformingconflict.org** – Transforming Conflict

**www.unicef.org** – UNICEF

**www.unison.org.uk** – UNISON

**www.voicetheunion.org.uk** – Voice: the union for education professionals

# School life

## My story Cerys

I have been working in my school for a couple of years supporting Ioanna, who has communication difficulties. As well as having a speech and language disorder, she speaks English as a second language. This meant that for some time her disorder was not picked up – when I first started to work with her, we really noticed a change in her progress. She is now nearing the end of Year 5 and starting to think about secondary school. Her parents have said that they want to send her to the local comprehensive school, as it is close to their house and easy to get to. However, we all feel at school that she would benefit enormously from going to a secondary school a little further away which has a speech and language unit attached. The SENCO and I tried to speak to Ioanna's mum a couple of times about this, but as her English is quite poor, we did not think that she had really understood how important it is for Ioanna to continue to have the close support of speech and language professionals.

After trying to speak to Ioanna's mum after school one day, the SENCO and I decided it would be useful to set up a meeting between the school, Ioanna's speech and language therapist, and her parents. We also invited a translator to help to explain to Ioanna's parents in more detail. We were able to discuss all the issues we wanted to and the parents also had the opportunity to ask questions about what was available to Ioanna. At the end of the meeting we all felt that it had been useful and the parents agreed to go and look around the speech and language unit with Ioanna.

## Ask the expert

**Q** Sometimes as a teaching assistant I don't feel able to make suggestions or say what I think to other adults in the school as I don't think it's part of my role – should I say what I think?

**A** You should always voice any concerns or take opportunities to put your ideas forward. As an individual support assistant in particular, you may have closer contact with the pupils than teachers do, so you have a clearer idea about what is needed. You may need to ask first if nobody seeks your opinion, but it should be a matter of course.

### VIEWPOINT

Do staff at your school have opportunities to say what they think? Support staff should have some opportunities to communicate and discuss their own ideas, whether this is through their own meetings or meetings with the whole school staff. If this is not available to you, ask for some time to be set aside and emphasise the importance of whole-school communication.

# TDA 3.2 Schools as organisations

You need to know and understand the structure of schools and how they work, and how schools fit in at a local and national level. You should know about your own school's mission, ethos and values and the implication of these and the roles and responsibilities of others within and outside the school who contribute to the education process. You will have to understand the wider context of legislation which affects schools and the principles and policies which are needed.

## By the end of this unit you will:

1. know the structure of education from early years to post-compulsory education

2. understand how schools are organised in terms of roles and responsibilities

3. understand school ethos, mission, aims and values

4. know about the legislation affecting schools

5. understand the purpose of school policies and procedures

6. understand the wider context in which schools operate.

# Know the structure of education from early years to post-compulsory education

## Entitlement and provision for early years education

As part of the Every Child Matters agenda and the Childcare Act 2006, it became an entitlement of all 3- and 4-year-olds in England to receive a free part-time **early years education** of up to 15 hours per week for 38 weeks of the year. The government funds local authorities to ensure that every child receives up to two years of free education before reaching school age. Parents do not need to contribute to this, but will be charged fees for any additional hours the child receives.

Early years provision in school is about supporting very young children. It is distinct from Key Stage 1 in each country within the UK and is based on the concept of learning through play rather than more formal education, as play has been shown to be an important vehicle for children's early learning. Although you may not work with this age group, you should have some understanding of the early years curriculum and the statutory requirements of the Early Years Foundation Stage or the requirements of your home country. As a member of support staff, you may be asked to work with pupils in school nurseries as well as Reception classes. If you have not worked at all with children of this age range, you may need to attend specific training if you are to be there for any length of time.

### Early Years Curriculum Frameworks in your home country

In English schools, the Foundation Curriculum runs from the ages of 3 to 5 years and is therefore used in Reception classes and in school nurseries. The Early Years Foundation Stage, which was revised in England in September 2012, sets out one standard framework for learning, development and care for all children from birth to the end of the Reception year. The Early Years Foundation Phase in Wales extends from the ages of 3 to 7, and combines Early Years and Key Stage 1 of the National Curriculum (for more information, see http://nationalstrategies.standards.dcsf.gov.uk/earlyyears).

In Scotland, the curriculum is focused around the document *Curriculum for Excellence*. This document concerns the curriculum for 3- to 18-year-olds. The curriculum for 3- to 4-year-olds and the early primary phase (Primary 1) are presented as one level. This means that, although in Scotland there is a distinction between the phases, children will only move on to Primary 1 when they are ready. There is also a strong emphasis on active learning and on deepening pupils' knowledge.

In Northern Ireland, pupils in Years 1 and 2 are in the Foundation Stage. Key Stage 1 consists of Years 3 and 4 (P4 and P5) and Key Stage 2 of Years 5, 6 and 7 (P6, P7 and P8). Although the year groups are divided up differently from those in other countries, the Foundation Stage remains distinct from the Primary Curriculum and again only introduces children to formal learning when they are ready.

The way in which learning is usually managed in the early years is that adults work alongside children on focused activities that involve specific concepts, such as using numbers or carrying out writing or language activities. Children also work independently and self-select from a wide range of activities within and outside the classroom. This encourages them to develop their **autonomy**.

---

### Knowledge into action

If you do not work in the Early Years Foundation Stage, ask your Head Teacher if you can go and observe practice in the Nursery or Reception class in your school. Find out how the structure of the day there is different from that of the rest of the school.

---

### Key terms

**Early years education** — education for children up to the age of 5 in nurseries and reception classes

**Autonomy** — doing things in a self-governed way

*How does it help children's development for them to play independently?*

## The different types of schools in relation to educational stage(s) and school governance

There are four main types of mainstream state schools which will all be funded by local authorities and are known as maintained schools. They will all have to follow the National Curriculum, and include:

- **community schools** – these are run and owned by the local authority (or Education and Library Board in Northern Ireland). This will also support the school through looking to develop links with the local community, and by providing support services. They will also usually determine the admissions policy. They may develop the use of the school facilities by local groups such as adult education or childcare classes

- **foundation and trust schools** – foundation schools are run by their own governing body, which determines the admissions policy in consultation with the local education authority. The school, land and buildings will also be owned by the governing body or a charitable foundation. A Trust school, although a type of foundation school, will form a charitable Trust with an outside partner, such as a business. The school will have to buy in any support services. The decision to become a

Trust school will be made by the governing body in consultation with parents

- **voluntary schools** – these come under two types:
  - ○ voluntary-aided schools are mainly religious or 'faith' schools, although anyone can apply for a place. They are run by their own governing body in the same way as a foundation school, although the land and buildings are normally owned by a religious organisation or charity. They are funded partly by the governing body, partly by the charity and partly by the local education authority, which also provides support services
  - ○ voluntary-controlled schools are similar types of schools to voluntary-aided schools, although they are run and funded by the local authority which also employs the staff and provides support services. The land and buildings are usually owned by a charity, which is often a religious organisation

- **specialist schools** – these are usually secondary schools which can apply for specialist status to develop one or two subject specialisms. They will receive additional government funding for doing this. Around 92 per cent of secondary schools in England have specialist status (source: Teachernet: April 2009). Special schools can also apply for specialist school status to be given for an SEN specialism under one of the four areas of the **SEN Code of Practice**.

There are also other types of schools which are not funded directly by the local education authority (Education and Library Board in Northern Ireland).

> **Key term**
>
> **SEN Code of Practice** – document which sets out the requirements for the identification and monitoring of pupils with special educational needs

### Independent schools

Independent schools are set apart from the local education authority since they are funded by fees paid by parents and also income from investments, gifts and charitable endowments. Most therefore have charitable status, which means that they can claim tax exemption. They do not have to follow the National Curriculum, and the Head Teacher and governors decide on the admissions policy. There are approximately 2,300 independent schools in the UK, which are obliged to register with the Department for Education (DfE) so that they can be monitored on a regular basis, although this may not be by Ofsted but the ISI (Independent Schools Inspectorate).

## Academies

Historically, these have been set up by sponsors from business although in 2010 the government introduced more opportunities for communities to become involved in giving schools academy status. Academies have close links with the local education authority, although they are not maintained by it and have more freedoms than state schools. For more on academies, see Specialist Schools and Academies website at the end of the unit.

### Over to you!
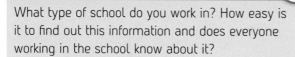

What type of school do you work in? How easy is it to find out this information and does everyone working in the school know about it?

### Functional skills

**English: Reading**
You could develop your reading skills by working in groups of three with people who come from different settings and carrying out a comparative study of admissions, prospectuses, policies and procedures, and general operation.

## Post-16 options for young people and adults

The opportunities for pupils aged 16 and over have traditionally been either to leave school and start employment, or to stay and continue with their studies. Although many pupils do still choose one of these options, it is likely that there will be more opportunities available as there has been an increased government focus on and funding of education

for 14- to 19-year-olds, and in particular a focus on reducing the number of young people not in education, employment or training (NEET) post-16. At the time of writing, the government guarantees that by the end of September of the year that each young person leaves compulsory education, they will have a place in further learning available. This 'September Guarantee' was implemented nationally in 2007 and was later extended so that 17-year-olds who have completed a short course or who have chosen to leave the activity they selected on completing school will have the opportunity to extend their learning.

### The September Guarantee

Under the last Labour government, the guarantee was as follows:

● full or part-time education in school, sixth form college, independent learning provider or further education (FE) college

● an Apprenticeship or programme-led Apprenticeship, which must include both the training element and a job or work placement

● Entry to Employment (E2E)

● employment with training to NVQ level 2.

The reason behind these requirements is that by 2013, all pupils will be required to continue in education or training to at least 17 years of age. This does not mean that they will be required to remain in school, but they should be following one of the pathways above. Under the coalition government this will rise to the age of 18 in 2015.

For more information and updates, go to the DfE website (www.education.gov.uk) and enter a search for 'Supporting young people'.

### Knowledge into action

Consider the wider educational environment of your school — for example, with regard to other primary and secondary schools, and further and higher education in your area. How do you think your school relates to other schools and colleges? Find out about any contact and joint projects.

**Functional skills**

**Functional skills**

**Maths: Representing**
While you are looking at and researching the facilities in your local area, you could carry out a mathematical study to see what percentage of different facilities there are in the area, and maybe compare this to other areas of the country. For example, you could create a pie chart.

# Understand how schools are organised in terms of roles and responsibilities

## The strategic purposes of members of the school team

### School governors
School governors are usually a team of 10 to 12 people, although there can be up to 20, who have

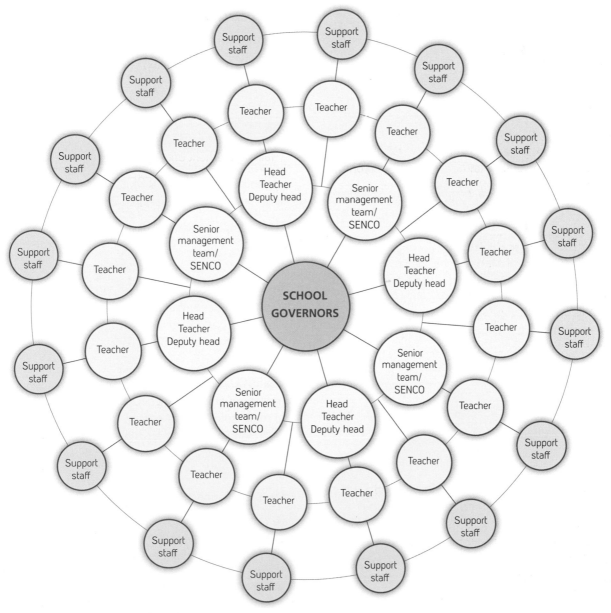

*Support staff are part of the whole school team.*

the responsibility of running the school. They will be made up of a variety of people who will have links with the school and local community. There should be at least one parent governor and at least one staff governor, in addition to the Head Teacher. There may also be a support staff governor. In addition there will be a local authority governor, appointed by the local authority (LA), and a local community governor who will usually work or live in the community served by the school. Governors will work closely with the Head Teacher and Senior Management Team, although you may not see them around the school often during the school day. Governors will be based on different committees which are responsible for various areas of school management – for example, the school site, personnel issues or **community cohesion**. They will meet in these committees and then report back to the full governing body. Their main duties are:

- to set aims and objectives for the school
- to adopt new policies for achieving the aims and objectives
- to set targets for achieving the aims and objectives.

You can find more information on school governorship and governor responsibilities at www.governornet.co.uk

## Senior management team

The school's Senior Management or Senior Leadership Team will work closely with the Head Teacher. The team will usually be made up of more experienced staff who have management positions – in a primary school this will probably be the deputy head teacher, year group leaders (if the school has more than one form entry), SENCO (Special Educational Needs Co-ordinator) and Foundation Stage leader. In a secondary school they may also be year group leaders and SENCOs, but may also be subject area leaders. They will usually meet once a week or on a regular basis to discuss issues which have come up and to make decisions concerning the running of the school or around the implementation of the **school improvement plan**. They will then discuss how this information will be spread to teachers and support staff.

## Other statutory roles

There will be other staff roles in school which are legally required to be fulfilled in terms of staffing.

Apart from the head teacher and deputy, the two main others are SENCOs and, in primary schools, the Foundation Stage manager.

The SENCO is responsible for managing and monitoring the provision for those with special educational needs within the school. This includes:

- 'ensuring liaison with parents and other professionals in respect of children with special educational needs
- advising and supporting other practitioners in the setting
- ensuring that appropriate **individual education plans** are in place
- ensuring that relevant background information about individual children with special educational needs is collected, recorded and updated.'

*SEN Code of Practice 2001: 4.15*

### Key terms

**Community cohesion** – the togetherness and bonding shown by members of a community, the 'glue' that holds a community together

**School improvement plan** – document which sets out priorities for the school over a four- or five-year period

**Individual education plan** (IEP) – targets and planned implementation strategies for pupils with special educational needs (see also pages 262–63)

The SENCO will also need to monitor and review the provision for pupils with special educational needs and make sure that the paperwork is in place for those who are on Early Years or School Action and Action Plus.

The Foundation Stage Manager must ensure that the Early Years Foundation Stage (that is, Reception and any Nursery classes) is being run according to the statutory requirements of the Early Years Foundation Stage document. They will be responsible for making sure that observations, assessments and record keeping are up to date, as well as ensuring that all staff in the Foundation Stage are trained in its implementation.

| Role of teacher | Role of teaching assistant |
|---|---|
| • To be responsible for planning and preparing to the National or Early Years Curriculum<br>• To teach pupils according to their educational needs<br>• To assess, record and report on the development, progress and attainment of pupils<br>• To take responsibility for all other adults within the learning environment<br>• To communicate and consult with the parents of pupils<br>• To communicate and co-operate with persons or bodies outside the school<br>• To participate in meetings arranged for any of the above purposes<br>• Usually to be responsible for managing an area of the curriculum, such as geography, as included in the job description | • To plan and prepare work alongside the teacher<br>• To support learning activities effectively as directed by the teacher<br>• To assess/evaluate pupils' work as directed by the teacher<br>• To report any problems or queries to the teacher<br>• To give feedback to the teacher following planned activities |

*Table 1: Some of the duties around planning and implementing learning activities of the teacher and teaching assistant.*

## Teachers

All teachers have the responsibility for the planning and preparation of the curriculum for pupils in their class. In a primary school, this will usually be for all subjects under the National Curriculum. As well as being responsible for their own class, teachers will generally also have another area of responsibility in school. This may be as a member of the senior management team, but in a primary school it could also be a subject area. In all schools each subject will need to be represented so that there is a person responsible for it; this means that in a smaller school with fewer teachers, staff may each be responsible for two or three subjects. They will be expected to know about any curriculum developments in their area and to feed back to all staff through staff meetings. They should also be available to advise and support other teachers in their subject, and monitor teaching. The local authority will also arrange subject leader forums which they will be expected to attend.

### Link

See also TDA 3.3 on supporting learning activities.

## Support staff roles

The number of support staff in schools has risen dramatically in recent years. The DfE's Statistical First Release in May 2010 shows the total number of teaching assistants across all LA maintained schools in England was 79,000 in 2000 and rose to 181,600 in 2009 (source: DfE: May 2010). This has been due to an increase in government funding which was based on the reduction of responsibilities on class teachers and a gradual increase in initiatives to raise pupil progress, many of which have been carried out by teaching assistants.

Types of support staff may be:

● breakfast, after-school or extended school staff
● midday supervisors and catering staff
● office or administrative staff
● caretakers or site managers
● teaching assistants
● individual support assistants for SEN children
● specialist or technicians (for example, in ICT)
● learning mentors and parent support workers.

The roles of each of these members of staff may be different and their job descriptions should reflect this.

## Functional skills

**ICT: Developing, presenting and communicating information**

You could produce a flow chart on a computer to show the roles and responsibilities of the staff in your school. This is something that you could display in the staff room for any new members or visitors to the school.

## Portfolio activity

Consider and write about the different ways in which you contribute to pupils' well-being and achievement in your school. Use records of pupil achievement for the groups with whom you work as evidence to support your response.

# Roles of external professionals

There will be a huge range of external professionals who may work with a school on a regular basis. If you are working with an individual pupil and collaborate with your school's SENCO, you are more likely to come into contact with different agencies or individuals. Even if you do not, you still need to be aware of the variety of people who may come into school to work with the Head Teacher and other staff. These include the following.

- The school should have an educational psychologist allocated to them through the local Special Educational Needs department. They will support the SENCO in providing assessments and observations to pupils each year and plan the provision for pupils who have additional needs. They may also lead meetings with parents and make recommendations for work with individual pupils.

- Speech and language therapists (SLTs) will work with pupils on speech, language and communication problems, in both producing and understanding language. There should be a number of SLTs working in your local area who have links with the school and in some cases are based there. However, most will work from an alternative location and will come into school to work with children, parents and teachers.

- Specialist teachers may come into school to

offer advice and support to pupils with a range of needs. These may be:

- ○ behaviour support needs
- ○ social and communication needs such as autism
- ○ English as an Additional Language needs.

- The Education Welfare Officer (EWO), sometimes known as Education Social Worker, will usually be based within local authorities. They will visit schools and work with the Head Teacher to monitor pupil attendance and to provide support with issues around absenteeism. They will also work alongside parents to support excluded pupils on their return to school.

- The School Improvement Partner (SIP) will come into school to advise and support the Head Teacher for three to five days each year. They will have previous experience of school leadership and/ or have worked in a senior advisory role in a local authority. They work alongside the local education authority and will support the Head Teacher in looking at ways of developing the school through both the **school self-evaluation** and pupil progress and attainment. This means focusing not only on academic factors but through looking at **extended school provision** and liaison with parents.

- Physiotherapists/occupational therapists may work with pupils outside school, but may also be asked to come in for meetings and discussions to support pupil progress.

You will also find that other teachers may visit your school for various meetings such as 'cluster groups'. These are designed to encourage teachers who have similar roles in schools in the local area to meet up and discuss their practice and ideas. This can be very useful — for example, if you are working in a one-form entry primary school (one class for each year group) and are the only teacher in your school who has expertise in the Foundation Stage.

## Key terms

**School self-evaluation** — document which looks at and evaluates the school's progress

**Extended school provision** — extra out-of-school activities, such as breakfast and after-school clubs

**Aims and Objectives**

- To provide a caring atmosphere in which our children can develop their skills and abilities in all curriculum areas and fulfil their potential.

- To ensure that staff and children will be able to participate in every aspect of school life, within the school community, whatever their needs or abilities.

- To foster an environment in which children and staff have high self-esteem and the confidence to achieve the highest standards.

- To harness our children's natural curiosity, encouraging a lifelong thirst for learning.

- To stimulate our children to develop enquiring minds and the confidence to pose questions and discuss ideas rationally.

- To help our children to understand that learning is an exciting challenge, part of which is taking risks and learning from mistakes.

- To encourage our children to take a pride in their achievements and appreciate the value of hard work.

- To promote an understanding of and care for the environment both within the school and the outside world.

- To encourage children and staff to have the confidence to grasp opportunities afforded by new technologies.

- To encourage parents to become partners in their child's education and support the school's focus on expected standards of behaviour.

- To enrich our children's knowledge and understanding of the diversity of the world we live in and develop a respect for other cultures, races and religions.

*(Source: Unicorn Primary School prospectus)*

*How do the aims of your school compare with those above?*

**Functional skills**

ICT: Developing, presenting and communicating information
You could produce an information booklet of names and contact details of each of these outside agencies that are linked to your school. You could do this by using a table within a Word® document that you could save then update later, as and when needed.

# Understand school ethos, mission, aims and values

You will need to understand the following terms as you will see them regularly on school literature and may be asked to define them for your own school. It is likely that your school prospectus or mission statement will outline them with regard to your particular workplace.

- **Ethos** – the school's values and beliefs and how it 'feels'; it is usually based on the philosophy or atmosphere of the school. This may also be affected by the type of school, for example, a church school may have a more spiritual ethos. The ethos should have been developed through discussion with staff, parents, pupils, governors and outside agencies or those in the community who have dealings with the school. Studies have shown that a positive school ethos is a key factor in raising pupil achievement, developing effective behaviour management and anti-bullying and peer support strategies.

- **Mission** — the school's overall intention, as set out by the Head Teacher. The school's mission is sometimes seen as a modern equivalent to a motto, in that it should be short and easy to remember. It will also overlap with the school's vision and aims.

- **Aims** — it is likely that the school's aims or vision will be in the prospectus and in other school literature. They will usually be set by the Head Teacher in collaboration with parents, staff and the community.

- **Values** — the values of the school are based on the moral code which will inform its development. Core values are at the heart of many communities and belief systems. Although there may be some differences in the way in which people view them, they will usually include respect for self and others and are related closely to Personal, Social, Health and Economic education (PSHE) and Citizenship Education. They may also be tied in with the school rules.

### Functional skills

**ICT: Using ICT**
Looking at your school's ethos, mission and aims, you could use a digital camera and take some photographs to evidence these in action. You could then produce a display of how your school fulfils its aims.

### Skills builder

Write a reflective account of your own school's ethos, mission and aims, giving examples of how these impact on your own day-to-day practice.

### Reflect

Everyone has their own values. They are an essential part of who you are. Think about your own values and how they may differ from those of parents, pupils and other staff. In what ways do they differ? Why is it important to be aware of this?

*It is good practice for everyone who works in the school to be aware of its ethos.*

## How ethos, mission, aims and values may be reflected in working practices

A school's ethos should always be reflected in the working practices of the staff. The school's literature may set out a very clear ethos, but it should be apparent from walking around the school that pupils and staff carry it out in their day-to-day practice.

- **Children at the centre of everything** — children should be valued in the school and there should be a culture that their learning and development is celebrated in a variety of ways.

- **Working together** — it should be clear that pupils collaborate with one another effectively to achieve both as part of the learning process and in forming relationships with others.

- **Attitudes of pupils and staff** — there should be a positive atmosphere in the school, demonstrated through the way in which pupils and staff take pride in their surroundings and in the way in which learning takes place.

- **Community cohesion** — this is the way in which the school forms links with external members of the community and through partnerships with others to advance children's learning.

- **Inclusive environment** — a positive recognition of the importance of diversity and equal opportunities should be part of the school's commitment to a safe and secure learning environment for all pupils.

## Methods of communicating a school's ethos, mission, aims and values

The school's aims and values will need to be communicated as much as possible in school literature and on its website as well as in school. This is because these sources will be where parents and others gain their first impressions. You will need to make sure that you have considered how schools, and in particular your own, communicate their aims and values, and whether they do this successfully.

## Know about the legislation affecting schools

### Laws and codes of practice and how schools are affected by legislation

Schools, as with any other organisation, are obliged to operate under current legislation. Although you may not need to know about these in depth, it is helpful to have some idea about why schools will need to work in a particular way, or why they have to draw up particular policies or documents. Some of the key pieces of legislation which you should know about are the:

- Data Protection Act 1998
- UN Convention on Rights of the Child 1989
- Education Act 2002
- Children Act 2004
- Childcare Act 2006
- Freedom of Information Act 2000
- Human Rights Act 1998
- Special Educational Needs (SEN) Code of Practice 2001 and Disability Discrimination Act 1995/2005/Equality Act.

### The Data Protection Act 1998

The Data Protection Act 1998 means that schools need to keep and use information only for the purpose for which it was intended. It also needs to be kept securely on site, either locked in filing cabinets or on password-protected computers. If you are asked to update any pupil information, you should do this while you are on school premises and not take any information off site. You should consider all information about pupils as **confidential** and ensure that you do not share it with others without parental consent. When discussing pupils with others — for example, if you are working as an individual support assistant — you should take care to ensure that you only share necessary information. Adults working with a particular pupil will need to receive information, while those who are merely curious do not.

### The UN Convention on Rights of the Child 1989

The UN Convention on Rights of the Child 1989 (UNCRC) was drawn up in 1989 and ratified by the UK in 1991. There are 54 articles included; those which relate directly to schools are as follows.

- Article 2 – children have a right to protection from any form of discrimination.
- Article 3 – the best interests of the child are the primary consideration.
- Article 12 – children are entitled to express their views, which should be given consideration in keeping with the child's age and maturity.
- Article 13 – children have a right to receive and share information as long as that information is not damaging to others.
- Article 14 – children have a right to freedom of religion, although they should also be free to examine their beliefs.
- Article 28 – all children have an equal right to education.
- Article 29 – children's education should develop each child's personality, talents and abilities to the fullest. They should also learn to live peacefully and respect the environment and other people.

For more information, see www.unicef.org/crc

## Education Act 2002

There have been a number of educational acts and these will continue to be updated with the corresponding year. The 2002 Act brought in several changes to school regulations, staffing and governance, and was further amended in 2006 to include a duty of schools to promote community cohesion. This means that schools are required to work alongside other community-based organisations and to develop links and a 'shared sense of belonging' while valuing the contributions of 'different individuals and different communities'. For more information, see www.teachingcitizenship.org.uk/dnloads/comm_cohesion_doc.pdf

## Children Act 2004 and Childcare Act 2006

The Children Act 2004 came in alongside the Every Child Matters framework and had a huge impact on the way in which schools address issues of care, welfare and discipline. It took its root from the Victoria Climbié inquiry. Under the joint requirements, agencies such as Social Services and Education work together to take on more responsibility for pupil welfare. There are five basic outcomes for children and young people under Every Child Matters, as Table 2 shows.

The Childcare Act 2006 places more responsibility on local authorities to:

- improve well-being for young children, and reduce inequalities
- ensure that there is sufficient childcare to enable parents to work

| Outcome | Description |
| --- | --- |
| Be healthy | Children should be physically, mentally, emotionally and sexually healthy. They should have healthy lifestyles and be able to choose not to take illegal drugs. |
| Stay safe | Children should be safe from neglect, violence, maltreatment, bullying and discrimination. They should be cared for and have security and stability. |
| Enjoy and achieve | Children should be ready for, attend and enjoy school. They should achieve national educational standards at both primary and secondary school. They should be able to achieve personal and social development, and enjoy recreation. |
| Make a positive contribution | Children should engage in decision making and support the local community. They should show positive behaviour in and out of school. Children should be encouraged to develop self-confidence and to deal with significant life changes and challenges. |
| Achieve economic well-being | Children should engage in further education, employment or training on leaving school. They should be able to live in decent homes with access to transport and material goods. They should be free from low income. |

*Every Child Matters: Change for Children – DfES-1109–2004*

*Table 2: The five outcomes under Every Child Matters.*

- provide information to parents about childcare
- ensure that local childcare providers are trained
- introduce the Early Years Foundation Stage for the under-5s
- reform the regulation system for childcare, with two new registers of childcare providers, to be run by Ofsted.

Your work will have been affected directly by the Children Act 2004 and the Childcare Act 2006 and you should have had some training or guidance in their implementation. One of the main outcomes for schools is that there is more 'joined-up' work between schools and other agencies for the best interests of children. There have also been many more breakfast and after-school clubs through the introduction of extended schools (see www.teachernet.gov.uk/wholeschool/extendedschools for more about these).

## Freedom of Information Act 2000

This Act was introduced in January 2005 to promote transparency and accountability in the public sector. It is fully retrospective, which means that information can be sought from any time in the past. Any person may request information held by a school, although this must be done in writing. Schools have a duty to provide advice and assistance to anyone who requests information; however, there are some cases in which schools will need to protect information which may be confidential. At the time of writing, the DCSF has produced guidance for schools and governing bodies to give advice when dealing with requests for information. For more information, visit www.teachernet.gov.uk and search for 'freedom of information for schools'.

## Human Rights Act 1998

There are a number of equalities laws which may affect schools. These are designed to ensure that inequalities do not exist and that all children will have the same entitlements to education. The Human Rights Act 1998 is linked to the 1950 European Convention on Human Rights. This came in after the end of the Second World War, and although it was a binding international agreement, it was not law. Under the Human Rights Act, individuals in the UK have particular rights and freedoms, but these must be balanced against the rights and freedoms of others. A key provision of the Act is that, 'It is unlawful for a public authority to act in a way which is incompatible [not in line] with a Convention right'.

Some of the articles which have a direct link to school provision are:

- Article 2 of Part II: The First Protocol – the right to education (although this does not mean the right to go to a particular school)
- Article 8 – the right to respect for private and family life
- Article 10 – the right to freedom of expression.

Restraint of pupils is permitted under the Act, to protect the rights of others or to prevent crime or injury. However, your school or local authority should have a policy on this and you should read it so that you are aware of guidelines for its use. There is a guidance leaflet for schools setting out their responsibilities under the Act: http://nihrc.org/dms/data/NIHRC/attachments/dd/files/42/HRAguide_schools.pdf

## The Special Educational Needs (SEN) Code of Practice 2001 and Disability Discrimination Act 1995/2005/Equality Act 2010

Under the SEN Code of Practice, parents and SEN children have an increased right to a mainstream education. This has had an impact on the number of children who have special educational needs being included in mainstream schools and on the number of individual support assistants who support them. It has also had training implications, as in order to support inclusion, schools must now manage pupils with a more diverse range of needs. This has meant that more children are integrated into mainstream schools, which has had a positive effect.

The Disability Discrimination Act and subsequent legislation regarding access for all has meant that all schools built from this date have had to make provision for pupils with disabilities – for example, they will need to have ramps, lifts and disabled toilets. Existing schools built before the Act was first introduced do not need to do this unless they have modifications to existing buildings, such as extensions or new blocks. The Act also means that pupils should not be excluded from any aspect of school life due to disabilities, for example, school trips or other outside provision.

Legislation will affect how schools work as they will need to comply fully with all legal requirements. They will also affect your work with children, although this may seem to happen indirectly. As laws and codes of practice affecting work in schools change regularly, it is not possible to list them all here. However, you should know that schools may need to seek advice and guidance if and when needed. This will often be through the governing body.

## Regulatory bodies relevant to the education sector which exist to monitor and enforce the legislative framework

### The Health and Safety Executive (HSE)

The Health and Safety Executive provides guidance and monitors the legislative framework for all organisations, whether these are industrial, business or education based. Schools are required to comply with the Health and Safety at Work Act (1974). This means that they will need to comply with health and safety law in a number of ways. The employer is responsible for health and safety and this will depend on the type of school, and is required to:

- carry out risk assessments and appropriate measures put in place in new situations or those which may pose an increased risk to adults or children such as on school trips
- complete and hold appropriate paperwork (such as accident recording) which may be requested for inspection under the Act
- have a school health and safety policy, and alert all staff to this.

### School-specific regulatory bodies

Ofsted (the Office for Standards in Education, Children's Services and Skills) was brought in to regulate and inspect the provision and education of children and young people, and to report their findings. They report directly to Parliament and all school inspections are obtainable through their website.

All registered teachers in England are required to be members of the General Teaching Council (GTC). Its functions are that of a regulatory role of the teaching profession. There is a Code of Conduct and Practice to which teachers are required to adhere.

The Independent Schools Council (representing independent schools in the UK) exists to provide information on independent schools, and also to inspect and regulate them. There is a separate Independent Schools Inspectorate (ISI) for each UK country.

## Understand the purpose of school policies and procedures

### Why schools have policies and procedures

All schools, as with other organisations, are required to have clear **school policies** and procedures. This is so that parents, staff, governors and others who are involved in the running of the school are able to work from a comprehensible set of guidelines. There are likely to be a large number of policies and you should know where to find them in your school so that you are able to refer to them when necessary. Although each school will have a slightly different list or they may have varying titles, each will need to outline its purpose and aims, and the responsibilities of staff.

**Key term**

**School policy** – the agreed principles and procedures for the school

### Policies and procedures schools may have

Schools may have polices and procedures relating to:

- staff
- pupil welfare
- teaching and learning
- equality, diversity and inclusion
- parental engagement.

## CASE STUDY: When policies are needed

Shanna is working as a midday supervisor and individual support assistant in an infant school. She had been there for two months when a child had an accident at lunchtime. Shanna was unable to find a senior member of staff. She had not been inducted properly and needed to act quickly, but did not know what to do.

- What should have happened in this instance?
- How could this situation have been averted?

### Functional skills

**English: Speaking, listening and communication**
This case study could be completed in the form of a discussion to develop your speaking and listening skills. Remember to listen carefully to what others are saying, so that you can respond in an appropriate way.

### Portfolio activity

You will need to know about each of these policies and how they relate to you and your school. In your groups, allocate two or three policies so that each of you can find out about them to give a presentation to others. Make notes on each during the presentations, for your portfolio.

| Area | Policies |
|---|---|
| Staff | Pay policy <br> Performance management policy <br> Grievance policy |
| Pupil welfare | Safeguarding policy <br> Health and safety policy <br> Drugs awareness policy <br> Behaviour management policy <br> Personal, social, health and economic education policy <br> Anti-bullying policy |
| Teaching and learning | Curriculum policies (a policy for each subject, such as history, maths, art) <br> Early years policy <br> Teaching and learning policy <br> Planning and assessment policy <br> Marking policy |
| Equality, diversity and inclusion | Equal opportunities policy <br> Race equality and cultural diversity policy <br> Special educational needs (or inclusion) policy <br> Gifted and talented policy <br> Disability and access policy |
| Parental engagement | Homework policy <br> Attendance policy <br> Home–school agreement |

*Table 3: Policies and procedures relating to different aspects of a school's running.*

## How school policies and procedures may be developed and communicated

Schools need to ensure not only that policies are in place, but also that they are revised and updated on a regular basis. It is likely that each policy will be dated and also have a date for its revision. There are a large number of 'model' policies available through local education authorities as well as through the Internet to assist schools in drawing them up, as this can be a time-consuming process. Depending on the policy, the school's senior management team or person responsible for a curriculum area (for example, the literacy co-ordinator) may draft a policy and then have it checked by other staff during a staff meeting. It will then need to be agreed or ratified by the governing body before it takes effect. Although you will not be required to know the contents of every school policy, you should have read and know your responsibilities, in particular regarding the:

- safeguarding policy
- health and safety policy
- behaviour management policy.

**Responsibilities**

Final responsibility for health and safety within the school lies with the Head Teacher.

The Site Manager (or in her absence the Head Teacher) is responsible for the following areas:

- Admin. areas
- Boiler room
- Classrooms
- Corridors, foyers
- ICT suite
- Kitchen and servery
- Libraries
- Hall
- Deputy Head's room
- Shared learning areas
- Playground and garden areas
- Toilets

It is the duty of every member of staff, both teaching and non-teaching, to report any unsafe conditions to the Head Teacher, Site Manager or the Administrative Officer in their absence. In addition, an attempt should be made to eliminate the danger before reporting it, without causing undue risk to self.

All employees have the responsibility of co-operating with the Head Teacher to achieve a healthy and safe workplace, and to take reasonable care of themselves, pupils and others. Health and Safety issues will be raised as a regular agenda item at the staff briefing meetings, which are held each Friday afternoon.

**Review of Training Needs**

The Head Teacher is responsible for keeping under constant review the safety training needs of staff within their jurisdiction. This includes induction and update training. As soon as possible after joining, the induction Co-ordinator ensures new staff are made aware of emergency procedures and fixtures relevant to their place of work, that they receive all necessary documents and are aware of Health and Safety procedures. The deputy is in charge of ensuring Cub organisers commit to following these procedures.

*Excerpt from a school's policy.*

You should also know the contents of any policies with which you work on a regular basis. For example, if you are a SENCO assistant, you should know the SEN policy, or if you work with numeracy groups, you should have read the numeracy policy.

**Reflect** ?

Following school policy helps you to remain professional in your approach at all times. How much are you and other support staff aware of policies in your school? To what extent do you think it is important that staff should be involved in drawing up new policies?

# Understand the wider context in which schools operate

## Roles and responsibilities of national and local government

### National government

The role of the DfE (Department for Education) is to be responsible for education and children's services. This means that as well as being responsible for drawing up education policy — for example, in setting the National Curriculum and Early Years Foundation Stage from which schools and nurseries operate — it is also looking into new ways of developing the quality of services available to children under the five outcomes of Every Child Matters. It has also set up and administers the schools' league tables.

Other aspects of its role include:

● funding research into education-based projects and those which are concerned with children and young people
● developing workforce reform
● promoting integrated working for all those who work with children and young people
● developing the role of the third sector (those who are non-governmental — voluntary and community organisations, charities and others who work with children).

For more information, see the DfE website: www.education.gov.uk

## Local government

Local government departments for education will provide services to schools in the area in the form of advice and support. The local education authority is responsible for providing accessible local services for:

● staff training and development
● special educational needs
● the curriculum, including early years
● promoting community cohesion
● school management issues
● behaviour management
● the development of school policies.

Local authorities will need to provide documentation which outlines their own vision and plans for the development of government-based initiatives. This will be through, for example, their local Children and Young People's Partnership (CYPP) plan, which will set out the way in which children's services are integrated and describe how and when improvements will be achieved in the local area. In a similar way to school policies, local authorities will also have policies which relate to wider issues, such as their own guidelines for schools for the use of restraint or guidance on the use of medicines.

Most local education authorities will employ specialist advisors to deal with different curriculum areas such as maths or ICT, or to advise on areas such as special

---

**CASE STUDY:** Promoting integrated working

Ali is working as a teaching assistant in a reception class. There is a child in the class that she has been asked to keep an eye on as he has been affected by his parents' divorce and lack of contact with his mother. Although she does not know all the details due to confidentiality, Ali is aware that the boy's father is his carer but the boy also has to look after his disabled sister, and he can find his responsibilities challenging. The class teacher has set up a meeting between Social Services, the boy's father and the school so that they can discuss the main concerns which they have.

● How might this be beneficial to all parties?
● Is there anything Ali could do in preparation for the meeting?

---

| Organisation | Description |
|---|---|
| Social services | Social services will link with schools in cases where it is necessary for them to share information or prepare for court hearings. They may also liaise with your school's family worker or have meetings with teachers. |
| Children's services | These are linked to the five outcomes of Every Child Matters, but may be from a range of providers including education, health, social services, early years and childcare. |
| Youth services | These will have more impact on secondary schools but will be concerned with training and provision post-14, the Youth Matters programme and Targeted Youth Support. |
| National Health Service | Many professionals who come into and work with schools may be employed by the National Health Service and Primary Care Trust, including speech therapists, physiotherapists and occupational therapists. |

*Table 4: Organisations which come into contact with schools. Have you been involved with these or any others?*

educational needs or the Foundation Stage. They will also have specifically trained teachers who will provide support for pupils who, for example, have behaviour needs, or require to be assessed for a specific learning need such as dyslexia. They will sometimes provide these services free to schools, but in some cases schools may be expected to pay for them, in particular if specialist teachers need to come into school to advise teachers or work with specific children.

If there is a change in education policy which all schools need to know about, the local education authority will be expected to pass on this information to schools and offer training to key staff through their local education development centre. They may also come on site and deliver whole-school training or INSET (In-Service Education and Training) to all staff if needed.

## Over to you!

Investigate whether your local authority has developed a Children and Young People's Partnership plan. If so, what are their priorities according to the plan?

## The role of schools in national policies relating to children, young people and families

Schools are expected to know about and show that they are working from national policies which relate to children, young people and families. An example of this is the Every Child Matters framework, which has had a wide-ranging impact on provision for children and young people nationally. As part of this and community cohesion, schools have been developing their central role in local communities through projects such as the extended schools programme, and Ofsted will also inspect against this criterion. Schools need to develop their own policies in line with national requirements, such as child protection and safeguarding children, following guidelines from local education authorities.

## Knowledge into action

Show how your school has developed policies with regards to the following and what national policies they may be linked with:

- school trips
- safeguarding
- premises and security.

## Roles of other organisations working with children and young people

Since there is a wide range of organisations which work with children and young people, it makes sense that they should liaise with one another and share their knowledge and experience. As well as developing links with one another for pupil support and community cohesion, it is likely that meetings will also be held between different services. Although they will work with and alongside schools, they may work in a different way, and all parties will need to be aware of this. However, the impact of a closer working relationship between organisations can only be beneficial to all concerned and is in the best interests of the children.

## Getting ready for assessment

You will need to show that you understand the ethos, policies and working practices of your own school and how it fits into the wider community. You can present your evidence in different ways, such as:

- writing a short report about your school

- having a professional discussion with your mentor or an expert witness and keeping a record of this (this may be a written record or a recording) to use as evidence

- using witness testimonies from colleagues in school or professionals from outside agencies to show how you have liaised or communicated with them

- using any other evidence of meetings you have set up or been involved in, such as emails or letters.

### Websites

**www.governornet.co.uk** – this site gives useful information for school governors
**www.education.gov.uk**
**www.tda.gov.uk** – up to date advice on all areas of education and training
**www.ssatrust.org.uk** – specialist schools and academies trust
**www.teachernet.gov.uk/wholeschool/extendedschools** – advice and information about extended schools provision

## Check your knowledge

1. Name the four different types of mainstream school.

2. What are all children in early years education entitled to?

3. What is a school's ethos?

4. What are the role and responsibilities of a school governor?

5. Why do some schools adopt specialist status?

6. Explain the term 'community cohesion'.

7. What is the role of the Foundation Stage Manager in a school?

8. Which of these organisations or professionals might come into schools to liaise with staff?

   a. speech and language therapist

   b. health and safety executive

   c. school improvement partner

   d. community cohesion officer.

# School life

## My Story Louise, Year 5/6 teaching assistant

I had been a teaching assistant at a two-form entry mainstream primary school for three years when I decided to take on the role of support staff governor. I didn't know much about what governors actually do but a colleague who has worked in another school for some time told me it would be a useful experience for my own professional development. After I'd been voted for and approved by others, I had some initial training run by the local education authority. I started to attend governors' meetings and was surprised at the amount of things I learnt about how schools are run even from the very earliest stages. I've now been support staff governor for three years and am on two committees, school site and curriculum, and attend regular meetings to discuss current issues. Being a governor means I can contribute to the running of the school in a different way. I feel I have a better understanding of the whole process, and a real appreciation of the amount of work governors do, often behind the scenes.

## Ask the expert

**Q** What happens if I want to be a governor but don't think I know enough about it? How can I find out more?

**A** If you are interested in being a governor you should as a first point of contact talk either to your Head Teacher or to someone else who is on the governing body. They will be able to tell you more about what is involved and the expected level of commitment in terms of time, meetings and so on at your particular school. Your local authority will also be able to provide you with literature and information on the work of a school governor.

**VIEWPOINT**

Governors play a crucial role in schools although their contact with school staff may be limited as they are likely to mainly work in another job. How much are your governors visible in your school to staff and pupils? What do you think about this?

# TDA 3.3 Support learning activities

You should be taking part in regular planning meetings with the teacher as well as discussing pupil progress and evaluating the work you have done. The activities you carry out may be in any learning environment, including educational visits and extended school provision. You should be able to show how you contribute to meetings with teachers or others in the school. You may also like to look at this unit alongside TDA 3.10 Plan and deliver learning activitives under the direction of a teacher.

## By the end of this unit you will:

1. be able to contribute to planning learning activities
2. be able to prepare for learning activities
3. be able to support learning activities
4. be able to observe and report on learner participation and progress
5. be able to contribute to the evaluation of learning activities
6. be able to evaluate own practice in relation to supporting literacy, numeracy and ICT.

# Be able to contribute to planning learning activities

## The planning, delivery and review of learning activities

In your role as a teaching assistant, you may be asked to help with the planning of learning activities in the learning environment. **Planning**, teaching and **evaluating** follow a cycle which gives structure to the learning process, as the following diagram shows.

It could be that the teacher plans for the long and medium term, and that you are involved in short-term or daily plans, or plans for individual sessions. You should know the learning objectives so that you are clear about what the children will be expected to have achieved by the end of the session.

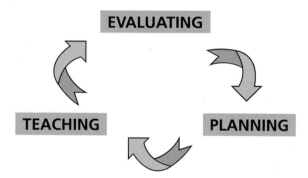

*The planning, teaching and evaluation cycle.*

Although the class teacher will have completed long-term plans for the class, you may be asked to work with them to discuss and plan activities for the week so that you are aware in advance of what you are required to do. You will need to work with the class teacher to ensure that the work you are covering fits in with activities and topics which have been planned for the term.

### Key terms

**Planning** – deciding with the teacher what you will do, when, how and with which pupils, to ensure that planned teaching and learning activities are implemented effectively

**Evaluating** – assessing how well the teaching and learning activities achieved their objectives

### Link

For the roles of the teacher and the teaching assistant, see TDA 3.2 Schools as organisations, pages 17–19.

Depending on your role, you may be invited to come to medium- or short-term planning meetings so that you have some idea of topics or themes before the planning itself takes place. At this stage, you should have an opportunity to give suggestions, as well as informing the teacher of any difficulties you anticipate

| Stage of planning | Purpose | Content |
|---|---|---|
| Long term (curriculum framework) | Shows coverage of subject and provides breadth | Summary of subject content |
| Medium term (termly or half termly) | Provides a framework for all subjects | Shows overview of activities and/or topics. Links to national primary strategy |
| Short term | Provides a plan for the week's lessons which can be broken down by day. | Should include:<br>• learning intentions<br>• activities<br>• organisation/differentiation<br>• provision for special educational needs (SEN)<br>• use of other adults<br>• rough time allocations<br>• space for notes |

*Table 1: There are three different types of planning which you may be involved with.*

**Medium-term Planning Sheet**
**Week 6**

Topic: Toys — Week beginning: 11/10/10

| Activities | Learning objectives | Learning outcomes | Comments |
|---|---|---|---|
| • Sort a collection of toys into old or new.<br>• Talk about characteristics of each set using adjectives, e.g. rusty, shiny, broken, dirty, ragged, clean | • How to decide whether an object is old or new<br>• Describe characteristics of old and new objects | • Sort objects into old and new sets<br>• Explain why they have grouped objects in a particular way | |
| • Discuss the meaning of words.<br>• Match adjectives to toys. | • Collections of words linked to topics | | |
| • Which would be the best paper for making a jigsaw (or a set of cards)?<br>• What would the material need to be like? Strong? Rigid?<br>• How could you find out which paper would be best?<br>• Test ideas with papers. Say what you did. | • Suggest how to test an idea about whether a paper is suitable for a particular purpose | • Make a suggestion of what a paper for making a puzzle should be like<br>• Suggest a way of testing the papers appropriate to the characeristic chosen | |
| • Make a paper sculpture. | | | |
| • Why do games have rules?<br>• What are they?<br>• What would be fair or unfair? | • Recognise choices they can make and the difference between right and wrong<br>• Agree and follow rules<br>• Understand how rules help them | | |

*A medium-term planning sheet.*

35

when considering the needs of the children. Your role and the role of the teacher should be in a partnership, where there are clear roles and responsibilities for working together to support the pupils. You may also be involved in planning a series of activities to be carried out over several sessions. This could be with the same group, if the children need to work on a particular idea, or with different children on a similar, perhaps differentiated, task. As you become more experienced, or if you are working with a child who has special needs, you may add some of your own ideas during the sessions so that the child or children builds on work done each time.

Following the session, both you and the class teacher should reflect on the effectiveness of the teaching and learning activities, and their success in relation to the learning objectives.

When evaluating, you will need to look at whether the children you were working with were able to meet the learning objective through their task. If the majority of children achieved the objectives but one or two found certain aspects difficult, it would be appropriate to record by exception, for example, 'All in this group were able to complete the task and had a good understanding, but George and Bayram could not understand the representation of 2p and 5p coins.' Similarly, if a child completes the task quickly and is more able than the rest of the group, this should also be recorded (see also page 108 on feedback). You may be involved in meetings or discussions with others in the year group during which you talk about topics or long-term plans for the year and whether you should repeat the same ideas the following year.

### Knowledge into action

Using a medium- or short-term plan which you have devised with others, annotate and highlight this where relevant, to show the input of both yourself and others in your team. You should also show how you have evaluated the effectiveness of the plan.

## Your own strengths and weaknesses

In primary schools, teachers and support staff have to work in many different subjects and situations, and everyone has different areas of strength. You are not just teaching the subjects of the National or Foundation Stage Curriculum, but also social skills, relating to others, being part of a school and so on. You are likely to feel more confident in some areas than others and this will subsequently impact on learning activities. However, if you are asked to do something which you are unsure or unclear how to approach, you should always speak to the teacher about it at the planning stage. You should be absolutely clear about what you are required to do and what the children are going to learn — if you are not sure, the outcome is unlikely to be satisfactory.

### CASE STUDY: Identifying strengths and weaknesses

Katy is an experienced assistant who has mainly worked in Key Stage 2 and has supported individual children as well as taking groups for intervention activities (programmes, such as after-school tutorials or reading programmes). She is currently supporting a pupil who has severe learning needs within Year 4, although the pupil is absent today. In Numeracy, the class teacher has said to Katy it would really help if she could take a group of six children who are struggling with decimal notation and do some number line work with them. Katy is not sure how to approach the concept, but takes the group for the activity.

- What is likely to happen?
- How could Katy have handled this situation differently?
- What are the implications for the group of Katy's chosen course of action?

## Use knowledge of the learners and curriculum to contribute to the teacher's planning

When planning, we should always take account of pupils' experiences and interests. Learning needs to be relevant to pupils in order to engage them and keep them motivated: we need to be able to relate what we are doing to their experiences, in order to ensure that what they are learning makes sense to them.

---

**CASE STUDY:** Meeting pupils' interests

You have been asked to work with a group of pupils on a project about the Romans in Year 3. This will take place over six weeks and the pupils will be required to make and set up a Roman market to show others in the school and provide a display.

You are working with six pupils and this is what you know about them.

1. Jack has average ability and enjoys working with others.
2. Toni is very quiet, but you know she is very creative and excellent at art. She also has average ability for her age.
3. Jamal has a tendency to lose focus very quickly. You think that he is a **kinaesthetic learner** who works best when he is moving around and engaged in 'active' learning.
4. Shirley has excellent numeracy skills, although she lacks confidence with writing.
5. Eleni speaks English as an additional language, but her ability is above average. She has been in school for two terms and goes for additional sessions to help with her understanding of language.
6. Ricky is immature and small for his age. He has an unsettled home background and often comes to school hungry and looking tired. He tries hard in school and has been particularly interested in this topic.
   - Show how you could use this knowledge to plan and deliver a series of lessons which would incorporate what you know about the pupils.

---

**Functional skills**

**English: Writing**
You could use the case study opposite to practise the planning skills you have learned about so far. Remember that when writing a plan, you need to present information clearly and concisely.

**Key term**

**Kinaesthetic learner** — someone who learns best through physical experience: touching, feeling and doing

## Constructive suggestions for own role in supporting planned learning activities

Ideally, you should be given this opportunity to input some of your own ideas into how you will carry out activities when they are at the planning stage. This is because you may have your own areas of expertise, or ideas which may help the teacher to create activities for children. This is especially true for assistants who support individual children with special needs, as there will be some activities in which these children need more structured tasks. You should also be aware of your own areas of weakness: if you know that you will find it difficult to take a group of children for an art activity on printing because you have not done this for a long time, for example, then say so. You should feel comfortable with what you are doing, because it is important to be confident when carrying out the activity. If you anticipate any other difficulties in carrying out the plan which the teacher has not foreseen, you should also point these out.

## Information required to support learning activities

Information required to support learning activities includes:

- relevant school curriculum and age-related expectations of pupils

- the teaching and learning objectives

- the learning resources required
- own role in supporting learning activities
- any additional needs of the children involved.

---

**CASE STUDY:** Offer constructive suggestions

Lucy is working in a Year 3 class with Josh, who has social and emotional needs. She regularly supports group activities and plans with the class teacher so that she can input into what she does both with Josh and the others in the group. The following week, the teacher is planning to do some work on Chinese New Year. As Lucy's husband is Chinese, she has some items at home which she suggests she can bring in to show the class and to start a discussion. She suggests that the children can then look at them in groups and, following their work, the items could be used for part of a display. The teacher then asks Lucy whether she has any other suggestions or if she can ask her husband about his experience of the traditional celebrations.

- Why is it important to discuss plans beforehand as much as possible?
- How will Lucy's involvement enhance the experience of the children?

---

Before carrying out learning activities, you will need to have an awareness of the curriculum and the stage at which pupils will be working. Depending on their age, pupils will be working at different stages within the Early Years Foundation Stage or National Curriculum (for a description of these stages, see also TDA 3.2 Schools as organisations). As you become more experienced with different age groups, you will develop your own knowledge and expectations about what pupils will be able to achieve.

You should have access to school records about pupils' learning, and be able to refer to paper or electronic-based records if required. This will give you details about pupils' educational background and will be particularly useful if you do not know the children well. Many classrooms now have a class file which other adults such as assistants can refer to so that they have access to information on pupils, and it is likely that the teacher will share this with you.

You may also gather information more informally through your own observations or discussions with other staff. You will, without realising it, pick up information in different ways all the time that you are in the class with the children.

If your plan is adequate and you have thought about resources beforehand, you should know exactly what is needed when you prepare for the activity. You should think about individual pupils and how they learn best when you are deciding what resources might be useful.

The teacher should make learning objectives and your role in each activity very clear, so that you know exactly what you are required to do and what the children should have learnt by the end of the session. This will also make evaluating the activities straightforward.

One advantage of planning is that you will be able to think about additional resources which you might have to buy or gather from outside school. It may be straightforward — for example, if you have been asked to use some artefacts to help you to discuss and find out about a religious festival and you know that these are always kept in the RE resources cupboard. However, if you have to think about and make or find resources to use, more preparation may be required.

When working with pupils who have particular needs, you may seek advice from specialist teachers or be able to borrow equipment or resources which are helpful (for more on this, see below).

# Be able to prepare for learning activities

## Select and prepare the resources required

The school should have different resource areas where members of staff will have access to equipment for each particular subject area, for example:

- maths equipment
- design and technology tools and equipment
- musical instruments

*Your school may use items to support the curriculum from a range of sources.*

- science **resources**
- art resources
- PE equipment
- geography/history resources
- CD-ROMs for computers
- RE resources
- personal, social, health and economic education (PSHE) resources
- textbooks and resource books for all subjects.

### Key term

**Resources** — furniture and equipment needed to support the learning activity, including classroom furniture and curriculum-specific equipment, such as computers for IT or apparatus for science

Some of these resources, such as PE equipment, may be immediately obvious. However, if there is a small subject area which you are not often required to support, you may need to ask other members of staff. You should make sure that you are familiar with how different items of equipment work before you come to use them.

You will also be responsible for more general classroom preparation, for example, ensuring that there are sufficient resources for planned activities within the classroom on a daily basis. This should have been discussed and directed by the teacher if there is anything specific or unusual required, for example, something that is topic based. You will also be expected to maintain the learning environment during and in between lessons. This may include jobs such as making sure there are adequate pens or sharp pencils, or keeping stocks of paper ready for use. It is important for you to be aware of items such as these, which are constantly in use and which may run out quickly. There will always be something to do in a classroom and when the class teacher is busy or unable to speak to you in between activities, you should always have the initiative to keep busy.

The types of **materials** which may be needed within the learning environment might include:

- written materials such as books or worksheets
- equipment for different curriculum areas
- general classroom items such as pencils, paper, scissors or glue sticks
- specific items, for example, artefacts for an 'Egyptians' topic
- outdoor equipment for playground use
- large resources such as sand and water.

## Develop and adapt resources

You will need to consider the needs of learners when planning learning activities, as some children will need specific resources to enable them to access the curriculum. The SENCO (Special Educational Needs Co-ordinator) may need to advise on how you achieve this if you have to support a child who has very specific needs. The school may already have some of the resources required, or they may be available through catalogues. However, in some cases it is likely that you will need to develop or adapt some of your own.

**CASE STUDY:** Adapt resources to meet the needs of learners

Consider the needs of the following pupils.

1. Ryan is a visually impaired child who has just started in the Reception class.
2. Sam is in Year 5 and has dyslexia.
3. Niamh has problems controlling her **fine motor skills** and needs additional support in the form of exercises and practice each day.

- How might you need to adapt learning resources for each of these pupils?
- Find out about any additional resources which you think could support them in their learning.

## Health, safety, security and access requirements

**Link**

See CYP 3.4 for more on health and safety.

Whatever the needs of children, they are entitled to a safe and secure learning environment. You should always be aware of health and safety issues, in particular when working with young children. It is a duty of all primary school employees to keep children safe, as many young children are not aware of hazards which may occur or the possible consequences. Schools will also have security measures in place, such as gates, and procedures for identifying any visitors who are in school, such as signing-in books and visitors' badges. If you encounter unfamiliar persons on school premises, you should always challenge them politely.

Sufficient storage space can be an issue in schools, but it is important that storage areas are locked and kept tidy so that they do not present an additional hazard. Spaces such as cleaning cupboards or areas where resources are kept can sometimes be untidy due to lack of time or staff being unsure of where items should be stored.

## Functional skills

### ICT: Using ICT

Using a video camera, you could carry out a short 'walk and talk' activity where you video the area in which you are about to carry out an activity with children and talk through the health and safety elements that you have considered. It is important that this activity is done prior to the children entering the area. Once you have recorded your footage, you could edit it and present it to your college group to show your understanding of health and safety.

---

**CASE STUDY:** Meeting health and safety requirements

Andrew has just started a new job in a primary school. He has been given a copy of the school's health and safety policy, which emphasises the importance and necessity of vigilance among members of staff. He is surprised to notice that this policy does not appear to be observed, however. The signing-in procedure is often ignored by office staff and visitors to the school are not identified. He knows that many parents help in the school and that the attitude of staff is: 'It's OK – it's only a parent, we know who they are.'

- Should Andrew say something and if so, to whom?
- Why is it important for the children that health and safety policies are not only in print but adhered to by all staff?

---

# Be able to support learning activities

## Learning support strategies

When delivering teaching and learning sessions, you will need to ensure that the methods you have selected will support and motivate all pupils. There should be a variety of delivery methods according to the needs of individual pupils. Some learners will need to have more practical tasks in order to stimulate and motivate them, whereas others will find that they work well researching through books or the Internet. As a general rule, it is best to devise sessions which incorporate different methods of teaching and learning, so that you will be able to meet the needs of all pupils.

Learning support strategies include:

- creating a positive learning environment
- managing behaviour
- encouraging group cohesion and collaboration
- prompting shy or reticent pupils
- translating or explaining words and phrases
- reminding learners of teaching points made by the teacher
- modelling correct use of language and vocabulary
- ensuring learners understand the learning tasks
- helping learners to use resources relevant to the activity
- providing individual attention, reassurance and help with learning tasks as appropriate to learners' needs
- modifying or adapting activities.

### Creating a positive learning environment

In order to establish and maintain a purposeful learning environment, you will need to develop positive expectations of pupils and encourage them to take responsibilities for their environment. They should respect the classroom or other learning environments in the school and take ownership of them, for example, through picking up litter or looking out for lost property. All members of the school community should have high expectations of the learning environment. If it is tidy and well organised, pupils will learn to take pride in their school surroundings. Having a purposeful learning environment means that the school should be conducive to learning, with clear, well-labelled displays, a welcoming atmosphere and clear behaviour boundaries of which all children are aware.

## BEST PRACTICE CHECKLIST: Establishing and maintaining a purposeful learning environment

- Resources and facilities should be accessible for all pupils, including those with special educational needs (SEN).
- The environment should be welcoming and contain clearly defined areas for different activities.
- Storage areas should be tidy and clearly labelled.
- Items hazardous to children should be stored safely.
- Displays and information should be at a height that all children can read.

### Functional skills

**ICT: Developing, presenting and communicating information**
Your ICT skills could support you in ensuring that the checklist above is complete. It is important when completing displays in schools that the font type and size you use on the computer is fit for the purpose.

## Managing behaviour

It is important to establish ground rules and high expectations of pupils from the start of your work with children, so that they have clear boundaries and are aware of consequences of their actions. It is important to praise good behaviour so that this is recognised, and you should ensure that any poor behaviour is challenged and dealt with straight away, so that learning can continue uninterrupted. If the behaviour persists, you should remove the child or children from the activity and refer to the teacher.

### Link

For more on boundaries, see TDA 3.4 Promote children and young people's positive behaviour.

## Encouraging group cohesion and collaboration

You will need to show that you encourage groups of pupils to work together where necessary in order to discuss different aspects of the task. If necessary, you may need to manage disruptions so that learning can continue.

## CASE STUDY: Managing disruptions within your group

Carole is working with a group of Year 6 pupils on a science activity. She is a very experienced assistant and regularly works with groups and individuals on activities set by the teacher. Today the group is quite lively and one pupil in particular is calling out and distracting the others. Carole uses all the strategies she knows to refocus the pupil, but he continues to disrupt the group.

- What would you do in this situation?
- Why is it important to refer incidents like this to the appropriate person?

## Prompting shy or reticent pupils

You will need to ensure that you include all pupils with whom you are working and in particular that you prompt those who are less keen to put forward their thoughts and ideas. You can do this by encouraging paired discussion to build their confidence and by direct questioning if this is appropriate.

## Translating or explaining words and phrases

In some cases, you may need to explain specific words or phrases where there is misunderstanding by pupils, particularly if they are very young, have communication difficulties or speak English as an additional language.

## Reminding learners of teaching points made by the teacher

As the task is progressing, you may need to 'bring pupils back' to remind them to keep on task and also make sure that they remember specific teaching points as they are working.

## Modelling correct use of language and vocabulary

Pupils will need to have an adult close to them who is able to model the correct use of language, as at primary level they will still be making some errors. They may also speak English as an additional language. You should not tell them that what they have said is wrong, but should repeat back to them using the correct language.

## Ensuring learners understand the learning tasks

Whenever starting a learning activity with pupils, you should clarify with them before they start the learning objective and what they are required to do. Some children, in particular those who are less confident, may start an activity even though they are not sure what they are required to do, because they are anxious about speaking out.

## Helping learners to use resources relevant to the activity

Always check that pupils know how to use specific resources which are part of the activity and do not assume that they have all used them before, in particular if the equipment is subject specific.

## Providing individual attention, reassurance and help with learning tasks as appropriate to learners' needs

You will need to be aware of the needs of the pupils with whom you are working so that you can provide them with the right level of support. This may mean that they have specific learning needs, or that their personality is such that they are either more or less demanding of your attention than other pupils. You should try to reassure less confident pupils through praise and encouragement, and extend all pupils through questioning. Although you are with the children to give support, you must remember that your role is not to do the work for them.

## Modifying or adapting activities

For learning to take place, information needs to be presented in a way that is relevant to the learner. As you get to know pupils, you will be able to identify how they learn best. The way in which you support their learning should depend on the learning styles and needs that they have. Some pupils may not be able to remain on task for very long, or may find written work more challenging than others. You may

need to spend time discussing activities with some pupils, or present information in a more visual way such as through photographs or artefacts in order to support their learning. It is also possible that the plan may not be appropriate for the needs of the children and that you need to change what they have been asked to do in order to help them achieve, perhaps at a different level than the one set. However, the most likely situation is that you will have a group of pupils with varying needs and you will need to maintain the interest of the group.

---

**CASE STUDY:** Adapting strategies for pupils' differing needs

You have been asked to work with a group of Year 4 pupils on an activity to look through a poem and identify the way in which the poet has described different experiences using his senses. You have read the poem to the pupils and they now have to think of some descriptive phrases of their own.

1. Emil has dyslexia and **dyspraxia** and is full of original ideas.

2. Clarice has some difficulty in remaining focused for too long.

3. Anya and William are of average ability.

4. Kelly is of average ability and very musical.

5. Liam is above average in maths, but finds language activities challenging.

- Looking at the best practice checklist at the end of this section, and bearing in mind the needs of the pupils, how could you adapt the strategies you used for the different pupils in the group?
- If planned carefully, how might this take some of the pressure off you as the adult?

---

### Key term

**Dyspraxia** — a brain condition causing co-ordination problems, poor concentration and poor memory

## How social organisation and relationships may affect the learning process

Social organisation and relationships include, for example:

- learner grouping
- group development
- group dynamics
- the way adults interact and respond to learners.

Another way in which pupil learning may be affected is by the group they are working with. Depending on the age of the pupils and their stage of development, they may be easily distracted or influenced by the opinions of others. Some pupils may be concerned about what their peers think of them and reluctant to put their ideas forward in case they are wrong. Others may want to show off to their classmates in order to gain attention. If there has been a disagreement or particular problem during playtime, pupils may be upset or agitated and therefore unable to concentrate on their learning. As the adult, you need to be aware of and manage these kinds of issues and their effects on pupils' learning.

### CASE STUDY: Managing circumstances that affect pupils' learning

You are working with a group of Year 6 pupils on a maths activity. They are working on a problem-solving activity and have been asked to look at different sequences of numbers using different-sized number grids. One of the pupils in your group is not at all engaged in the activity and as he appears upset, he disturbs the others in the group.

- What steps could you take to involve the pupil in the task?
- Are there any other strategies that you could use to make sure that he completes the activity?

## Give attention to learners balancing the needs of individuals and the group

When working with groups of pupils, you must make sure that you are able to give attention to all pupils, rather than to those who seek your support the most, or those who have particular needs. This can be difficult to manage, in particular if a child in your group is demanding or has behaviour issues, or if you are working with a larger group. However, there are a number of ways in which you can minimise queries and problems which may arise by speaking to the group before you start.

1. You will need to be very clear on ground rules and establish high expectations of behaviour at the start of your work with pupils.

2. You should ensure that you have clarified what children have been asked to do and that they understand and know the learning objective.

3. If pupils have been asked to work with any resources or artefacts, they should have some time to look at them before starting the activity.

You should then focus on any children who you think may need more support and then gradually move around the group, checking on each child's progress. If you are having discussions with the children, make sure all of the group are included and not just those who are more anxious to participate.

### Reflect

Using the information on the opposite page, think about how you could tailor the rest of the lesson to the strengths of the four children in the group. You may also find that although you are primarily working with an individual pupil, you are regularly asked to take groups of pupils to support their learning. This is because when working with children who have additional needs, it is important that they are not isolated by continually working on their own with an adult. What benefits do you think children get from working with others on group activities and listening to their ideas?

| | |
|---|---|
| | **Learning objective:** To be able to identify and label parts of a plant (Y2) |
| | **Teaching and learning methods** |
| General intro | Take all pupils for a walk in the school garden to look at different plants and their characteristics. Select some plants which look 'different' from each other and ask pupils to identify what is the same about them. Go back to class and label parts of plant. |
| Jack | Enjoys games and practical activities. Lower ability. Possibly dyslexic but no diagnosis. |
| Shola | Very creative, lively. |
| Suzanne | Good general ability and focus. |
| Warren | Difficult to engage in learning. Finds written work hard. |

*Do you make it clear to children what they have been asked to do and what the learning objective is?*

## Encourage learners to take responsibility for their own learning

### Link

See TDA 3.7 for more on assessment for learning.

It is important for pupils to understand what they are learning and its purpose. The now common practice of displaying learning objectives at the start of the lesson has supported the view that pupils are more likely to be engaged in their learning if they understand the aim of what they are doing. You can then encourage them at intervals during the learning process to think about how they are progressing.

**CASE STUDY:** Encouraging learners

Adam is in Year 3 (P4) and is a lively and happy boy. For some time, however, he has found school work challenging and has become less willing to participate, particularly in maths activities. When you have talked to him about it and tried to encourage him to carry on with his work, his response has been, 'I can't, I'm rubbish at maths.'

- Outline how you could help Adam to regain his confidence and present some ideas you could work on with the class teacher.
- Why is it particularly important that you monitor Adam's progress in this case?

## DVD activity

### Video clip 1 – Classroom preparation

In clip 1, the teacher and teaching assistant are shown together discussing and planning the activities for the following day. The assistant is seen checking the plans and putting forward her own suggestions. Identify how she shows an awareness both of the needs of the children and of general classroom issues when preparing the learning environment.

In addition, the assistant notices a health and safety issue in the classroom and reports this to the teacher. Find out who in your school is responsible for health and safety. Show how your school's health and safety policy is publicised in school to ensure that all staff are aware of its contents. Does it include guidance for the use of learning materials and their preparation? What opportunities does your school have for recycling and disposal of waste materials? Children will also need to be made aware of health and safety issues. Think about different subject areas (for example, PE, art, ICT) and outline some of the health and safety issues which may occur in these environments and how they can be prevented.

### Video clip 2 – Understanding shapes or measures

In clip 2, the teaching assistant is working with a group of four Year 1 pupils on an activity to encourage them to name and describe the properties of different 2D and 3D shapes.

1. List some of the factors of which you will need to be aware when supporting pupil learning. How does this assistant take into account the age of the children while managing the activity? Does she need to modify what she is doing in order to keep the children on task, and if so, how?

2. Think about your own experience when supporting learning activities. These may be during written work or more practical sessions, such as this one. How do you encourage independent learning in pupils while enabling them to achieve?

3. On this DVD there are several different clips of teaching assistants supporting learning in different environments (clips 2, 3, 6, 8, 9 and 10). Do any of these sessions demonstrate how support strategies are used and adapted to accommodate different learning needs as well as any problems in the learning environment? Give reasons for your answer.

4. What do you think of the way in which the assistant observes and reports on learner participation and progress? What methods has she used during the activity to monitor and promote pupil participation? How will this help when evaluating the children's learning?

Assessment for learning has become a regularly used motivational way of encouraging children to take responsibility for their own learning. It is a way of ensuring that learners are clear on the purpose of what they are doing, what they need to do and how close they are to achieving it. Research has shown that there is a clear relationship between being part of the process of assessment and pupil motivation. Those who are actively engaged with their progress will feel empowered to improve their performance, as they have more ownership of their learning.

## Support learners to develop literacy, numeracy, ICT and problem-solving skills

When supporting learning, whatever the subject, you should at all times encourage pupils to develop their skills in the areas of literacy, numeracy and ICT. This is because there will always be some overlap in what children are required to do. If you have opportunities, for example, to include ICT in a learning activity for another subject area, you could discuss ways of doing this with the teacher. When your assessor comes to see you working with pupils, you will need to think about how you show that you support these subjects in different ways, as well as through literacy, numeracy and ICT sessions.

### Functional skills

**Maths, English and ICT**
This information highlights the importance of including maths, English and ICT in all areas of your work. This is what makes functional skills so important.

### Link

See also TDA 3.11 and 3.12, Support literacy and Support numeracy development.

## Problem-solving skills

This method of learning involves groups of pupils working together to discuss or discover ideas. An example might be pupils finding the best material to make a bag to carry potatoes. Through doing this, they also learn how to work as part of a team and listen to others' views.

### Over to you!

Think about different types of problem-solving activities which you have undertaken with pupils. What do you consider to be the benefits of more open-ended activities?

### Functional skills

**English: Writing**
Considering one of these problem-solving activities that you have undertaken, you could evaluate the activity. When writing an activity evaluation, it is important that you present the information clearly and concisely, using language that is fit for purpose.

## Problems when supporting learning activities

It is likely that when you are supporting individuals, groups or the whole class, at some stage you will encounter problems when supporting learning activities. These could take different forms, but could relate to:

● the learning activities

● the learning resources

● the learning environment

● the learners.

### The learning activity

Sometimes the teacher may set activities that are not suitable for the pupils involved or you may not have clear or complete information to support the activity. You may need to change the activity to make it more achievable for the pupils by going back and checking with the teacher. If this is not possible, you may need to modify it yourself so that they are able to carry out the task (see the case study on page 43 regarding strategies for adapting work).

### Learning resources

The task usually requires certain resources such as pencils, paper, worksheets or textbooks, maths apparatus, paint pots, science equipment and so on. If you have been asked to set up for the task, make sure that you have enough equipment and that it is accessible to all the pupils. Also, where you have equipment that needs to be in working order, check that you know how to use it, that it is functioning and that pupils will be able to use it. If the teacher or another adult has set up for your task, it is still worth doing a check to ensure that you have everything you need. In this way you can avoid potential problems before they arise.

### The learning environment

This relates to the suitability of the area in which pupils are working. Problems may arise in the following circumstances.

● **Insufficient space to work:** If pupils are working on weighing, for example, and there is no room for them all to have access to the scales, they may quickly lose their focus on the task. There may not be space around the table or work area for the number of pupils that you have been asked to work with. Always ensure that you have sufficient space for people and equipment before you start.

- **Too much noise:** The pupils may be working with you in a corner of the classroom, but any other kind of noise will be a distraction, whether it is from other pupils in the room or from some kind of outside disturbance such as grass cutting or a nearby road. It may be possible in this situation for you to investigate another area within the school which is free from this kind of noise, or to inform the teacher that the noise level within the classroom is preventing the pupils from benefiting from the activity.

- **Disturbances from other children:** This can often be a problem if you are working in the classroom, because tasks with close adult supervision can often seem exciting to other pupils. They may be naturally curious to find out what the group or individual is doing, and if there is a continual problem, the teacher should be informed. A good diversion is often to say that they will all be having a turn as long as they allow others to have theirs.

---

### CASE STUDY: Managing disturbances outside your group

You have been asked to work in the classroom on a practical task of science investigation with a group of Year 6 pupils. Although you have sufficient space to carry out the activity, you quickly find that due to the interest generated, pupils from other groups are repeatedly disturbing your activities, because they are interested in finding out what is happening.

- How could you ensure that other pupils do not continue to disturb you?
- What could you say to the pupils with whom you are working?

---

### The learners

Here, again, there may be a variety of reasons why pupils are not able to achieve.

- **Pupils' behaviour:** If any pupils are not focused on the task due to poor behaviour, you need to intervene straight away. If they are able to continue interrupting, they will do so and you will be unable to continue with the task. Always praise the good behaviour of any pupils who are doing what is required of them, as this sometimes makes the others try to gain your attention by behaving well. If there is a particular child who is misbehaving and disturbing others, a last resort is to remove them from the group and work with them later.

- **Pupils' self-esteem:** Sometimes a child with low self-esteem may not think that they are able to complete the task that has been set. Some pupils are quite difficult to motivate and you need to offer reassurance and praise wherever you can to improve their self-esteem. However, it is very important to remember that your role is one of a facilitator and that you are not there to complete the task for the child. Some pupils may just need a little gentle reassurance and coaxing to have a go, while others may be more difficult to work with and require you to use your questioning skills.

- **Pupils' lack of concentration:** There may be a few reasons for pupils finding it hard to concentrate on the task that has been set. These could include an inability to complete the work (the teacher has made the task too difficult) or the pupil completes the task quickly and needs more stimulation. Some pupils, particularly younger ones, have a very short concentration span and the task may be taking too long to complete. If this is the case, you need to stop the pupil and continue with the task later.

- **Pupils' range of ability:** You may find that you are working with a class or group of pupils whose wide range of ability means that some of them are finished before others. In this situation, you may need to have something else ready for them to move on to. For example, if a group of Year 2 pupils are working on an activity to find words ending in -ing, you could ask those who finish early to use their words in sentences of their own.

*What knowledge have you picked up through observation?*

---

**BEST PRACTICE CHECKLIST:** Supporting children during learning activities

- Ensure both you and the pupils understand what you are required to do.

- Use a range of questioning strategies.

- Remind the pupils of the main teaching points.

- Model the correct vocabulary.

- Make sure you carefully and actively listen to all the pupils.

- Encourage the pupils to work together in pairs.

- Help pupils to use the relevant resources and ensure there are enough.

- Reassure pupils who are less confident about their ideas.

- Give praise wherever possible.

- Have high expectations of pupils.

- Adapt work where necessary.

- Inform the teacher of any problems that have taken place that you have been unable to resolve.

- Provide a level of assistance that allows pupils to achieve without helping them too much.

---

# Be able to observe and report on learner participation and progress

When you are supporting learning, you will also be observing how children are working and coping with the activity so that you are able to feed back to the teacher. However, you should not confuse this with more formal observations which the teacher may ask you to carry out and which require you to sit away from the children and not interact with them. Observations are important, as through them we can assess and evaluate pupil participation and progress even more closely.

## Monitor learners' response and assess their participation and progress

You will need to constantly monitor pupils' responses to learning activities and find new ways to engage them where necessary. Pupils will find some subjects more stimulating than others or need help to achieve learning objectives. It is important that you monitor their responses and check what they know, because you need to feed back to the teacher whether they have achieved the learning objective.

You might monitor and promote pupil participation in different ways.

## Record observations and assessments of learners' participation and progress

The teacher with whom you are working should give you information about the **format** of the observation you are carrying out and your method of recording. Observations may be presented in a number of ways depending on their purpose. Some different types of recording are discussed here.

### Key term

**Format** – the way in which results of observations are recorded and presented

- **Free description** enables you to write everything down during the period of the observation (usually five to ten minutes). It means that the observation will be quite short, as it will be very focused on the pupil. Free descriptions need to include what the pupil says to others, how they express themselves non-verbally and the way in which the activity is carried out. These are used when a lot of detail is required and are usually written in the present tense.

- **Structured description** may require the observer to record what the pupil is doing against specific headings or in response to planned questions. Structured descriptions are used to guide the observer on what needs to be recorded, for example, a series of steps towards achieving a task.

- **Checklists** used to check and record whether pupils can carry out a particular activity quickly and in a straightforward way. They usually require the observer to make a judgement on whether a pupil is able to achieve a task; the focus is not on how they do it, but whether or not they can. Checklists may take different forms and schools can devise their own easily, depending on what is being observed.

- **Event samples** are used to record how often a pupil displays a particular type of behaviour or activity. Event samples need to be carried out without the observer participating in the activity to retain objectivity.

| Method | Examples |
|---|---|
| Instructing pupils | • Talk through with pupils what they have to do.<br>• Give pupils a starting point so that they are able to focus. |
| Questioning pupils | • Use open-ended questions – what/when/why/how? – rather than questions that invite 'yes' or 'no' answers.<br>• Find out what the pupils already know or remember from last time.<br>• Involve all the pupils in a group.<br>• Probe, using questions, if pupils are unable to understand the task. |
| Explaining to pupils | • Explain any words or phrases that pupils are not clear about.<br>• Remind pupils of key teaching points.<br>• Model the correct use of vocabulary.<br>• Ensure all pupils understand the teacher's instructions. |

*Table 2: Methods of monitoring and promoting pupil participation.*

● **Informal observations** may arise if you are, for example, asked 'just to keep an eye' on a pupil or to watch them during breaktime, especially if there have been any specific concerns, and then feed back to teachers. In this case you can make your own notes, but should be careful about confidentiality if you are writing things down and remember not to leave notebooks lying around, particularly if you have recorded pupils' names.

### Skills builder

Ask your class teacher if you can carry out an observation on a pupil. Depending on why it will be useful, decide on the best format to use and keep as evidence for your portfolio, remembering to remove the pupil's name.

# Be able to contribute to the evaluation of learning activities

## The importance of evaluating learning activities

Evaluation is important as it feeds into the planning cycle mentioned at the beginning of this unit and enables both children and teaching staff to think about the learning that has taken place. When evaluating teaching and learning activities and outcomes, it is important that you look back to the learning objectives involved. We cannot measure what children have learned without knowing what we are measuring against. If we do not think carefully about learning objectives at the planning stage, it will not always be possible to evaluate whether pupils have achieved them. Learning objectives need to be clear for this to be possible.

● Learners must understand what the outcomes mean.

● They must be achievable.

● We must be able to assess pupils against them.

### Skills builder

Look at the following lesson objectives. Which of the following learning objectives can you clearly measure against? Try using the following words in front of them – 'At the end of the lesson we will be able to...'

* understand the water cycle
* form number bonds to ten
* cut and paste from the Internet
* understand the Great Fire of London
* be able to identify rhyming words in a poem
* find features of a map
* identify features of different shapes.

You should also have an idea about the success criteria when evaluating pupils' learning. Pupils may not meet the learning objective, but they could have a real enthusiasm for the subject and have participated fully in all aspects of the lesson – you will need to record this somewhere. You should also look at the resources you have used and whether these were successfully used.

## Use the outcomes of observations and assessments to provide feedback to improve practice

### Provide feedback to learners on progress made

After most teaching and learning activities with pupils, we will ask them about their learning and discuss with them the next steps. We may do this at the end of the session, or plenary, depending on the structure of the lesson and time available. However, depending on the age and needs of the child, we may also use assessment for learning (see TDA 3.7) as a tool to support them in assessing their own work. It is important for pupils to have time to think about their learning and to understand any feedback given before moving on with their learning.

# Teacher/TA Feedback Sheet

**Class:** Year 6

To be filled in by teacher:
**Teacher's name:** Maryam Radpour
**TA's name:** Joel Forbes

### Brief description of activity

Plotting different points and shapes using co-ordinates on x and y axis. Follow up to start reflecting shapes.

### How session is linked to medium-term plans

Using Primary Framework — Understanding Shape

### TA's role

To check understanding of how to plot co-ordinates.

### Important vocabulary

axis, perimeter, shape, diagonal, co-ordinate, edge, corner names of shapes

### Key learning points

To be able to plot points using co-ordinates.
To identify and reflect shapes.

### For use during group work:

| Children | D | H | Feedback/Assessment |
|---|---|---|---|
|  |  |  |  |
|  |  |  |  |
|  |  |  |  |
|  |  |  |  |
|  |  |  |  |
|  |  |  |  |
|  |  |  |  |

D = Can do task
H = Help required to complete task

*What do you think makes a feedback form most useful?*

## Provide the teacher with constructive feedback on the learning activities and on learners' participation and progress

It is very important that you give teachers constructive feedback on the learning activities which you have carried out with children. Finding time to give feedback to teachers can be very difficult. There is often little time in school to sit down and discuss pupils' work with teachers. Some teachers and teaching assistants will discuss the day's activities on the phone on a daily basis. Another way in which feedback can be given, if there is not time for verbal discussion, is through the use of feedback forms. If these are planned and set out correctly, you will be able to show whether pupils have achieved learning objectives, how they responded to the activity and how much support they needed. Issues such as problems you have faced during the activity should also be noted.

If you have carried out more formal observations as detailed at the end of the previous section, you may not need to give the teacher as much verbal feedback, as the purpose of these observations is different and they will give all the detail required.

You may need to be tactful when feeding back to teachers about learning activities. There may be a number of reasons why an activity has not gone well. However, if it is clearly due to planning, or the children have not found the task engaging, you may have to suggest this to the teacher. Depending on their personality and how well you get along with one another, this may or may not present problems. If you have a relationship which allows you both to give suggestions to one another and discuss any issues as they arise, you will find it easier. Sometimes, however, if you are more experienced than the teacher, or they are not used to working with other adults, it may be difficult.

Even if you believe you are right in your views about ways to support children, it is important that you are positive when you make suggestions or give feedback.

**Reflect**

Which phrase would you use in each of these situations?

1. 'There is no way that group will only take half an hour to do that piece of work; it's just too hard for them.'
   'Would you mind if next time I did that activity I made the introductory activity longer and the focused activity shorter? As I don't think the next group will be able to go straight into the main task.'

2. 'I knew that those two couldn't work together.'
   'What do you think about putting Charlie and Sam together, so that Charlie can guide Sam by reading the problems to him? Then I can swap some of the other pairs round too.'

3. 'Why don't we try it slightly differently with Kaleb so that he doesn't have to go straight into the abstract method?'
   'Kaleb just won't be able to understand it if we do it that way.'

## Reflect on and improve own practice in supporting learning activities

You should always reflect on what you have done with pupils, not only in order to evaluate what pupils have learnt, but also to consider the way in which you have managed different activities. You may find that sometimes you are not as satisfied as others with the outcome and this may be for a variety of reasons. It may be that there were unforeseen circumstances which meant that the session did not go as planned, as sometimes happens in school, or the task was inappropriate for the needs of the different children. You should not be disheartened about this — it happens to everyone — but you will need to consider why it did happen, so that you can learn from the experience. As well as looking at observations and assessments, a good way of doing this is to ask yourself the following questions at the end of an activity.

- How did it go?
- What was I pleased with?
- What did not go as well as I had planned?
- What would I change if I had to do the activity again?

This will then help you to move on and evaluate what you have done with children, which will in turn benefit your own practice.

### Link

See also SfCD SHC 32 Engage in personal development.

### Portfolio activity

Using a reflective account or your own school's evaluation forms, give an example of an evaluation you have carried out on a teaching and learning session you have planned alongside the teacher. Make sure you show whether pupils with whom you have been working have achieved the learning objectives.

### BEST PRACTICE CHECKLIST: Evaluation

- Pupils should have met the learning objectives.
- They should have participated fully in the session.
- Pupils should have understood the vocabulary or terminology used.
- The resources you used should have been appropriate for the session.
- You should have retained control of the session and the pupils should have responded well to you.

### Functional skills

**English: Writing**
Responding to the statements in the bullets on page 53 will allow you the opportunity to develop your report-writing skills. Be honest in your comments and share your evaluation report with others. You could even share your evaluation with your manager at your appraisal.

# Be able to evaluate own practice in relation to supporting literacy, numeracy and ICT

## How own knowledge, understanding and skills in literacy, numeracy and ICT impact on practice

In order to support pupils effectively, you should have a good level of competence in literacy, numeracy and ICT. Increasingly, schools are requiring those who support teaching and learning to have at least a level 2 qualification (GCSE level) in these three areas. This is because pupils should be given the best possible support in their learning. It is also of benefit to you, as it will improve your own confidence when working with pupils.

## Develop a plan for improving own knowledge, understanding and skills

As part of your qualification in supporting teaching and learning, you will need to think about how you can improve your own knowledge, understanding and skills in literacy, numeracy and ICT, and develop a plan. You should be able to discuss this with your line manager or other member of the Senior Management Team in school so that you can develop a plan together. If this is not possible, you should have access to a college representative, such as your tutor or assessor, who will know about the opportunities in your local area. Some local authorities offer additional literacy, numeracy and ICT courses at convenient times for support staff, to encourage them to undertake the training.

## Getting ready for assessment

In order to gather evidence for this unit, your assessor should ideally be able to observe you preparing for and supporting a learning activity which you have contributed to in some way. You should be able to show your assessor the plans and explain your contribution. If you are unable to do this, write a reflective account of a learning activity you have undertaken with a group of pupils. Looking carefully at the assessment criteria for this unit, include the following:

- information you had before the activity such as learning objectives, the needs of the pupils and any specific criteria you needed to follow
- how you selected and prepared learning resources or materials, and any adaptations you had to make to them
- the year group and stage of the curriculum at which the pupils are working and where the lesson fits into the daily or weekly plans
- how you included all the pupils and encouraged them to take responsibility for their own learning
- any problems that occurred and how you dealt with them.

Don't forget to include any observations or assessments you carried out, as well as your own evaluation of the activity and feedback to the teacher.

## Check your knowledge

1. Give three ways in which you might contribute to planning an activity.

2. What information will you need to have about the children before starting a learning activity?

3. What kinds of issues do you need to be aware of in any learning environment?

4. When might you need to develop and adapt learning resources for learners?

5. When would you use the following methods of observation:

    a) checklist

    b) free description

    c) event sample?

6. Outline some of the benefits of evaluating learning activities for:

    a) you

    b) the teacher

    c) the pupils.

7. When might you use assessment for learning with pupils?

### Websites

**www.ccea.org.uk** – National Curriculum documents (Northern Ireland)
**http://curriculum.qcda.gov.uk** – National Curriculum documents (England)
**www.dcsf.gov.uk/everychildmatters** – Every Child Matters (Green Paper)
**www.ltscotland.org.uk** – National Curriculum documents (Scotland)
**www.wales.gov.uk** – go to 'education and skills' and then 'schools' for information on the Welsh curriculum
**www.qcda.gov.uk** – Qualifications and Curriculum Development Agency (QCDA): this website has plenty of information and references around assessment for learning and suggestions for further reading

# School life

## My story Aysel

I work in a large inner-city primary and have been at the school for about a year. I mainly work in years 2 and 3 and am also a midday supervisor. Although I get on really well with the teachers, when I first came to the school I found it quite difficult, as I was never given any advance notice about the support I was going to be giving the children. I literally went into the lesson without knowing what was going to be taught or having any idea about the plans or the learning objective. I found this very hard, as I could not get myself ready and often thought afterwards, 'If only I had known before, I could have done that.' I have a good relationship with my line manager and it came up at my performance management review that I did not feel I was doing my job properly, as I couldn't support the children effectively without seeing the plans. We had a meeting with my class teacher and I said how I had the plans in advance at my last school, which really helped me. Now the teacher sends me through the plans as soon as she does them, and I can prepare better for the lessons. The teacher says she has noticed a difference too.

## Ask the expert

**Q** What if the teacher can't send the plans in advance?

**A** In some schools the teacher will put plans on the wall of the classroom or will print out plans at the beginning of the week for support staff. This may also depend on when they do their planning, as some will wait until the weekend to get it done. In some schools there are planning meetings to which only teachers are invited – if this is the case in your school, you can ask if you can also be present so that you are more aware of plans in your class. You should always speak out if you are unable to share plans, as you should be working in partnership with the teacher to ensure that pupils are getting full access to the curriculum.

### VIEWPOINT

If you have a difficult working relationship with your class teacher it is likely that this will be based around personalities – however, you must remember that you will need to remain professional and that you are both there for the children. Could you speak to the teacher or set aside some time each week so that you can discuss plans? Remember that avoiding speaking will only make the problem worse.

# TDA 3.4 Promote children & young people's positive behaviour

For this unit you will need to demonstrate that you are able to promote positive pupil behaviour in a variety of contexts. You will need to be able to show that you understand and implement agreed classroom management strategies and are part of a whole-school approach to encourage positive behaviour. You will also need to be able to encourage pupils to take responsibility for their own behaviour within the framework of a code of conduct. For more on behaviour management, see TDA 3.20 Support pupils with behaviour, emotional and social development needs.

## By the end of this unit you will:

1. understand policies and procedures for promoting children and young people's positive behaviour

2. be able to promote positive behaviour

3. be able to manage inappropriate behaviour

4. be able to respond to challenging behaviour

5. be able to contribute to reviews of behaviour and behaviour policies.

# Understand policies and procedures for promoting children and young people's positive behaviour

When managing pupils' behaviour, all staff will need to be aware of school policies. This means that you should know where they are and have read them, so that the children will understand when you apply **sanctions** and behaviour management strategies. Although the main policy dealing with behaviour will be the behaviour policy, other school policies will also have an impact on managing behaviour — for example, the health and safety, child protection, and anti-bullying policies.

## Policies and procedures of the setting

### Behaviour policy

The school's behaviour policy is important as it gives guidelines to all staff on how they should manage pupil behaviour. All staff need to be familiar with school policy so that they can apply it consistently in the school.

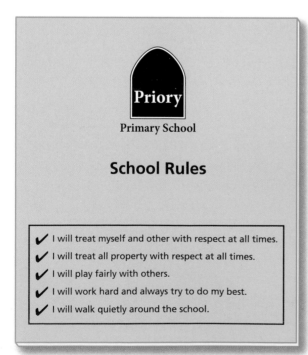

### Priory

**Primary School**

**School Rules**

✔ I will treat myself and other with respect at all times.
✔ I will treat all property with respect at all times.
✔ I will play fairly with others.
✔ I will work hard and always try to do my best.
✔ I will walk quietly around the school.

*A simply and attractively laid out code of conduct will appeal to pupils.*

## Code of conduct

It is likely that your school will have a set of rules or **code of conduct**. It is imperative in any school for children to have guidelines so that they have a clear understanding of how to behave. Children need to be aware of the boundaries within which to manage their behaviour, so that they understand what is expected of them.

These rules should be written in such a way that the children are given positive targets, for example, 'I will walk quietly around the school' rather than the negative 'Do not run in school'. Where the language may be difficult for young children to understand, for example, 'treating others with respect', staff should make sure that the children understand its meaning. Staff should discuss the rules frequently with the children, both in class and during assembly times, so that they remember them.

As well as this list of school rules, staff should encourage pupils to behave in a positive way through watching the behaviour of adults. Children will soon notice if an adult is not acting in a way that they would expect, or if there are inconsistent expectations between adults. When a child is behaving particularly well, you should remember to praise this behaviour so that it is recognised. Children need to be praised for work, behaviour, effort and achievement genuinely and frequently. This will reinforce good behaviour and build self-esteem.

### Rewards and sanctions

Your school should have a scale of sanctions for instances when behaviour is undesirable despite modelling and encouraging good behaviour. All staff should be able to apply these sanctions and pupils should be aware of this. There should be a clear, structured approach, which defines what is expected and the consequences of **inappropriate behaviour**.

### Key terms

**Sanctions** — penalties for disobeying rules

**Code of conduct** — an agreed set of rules by which all children are expected to behave

**Inappropriate behaviour** — behaviour that conflicts with the accepted values and beliefs of the school and community

Consequences could be:

- time out or name on the board
- miss one minute or longer of playtime
- be sent to the deputy head
- be sent to the head teacher or have the teacher speak to the parents.

Your school's behaviour policy should give a clear indication of the procedures you can use when implementing rewards and sanctions. You should make sure that both you and the children are aware of what will happen if their behaviour is not acceptable.

All adults in the school should be able to give rewards and sanctions, although some will be specific to certain members of staff. An example of this might be certificates, which may only be handed out by the head teacher in Friday assembly. If, as a member of support staff, you are not sure about what you can pass on to children, you need to find this out so that you are ready at the appropriate moment.

### Dealing with conflict and inappropriate behaviour

It is likely that your school policy will give you guidance and information about how you should manage more difficult behaviour. It is important that children see a clear structure to what will happen if they choose not to pay attention to the school rules that are in place. They will be much more likely to keep to the rules if they know exactly what will happen if they do not. In this situation, adults are prepared for the types of behaviour which may occur and are teaching children that they are responsible for their actions (see also page 63).

### Anti-bullying

This policy may be addressed as part of the behaviour policy, but should set out school procedures for dealing with any incidence of bullying within or outside the school. Bullying can take many forms, particularly through cyber-bullying with the increase in technologies such as mobile phones and the Internet, and increasing numbers of young children have access to these.

### Attendance

The attendance policy will set out how the school manages issues around attendance. In all schools, attendance is monitored closely and recorded on computer systems so that patterns can be noted and parents or carers informed if attendance falls below a certain percentage. In some cases, schools will award certificates to classes or individual pupils for full attendance during a term or half-term.

**Over to you!**

Using your school's behaviour policy, find and photocopy for your portfolio:

- any school rules or codes of conduct
- rewards and sanctions used within the school
- your responsibilities under the policy.

If you are unable to copy the policies, you may wish to write a reflective account to explain both your responsibilities and the school's procedures.

## How the policies and procedures of the setting support children and young people

You will need to evaluate how your own school's policies and procedures support children and young people and can do this by carrying out the portfolio activity below.

**Portfolio activity**

Using the following table, consider and fill in showing how your school's policies and procedures ensure that children are supported in each of the above ways. Justify each of your points.

| | |
|---|---|
| Feel safe | |
| Make a positive contribution | |
| Develop social and emotional skills | |
| Understand expectations and limits | |

# Benefits of all staff consistently applying boundaries and rules in accordance with policies and procedures

If all members of the **school community** are using the same principles and strategies when managing behaviour, it is far more likely that the children will respond positively. Children will know the scale of rewards and sanctions, and the order in which they will be applied, whoever is speaking to them about their behaviour. Workforce remodelling has had an impact on the number of different professionals who are now working in schools. Support staff and midday supervisors, as well as those running extended school provision, should know the importance and impact of consistent strategies. It is also important that support staff are given status within the school so that they are respected in the same way as teaching staff.

## Key term

**School community** — all personnel contributing to the work of the school including pupils, teachers, support staff, volunteer helpers, parents and carers, and other professional agencies

## Reflect

How do children in your school address teaching assistants and other support staff? Do they use first names or surnames (for example, Mrs Jones)? Do you think this makes any difference to the way in which children in the school perceive the responsibilities of support staff?

## DVD activity

### Video clip 3 – Restorative justice

In the DVD clip, teaching staff are shown using the restorative justice technique (see also page 68) to help them to manage unwanted behaviour in school. The teacher is also shown talking about bullying during a 'circle time' session.

At Rathfern School, there is a consistent approach to behaviour management: all of the staff are aware of the school policy and have equal and shared responsibilities when managing behaviour.

1.  Write a reflective account about how your school manages behaviour; examine the expectations of support staff. In your account, you should include references to your school's behaviour policy and state how you have implemented different aspects of this. Why is it important for all school staff to be consistent when applying behaviour management strategies?

2.  Circle time is a forum for pupils to discuss a range of issues in a non-threatening way. Thinking about the restorative justice technique,

reflect on the experience of the two children at the end of the clip. Restorative justice encourages pupils to take responsibility for their own behaviour. What do you think of the way that the assistant managed the situation? If you had been speaking to these children, are there any aspects which you might have managed differently? What strategies does your school use for dealing with inappropriate behaviour?

3.  Discuss some of the ways in which you have recognised and rewarded positive behaviour in school. Outline the reasons why this is an important aspect of behaviour management.

4.  In your role, you may also find that you have to deal with often challenging behaviour from pupils and this may include risks to the safety of both yourself and others. Write a reflective account stating how you reacted to and managed the situation, and if you needed to refer to others within the school. What strategies does your school have in place for meeting the needs of pupils with learning and behavioural difficulties?

# Be able to promote positive behaviour

## Benefits of actively promoting positive aspects of behaviour

It is important for all pupils, but especially for those who tend to be reprimanded more than others, that we recognise and reward positive behaviour. Even as adults, we like to be noticed for something good that we do. Research has shown that we need to be given six positives for every negative in order to balance this out. It is always much easier for us to focus on negative aspects of a child's behaviour and react to these. When recognising and rewarding positive behaviour, however, you must not forget to notice those children who always behave appropriately.

These ideas are linked to behaviourist theory, which was developed by B.F. Skinner in the 1940s. He suggested that children will respond to praise and so will repeat behaviour that gives them recognition or praise. This may take the simple form of verbal praise, which is very powerful, or stamps, stickers or merit marks. Children who receive praise or attention for positive behaviour, such as kindness towards others, are more likely to repeat this behaviour.

Children may also attempt to gain attention through undesirable behaviour, so you will need to be aware of this and try to ignore it where possible, instead giving attention to those children who are behaving well.

**CASE STUDY:** Promoting positive behaviour

Billy is in Year 5 and is new to the school. He seems to be a lively and likeable member of the class. However, he can sometimes need to be reminded about school rules. You notice one day that he has been particularly helpful to another child during a science lesson when she has found the concept difficult.

- What will be the benefits of praising Billy?
- Why is it important to do so?

## Ways of establishing ground rules which underpin appropriate behaviour and respect

Where possible, pupils should be involved in devising school or classroom rules so that they have more ownership of them. You can do this by inviting them to put forward their ideas and to say why, and then ask others to vote for them. Alternatively you can give them a range of different ideas or think about and discuss rules from other schools, so that they can see a range of different approaches. This will be beneficial as you will agree as a group how pupils should behave, and the children will understand why ground rules are important. You will be able to say to them, for example, 'As a class we agreed that taking other people's property is not acceptable' rather than 'Leave Sajida's things alone'. This will also encourage them to take responsibility for their actions.

**Skills builder**

The next time you are working with a new group of pupils, make sure you establish ground rules before you start. Encourage pupils to contribute their own ideas and take responsibility for the rules. What difference do you think this makes to the activity?

## Promote positive behaviour, demonstrate realistic, consistent and supportive responses, and provide an effective role model

You will need to demonstrate that you are a good role model in all areas of behaviour within the school. Children will take their lead from adults and need to see that they too are behaving appropriately and responsibly. We cannot ask them to behave in a certain way if our own behaviour is not appropriate. This is also true for good manners! Be careful when speaking to other adults and pupils that you are showing the same respect that we are asking children to show others.

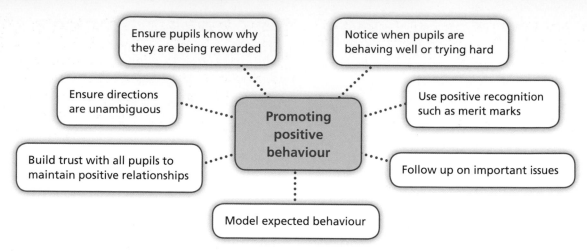

*How many of these strategies do you apply in your school?*

## Notice when children are behaving well or trying hard

This is important because it will help to build positive relationships and shows that you care about the child. If you do not notice, they may think that it is not worth repeating the behaviour or that it is not important.

## Ensure responses are realistic

When managing behaviour, you should ensure that you do not give children unrealistic targets. They should be able to achieve any requirements which are set, so that they do not become disheartened and stop trying.

## Use positive recognition such as merit marks

Most schools use these kinds of systems and will have assemblies and evenings to celebrate work and behaviour.

## Follow up on important issues

You should always make sure you follow up, particularly if you have said that you will. There is little point in saying to a child that you will be telling their teacher how pleased you are with their behaviour if you then forget to do so. The child will then think that you do not really believe it is important.

## Build trust with all pupils to maintain positive relationships

Do all you can to show pupils that you are interested in and value them. As you get to know them, you will remember particular things about them. Giving your trust to pupils encourages them to take more

responsibility, for example, taking the register down to the school office.

## Ensure children know why they are being rewarded

You must be clear on exactly what you are praising or rewarding, for example, 'I am giving you this merit mark because you have been so helpful to others this morning.'

## Making sure directions are unambiguous

You should make sure that you communicate clearly to children so that they understand what you are asking. Young children, especially, may find directions confusing, especially if there are too many instructions at once or if they are occupied doing something else. If you communicate through questioning, for example, 'Is it nearly hometime?', pupils may think that there is some choice involved. If we want children to do as we ask, we need to say things as though we mean them!

## Use of school councils

School councils are also being increasingly used in both primary and secondary schools and are linked to the Citizenship curriculum. In Wales they have become a compulsory part of school life, following legislation by the Welsh Assembly. They discuss a range of issues, but a report by Ofsted in November 2006 cited them as having one of the most positive impacts on whole-school behaviour; as pupils have a voice in managing issues which affect them. Councils comprise an elected representative group of pupils who play an active role in dealing with issues such as bullying. An organisation called School Councils UK has the support of the Department for Education (DfE) and gives advice and guidance for setting up and running councils.

# Be able to manage inappropriate behaviour

## Minimising disruption through inappropriate behaviour according to policies and procedures

An error which is often made when starting to work with young children is to try to befriend them first as a way to gain their approval. This not only does not work, but will make behaviour management very difficult. It is more important to set boundaries and limits first so that pupils know where they stand. This will ultimately make your job easier — there is plenty of time to be friends later! As well as being aware of school policies and any scale of sanctions which you are able to use, you should also be able to show that you mean what you say — never use empty threats, as this will prevent children from listening to you in the future. (See the best practice checklist at the end of this section for more strategies.)

**Functional skills**

**English: Speaking, listening and communication**
You could share your experiences and responses to the case study in the form of a class discussion. Remember to listen carefully to what others are saying, so that you can respond in an appropriate way.

## Apply rules and boundaries consistently and fairly, according to age, needs and abilities

You will need to be able to adapt how you manage the behaviour of children, as their behaviour will depend on their age and stage of development. Depending upon the age and/or needs of pupils, your rewards and sanctions may be very different — this is to ensure that they are age-appropriate. Pupils in years 5 and 6, for example, will probably not be as worried about having their name put on the board as younger pupils — in a similar way, very young pupils will be unlikely to be given a detention. Your school should have a scale of sanctions for you to use with pupils when their behaviour is inappropriate.

### Age and ability of children

Children will have an 'average' rate of development and achieve **milestones** at broadly the same time, but their behaviour will be affected by their intellectual stage of development. For example, younger or more immature children may not be as keen to please their peers and fit in with others, but this will be very important to children in Key Stage 2. Children who are younger or who have special educational needs may, for example, need to be reminded more often about their behaviour. The rules and boundaries will also need to be worded differently so that pupils understand them clearly.

**Key term**

**Milestones** — measureable points in development; the term is usually used to describe stages in children's development where progress can be measured

**CASE STUDY:** Managing inappropriate behaviour

John is working in Year 6 for the first time — in the past he has only worked in Key Stage 1. Today he has been given a literacy group to work with for the first time and some of the pupils have started to talk over him and not listen to what he is saying. John asks them to stop and says that if they do not, he will have to send for the teacher. They do not stop and he threatens to keep them in at playtime.

- Why will John's second strategy not work either?
- Do you think he considered the policy of his school in this case?
- What should John have done?

**Functional skills**

ICT: Developing, presenting and communicating information

English: Writing

You could look at the rules and boundaries in your school and produce two differentiated posters: one for Year 6 children and one for Reception children, each outlining what their rules and boundaries are. This would provide you with the opportunity to practise writing for a different purpose and also differentiating your language to include all children.

## Needs of children
### Physical stage of development

You may have to take pupils' physical stage of development into account when managing behaviour. Sometimes if children's growth patterns are very different from those of their peers, this may have an effect on their behaviour. For example, children in the last two years of primary school may start to become taller and develop some of the first signs of puberty. Girls in particular can become much taller than boys and this can put pressure on them to behave differently. There may need to be additional provision made in this instance, for example, when getting changed for PE. If there are physical difficulties, for example, a visual or hearing problem, these may affect the way in which children relate to others and cause a delay in their overall development which you may need to take into consideration.

### Social and emotional stage of development

The social and emotional development of children is directly linked to the way in which they begin to relate to others. Children need to interact with others so that they have opportunities to gain confidence. For example, they may withdraw socially, find communicating difficult or suffer a language delay. All of these could have a negative effect on their developing self-esteem and on their behaviour, and you may need to take this into account. The rate at which a child will develop socially and emotionally will also depend on the opportunities which have been given for them to interact with others. Where a child has come from a large family, for example, there may have been many more opportunities to play with others and form relationships. If a child has had very little contact or social interaction with other children, it may be more difficult when starting at a school or nursery to understand how relationships with others are formed. There also may be less

*In what ways are interactions with others linked to children's emotional and social development?*

understanding of social codes of behaviour, such as taking turns or waiting for others to finish speaking, or alternatively negative behaviour in order to gain attention (see also on page 66).

(see also on page 66)

### Reflect ?

Write an account of a situation in which you have had to manage pupils' negative or inappropriate behaviour. Consider whether you took into consideration the ages, needs and abilities of the children. Make sure you include your school's strategies and how you have implemented these in stages.

### Functional skills 💬

**English: Reading**
You may need to read round the area in textbooks, policies or the Internet prior to writing your account. Reading to obtain information from at least three different documents will help to develop this area of your functional skills.

### CASE STUDY: Considering pupils' needs

Joe is working as an individual support assistant to Anna, who is in Year 3. She has a developmental disorder which means that she finds it difficult to keep up with her peers intellectually and socially. She is in the playground and has upset two other girls in her class, who tell Joe that she keeps following them and they do not want to play with her.

- How should Joe address Anna's behaviour in this instance?
- What should he say to the other girls?

## Support colleagues to deal with inappropriate behaviour

You should be aware that behaviour management is the responsibility of all adults in the school. This may mean that you are called upon to support

colleagues in different situations, or that you will need to act spontaneously if needed. You should always check if you find that you are close to others who are managing behaviour, to see whether they may need assistance. It is also important to back them up if required, for example, if you are passing and a situation is happening where this would be helpful.

### CASE STUDY: Providing support for colleagues

Lizzie is a new teaching assistant who has been working at your school for two terms and is working towards her level 2 qualification. You are coming down the Key Stage 2 corridor and notice that she is having to speak to a couple of boys about an incident of bad language. She seems to be managing the situation well.

- Would you do anything as you passed Lizzie?
- What might you do if the children were not responding positively to what Lizzie was saying?

## The sorts of behaviour or discipline problems that should be referred to others

Depending on your experience, confidence and how long you have been in the school, you may feel comfortable in dealing with inappropriate behaviour yourself. However there are some situations in which support staff should always refer to others. These are if:

- pupils are a danger to themselves and/or others
- you are dealing with a difficult situation on your own
- you are not comfortable when dealing with a pupil, for example, if they are behaving unpredictably
- pupils are not carrying out your instructions and you are not in control of the situation.

Depending on the situation, you may have to refer to different people – sometimes it may be enough just to have support from another adult within the school.

However, there is also a wider range of specialist support you may be able to call upon:

- within the school:
  - ○ the SENCO or supervisor should be the first point of contact for behaviour support and devising additional strategies for use within the classroom. They will also contact other professionals outside the school
  - ○ other class teachers may also be able to offer support, particularly if they have had to deal with similar behaviour patterns
  - ○ head teacher or deputy — you should be able to speak to those in the Senior Management Team of your school if you have particular concerns about a child or situation

- outside the school:
  - ○ Behaviour Unit — this unit is usually run by the local authority and will offer support and suggestions for dealing with pupils who have behaviour problems. They may also come into schools to observe or work with specific children
  - ○ educational psychologists visit all schools regularly to support children and the adults who work with them. They offer help and advice on a variety of special needs problems, and may assess children and devise individual programmes. They are also involved with assessing those children who may need a statement of special educational needs.

## BEST PRACTICE CHECKLIST: Managing unwanted behaviour

- Intervene early so that the problem does not escalate. If you are the first to be aware of a situation, intervene straightaway.
- Repeat directions calmly rather than reacting to what the child is saying or doing.
- Send for additional help if needed, especially if there are health and safety issues.
- Make eye contact with the child who is misbehaving, so that they see an adult is aware of what they are doing.
- Relate any negative comments to the behaviour, rather than the child, for example, 'Simon, that was not a sensible choice', is more acceptable than 'Simon, you are not a sensible boy'.
- Remove items that are being used inappropriately. The child should then be told why the item has been removed and when they will be able to have it back.
- Use proximity; move closer to a child who is misbehaving so that they are aware of an adult presence. You can use this practice in whole-class teaching time, when the teacher is at the front, to calm or prevent inappropriate behaviour by having an awareness of whom to sit beside.
- Use time out if older children are consistently misbehaving and need to be given some time to calm down before returning to a situation. It can be applied within the classroom or on the playground.
- Use an agreed scale of sanctions of which all in the school community are aware.

## Skills builder

In pairs, look at the scenarios below. Decide which of these you would be comfortable dealing with yourself and which you would need to refer to others.

- A reception child has a temper tantrum because her mother has just left.
- A special needs child is refusing to join in with your group's activity.
- A playtime argument between two Year 6 boys over a football has become aggressive.
- A case of bullying which you have discovered during your speech and language group activity.
- An incident you have come across in the corridor which has left a Year 4 child very upset.
- A child has reacted unch.teristically when being told she has to stay and finish her work.

How would you deal with the situations you could manage yourself?

# Be able to respond to challenging behaviour

## Recognise patterns/triggers for inappropriate behaviour and act to avoid them

As you get to know pupils, you may find that you are able to identify triggers to their inappropriate behaviour. Knowledge of the pupil will also help you when dealing with this, as you will be able to predict what works and what does not. For example, with young children, it may be enough to remove them from the situation. An awareness of the child's needs will be very important if they have specific behavioural difficulties.

## Use agreed strategies, assess and manage risks to own and others' safety

You will need to know how to manage risks to yourself and others. If you are in any doubt about your ability to do this, you must always refer to another member of staff. Your school's behaviour and health and safety policies should give guidelines for dealing with **challenging behaviour** and also the use of restraint, which may be based on local guidelines.

**Key term**

**Challenging behaviour** — behaviour which may involve verbal or physical abuse, or behaviour which is illegal or destructive

Children will not always be aware of risk and dangerous situations, particularly if they are very young or are caught up in what they are doing. Therefore, when speaking to them you should always point out the consequences of their behaviour.

When you are assessing risks to safety, these may be due to:

- a child who is violent or aggressive
- a situation which has got out of control, for example, an argument.

## Support others to identify the circumstances which trigger inappropriate behavioural responses

When working within classes or with individual children who have particularly negative behaviour on a regular basis, it may be helpful to keep a log of any situations which they find difficult or triggers to their behaviour. If you become aware of triggers to inappropriate behaviour, you should always mention it to others so that the situation can be avoided if possible. You may need to remove the child from the situation or speak to them if you see the warning signs that they are becoming distressed. If you are supporting a child who has behavioural needs, you should be able to discuss with them the kinds of situations which they find difficult to manage. In this way, you may be able to support them in managing their own behaviour. Alternatively you may discuss the situation with your SENCO and decide to bring in help from an outside professional in order to evaluate different strategies.

## Deal with bullying, harassment or oppressive behaviour according to policies and procedures

Research for Childline and the DfES in 2003 found that 51 per cent of children in primary schools and 54 per cent of children in secondary schools feel that bullying is a 'big problem' or 'quite a big problem' in their school. The NSPCC reported that 31 per cent of children have experienced bullying by their peers during childhood. As you have close contact with children, you may find yourself in a situation in which you need to act straight away in order to deal with bullying and/ or oppressive behaviour. This may take place on the playground or in other places outside the classroom, or it may be less obvious. You should, however, know your school's policy for dealing with bullying so that you act appropriately. Bullying can start from a very young age and all schools should have a definite plan of action in order to create an environment in which children feel safe. Your school may have a separate anti-bullying policy or this may be linked with the policy for behaviour.

You should also remember that although traditionally bullying has meant issues such as playground name-calling or taunts, it can also mean email, texts or hurtful comments through social networking sites. If a child confides in you that they are being sent hurtful or distressing messages, you should not discount the seriousness of this and you should always report it.

The NSPCC have devised a distance learning programme for dealing with bullies in schools which was launched in November 2008 – details of the website are at the end of this unit.

### Functional skills

**Maths: Analysing and interpreting**
You could create a questionnaire and hand it out to children about whether they feel bullying is an issue to them at school. You could collate your results in the form of percentages and then produce a pie chart of results. This research will not only develop your mathematical skills, but your findings could also feed into the personal, social, health and economic education (PSHE) programme at school.

# Be able to contribute to reviews of behaviour and behaviour policies
## Supporting children and young people to review their behaviour

Rather than simply telling off children, it is likely that you will be asked to support them in reviewing their behaviour and consider why they have acted inappropriately. It is important for children to learn to understand and respect the feelings of others. In many schools, the programme of **restorative justice** is used to ask pupils to sit down with the person with whom they have had a conflict or disagreement in order to help them to learn to understand how the impact of what they do affects others.

### Key term

**Restorative justice** – programme in which pupils are encouraged to consider the impact of their actions or words on others

Children also need to be able to understand how their own feelings may affect their behaviour and you may also need to talk to them about this. For example, saying to a pupil 'I know you are upset because you could not do cooking today' will help them to make the link between emotion and behaviour. In this way, they are more able to understand how to think about others.

*What kinds of situations have you had to deal with which may constitute bullying?*

## Supporting children and young people to identify and agree behaviour targets

You may need to work alongside your class teacher or SENCO as well as the child concerned to devise targets for **behaviour support plans** or individual education plans. Usually these plans will be specific and outline the steps to be taken by staff to support the pupil when working towards the target, and the resources used. There may have been suggestions for targets you can work on from outside agencies. When working with and setting targets, you should make sure that they are SMART (specific, measurable, achievable, realistic and time-bound) and that the pupil is aware of why they need to work on them. It is also important to have realistic expectations of both pupils and staff. When working towards the targets, you will then be able to discuss with pupils why they have agreed these and ask them about any issues which arise. You may also be able to help pupils who do not have specific support plans to think about how they can improve their behaviour if this is starting to become an issue.

It can also be helpful with older pupils to draw up a contract for behaviour so that they can recognise and proactively take responsibility for their actions. It will then be clearer to them exactly what they are required to do.

### Key term

**Behaviour support plan** – plan setting out arrangements for the education of children and young people with behaviour difficulties

---

### Swingate Primary School

Summer Term 2012

Support Began: Jan 2010

### Behaviour Support Plan

School Action/Action Plus

Review date: July 2012

Name: ..................................................    Class: ....................................................

Supported by ....................................................

Targets

1. To come into class without disturbing others
2. To work in a group with adult support and remain on task for 5 minutes

Signed ...........................(teacher) ...............................(pupil) ...............................(parent)

---

*An example of a behaviour support plan. Is the format different in your school?*

Have you been involved in drawing up behaviour support plans or other kinds of behavioural targets for children? If so, evaluate how successful they have been and whether you would use the same strategy next time. If not, describe a time when you have had to discuss with pupils how they will behave in future and how you have followed this up alongside other staff.

## Contribute to reviews of behaviour policies and the effectiveness of rewards and sanctions

If you have pupils in your school who have specific behavioural difficulties, they should be invited to review their behaviour and any targets they have on a regular basis. This will give them the opportunity to think about and discuss the impact of what they do. If you are involved in reviews with pupils, you should know them well and they should be comfortable working with you. Your role, when reviewing behaviour, will be to encourage pupils to think about what they have done and the consequences of their actions for themselves and for others. This will be in relation to the impact their behaviour has had on themselves and others, and on their learning and achievement. When reviewing targets and asking children about their progress, you will need to be sensitive in the way you approach them

and the kind of questioning you use. It is likely that other members of staff and the child's parents will also be involved and that the review will also feed in to developing new targets if necessary.

## Provide feedback on the effectiveness of behaviour management strategies to inform policy review and development

Evaluation of behaviour strategies should be an ongoing process. What works one week with a child or group of children may not always work in another. You should work with the class teacher and other staff to evaluate the kinds of systems which are used within the class and the school as a whole. Behaviour management strategies should be reviewed through careful monitoring of outcomes. You should also be involved in the **review of behaviour management**, which the school should undertake with all staff when reviewing the behaviour policy.

### Key term

**Review of behaviour management** – opportunities to discuss and make recommendations about behaviour, including bullying, and the effectiveness or rewards and sanctions, including class, year and school councils, class or group behaviour reviews, and whole-school policy reviews

### CASE STUDY: Reviewing behaviour support plans

Genette is working with Michael, a Year 2 child who has some social and emotional difficulties. His behaviour has improved slightly since having a support plan and this is reviewed every three weeks, which reminds everyone how he is managing. Just before the latest review is set to take place, Michael has a particularly bad day and his parents have to be called in to take him home.

- What impact will this have on the review?
- Should any different action be taken in your view?
- Outline how you would tackle this issue if you were Genette.

### CASE STUDY: House points system

Hilden Primary School has recently decided to implement a house points system in order to help promote positive behaviour in the school. Although behaviour is not a serious issue in the school, the staff have decided that it is important to recognise when pupils are making special efforts with their behaviour. The programme has been running for two terms when there is a staff meeting to discuss how it is going. The whole school staff are invited and are given the date well in advance.

- Why is this meeting important?
- What might it be helpful to do before the meeting?
- Why is it important to invite all members of staff?

## Getting ready for assessment

Write a reflective account of a situation in which you have had to manage risk to yourself or others due to pupil behaviour. Outline the background and events leading up to the incident. In order to cover the knowledge required, make sure that you indicate how you followed school policy, assessed and acted on the risk involved and took into account the needs of any pupils who have learning and behavioural difficulties. You should check with your assessor that you have covered as much of the assessment criteria as possible.

### Websites

**www.dcsf.gov.uk/everychildmatters** – Every Child Matters (Green Paper)

**www.nspcc.org.uk/pbb** – Information on NSPCC Educare programme to prevent bullying

**www.schoolcouncils.org** – School Councils UK

**www.teachernet.gov.uk/teachingandlearning/ socialandpastoral/seal_learning** – Teachernet, Social and Emotional Aspects of Learning (SEAL)

## Check your knowledge

1. What policies will be relevant to managing pupil behaviour in school?

2. How does your school make pupils aware of school and class rules? Are these reviewed regularly and how?

3. Think about the ways in which you promote positive behaviour on a regular basis. How does this encourage pupils to behave appropriately?

4. Which of these might you use to manage unwanted behaviour?

   a) eye contact with a child who is misbehaving

   b) send for additional help

   c) repeat instructions calmly to a child who is behaving inappropriately

   d) intervening early

   e) remove any items which the child is using to distract someone else

   f) move closer to a child who is misbehaving, for example, during assembly.

5. What are the names of other professionals who may be able to support pupils who have behaviour issues?

6. How can pupils be encouraged to discuss their behaviour and identify reasons for continued misdemeanours?

# School life

## My story: Amal

I started working at Stoneycroft Primary in January, as a learning mentor. I was really keen to support the children as much as possible – many of them come from backgrounds which had led to poor behaviour. I decided to set up a group at lunchtimes where they could come just to have a chat, and to be available every day. I use one of the classrooms and just call it my 'listening ear club', and they know that they can come and talk to me about anything which is worrying them. Over the last couple of terms I have helped to sort out a bullying issue, as well as helping a child who was under pressure at home as he was a carer for his mum, who is ill. As a result of what the children said, I also suggested to my line manager that we had a blitz on behaviour management in the school, as many children did not seem to know school rules and staff have not been consistent in applying sanctions or rewards. This has been a big success, we have had staff meetings on behaviour management and reviewed our policy, which has led to an improvement in the school and on the playground. It has been great to be a part of this.

## Ask the expert

**Q** What can I do if there is one particular child who always seems to be getting into trouble?

**A** Make sure that you look out for times when the child is trying hard to do the right thing and praise them – in this way they will receive positive rather than negative attention.

### VIEWPOINT

This can be a problem, in particular if different adults apply different rules. Children need to be clear on boundaries and know what the consequences will be if they do not. Do you think there are behaviour issues in your school? How can you work closely with other staff to make sure that pupils know what is expected of them?

# TDA 3.5 Develop professional relationships with children, young people & adults

This unit looks at how you work with others in school and develop professional relationships with them. All five learning outcomes will need to be assessed in the workplace and your assessor will need to see you show how you meet them. However, much of the knowledge you will need for this unit will be found in TDA 3.1 and will be cross-referenced to help you.

## By the end of this unit you will:

1. be able to develop professional relationships with children and young people

2. be able to communicate with children and young people

3. be able to develop professional relationships with adults

4. be able to support children and young people in developing relationships

5. be able to comply with policies and procedures for confidentiality, sharing information and data protection.

# Be able to develop professional relationships with children and young people

You may find it easy to explain why you work with children — usually this is because you find communication with them comes naturally to you. However, being able to develop professional relationships so that you can work effectively with pupils can sometimes prove more of a challenge, particularly if the child or group with whom you are working has particular needs or issues which make communication difficult.

## Establish trusting relationships with children and young people and demonstrate supportive responses to their questions

### Link

See TDA 3.1 for more on communication with children.

You will need to ensure that whenever you communicate with children, you are actively listening to what they are saying. In busy situations adults can have a tendency to speak to children without doing this, which may make the child feel that what they are saying is not valued. Responding appropriately to children reinforces self-esteem, values what they are saying and is a crucial part of building relationships. Making conversation and finding out the answer to questions also builds on the language skills that are vital to a child's learning.

Children of all ages need to feel that they are heard. This is particularly true if they have concerns or are distressed about something. You may need to reflect on how you do this and the opportunities you give pupils to talk.

**CASE STUDY:** Supporting children's concerns

Alicia is working in Year 5 in the mornings and takes out small groups. One morning after the group session she is approached by Fern, one of the girls she works with regularly, who asks whether she can speak to her about something. Fern seems quite distressed. Alicia is having a particularly busy day and says that she will talk to her after play, but there is an incident at playtime which she deals with as she is on duty and she only remembers on her way home at lunchtime that she has not had a chance to speak to Fern.

- What should Alicia have done?
- Is there anything she can do now to resolve the issue?

## Support children and young people in making choices for themselves

An important part of learning is for children to learn to make choices for themselves. In the earliest stages of school, making choices is part of the curriculum and they are given opportunities to practise this in their selection of play activities. They are encouraged to have some control within the boundaries of the setting. As they become older, pupils should continue to be encouraged to participate in decision making. This is because a strict and authoritarian structure is likely to cause problems later on, as children will become frustrated by constantly being told what to do. One strategy which is often used with children is discussing targets for work and behaviour with pupils, and involving them in setting their own, so that targets are not imposed on them without their involvement. Another strategy, which is regularly used with older pupils, is the use of school councils. These work very effectively in encouraging pupils to think about and discuss different sides of an issue and then come to a decision which will then be adopted by the school.

## CASE STUDY: Supporting children in making choices

It is the beginning of the new school year. The class teacher and yourself need to speak to the new class about the kind of behaviour you expect to see in the class. You have decided that you will involve the pupils in discussing a set of class rules.

- Why might this be a worthwhile exercise?
- What support would you need to give the pupils?
- Have you been involved in similar activities in your own school?

## Give attention to individual children and young people in a way that is fair to them and the group

When you are working with groups of children, you may find it difficult to balance the needs of individuals with those of the group. This will be because often children seem to require different levels of attention: some may be able to work and organise themselves independently, whereas others may need the reassurance of an adult. You will need to arrange the position of different children in the group, as well as your own, so that you are able to give this reassurance at times just by your physical nearness. If you encourage children to work and make decisions for themselves, they will not need as much adult support and will have more confidence.

## BEST PRACTICE CHECKLIST: Giving attention to individual children

- Encourage all children to put forward their own ideas.
- Know the names of all children.
- Acknowledge that some children will have strengths in a particular area and encourage this.
- Know the needs of all children (for example, any special educational needs).
- Enable children to express themselves in different ways — for example, through creative activities.
- Sit close to children who need more reassurance.
- Be sympathetic if individuals find some things difficult.

# Be able to communicate with children and young people

## Forms of communication to meet the needs of children and young people

It is likely that you will use different forms of communication with children on a regular basis. Although spoken language will be appropriate for most children, in school we often need to use body language and gestures to get our point across. This is particularly true in situations where a teaching assistant needs to communicate with a child from the other side of the classroom — for example, through making eye contact with them and raising their eyebrows to let them know they have seen them talking! In order to communicate with children, you may find that in some cases you will need to go for additional training — if a child who you support uses British Sign Language or Braille, for example, or uses electronic methods of communication. You may also need to speak to the class teacher or SENCO (Special Educational Needs Co-ordinator) if you have concerns about a particular child around issues of communication; even if speech is the most appropriate form of communication, some children may have speech and language difficulties and need additional support.

## CASE STUDY: Using appropriate communication methods

Daniel is working as an individual support assistant in Year 1 for Helen, who has a range of learning difficulties. Although Daniel is very experienced, because of the range of Helen's needs he feels that he is finding it difficult to communicate effectively with her. He has spoken to the SENCO who has given him some ideas, but Daniel still does not feel equipped to support Helen as effectively as he might.

- Is there anything else Daniel could do?
- Where else might he go for help?

## How to adapt communication

### Link

For information on how to adapt communication see TDA 3.1, page 5.

## Strategies to promote understanding and trust in communication

As well as building positive relationships with children, you can promote understanding and trust with them in other ways. Where miscommunication occurs, particularly with younger children, it can affect their confidence and this can be difficult to restore. Strategies and techniques to promote understanding and trust in communication include, for example:

● active listening

● avoiding assumptions

● using questions to clarify and check understanding

● summarising and confirming key points.

### Active listening
You need to show that you are interested in what children are saying and that you are actively listening. It is very frustrating when we are talking to another person and find that they are not listening and we need to repeat what we have said. We can also show that we are listening through the use of body language and the amount of interest we display, including how we respond. It is important for children to gain the approval of adults and most will respond better to a member of staff who is taking the time to listen to them. This also means that pupils are more likely to talk to staff and confide in them if there is anything wrong.

### Avoiding assumptions
You should always ensure that you do not make assumptions when you are speaking to children, as this can cause misunderstandings and sometimes confusion, particularly with younger pupils. This means that you should not assume that they know what you are referring to or what you mean when you are speaking to them.

### Using questions to clarify and check understanding
You should always use questions to check that pupils understand key points and know what they are required to do. It also helps if you avoid asking closed questions which require 'yes' or 'no' answers in order to encourage children to respond in more depth.

---

**CASE STUDY:** Using questions to check understanding

Vijay is in Year 3 and has been in school for six months. He did not speak English when he started in the school, but has picked up quite a lot and is managing well. The teacher has just given the class a complicated list of things to do at the beginning of the session and you notice that Vijay seems unsure what to do and is looking worried.

● Why is it important that you go and speak to Vijay?

● What strategies could you use to help him and others in the class to check their understanding?

## Functional skills

**English: Writing**
In order to achieve your functional skills in English, you need to be able to present complex information clearly and concisely. Looking back at the case study opposite, could you clearly present the teacher's list of things to do in a way that Year 3 children would understand?

## Summarising and confirming key points

It is always worth repeating and summarising key teaching points to pupils when you are working with them, in case they have not picked them up. When giving children instructions, go over what they need to do or ask them to do it for you. In this way you can be sure that they have understood the requirements of the task.

## Making sure you carry out anything you say you will

You should always follow up on anything which you tell children is going to happen. This may range from telling a teacher about something good or disappointing that a pupil has done to remembering that you would pick up their PE kit which their parent has left in the office.

## Being sympathetic and responding to children's needs

If you take time to listen and respond to pupils appropriately when they are speaking to you, you will develop trust. They will feel that you are approachable and be more likely to want to speak to you.

## Functional skills

**English: Speaking, listening and communication**
It is really important when responding to children that you adapt your responses to suit the age range of the child and refrain from using slang that they could repeat.

*Why should you always take time to listen to pupils and ensure you are approachable?*

# Be able to develop professional relationships with adults

## Establish rapport and professional relationships

When working with other adults, whether this is within or outside the school environment, you will need to be able to work in an environment of mutual support and openness. In school surroundings you will not be able to work independently of others, nor would it be practicable to do so. Although you will need to maintain your professionalism in a school environment, you should also be able to support other adults in a practical and sensitive way.

The support you will be required to give other adults will be on several levels (which you can remember with the acronym PIPE).

- **Practical:** You may be working with others who are unfamiliar with the classroom or school surroundings and need to have help or advice with finding or using equipment and resources.

- **Informative:** You may need to give support to those who do not have information about a particular situation. Alternatively, you may be asked to prepare and write reports about specific pupils.

- **Professional:** You may be in a position to support or help others with issues such as planning, or you may be asked whether others can observe your work with pupils or discuss your work with them.

- **Emotional:** It is important to support others through day-to-day events and retain a sense of humour!

The school should also support and encourage good lines of communication between all staff as this is one of the most effective ways of maintaining positive working relationships.

### Functional skills

**English: Writing**
Looking at the PIPE levels of support, you could have a go at writing an evaluation of your job role and identify how you fulfil each of the areas outlined above. This is writing for a different purpose, so consider the choice of layout carefully and ensure you use the correct punctuation, spelling and grammar.

### BEST PRACTICE CHECKLIST: Establishing and maintaining professional relationships

- Remain professional in the school environment and when communicating with other professionals in contact with the school.
- Treat others with respect.
- Notice the efforts and achievements of others.
- Give practical support where needed.
- Avoid speaking about others in a negative way such as gossiping.

## How to adapt communication with adults for cultural/social differences, context and communication differences

### Cultural and social differences

It is likely that you will be aware of any cultural or social differences when communicating with adults and will adapt how you speak to them accordingly. However, there may also be school policies in place where you have a large number of parents who are from a particular culture or speak English as an additional language, and you will have support and guidance from your local authority as to how you might adapt your communication skills accordingly.

You may also find that there are social differences in the way in which some individuals approach certain situations. Where this occurs, you will need to make sure that you respect the views of others.

## DVD activity

### Video clip 4 — Communicating with other adults

In the DVD clip, the teaching assistant is seen relating to parents, pupils, carers and teachers in school.

1. While watching the clip, consider the following questions.

   - How does she demonstrate that she considers the needs of those with whom she comes into contact?

   - Does she need to adapt her approach in any of the situations shown here?

2. For your NVQ, it is important that you are able to show you have good working relationships with others. In a busy school environment, it can be difficult both to remember and to have time to pass on information to the appropriate person. How can you be sure that you prioritise so you will be able to do this? What school systems are in place to help you?

3. Think about the range of adults and pupils with whom you come into contact as part of your role. Show how you demonstrate to pupils the value and importance of having positive relationships with others, and of respecting individuality, and how this is promoted in your school setting.

4. Outline any areas of conflict between adults which you have experienced during the course of your professional work in school. How have these been resolved? (You will need to remove names or have a professional discussion with your assessor about this so that they do not appear in your portfolio.) Have they helped you to deal with any issues between children as they arise?

Also watch clip 6, which shows the same assistant working alongside a teacher to plan a series of lessons for the following week. At level 3, you should be able to be involved in planning alongside teachers and in putting forward your own ideas. How will this kind of activity help to promote positive professional relationships and clear communication? Why is this so important?

Look at clip 10 of the individual support assistant (ISA) supporting a child with communication difficulties. How does she show sensitivity to his condition while also developing a positive relationship with him?

## The context of the communication

You will adapt your communication skills to the context of the communication when you change the way in which you communicate according to the situation. This may simply mean formal or informal verbal communication, but could also be through other means, for example, written — emails, letters, newsletters, notices and so on. You should ensure that however you communicate, the information is accessible to all those for whom it is intended.

## Functional skills

**English: Writing**
**ICT: Using ICT**
Have a go at writing the letter to parents that is mentioned in the case study on the next page about the school football club. The layout and language is essential in this situation. You could email your letter through to your assessor as an attachment.

**CASE STUDY:** Context of communication

Mike is setting up an after-school football club for children in Years 5 and 6. He has sent letters out to parents both through teachers and via 'parentmail', which is the school email system. However, several parents have complained to the school office that they have not seen the letters. Two children were away when it was given out, several children and their parents speak English as an additional language and do not read letters from school, and they have consequently missed the chance to join the club.

- What could Mike have done to ensure that everyone was given a letter?
- How else could he ensure that others for whom English is a second language are able to access communications like this, so that children are not excluded?

**CASE STUDY:** Developing understanding and trust with others

A new learning support assistant in your school, Mary, has come to speak to you because she has had a disagreement with a physiotherapist who has come to visit one of the children. She tells you that the physio has given her a long list of exercises to do with the child and that she does not have time to do this and has told the physio so. Moreover, she says that the physio became unhappy when Mary got her name wrong and addressed her incorrectly. Mary says that it is enough to try to remember the names of all the children and she should not be expected to learn longwinded surnames of everyone that comes into school.

- What issues need to be considered here?
- What might you say to Mary?
- Should you speak to anyone else about this?

## Strategies to promote understanding and trust in communication

Understanding and trust for others is a crucial part of being able to have a positive relationship with them. We cannot do this unless we value others, respect their views and show that we do this. We can do this in a number of ways.

- Actively listen to all adults and let them put their ideas forward – encourage discussion.

- Avoid assumptions about adults, particularly if we know very little about them or their backgrounds.

- Find out how individuals like to be addressed and then speak to them in the correct way – for example, Ms Malone, Miss Matharu.

- Use questions to clarify and check understanding wherever this is unclear.

- Summarise and confirm key points when you have finished speaking to adults to ensure that you are clear on what is to happen.

It is important for you to remember that we are all individuals and that you should not expect others to share the same ideas.

## Use skills to resolve misunderstandings and conflicts constructively

Areas of conflict can occur when communication has not been effective. The best way to resolve areas of poor communication is to discuss them to establish the cause. It is important not to ignore the problem.

**Link**

See TDA 3.1 for more on resolving misunderstandings and conflicts.

# When and how to refer others to further sources of information, advice or support

You may find that you need to refer other adults to further sources of information, advice or support. This may be because you are working with an individual child and have developed a relationship with their parents, or in the case of a family worker, are more likely to be asked for advice. You should ensure that you maintain your professionalism and that you are passing on the correct information. If you are at all unsure you will need to say so, or let them know that you will find out and then get back to them. There are a number of social services which may be able to help in different situations. If at all unclear, you should speak to your SENCO or another member of the Senior Management Team.

## Key term

**Global developmental delay** – a brain disorder where an individual may struggle with, for example, speech and fine/gross motor skills

**CASE STUDY:** Referring other adults for further support or advice

Linda is working with Raoul, who has **global developmental delay**. His mother also has some special needs. Linda has been working with Raoul for a term when she is approached by his mother. She asks Linda to help her as she wants to take him to swimming lessons, but does not know how to go about it. She tries to give Linda some money and asks her whether she can arrange the lessons for her son. She has sought Linda's help on other occasions too and is often outside the classroom during lesson time or looking through the lost property. She has also asked Linda to do some shopping for her and has asked her to come to the house.

- Should Linda help Raoul's mother in this way?
- Where else could Linda seek help or find out how to support her?

*You must be professional at all times – remember your actions set an example.*

*As you spend more time with pupils, you will get to know their personalities and backgrounds.*

# Be able to support children and young people in developing relationships

## Help children and young people to understand the value and importance of positive relationships

As adults working with children, we need to help them to understand the value and importance of positive relationships. Children will learn to do this over time in different ways in school. They will be encouraged to work in pairs, groups and as a class to listen to one another and acknowledge ideas. They will learn to think of others and have respect for others' feelings. They will also find out how positive relationships with others will enhance what they do. By observing our interactions with children and other adults, they should be able to see the effects that positive relationships with others have.

## Provide an effective role model in own relationships

As adults, we need to show children how to get along with one another and model the kind of behaviour we expect from them. If we are able to show them that we value and respect others, they are much more likely to learn to do the same. You should be consistent in your behaviour and relationships so that children learn to do this.

Having positive relationships with others is also important because we will be more likely to communicate information to one another. Parents and other professionals who come into the school will be more likely to offer support if communication is strong and effective. This will in turn benefit the children.

# Encourage children and young people to respect individuality, diversity, feelings and points of view

It is important that schools encourage pupils to learn to value and embrace diversity and individuality. The learning environment should be one in which all cultures, ages and personalities are valued and respected. Often as pupils become older and form friendship groups, they can become nervous about being different and standing up for what they think. Adults need to encourage them to speak confidently and listen to what they have to say.

It is important for children to learn to understand and respect the feelings of others. Young children will find this harder as their understanding will not be developed enough for them to put themselves in the position of others. By school age they may have a greater or lesser experience of this. We often speak to them in school about thinking through the consequences of their actions and how they might have affected others. Through stories, assemblies and role plays we might encourage them to consider the feelings of others.

Children also need to be able to understand how their own feelings might affect their behaviour and you may need to talk to them about this. For example, saying to a child 'I know you are upset because you could not do cooking today' will help them to make the link between emotion and behaviour. In this way, they will be more able to understand how to think about others.

One effective way of encouraging children to understand and respect the feelings of others is through discussion and activities such as 'circle time'. Although this may not always be practical with very young children, as they are often required to sit for a long time and wait for their turn before speaking, older children will benefit from talking through issues as they occur. A whole-class forum is often a good way of doing this.

Strategies such as restorative justice programmes are also popular in schools. These are taken from the criminal justice system and have worked well as a method of resolving behaviour issues and learning from what happens. Table 1 below, taken from the Transforming Conflict website, an organisation which promotes restorative justice, shows how you can encourage and support pupils as they learn to understand how the impact of what they do affects others.

| Retributive justice | Restorative justice |
| --- | --- |
| Negative behaviour is 'breaking the rules' | Negative behaviour is adversely affecting others |
| Focus on blame/guilt/who was the culprit | Focus on problem solving and expressing needs and feelings |
| Adversarial relationships | Dialogue and negotiation |
| Imposition of pain/unpleasantness to punish and deter | Restitution leading to reconciliation |
| Attention to rules | Attention to relationships |
| Conflict represented as impersonal and abstract | Conflict identified as interpersonal with value for learning |
| One social injury replaced by another | Focus on repair of social injury |
| School community as spectators | School community involved in facilitation |
| People affected by behaviour are not necessarily involved | Encouragement of all concerned to be involved |
| Accountability defined in terms of punishment | Accountability defined as understanding the impact of the action |

Source: www.transformingconflict.org – restorative justice in schools.

Table 1: Retributive justice versus restorative justice.

## CASE STUDY: Respecting others' individuality

It is lunchtime and you are in the dining hall with children from Year 6. You notice that some children are huddled around a child who is not eating. When you go over to find out what is happening, he tells you that he is fasting because it is Ramadan. The other children ask you what this means and why he cannot have any lunch.

- How would you deal with this in the short term?
- Why should you follow this up, and how would you do this?
- What procedures does your school have in place for supporting children who celebrate different religious festivals?

### Portfolio activity

Write a reflective account of the different ways in which your school supports the development of positive relationships between children.

- How have you been involved?
- What kinds of activities does the school encourage and have you seen benefits of this way of working?

If you have had any specific training, you should also mention this.

### Functional skills

**ICT: Developing, presenting and communicating information**
Once you have written your reflective account, you could present your account in the form of an idea-sharing presentation done in PowerPoint®. This would give you the opportunity to gather tips from each of your peers to support you in your role.

*How can you encourage children to consider the feelings of others?*

**CASE STUDY:** Encouraging children to solve conflict themselves

You are working close to a group of Year 6 pupils who are carrying out an investigative activity. They have to discuss and find out about reversible and irreversible changes in materials. The children have started well but are now arguing about the best method they can use to test the materials and which materials to look at. You are observing them and decide to wait and see whether they are able to resolve the argument themselves. After some time, one of them suggests that they work in pairs and each consider different materials, as this will be a better use of time.

- Do you think that this is the best outcome?
- Would the children have benefited from adult intervention? If so, how?

## Encourage children and young people to deal with conflict for themselves

Conflicting points of view and ideas will be a natural outcome of encouraging children's individuality. We all have our own thoughts and feelings, and children need to learn how to deal with this. They will also have to learn what behaviour is acceptable in the school environment, and be able to listen to and respect the thoughts of others. Older children should be encouraged to have discussions and debates around different points of view, as this will give them perspectives other than their own. Learning to talk through and resolve issues themselves will give them a valuable skill.

### When you should intervene

You will need to recognise that adults should not always intervene when there are areas of conflict and that if we want children to learn to resolve issues, we need to give them opportunities to do so. The best strategy is for them to discuss or negotiate issues themselves. However, there are times when you need to intervene and speak to pupils, for example, if at any time they become aggressive or unkind to others.

Children who are very young or immature may find it hard to put themselves in the place of others. You may need to point out how important it is to be considerate of how others may be feeling. For example, if they want to take part in an activity which another child is doing, they will have to wait. Learning to share can be difficult for some children who may not have had much experience of this before coming to school.

If children have specific needs or abilities, for example, if they are autistic, they may find empathy with others very difficult. You will need to adapt how you respond in order to support them and you may need to ask for specialist advice. Where pupils have limited understanding due to their needs, it may be more difficult to explain to them and you may have to speak to them sensitively to resolve conflict.

## Encourage other adults to have positive relationships with children and young people

It is very important for you to support positive relationships between children and other adults in the setting. You are in a position in which children will notice and take their lead from your behaviour and the way in which you relate to others. If they see adults modelling negative behaviour and comments, they will learn to think that this is acceptable. You should always make it clear that you have positive views about others when working with them.

> ### CASE STUDY: Supporting other adults to have positive relationships with children
>
> You are working in a Year 5 class alongside the class teacher. On one afternoon each week the teacher has planning, preparation and assessment (PPA) time and the children have another teacher, Mr Knightley, who does part-time supply work at the school. Although the class like Mr Knightley, you have noticed that some of them are making negative comments about him and this has started to affect their behaviour during the afternoon session.
>
> - Is there anything you can do to support the teacher both in the session and outside it?
> - Why is it important to try to keep the relationship positive?

school policy for the formal recording and storage of information. You may also need to report to others on something which has happened, for example, on the playground, if information needs to be passed on quickly. However, you must make sure that you also have a formal record and that information is also passed to parents.

> ### CASE STUDY: Recording and reporting information
>
> Elise is a Year 2 teaching assistant who also works as a midday supervisor. One of the children in another class has fallen over during lunchbreak and cut her head. Elise reports and records the incident in three ways.
>
> 1. She takes the child straight to first aid and tells them what has happened.
> 2. She writes the incident in the 'Head' book so that there is a record in school.
> 3. She fills in a form letting the parents know and puts this in the child's book bag.
>
> - Is there anything else which Elise could do?
> - Why is it important to follow school procedure in this situation?

# Be able to comply with policies and procedures for confidentiality, sharing information and data protection

## Apply the setting's policies and procedures for sharing information, confidentiality and data protection

### Link

For more on sharing information, confidentiality and data protection, see TDA 3.2 Schools as organisations, page 23.

### Knowledge into action

Find out about your school's systems for recording and storing information, and the responsibilities of staff. When your assessor comes into school, show them examples of any records which you have updated.

### Functional skills

ICT: Using ICT
It is important to remember that any electronic records that contain confidential information should be password protected. It is important to keep a password as strong as possible. You can do this by ensuring the password contains lowercase letters, uppercase letters and numbers.

## How to report and record information formally and informally

There will be a number of different ways in which you will record information in school, both formally and informally. If you are keeping school records on a child for any reason, you will need to follow

## Getting ready for assessment

In order to gather evidence for this unit, you will need to demonstrate how you develop professional relationships with children, young people and adults. Learning outcomes will need to be assessed in the workplace and you should encourage your assessor both to observe you working with others and to interview witnesses who will verify your positive relationships with adults and children. Make sure you set up plenty of opportunities for this to be observed, both formally in the classroom or in a meeting, and informally — for example, in the staffroom during break.

### Websites

**www.direct.gov.uk** – you can find more on the Data Protection Act 1998 here
**www.transformingconflict.org** – Transforming Conflict
**www.education.gov.uk** – put Information sharing into search engine for more links

## Check your knowledge

1. Give three examples of how you might establish trusting relationships with children and young people.

2. How can we show as adults that we are supportive and respectful of children's questions, ideas and concerns?

3. What can we do to balance the needs of all children when working with them as a group?

4. Which of the following are strategies to promote understanding and trust in communication with children?

   a) active listening

   b) talking to their parents every day

   c) questioning them to check their understanding

   d) being sympathetic to their needs.

5. Give two examples of how you might support other adults in school.

6. What are the main sources of conflict between adults? Give two ways in which you might go about resolving these.

7. Give three ways in which you might demonstrate to children that you are an effective role model.

8. How can you encourage pupils to deal with conflict for themselves?

9. Where would you find your school's policy for confidentiality and data protection?

# School life

## My story Lynne

I came to my school a long time ago when my children were small – I think it's about 23 years now. I have always really enjoyed my work with the children and like to think that there are a lot of people in school that I get along with. However, recently a few people left that I have been quite close to and some new people came to the school this term. They all have new qualifications (I have never bothered with those as I have plenty of experience which I think counts for a lot) and seem to think that they know better than me as a result. I am starting to feel really uncomfortable in the staffroom as they are always in there and when I walk in it goes quiet.

## My story Sandy

I am new at the school and have been put in a class with a real 'old school' teaching assistant. She has been here for ages and thinks she knows it all. I like her, but whenever we talk she seems to think I don't know anything about children and she can be really patronising. I have talked to other TAs about it and they have told me to ignore her and just get on with my job.

## Ask the expert

**Q** How can we get along?

**A** These two members of staff want to get on with each other, but each has their own preconceived ideas about the other. They have not tried talking through how they feel and this is likely to continue to be a difficult working relationship unless they do. In this type of situation it is important to think about things from the other person's point of view and try to work together, as it is unlikely that the children will benefit from this kind of animosity among the adults who work with them.

**VIEWPOINT**

How else can this be resolved? Think about what else could be done by other members of staff and by Lynne and Sandy to help them to work together in the best interests of the children.

# TDA 3.6 Promote equality, diversity & inclusion in work with children & young people

You should be aware of national legislation and codes of practice relevant to your work with children and the importance of ensuring that all pupils have equal access to the curriculum. You need to understand the impact of prejudice and discrimination and actively encourage and demonstrate positive relationships within school. When your assessor comes into school, you will need to show that you promote equality and diversity through your work and the way in which you interact with children.

## By the end of this unit you will:

1. be able to promote equality and diversity in work with children and young people
2. understand the impact of prejudice and discrimination on children and young people
3. be able to support inclusion and inclusive practices in work with children and young people.

# Be able to promote equality and diversity in work with children and young people

## Current legislation and codes of practice

Areas of legislation are ever-changing but it is important to be able to identify current and relevant aspects of those which promote equality and value diversity. You are not expected to know the details of each but should be able to identify their main points and their relevance to the school environment, and show that you are aware of them in your practice.

### Every Child Matters 2003 and Children Act 2004 updated in 2010 to Help Children Achieve More

These were put into place to ensure that all organisations and agencies involved with children between birth and 19 years should work together to ensure that children have the support needed to be healthy, stay safe, enjoy and achieve, make a positive contribution and achieve economic well-being. The acronym SHEEP can help you to remember this:

- **S**tay safe

- **H**ealthy

- **E**njoy and achieve

- **E**conomic well-being

- **P**ositive contribution.

### Functional skills

**ICT: Developing, presenting and communicating information**
The Every Child Matters framework lends itself to being converted into a poster that could be displayed within your setting. This also provides a good opportunity to practise a range of different layout techniques including text, images and other digital content.

Following the Every Child Matters framework, the Children Act 2004 required that these recommendations become a legal requirement. The key aspect of the Act was to overhaul child protection and children's services in the UK. Every Child Matters has been further developed through the publication of the Children's Plan 2007 which sets out to improve educational outcomes for all children. Its name was changed in 2010 to 'Help Children Achieve More' although the key ideas and five outcomes remain the same.

### Link

See also CYP 3.3 on safeguarding children.

### Equality Act 2010

The Equality Act was introduced in October 2010 to replace a range of anti-discrimination legislation which existed prior to this time. It aims to bring together the Equal Pay Act 1970, Sex Dicrimination Act 1975, Race Relations Act 1976 and the Disability Discrimination Act 1995 in order to protect people and to prevent services from discriminating against any group — be that gender, race, or disability. The way in which this Act relates to schools is that they are required to promote inclusion and disability and race equality for all. It is against the law for anyone to discriminate, either directly or indirectly, and schools should actively promote equal opportunities and positive relationships between all groups of children. It is also a statutory requirement for schools to encourage the inclusion of children with disabilities into mainstream schools.

### SEN Code of Practice 2001

The Special Educational Needs and Disability Act 2001 (SENDA) strengthened the rights of parents and SEN children to a mainstream education. It made significant changes to the educational opportunities that are available to children with disabilities and special educational needs. This means that it is more likely for these children to be in mainstream schools.

| Inclusion | Separation |
|---|---|
| Equality – all children receive the support they need to build on and achieve their potential | 'Special' or different treatment |
| Learning assertiveness | Learning helplessness |
| Participation of all | Participation of some |
| Involves all members of society | Builds barriers in society |

*Table 1: Advantages of inclusive education (Source: Disability Equality in Education).*

## Human Rights Act 1998

The United Nations first set a standard on human rights in 1948 with the Universal Declaration of Human Rights. This was accepted by many countries around the world and highlighted the principle that all humans have the same rights and should be treated equally. In 1998 the Human Rights Act gave a further legal status to this. Your basic human rights are:

- the right to life

- freedom from torture and degrading treatment

- freedom from slavery and forced labour

- the right to liberty

- the right to a fair trial

- the right not to be punished for something that wasn't a crime when you did it

- the right to respect for private and family life

- freedom of thought, conscience and religion, and freedom to express your beliefs

- freedom of expression

- freedom of assembly and association

- the right to marry and to start a family

- the right not to be discriminated against in respect of these rights and freedoms

- the right to peaceful enjoyment of your property

- the right to an education

- the right to participate in free elections

- the right not to be subjected to the death penalty.

(Source: Direct.gov.uk – Human Rights Act)

## UN Convention on the Rights of the Child 1989

The UK signed this legally binding agreement in 1990. It leads on from the Human Rights Act and sets out the rights of all children to be treated equally and fairly and without discrimination. (For more on this Act, see CYP 3.3 on safeguarding.)

### Over to you!

Choose one area of legislation and show in more detail the impact it has had on provision available for pupils in schools.

### Functional skills

**ICT: Finding and selecting information**
Completing this task may require you to research further around legislation on the Internet. Try using a variety of search engines in order to expand your results. Always remember to check the copyright of the information that you are using.

## The importance of promoting the rights to participation and equality of access

All pupils should be able to fully access all areas of the curriculum. The advent of the Every Child Matters framework and the focus on personalised learning in all sectors of education has also made this high on the agenda. The reasons for this are:

- human rights
  - all children have a right to learn and play together

○ children should not be discriminated against for any reason

○ **inclusion** is concerned with improving schools for staff as well as pupils

● equal opportunities in education

○ children do better in inclusive settings, both academically and socially

○ children should not need to be separated to achieve adequate educational provision

○ inclusive education is a more efficient use of educational resources

● social opportunities

○ inclusion in education is one aspect of inclusion in society

○ children need to be involved and integrated with all of their peers.

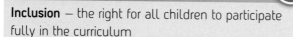

## Key term

**Inclusion** — the right for all children to participate fully in the curriculum

All schools should have codes of practice and policies around equal opportunities and inclusion. These sometimes form part of the policy for special educational needs but are usually separate. You should be familiar with these policies and know where to find them in school.

## Functional skills

### English: Reading
You could locate and read the codes of practice and policies around equal opportunities and inclusion for your setting, and then compare them against the policy for special educational needs. Not only will this comparison highlight the relationships between the policies, but it will also give you a good opportunity to develop your reading skills further.

Always be aware of the needs of different pupils, whatever these may be. Remember that these may become more apparent as you get to know particular pupils. Those who may be vulnerable could include pupils:

● who have special educational needs (SEN)

● who speak English as an additional language

● who are new to the school

● who are gifted and talented

● whose culture or ethnicity is different from the predominant culture of the school

● who are in foster care

● whose parents' views are not consistent with those of the school.

## Reflect

- What can you say about inclusion in your school?

- How effective is it, in your experience?

- Do you think that its advantages outweigh any disadvantages that you can identify?

## The importance and benefits of valuing and promoting cultural diversity

Schools will all be aware of the importance of valuing and promoting cultural diversity. Most will actively include a number of strategies to ensure that children from all cultures feel welcome in school. These may be:

● 'Welcome' displayed in a variety of languages in the entrance hall, and other signs in different areas of the school

● other languages spoken in different lessons or during registration

● representations from other cultures found in books and learning resources, and displayed around the school

- festivals and celebrations from other cultures discussed and explored

- parents involved in 'finding out' sessions with children.

Measures such as these will have a number of benefits for children – mainly that they will grow up in an environment which values cultural diversity and enables us to learn from one another. Children will also become used to finding out about other cultures and belief systems from an early age. In this way they will not grow up thinking that their own and their family's culture is the same as everyone else's.

Children from all backgrounds need to know that their culture and status is valued as this helps them to feel settled and secure; this in turn contributes to their being able to learn. If they feel isolated or anxious, it is more likely that learning will be difficult for them.

## Interact in a way that values diversity and respects differences

You should always ensure that when interacting with children, you value diversity and respect their backgrounds and beliefs. Children will quickly pick up

---

**CASE STUDY:** Valuing and promoting cultural diversity

Omar is in the Reception class and his mother comes in regularly to cook with the children. The class teacher notices that they will be looking at weddings as part of their topic and asks Omar's mother if she would be able to come in and talk about a Hindu wedding. She agrees, and brings in photographs, saris and other artefacts to talk about what happens and show them to the children.

They have an 'Indian afternoon' which results in paintings, cooking, discussion and exploration of a number of aspects of the culture relating to weddings.

- In what ways will this be beneficial to the children?
- How might the class extend what they have learned during the afternoon?

---

*How can you actively value and respect the diversity of the children you work with?*

on any discriminatory comments or opinions in the school environment. You should also be aware that your own thoughts and opinions have been shaped by your experiences and background — self-awareness of your own values and beliefs is an important part of your work with others. Make sure that you react and respond to children appropriately at all times.

## Reflect

Consider and discuss how you feel about:

- the movement of several traveller families into the school catchment area

- the request from a parent of a Muslim child that she fasts during Ramadan

- a Catholic pupil who is not allowed to eat any meat on Ash Wednesday

- a request from a Sikh parent that her child is able to wear his Kara (a bangle) at all times, including during PE lessons.

## Functional skills

**English: Speaking, listening and communication**
This reflection provides excellent discussion topics that you may have had similar experience of in your setting. Listen carefully to what others say so that you can move the discussion on. Maybe you could take on the roles of different people — for example, the view of the Sikh parent, the health and safety officer, class teacher and the other children in relation to the bangle being worn for PE.

# Ways of applying the principles of equality, diversity and anti-discriminatory practice

This assessment criterion will need to be assessed in the workplace.

You will need to be able to show how you apply these principles within your day-to-day practice in school, so

*What sort of support will children with special educational needs require?*

that all children are included in all aspects of school life. When working with pupils who have additional needs, you may need to ensure that they have equal opportunities to others in a number of ways, which may include:

● adapting and modifying learning materials for them so that they can fully access the curriculum.

● using additional resources or specific equipment such as new technologies

● going for specific training – this may be learning to sign or use Makaton or PECS (Picture Exchange Communication System, relating to autism), or how to use a Braille machine

● giving them extra time to complete tasks if required

● working with them on intervention programmes.

**Anti-discriminatory practice** forms the basis of an environment in which there is no discrimination towards individuals on the basis of race, ability, gender, culture or ethnicity. No children should be the victims of discrimination and fair treatment should be given to all individuals. The term 'inclusion' is often used when referring to children who have special educational needs, but it is also used in a wider sense to describe equal opportunities for all in the learning environment. It is through the development of trust and positive relationships that children will learn to respect one another. You can apply the principles of anti-discriminatory practice through the way in which you form relationships in school, both with adults and children, and through acting as a role model at all times. However, you must also make sure that you challenge any discriminatory comments or behaviour made by others.

---

**Key term**

**Anti-discriminatory practice** – taking positive action to counter discrimination, which involves identifying and challenging discrimination, and being positive in your practice about differences and similarities between people

---

**BEST PRACTICE CHECKLIST:** Promoting equality and diversity

● Have high expectations of pupils and develop their attitudes of self-belief through appropriate challenges.

● Celebrate and value diversity.

● Be aware that all pupils have more in common than is different.

● Encourage the participation of all pupils in the curriculum and social life of the school.

● Work to include all pupils in the main activities of the class wherever possible.

● Develop 'can do' attitudes in pupils through appropriate degrees of challenge and support.

---

# Understand the impact of prejudice and discrimination on children and young people

## Ways in which children and young people can experience prejudice and discrimination

There are many ways in which children can experience prejudice and discrimination in school. There are so many pressures on children to fit in and to conform with expected appearances and behaviour that they may be discriminated against and bullied if they do not. This can start at a surprisingly young age and staff in schools need to be vigilant to ensure that children respect and embrace diversity. Children can experience prejudice and discrimination in the same way as adults due to race, religion, age, sex, culture or ethnicity.

In particular look out for:

● comments about a child's appearance or clothes

● children not playing with others who may be 'different'

● children being excluded because they are boys or girls

● children only playing together with others of the same race or ethnicity.

## CASE STUDY: Prejudice and discrimination

Rania has just been appointed as a bilingual assistant in Year 4 to work with Tariq, who speaks English as an additional language and has a speech and language disorder. Tariq is lacking in confidence as a result of his needs, but Rania is aware that she must not be at his side too much, as this will prevent him from developing his independence and making friends. On the playground one morning she notices that Tariq is trying hard to join in, but overhears a group of children making fun of him and speaking to him with a strong accent when he has asked if he can join in with their game of basketball.

- Should Rania intervene on this occasion?
- What could she say to the group?
- How can she balance the development of Tariq's independence while ensuring that he does not become reliant on her?

## The impact of prejudice and discrimination

Although it may sound obvious, an environment of prejudice and discrimination will have a very negative impact on children. Depending on how long it goes on and the form it takes, a negative atmosphere will have an effect on the following for a child.

### Self-esteem and social and emotional development

A child who is discriminated against for whatever reason will feel that they are not valued as a person and will start to lose confidence in themselves. This may mean that they start to withdraw socially, becoming less able to join in with activities with their peers, as they will not want to draw attention to themselves.

### Learning

A child who does not feel part of the class and their peer group due to discrimination or prejudice will not

*What effects does low self-esteem have?*

---

**CASE STUDY:** Challenging discrimination

Mike is working in an inner-city junior school which has very few children who are from white British backgrounds. Although the school has an inclusive policy and has a 'no tolerance' view on any form of discrimination, Mike has sometimes had to deal with some incidents of bullying and racial discrimination on the playground. On this occasion, a white child who is new to the school has come up to him and told him that a girl has said to her that she cannot play with them because she won't understand their game as she is white.

- What should Mike do?
- What should he say to the group of girls?
- Should he follow up the incident in any way?

---

be happy and settled in school. This will mean that their learning will be affected and they will find it difficult to focus on their work.

### Relationships with others

A child who lacks confidence and who does not want to participate in activities with others as a result is likely to develop fewer positive relationships with their peers or with adults.

---

**Skills builder**

Can a school ensure that prejudice and discrimination do not occur? Think about and list ways in which they may be able to prevent them from happening.

---

## Evaluate how own attitudes, values and behaviour could impact on work

You will need to be able to consider how your own attitudes, values and behaviour could impact on your work. In some cases this may not have been necessary before but you should think about whether you are treating pupils differently because of your own inbuilt ideas.

## How to challenge discrimination

You must always challenge discrimination whenever you come across it and in many schools you will also need to record and report discriminatory behaviour and comments. Young children will sometimes say things without understanding the implications, in particular if they have heard them said by others. It should be made clear to them that their comments are not acceptable and that everyone in school should be treated fairly and with respect.

# Be able to support inclusion and inclusive practices in work with children and young people

## What is meant by inclusion and inclusive practices

As already identified, pupils all have an equal right to education and learning. Equal opportunities and inclusion should take account not only of access to provision on school premises, but also to facilities outside the school setting, for example, on school visits. Schools and other organisations that offer educational provision must by law ensure that all pupils have access to a broad and balanced curriculum. The school should ensure that inclusive practices are a matter of course within day-to-day provision and that any barriers to inclusion are identified and removed.

## Barriers to children and young people's participation

**Barriers to participation** may include:

- **physical barriers** — lack of access, equipment or resources

---

**Key term**

**Barriers to participation** — anything that prevents the pupil participating fully in activities and experiences offered by the setting or service

---

- **organisational barriers** – school policies, lack of training, lack of diversity within the school curriculum
- **attitudes within the school community** – staff, parents, other pupils.

## Physical barriers

These include lack of equipment or resources which may be needed by the child to enable them to participate fully. Physical barriers may also be present in the school environment if it has not been properly adapted to cater for the needs of all pupils. Examples of these adaptations are ramps, disabled toilets, lifts for wheelchair users and hearing loops for hearing-impaired pupils. As a result of the amendments made to the Disability Discrimination Act in the Special Educational Needs and Disability Act 2001, all schools built from 2001 need to have physical access for all pupils.

## Organisational barriers

These mean that policies within the organisation have been not set up effectively to ensure that all pupils are included effectively. Reasons may be lack of training within the school, insufficient use of support which may be available or lack of understanding.

## Attitudes within the school community

There may be barriers within the attitudes of staff, parents, governors or other pupils. This means that they may hold views which are inconsistent with those of the school and which mean that pupils

may be discriminated against. Attitudes such as these can mean that children become confused about the school's values, as they will be receiving conflicting messages. This may also give them a reason to behave in a way which the school does not agree with.

# Ways of supporting inclusion and inclusive practices

This assessment criterion will need to be assessed in the workplace.

> **Link**
>
> See also TDA 3.5, Develop professional relationships with children, young people and adults.

You will need to be able to show that you support inclusion within your school and that you are committed to inclusive practices. This will principally affect your work with children but you should also be aware of it in your dealings with adults. Your school will in all likelihood already demonstrate positive policies for supporting inclusive practice, but you should know how it does this and what it means for the school community.

You can support inclusive practices by:

- knowing and following your school's inclusion or equal opportunities policy
- demonstrating positive relationships with all children and adults
- actively showing that you respect and value individuals through your day-to-day communication with them
- supporting pupils who have additional needs
- respecting individuality and encouraging pupils to do the same
- challenging any discrimination when it occurs.

### Knowing and following your school's inclusion or equal opportunities policy

You can show that you do this by reading and highlighting your school's policy and showing it to your assessor to demonstrate that you know and understand key points.

---

**CASE STUDY:** Barriers to participation

You have just started to work with Kayleigh in Year 3, who is a wheelchair user. One of the parents in the class comes to see you and says that Kayleigh will not be able to go on a week-long residential trip due to take place early in Year 6, as there are no facilities for 'children like that'. You are concerned both by the attitude of the parent and by the possibility that Kayleigh may not be able to go on the trip.

- What would you do?
- How can schools go about removing social barriers such as these if they exist?

# Inclusion Policy

## Introduction

(To be read in conjunction with the following school policies: English as an Additional Language; Equal Opportunities; Gifted and Talented Children; Racial Equality; Special Educational Needs.)

In our vision for our school we talk about creating an attractive and exciting learning environment in which our children are stimulated to learn. Importance is placed on high self-esteem as we are committed to giving all of our children every opportunity to achieve the highest of standards. We do this by taking account of pupils' varied life experiences and needs. We offer a broad and balanced curriculum and have high expectations for all children. The achievements, attitudes and well-being of all our children matter. This policy helps to ensure that this school promotes the individuality of all our children, irrespective of ethnicity, attainment, age, disability, gender or background.

## Aims and Objectives

Our school aims to be an inclusive school. We actively seek to remove the barriers to learning and participation that can hinder or exclude individual pupils, or groups of pupils. This means that equality of opportunity must be a reality for our children. We make this a reality through the attention we pay to the different groups of children within our school:

- girls and boys
- minority ethnic and faith groups
- children who need support to learn English as an additional language
- children with special educational needs
- gifted and talented children
- children who are at risk of disaffection or exclusion
- travellers and asylum seekers.

We offer a broad curriculum which meets the specific needs of individuals and groups of children. We meet these needs through:

- setting suitable learning challenges
- responding to children's diverse learning needs
- overcoming potential barriers to learning and assessment for individuals and groups of pupils
- providing other curricular opportunities outside the National Curriculum to meet the needs of individuals or groups of children (such as work-based learning, personal, social health and economic education)
- working with other agencies to provide additional advice and support such as speech and language therapy and mobility training.

We achieve educational inclusion by continually reviewing what we do, through asking ourselves these key questions.

- Do all our children achieve their best?
- Are there differences in the achievement of different groups of children?
- What are we doing for those children who we know are not achieving their best?
- Are our actions effective?
- Are we successful in promoting racial harmony and preparing pupils to live in a diverse society?

*Part of a school's inclusion policy.*

## Demonstrating positive relationships with all children and adults

You should be approachable and show sensitivity in your relationships with others, in particular if you notice something where others do not seem to be aware that there is anything wrong.

---

**CASE STUDY: Supporting inclusive practice**

Kwakye is a male teaching assistant in a primary school. He enjoys his job and working with his female colleagues, and is a valued member of staff. However, you have noticed that he is often teased and almost bullied in the staff room by female colleagues. They often say that he is a man, so is unable to multitask, or that as a man he won't be able to deal with sensitive issues. You have noticed that lately he seems to be spending less and less time in the staffroom.

- Do you think that these kinds of comments matter?
- Would you say anything to Kwakye?
- Why is it important that these kinds of issues are addressed?

---

## Actively showing that you respect and value individuals through your day-to-day communication with them

You should be self-aware and think about the impact your words and behaviour will have on others. This may be in your interactions but can also be through other forms of communication such as letters, emails, texts and notices. It may be that you say something which you had intended as a joke but which others might take to heart – it is better not to do it in the first place.

## Supporting pupils who have additional needs

You may need to do this through differentiating work, modifying materials and resources, or in the way which is most appropriate to the child and their needs. You will work alongside your SENCO and class teacher in order to establish what will be in the child's best interests.

## Respecting individuality and encouraging pupils to do the same

When you find that issues of individuality come up in your day-to-day work with children, it is worth discussing and thinking about it with them. In this way any questions can be answered and children who may feel 'different' from others will have an opportunity to talk about their beliefs if they would like to.

---

**Functional skills**

**ICT: Developing, presenting and communicating information**
**ICT: Using ICT**
Using PowerPoint®, you could create a new presentation entitled 'Supporting Inclusive Practice', then link it to your role in school through examples of your day-to-day work. You could try to include relevant digital pictures, film or images that you have scanned in to your presentation. As you develop your knowledge and skills, you will take on more responsibilities and you can add these to your presentation at a later date.

---

**CASE STUDY: Respecting individuality**

You are working in Year 1 and are starting to talk about Diwali. One of the children in the class puts up his hand and says that they will be celebrating Diwali at his house and they do every year. One child says, 'Diwali, that's a funny word.' Another says, 'What do you have to do?'

- Why is this a useful learning opportunity?
- How could you make the most of this opportunity to respect individuality in the classroom?

---

## Challenging any discrimination when it occurs

Whether this has been reported to you or if you have heard or seen it yourself, you must always ensure that you challenge anyone who is discriminatory towards others. This will occur rarely, but incidents of discrimination should not go unchecked.

## Getting ready for assessment

Think about the ways in which your school supports inclusion and celebrates diversity. You may want to look at policies, discuss particular aspects of your school and its catchment area, look at the assembly timetable, or show how the school involves parents and the community. You can then show your assessor when they come into school or write up a reflective account and use it for your portfolio.

### Websites

**www.dcsf.gov.uk/everychildmatters** – Every Child Matters framework
**www.direct.gov.uk/surestart** – government programme to deliver the best start in life for every child
**www.homeoffice.gov.uk/equalities/equality-act/** – Home office information about Equality Act 2010
**www.institute.nhs.uk/building_capability/breaking_through/race_relations.html** – Race Relations Act
**www.ncb.org.uk** – National Children's Bureau, supporting parents and children

## Check your knowledge

1. Identify three areas of legislation which have impacted on the promotion of equality and diversity in schools.

2. Why is it important for schools to have policies in place with regard to equal opportunities?

3. How would you define the term 'inclusion'?

4. Outline how schools can show that they value diversity in the learning environment.

5. Why is it important to promote and value diversity in schools? (Choose all that apply.)
   a) It makes all children feel valued.
   b) It keeps everyone happy.
   c) It enables children to learn from one another.
   d) It means that we can find out about other cultures.
   e) It shows the importance of inclusion in society.

6. Why should we think about our own values and attitudes when considering anti-discriminatory practice?

7. Name four ways in which you as an individual have demonstrated that you promote equality and diversity.

8. What impact might prejudice and discrimination have on a child?

9. How can you support inclusive practices in school?

# School life

## My story Emil

I am a very experienced bilingual assistant working in a school which has a high number of speakers of other languages. I have been here for some years and enjoy my work with children, in particular the one-to-one sessions with children who have specific targets and I can really see their progress. I also work in a Year 3 class two mornings a week, supporting the class teacher during literacy and numeracy sessions. During these sessions I usually sit with those children who need some extra support. When I first started working in the class, there was a large group of eight children who always sat together and whom I was asked to support – the class teacher had put them together because they all spoke different languages. I found this quite challenging because although they were all bilingual, their abilities varied enormously and as they were such a large group, I did not feel that I was supporting them effectively. Also I felt that it was a form of discrimination, as the teacher did not seem to see beyond the fact that they did not speak English as a first language.

I decided to speak to her, but had to be careful how I approached the issue as I did not want her to feel that I was criticising or undermining her; also, as I am not in the class all the time, I do not have much chance to speak to her outside lessons. I was able to arrange to meet up with her and said that as the group was so large it wasn't really working due to its size and the range in abilities – also two of the group were quite able and managed without my support most of the time. To be fair to the teacher, she was fine about it and thanked me for bringing it to her attention – it's hard to keep tabs on everything with a class of 33!

## Ask the expert

**Q** Can I tell the teacher what I think?

**A** It's fine from time to time to say what you think to the teacher, as long as you are not overtly critical, and in particular if they ask you what you think – you are working as a team and you have close contact with their class. However, you should also bear in mind that there are likely to be reasons for them to work in a particular way and you may not always be aware of these. However, if you have ongoing concerns about anything, you should always say something, either to the teacher or to your own line manager.

### VIEWPOINT

In any work situation you may find that there will be people you get on with better than others, and schools are no exception. You should remember that it is unlikely that you will work with the same teacher for more than a year and that all relationships will be about compromise. You may also find that you get on better than you had anticipated and that you learn a lot from the experience! Remember to remain professional and that communication is very important.

# TDA 3.7 Support assessment for learning

As part of the assessment for learning process, you will need to know the kinds of strategies that teachers use to inform assessment. You will then need to show how you involve pupils in checking and reviewing their progress, and enable them to apply self-assessment strategies to check their learning as they work.

## By the end of this unit you will:

1. understand the purpose and characteristics of assessment for learning

2. be able to use assessment strategies to promote learning

3. be able to support learners in reviewing their learning strategies and achievements

4. be able to contribute to reviewing assessment for learning.

103

# Understand the purpose and characteristics of assessment for learning

## Compare the roles of the teacher and the learning support practitioner

One of the main responsibilities of the class teacher is to monitor and assess pupil achievement. They will need to know how all children in their class are progressing and be able to report back to parents and other staff. Assessment is an ongoing process which will take different forms and in your role as a teaching assistant, you will need to be able to support teachers with the process.

---

### Functional skills

**Maths: Interpreting**
Thinking about one of the subjects that you support a group of children with, you could apply a number of mathematical skills to do the following.

- Find out what fraction and percentage of the class are on, above or below target in this area.

- Investigate the ratio of boys to girls on, above or below target, and then link to any research around gender and this subject.

- Create a graph to track targets on visually in order to show how over time the children have moved on with your support.

---

Teachers will plan lessons and schemes of work which should set out clear objectives so that learner progress can be measured. Both children and adults in the class will need to be clear about what these objectives are and it is good practice for teachers to set out and display the learning objective at the start of each session. In this way you will be sharing with all children what they are going to learn as well as having a clear understanding of what you are supporting.

## The difference between formative and summative assessment

### Formative assessment strategies

As pupil learning takes place, you will need to measure it against these objectives using ongoing methods of assessment. These are known as formative assessment methods and can be used to check the learning in any lesson.

- **Using open-ended questions** – this will encourage children to put their ideas forward without being 'led' by adults, for example, 'Tell me how you are going to...'

- **Observing pupils** – we will gather much of our knowledge of how pupils are achieving through watching them work and noticing the kinds of strategies they are using to work things out or what they find more difficult. This can take place on a daily basis or can be carried out more formally through direct observations.

- **Listening to how pupils describe their work and their reasoning** – through doing this we hear about the methods which pupils use.

- **Checking pupils' understanding** – we can do this through questioning pupils about their learning and asking them what they know.

- **Engaging pupils in reviewing progress** – this should take place throughout each session, when pupils should be encouraged to think about what they have learned and measure it against learning objectives, and how they might apply this knowledge in the future.

### Summative assessment

The other main form of assessment which teachers use to check learning is summative assessment. This occurs at the end of a term or scheme of work when it is important to know what pupils have achieved at a particular time. It could take the form of end of Key Stage SATS or an end of year school report, and informs a range of people about the level of a pupil's work. It could really be called assessment *of* learning.

## The characteristics of assessment for learning

**Assessment for learning** informs and promotes the achievement of all pupils, as it encourages them to take responsibility for their own learning. The process involves explaining learning outcomes to pupils, giving them feedback on their progress and enabling them to develop their self-assessment skills so that they are ultimately able to reflect on and recognise their own achievements. This will usually start with pupils taking part in peer assessment to build up these skills and discuss their work before moving on to thinking about their own work. Pupils will need to be able to consider their learning carefully throughout the process and keep coming back to the learning objective or what they are expected to learn.

### Key term

**Assessment for learning** — using assessment as part of teaching and learning in ways which will raise learners' achievement

### Reflect

How are pupils encouraged to think about their learning during the process? Are they clear about learning objectives? Do they review this at the end of each lesson?

### Functional skills

**ICT: Developing, presenting and communicating information**
Using a suitable software package on the computer (Word® or Publisher®), you could have a go at devising a self-assessment sheet that you could use with the age of children that you work with. The sheet would need to contain a simple way of recording — for example, circling smiley faces for how they feel about their work and then maybe writing some bullet points to say how they would make it better.

## The importance and benefits of assessment for learning

Research has shown that there is a clear relationship between being part of the process of assessment and pupil motivation. Children who are actively engaged with their progress will feel empowered to improve their performance, as they will feel more ownership of their learning. This will in turn develop their self-esteem and motivation — children who feel that they are not part of the learning process are far more likely to become disengaged and consequently lose interest. Effective feedback also ensures that adults are supporting more able as well as less able children by giving them the tools to achieve to the best of their potential. Assessment for learning is a device to enable pupils to understand the aim of what they are doing, what they need to do to reach that aim and where they are in relation to it.

## How assessment for learning can contribute to planning for future learning

Assessment for learning must by definition contribute to future planning for all who are involved in the learning process. As such it is a valuable tool, and it will mean that all concerned will learn from the experience.

● For the teacher, effective assessment for learning will enable them to pass on the responsibility to the child over time for managing their own learning, so that they will become more actively involved in the process.

*Pupils need to learn to reflect on and assess their own learning.*

● For the pupil, the process will inform them about how they approach learning and tackle areas on which they need to work. They will be able to consider areas for improvement by looking at assessment criteria and develop their ability to self-assess. Their increased awareness of how to learn will develop their confidence and help them to recognise when to ask for support.

● For you, assessment for learning will inform how you approach pupil questioning based on what you have discovered about how they learn. You may need to pace the progress of learners depending on their needs, so that less able pupils are given opportunities to revisit areas of uncertainty.

# Be able to use assessment strategies to promote learning

## The information required to contribute to assessment for learning

Information required includes:

● the learning objectives for the activities

● the personalised learning goals for individual learners

● the success criteria of the learning activities

● the **assessment opportunities and strategies** relevant to own role in the learning activities.

### Key term

**Assessment opportunities and strategies** – the occasions, approaches and techniques used for ongoing assessment during learning activities

At the start of any activity, pupils will need to be clear about what they are going to learn and how they will be assessed. For assessment for learning to be effective, pupils will need to know what they are learning, why they are learning it and how assessment will take place. Pupils should discuss these with you at the start of each session and will need you and the class teacher to give them specific criteria against which their learning will be measured. As pupils take on more responsibility for their learning, they will find it easier to look at learning objectives to see whether these have been met. A simple example of this might be a literacy activity

in which pupils are learning to use capital letters and then filling in gaps in sentences to check their knowledge (see below). You may or may not make pupils aware of the success criteria for the activity, which will be how they apply the learning objective in their subsequent work.

As well as knowing the learning objective, pupils will need to think about their own personalised learning goals, if they have these, so that they can integrate them in the process. For example, if a pupil's learning goal for literacy is to use full stops, this will tie in well with the literacy activity listed below. However, if the goal does not tie in, it can still be part of the process, as thinking about their target will still encourage them to be aware of their learning needs.

● **What pupils are learning** – where capital letters need to be applied.

● **Success criteria** – pupils able to use capital letters consistently.

● **Why they are learning it** – to enable them to use the correct form of written English.

● **How assessment will take place** – teacher and teaching assistant will check that pupils are using capital letters consistently in their written work.

It may be helpful, particularly with older pupils, to ask them to look at exemplar pieces of work which show what they need to do in order to meet the success criteria. In this way they will start to see what is being asked for.

As you support learners through the process, you will also need to use a variety of assessment opportunities to guide them in thinking about their work and their progress – for examples of these, see opposite.

### Functional skills

ICT: Developing, presenting and communicating information
You could convert individual targets into charts so that the individuals have a visual target grid that they can use to help them to see their own progression. For example, if you have a pupil with six literacy targets, you could produce a pie chart divided into six equal pieces (60° each). As the child achieves each target, they could take responsibility for colouring that section in.

## Personalised learning goals and criteria for assessing progress with learners

It is likely that all children in primary school will have **personalised learning goals** for literacy and numeracy. These may be updated on a termly or half-termly basis, depending on school policy. The class teacher will usually give similar targets to children who are of the same ability so that work can be tailored for their needs as a group. Pupils will usually have them printed out, either in the front of their books or on a laminated card for easy reference.

Children who have additional needs will also have personalised learning goals, but these may be recorded on an individual or personalised learning plan which will have been agreed and signed by pupils, parents and teachers.

Before starting work on an activity, you will need to discuss and ensure that pupils know and understand their own learning goals as well as the learning objectives.

### Key terms

**Personalised learning goals** — goals which reflect the learning objectives of activities and take account of the past achievements and current learning needs of individual learners

**Dyscalculia** — a learning disability or difficulty involving innate difficulty in learning or comprehending mathematics

**CASE STUDY:** Clarify personalised learning goals for assessing progress

Sam is working regularly with Lydia in Year 6, who has dyslexia and **dyscalculia**. Lydia is aware of her needs and knows that she needs to take longer over her work, although she does not have an individual education plan (IEP). Her maths target this term is to use known facts and place value to answer simple calculations involving decimals. Today Lydia is in Sam's group and the learning objective is to solve multi-step word problems. There are some opportunities in the task to tie the learning goal in with the objective.

- How might Sam approach this with Lydia?
- Should Sam focus on the learning objective or Lydia's personal learning goal?

## Use assessment opportunities and strategies to gain information and judge learners' participation and progress

In order to help you to review pupils' progress, it may be helpful for you to follow a checklist like this.

- Ensure pupils understand the learning objectives and any individual learning targets so that they can assess their own progress to meeting these as they proceed.

- Talk to pupils about what they have to do and whether they need to hand work in.

- Inform pupils how they will be assessed and ensure they understand.

- Give examples of work produced by other learners if possible, so that pupils can see how the assessment criteria are applied.

- Provide individual support and oral feedback as pupils are working, praising learners when they focus their comments on their personalised learning goals for the task.

- Ensure that there are opportunities for either peer or self-assessment.

- Encourage learners to review and comment on their work before handing it in or discussing it with the teacher.

- Provide written feedback.

For further assessment strategies to use with pupils, see 'Formative assessment strategies' on page 104.

You do not need to use all the points above, but they are indicators for you to make sure you have not missed any of the opportunities to support assessment for learning.

### Portfolio activity

Using the list above as a guide, reflect on how you have supported either an individual or a group of pupils through a learning activity.

## Provide constructive feedback to learners

For assessment for learning to be effective, it is essential that children receive constructive feedback from adults which focuses on strengths as well as supporting and guiding pupils through any difficulties they may have.

You will need to give feedback which:

- gives information to a pupil which focuses on performance

- is delivered positively

- is not personal, but based on facts.

There are different types of feedback which we should give pupils during and following learning activities.

- **Affirmation feedback** should be delivered as soon as possible: 'Well done, you have remembered to include all the points we discussed!' This type of feedback helps to motivate pupils.

- **Developmental feedback** will suggest what to do next time: 'Nathan, try to remember to get all the equipment you will need before starting the activity.'

Both types of feedback can be written or oral, but for feedback to be effective, it should be given as promptly as possible. If feedback is given too long after an activity has been completed, children will

find it harder to apply it to their learning. This may be particularly true in the case of marking, which should be done as soon as possible after an activity is completed, if possible with the child present.

### Reflect

Think about and discuss in groups some feedback you remember from when you were at school. It is possible that you have received some feedback which focused on negative rather than positive points. What effect did this have on you as a learner?

### Functional skills

**English: Speaking, listening and communication**
In order to develop your confidence in this area, you could role-play giving and receiving feedback in pairs. This will support you in the classroom with the children if you have tried out some suitable phrases first.

### BEST PRACTICE CHECKLIST: Providing feedback

- Remain non-judgemental.

- Focus on strengths.

- Work through one thing at a time.

- Give constructive advice where needed and guidance on how a child can improve.

- Link feedback directly to what has been observed or written.

- End positively.

### CASE STUDY: Encouraging through feedback

You have been working with a group who are finding a task quite difficult. You have tried praising them for the work they have done so far, but they are continuing to struggle and you are concerned that they might not want to continue.

- What kind of feedback should you be giving the group?

- Outline the steps you might go through to encourage them back on task.

## Provide opportunities and encouragement for learners to improve upon their work

An important aspect of assessment for learning is that children's progress will be measured against their own previous achievements rather than being compared with those of others. Pupils' learning should be set at a level which ensures that they are building on what they learn. This means that they should be starting from a point of previous understanding and then extending their learning to take in new information. Pupils will benefit from discussing previous learning experiences to consolidate what they know and reinforce their understanding before moving on to take in new concepts and ideas. You will need to encourage and motivate pupils, in particular if they are finding it difficult to understand or there are other factors which are impacting on their learning. It is important that you show them that you believe in them and are able to support them as they start from what they know.

If you have pupils with low self-esteem, or who have tried to learn in a particular way before which has been clearer to them, you may need to adapt or modify what they have been asked to do in order to help them.

### Knowledge into action

Ask learners to think about a piece of work that they have completed well and which they feel proud of. Encourage them to think about the learning objectives and success criteria of the session, and evaluate it against their targets. They should then be able to feed back to others about their learning.

## Be able to support learners in reviewing their learning strategies and achievements

### Help learners to review learning strategies and future needs, and encourage them to communicate needs and ideas

When we talk about reviewing learning, we sometimes assume that it is going to be at the end of a session or unit of work. However, the learning process is such that we should be reviewing learning with children throughout learning sessions. It is good practice during any session for adults to review with pupils what they are learning, but this can be harder for you to do in some learning situations than in others. This may be due to time but might also be due to the way in which the activity has been presented to pupils. Where possible, you should encourage pupils to measure their achievements against the learning objectives and think about how they might approach their learning in the future based on this. For example, they should consider their work at each stage against the final outcome to see whether it has met the objective. This may be part of a whole-class discussion or pupils may work in their groups or with partners on reviewing their learning during activities. There may also be whole-school strategies which are used to check on pupil learning. Some examples are listed below.

- **Traffic lights/smiley faces/thumbs up** — these can be used as a means of reviewing pupil learning and are good visual tools for younger children. They hold up a traffic light/smiley face or thumb to show how they are feeling about their learning at different points in the session. A red light, sad face or thumb down means they do not understand, and so on.

- **Foggy bits** — pupils are given the opportunity to write down or articulate the parts of the session or activity which have not been clear.

- **Write a sentence** — children are able to put in a sentence the key points of their learning at the end of a unit of work or learning activity.

- **Talk partner review** – children talk to their partner about their learning and parts that they enjoyed or found difficult. They can also do this at the beginning of a session or topic to see what they already know.

- **Post-it notes/whiteboards** – children can write down on post-its or whiteboards what they have learned, what they found easy and what they found hard.

## Support learners in using peer assessment and self-assessment

When supporting pupils during self-assessment, you will need to structure learning activities so that their purposes and outcomes are very clear. The younger the child, the more you may need to do this. However, if pupils understand why they are doing something, it is far more likely that they will want to learn. Children will need to be able to look at simple specific criteria to start with, so that they can measure their learning against this. Self-assessment for younger children is more difficult and it will be better for them to start by using peer assessment to encourage them to think about learning aims. Older pupils too will benefit from using peer assessment as a starting point (see below).

### Keep assessment criteria simple

You need to be very clear on what pupils are being assessed against. If you have more than two criteria, you will need to make them very specific. Clarify the purpose of the task so that pupils understand why they are doing it. Ask pupils to tell you what they think they are doing and why. This enables you to check that children have understood the task and how their learning will be measured. Encourage pupils to check learning periodically against the criteria – this will keep them focused on what they have been asked to do.

### How to promote the skills of collaboration in peer assessment

Pupils will build up their assessment techniques through working with adults and their peers so that they can ultimately begin to assess their own learning against learning outcomes and to look more objectively at their achievements. Peer assessment is not supposed to compare the achievements of children or cause them to grade one another according to their performance. For this reason, it is very important that children are clear on what they will be assessed against. Pupils should look at one another's work and notice how it relates to the assessment criteria. They can discuss what they have been asked to do and how their work reflects this. In this way it

**Clarify the purpose of the task**
- This is so that pupils understand why they are doing it

**Keep assessment criteria simple**
- Be very clear on what pupils are being assessed against. If you have more than two criteria, make them very specific

**Supporting pupils with self-assessment techniques**

**Ask pupils to tell you what they think they are doing and why**
- This enables you to check that children have understood the task and how their learning will be measured

**Encourage pupils to periodically check learning against the criteria**
- This will keep them focused on what they have been asked to do

*Supporting pupils with self-assessment techniques.*

> **CASE STUDY:** Promoting skills of collaboration
>
> You have been asked to work with Year 5 and support them as they critically evaluate their own work against a list of assessment criteria during an art session. They are working on a series of activities to look at the local environment and record sketches of details in building, patterns which they notice, textures and other details. The assessment criteria have been defined as follows.
>
> 1. Choose six interesting features of the local environment and record them in your sketch book.
>
> 2. Look at proportions, lines and shapes, and draw attention to these.
>
> 3. Show two ways in which light has affected the different features.
>
> - How would you start the children off so that they were not asked to self-evaluate straight away?
> - How could this start as a peer assessment and then move on to a self-assessment activity?
> - How would you ensure that you did not emphasise children's weaknesses and damage their self-esteem?

will start to bring their attention to what teachers are looking for when measuring achievement.

Through looking at the work of others, they may be able to see more easily how assessment criteria can be used to measure learning.

## Support learners to reflect on learning and identify progress, needs, strengths and weaknesses

### Reflect on their learning

When you are supporting learning, you will need to encourage pupils to think about and reflect on their learning throughout the process, and not just when they have finished their work. This is because they may need to think about the approach they are taking and whether this is the best way to tackle the task. You will need to do this through effective questioning and checking their understanding of the objective against what they are doing. You may also like to use the tools suggested on pages 109–10.

### Identify the progress they have made

You will need to check that the children are able to assess the progress that they have made when working. They might do this through peer or self-assessment, as already discussed, or you may need to question them about their learning by asking them to:

- put their hand up if they have a question about the activity and then asking if any of the others can answer it for them rather than answering yourself
- write down areas which they still feel unsure about
- tell you what they have learned during the session.

### Identify emerging learning needs, the strengths and weaknesses of their learning strategies, and plan how to improve them

As children reflect on their learning, they will start to be able to identify what they need to do to improve. Where they are used to doing this, they may find it straightforward, but children who have a fear of 'getting it wrong' may find the process challenging and you may need to support them though it. One way of doing this is to use misconceptions or incorrect ideas as a discussion point so that pupils can talk about how they approached the task and what led them to their answer. This can lead to a more positive approach to learning from mistakes and seeing it as an opportunity rather than something to be feared. Another way of supporting pupils might be to keep a record of their learning through a journal or diary in which they have the opportunity to think about their learning. They could also use this as a place to write or keep any of their own personalised targets.

**CASE STUDY:** Supporting learners to reflect on their learning

You are supporting a group of pupils in Year 6. The group has just completed a learning activity where pupils have been required to work collaboratively on a science investigation on circuits and follow up with a discussion on what they have learned. Although the investigation has gone well, there is some confusion from different children about exactly what they have learned from the investigation and how they should record their learning.

- Why do you think the pupils might be confused about their learning?
- How might you support the learners through assessment for learning?
- What might you do differently next time?

# Be able to contribute to reviewing assessment for learning

## Provide feedback to the teacher on learners' participation and progress

When using assessment for learning techniques, you need to work closely with the teacher so that you can discuss and review how you present learning activities to pupils and the kinds of opportunities which are available for assessment for learning. You will need to consider how pupils have responded to the process and which strategies you have found useful and thought-provoking for pupils. In this way you will be able to develop the opportunities available for use in the future.

As you will need to give feedback to the teacher, it is important to consider the different aspects of assessment for learning. The teacher will need to be aware of pupil engagement in the process and any difficulties which they have. It is likely that you will be giving the teacher feedback on learner participation and progress in the learning activities in any teaching and learning activity. This may be done verbally or using a feedback sheet, but you need to include all aspects of the learning process. It can be useful to note down either on post-its or small pieces of paper any interesting or useful comments

which pupils make during the learning process so that these can also be fed back. It will be useful to observe and feed back whether assessment for learning makes pupils more eager to participate in the learning activities and whether it makes a difference to pupil engagement.

An alternative way of giving feedback to teachers is through group feedback, in which the learners discuss the results of peer assessment with adults. In this way you will find out about their learning and feed back to the teacher at the same time.

### Reflect

How do you feed back to teachers when carrying out assessment for learning tasks? Do you ever change the way in which you do this? Does it work well both for you and for the teacher?

## Use the outcomes of assessment to reflect on and improve own contribution

Following learning activities, you will need to look at the outcomes of assessment for learning so that you can judge whether the way in which you have approached the process has been successful. In other words, you should be able to check that it has enabled pupils to take more responsibility for the learning experience and has influenced what they have learnt. You will also need to be able to reflect on your own learning and experience when supporting pupil learning, so that you can adjust your approach if necessary. You should think about:

- how you questioned pupils and encouraged them to look closely at the assessment criteria
- how you gave feedback to pupils
- how you supported both peer and self-assessment.

It may help to look again at the checklist on page 108 so that you can see whether different strategies may have worked better with pupils.

You will also need to discuss with the teacher the pupils' responses to the process, as some will have found it easier to manage than others and teachers may have suggestions as to how this may be developed. Depending on the ages and needs of the pupils, the use of peer or self-assessment may need to be altered.

## Getting ready for assessment

As learning outcomes 2–4 need to be assessed in the workplace, it would be helpful if your assessor could witness your planning and carrying out an assessment for learning lesson in which you encourage pupils to look at their progress against learning objectives and their own personal targets. If you can also encourage pupils to review their work, this will enable you to gather evidence for many of the assessment criteria.

### Websites

**www.education.gov.uk/publications/eOrderingDownload/ DCSF-00341-2008.pdf** – DCSF booklet on the Assessment for Learning Strategy
**www.teachers.tv** – Teachers' TV
**www.tes.co.uk** – the *Times Educational Supplement* (TES) website also has some useful ideas on assessment for learning

## Check your knowledge

1. How would you define assessment for learning?

2. How can assessment for learning help pupils when they are carrying out learning activities?

3. What is the difference between formative and summative assessment?

4. What kind of information do we need in order to carry out assessment for learning?

   a) the teacher's long- and medium-term plans

   b) information on the child

   c) learning objectives for the lesson

   d) success criteria for the objectives.

5. What kinds of assessment strategies might you use to find out how well learners are participating in the session?

6. How would you use peer assessment in a lesson?

7. How can we encourage pupils to feed back to us about their learning?

8. How might we develop opportunities for assessment for learning in the classroom?

# School life

## My story Jess

Our school recently had a blitz on assessment for learning and all staff were asked to ensure that it was implemented in classes. The teachers were all sent on training and the head emphasised its importance and the need for a 'whole-school' approach. However, I really did not feel able to implement the requirements and did not really understand what it was all about. I found some clips on Teachers TV which were good and also an article in the *Times Educational Supplement,* but did not really think I was getting enough support from the school for something that we were all supposed to be doing. I spoke to my head teacher as I get on well with her and said that a few of us didn't feel able to implement something which was clearly a priority without more information and training. She apologised and said that it was a misunderstanding as she had thought that teachers were going to pass on the information to support staff, whereas in reality this had not been organised. We were then able to set some time aside for training and now I am getting used to the process, I think it is very beneficial to the children, as it builds on what we were doing anyway.

## Ask the expert

**Q** What should I do when I am not sure about what I have been asked to do, but no one has time to talk to me?

**A** You must always speak out if you do not know what you are required to do – you will not be able to support children effectively if you are not clear about what you are to do with them. In a similar way the children may also be confused or unclear about their work, which will affect their learning. Although staff in school are always busy, there will be someone who will be able to listen to you and hear your concerns. Choose your moment carefully though – sometimes it is not possible to drop everything!

## VIEWPOINT

In the situation above, do you think the responsibility for passing information on lies with the head teacher or the staff below them? Remember that your colleagues have their own priorities and pressures, and if information has not been passed on to you, you may need to approach the relevant person for it in a tactful manner, rather than suggesting they are not doing their job properly.

# SfCD SHC32 Engage in personal development

This unit is about how to engage in your own continuing professional development. As part of your qualification you will also need to have some form of professional appraisal which includes thinking about your practice and setting targets for development: many schools are doing this already for teaching assistants. Appraisals will usually be carried out by your line manager, and some schools are asking their higher level teaching assistants (HLTAs) to appraise other assistants.

## By the end of this unit you will:

1. understand what is required for competence in the learner's own work role within the sector

2. be able to reflect on practice

3. be able to evaluate own performance

4. be able to agree a personal development plan

5. be able to reflect on how learning opportunities contribute to personal development.

# Understand what is required for competence in the learner's own work role within the sector

## Duties and responsibilities of own role within the sector

To support pupils effectively, you should have a very clear idea about the school structure and your role within it. You should have an up-to-date job description which is a realistic reflection of your duties. A starting point for thinking about your role will then be to look through it and think about any changes which have taken place over the past year.

### Link

See also TDA 3.2 Schools as organisations, for more on how schools are organised and the roles of different members of staff.

**London Borough of Lewisham**
**Job Description**
**Title: Teaching Assistant**
**Post: Level 3**

**Main purpose of the job:**

Under guidance of teaching staff: implement work programmes to individuals/groups (this could include those requiring detailed and specialist knowledge in particular areas); assist in whole planning cycle and management/preparation of resources; provide cover for whole classes for short periods under an agreed system of supervision.

**Summary of responsibilities and duties:**
**Support for pupils**

- Use specialist (curricular/learning) skills/training/experience to support pupils.
- Assist with the development and implementation of individual education plans (IEPs).
- Establish productive working relationships with pupils, acting as a role model and setting high expectations.
- Promote the inclusion and acceptance of all pupils within the classroom.
- Support pupils consistently while recognising and responding to their individual needs.
- Encourage pupils to interact and work co-operatively with others, and engage all pupils in activities.
- Promote independence and employ strategies to recognise and reward achievement of self-reliance.
- Provide feedback to pupils in relation to progress and achievement.

**Support for teacher**

- Work with the teacher to establish an appropriate learning environment.
- Work with the teacher in lesson planning, evaluating and adjusting lessons/work plans as appropriate.
- Monitor and evaluate pupils' responses to learning activities through observation and planned recording of achievement against predetermined learning objectives.
- Provide objective and accurate feedback and reports as required to the teacher on pupil achievement, progress and other matters, ensuring the availability of appropriate evidence.

*An example of a level 3 teaching assistant job description. What are the similarities and differences from your own?*

Sample teaching assistant job descriptions are also available on www.teachernet.gov.uk; click on management, staffing and staff development, job descriptions.

As well as a job description, there may also be a person specification, which should set out personal qualities which are relevant to the particular post. It may include some of the strengths listed below. You do not have to use these for your performance review, but it may be worth looking at them and bearing them in mind.

### Knowledge into action

Find a copy of your own job description. Has this changed at all since you started in your role? If so, write a short paragraph describing the changes and ask your line manager to sign it. What are your main duties and responsibilities? Copy the job description and changes if necessary to put in the front of your portfolio.

## Be a good communicator/enjoy working with others

It is vital that an assistant is able to share thoughts and ideas with others, and is comfortable doing this.

## Use initiative

Assistants will need to be able to decide for themselves how to use their time if the teacher is not always available to ask. There will always be jobs which need doing in a classroom, even if this just means sharpening pencils or making sure that books are tidy and in the right place.

## Respect confidentiality

You should remember that in a position of responsibility, it is essential to maintain confidentiality. You may sometimes find that you are placed in a position where you are made aware of personal details concerning a child or family. Although background and school records are available to those within the school, it is not appropriate to discuss them with outsiders.

## Be sensitive to children's needs

Whether an individual or classroom assistant, it is important to be able to judge how much support to give while still encouraging children's independence. Children need to be sure about what they have been asked to do and may need help organising their thoughts or strategies, but it is the child who must do the work and not the assistant.

## Have good listening skills

A teaching assistant needs to be able to listen to others and have a sympathetic nature. This is an important quality for your interactions, both with children and other adults.

## Be willing to undertake training for personal development

In any school, there will always be occasions on which assistants are invited or required to undergo training; these opportunities should be used where possible. You may also find that your role changes within the school due to movement between classes or changing year groups. You will need to be flexible and willing to rise to different expectations.

## Be firm but fair with the children

Children will quickly realise if an adult is not able to set fair boundaries of behaviour. Adults should always ensure that when they start working with children they make these boundaries clear.

## Enjoy working with children and have a sense of humour

Assistants will need to be able to see the funny side of working with children; a sense of humour is often a very useful asset!

### Functional skills

ICT: Developing, presenting and communicating information
English: Writing
These are all key skills that teaching assistants need to have. You could produce an information booklet on the computer outlining these skills and why they are important. This information booklet could be used to give to other people who are considering a career in this area. Make sure you present the information clearly and concisely.

## Expectations about own role in relation to relevant standards

Each work role will have its own set of **standards**; there is a list of standards for classroom teachers and there are also standards for school support staff, depending on their role. You will need to look at these together with your line manager as well as your assessor, as you will need to meet the standards in order to gain your qualification.

The National Occupational Standards for Teaching Assistants offers guidance on the wider aspects of competent performance. It also forms the basis for the NAPTA (National Association of Professional Teaching Assistants) Profiles, which some schools are asking their teaching assistants to complete (see www.napta.org.uk). The Support Work in Schools qualifications at levels 2 and 3 are also based on the National Occupational Standards. Other models of performance which are accessible to assistants include local and national guidelines for codes of practice, provided by government bodies such as the DfE and Ofsted. These are often available in school or through the DfE and Ofsted websites (www.education.gov.uk and www.ofsted.gov.uk).

It is important to be able to look through the standards and think about how they are relevant to you in all areas of your role. For example, each mandatory unit in this book relates to national standards against which you will need to be assessed. You will then need to choose those optional units which are more closely relevant to your own role by looking through and considering the requirements of each one.

### Functional skills

**English: Reading**
Read through the standards for teaching assistants at level 2 and level 3. Summarise the differences in the role, responsibilities and expectations for teaching assistants working at level 3.

# Be able to reflect on practice

## The importance of reflective practice in improving the quality of service provided

The role of the teaching assistant has in recent years become that of a professional. As part of any professional job role, it is important to be able to carry out reflective practice. This will be especially important when working with children, as your personal effectiveness will have a considerable impact on them and their learning.

**Reflective practice** means thinking about and evaluating what you do and discussing any changes which could be made. It relates not only to your **professional development** but also to how you carry out individual activities with children and other aspects of your role. You will need to reflect on a regular basis and should have opportunities to discuss your thoughts and ideas with your colleagues. By doing this you will be able to identify areas of strength as well as exploring those which need further development. Teaching assistants have quite diverse roles within schools and inevitably you will find that you are more confident in some situations than

### Over to you!

Choose one aspect of the standards for supporting teaching and learning (for example, those for personal development) and compare them with the corresponding standards for classroom teachers which may be found on the Training and Development Agency for Schools (TDA) website (www.tda.gov.uk). What similarities and differences do you notice?

### Key terms

**Standards** — statements about how tasks should be carried out and the minimum acceptable quality of practice that should be delivered

**Reflective practice** — the process of thinking about and critically analysing your actions with the goal of changing and improving occupational practice

**Professional development** — ongoing training and professional updating

*It will help to discuss your reflections with others.*

others. By reflecting on your practice and how you work with others, you will come to be more effective in your role and gain in confidence.

## The ability to reflect on practice

Reflecting on your work will give you opportunities to improve your practice and therefore will empower you, as you are using skills which you have developed yourself. It is important to take time out to think about what you are doing in your work with children; you have a professional duty to consider the impact of what you do. By thinking about this and knowing why particular strategies or approaches have worked, you will then be able to repeat them. In identifying aspects which have been less successful, you will be able to ask for more support. Remember that it is not a question of whether you got it 'right' or 'wrong', but making sure you can build on all the positive aspects of the work you do as a positive means of developing your career. Effective questioning of your experiences will help you to find a starting point for your reflective analysis. As a tool, it enhances your experiences as it enables you to take more control over what you do and develops your confidence.

In all aspects of your role, you will need to be able to think about your practice. Your school will be able to offer you support and will provide you with the experience you need. Taking a step back and looking at things from a different point of view is often an enlightening exercise — the important thing to do is to ask the right questions so that you are learning from the experience. You may also have the opportunity to benefit from other tools such as observations of your practice, peer assessment and feedback from your assessor. These are all useful ways of helping you to think about how your practice comes across to others. You may find that some of your reflections come as a surprise and you were not expecting to find out some things. If the school has an ethic of reflection anyway, it will be easier for you to engage in personal reflection, as you will be more used to the process. This is particularly true when it comes to uncovering the difference between words and actual practice — if the school has an open and accepting ethos where everyone is engaged in reflection and expects to learn through mistakes, the process will be less threatening.

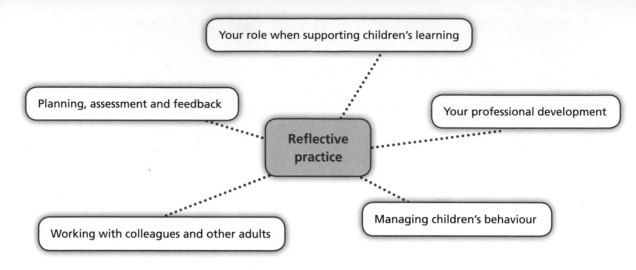

*You will need to reflect on different aspects of your role.*

It is important to remember that in your work with children, you are part of a whole school. If you are reflecting on your practice and find that you need to change or develop the work that you are doing, you will need to discuss this with others with whom you work, as this will also affect them. This could mean that if you are in a school which is less receptive to change or where staff do not reflect on their work as a matter of course, it may be difficult for you to approach others. You may need to be very tactful and sensitive in order to put your ideas across in a way which does not appear threatening.

A good starting point might be speaking to your class teacher or line manager, as they may be able to advise you on your ideas. Staff or year group meetings may also be an opportunity for you to put forward proposals, and this will also give others the chance to respond. You will need to think

about how you communicate your thoughts so that you do not appear to be criticising the way others operate. Always ensure that you build in a means of reviewing and evaluating any changes which are considered.

**BEST PRACTICE CHECKLIST:** Reflective analysis

- Be honest with yourself and others.
- Make sure you evaluate successes as well as failures.
- Include all areas of your work.
- Ask a colleague for help if required.

## How own values, belief systems and experiences may affect own working practice

As you examine your existing practice, you may find that the process is challenging and sometimes hard. You will need to reflect not only on the practical side of your work with children, which can be a difficult process in itself, but also on your own attitudes and beliefs. Reflection can lead you to reconsider issues which you may not even have thought of as relevant. When you start to think about all aspects of your role, you may find this hard, as beliefs can be very

*How often do you take the opportunity to discuss your ideas with the class teacher?*

difficult to change. You may also come across parents who have very different views from yourself or from those of the school. You will need to maintain your professionalism at all times.

**CASE STUDY:** How your values and opinions may affect working practice

Remy works in Year 1 in a church school as their general teaching assistant. Assistants are not usually required to go to assembly, but today Remy has been called upon to support Daniel in her class, who is autistic, as she knows him and his assistant is unwell. She has been asked to accompany him to assembly as he is unable to cope without adult support. Remy says that due to her own beliefs she is not prepared to go to assembly and that someone else will have to do it instead.

- Should Remy have been asked to go to assembly?
- Do you think that she was right to refuse to go?
- What do you think about the situation?

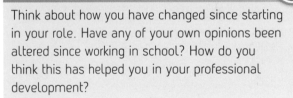

**Reflect**

Think about how you have changed since starting in your role. Have any of your own opinions been altered since working in school? How do you think this has helped you in your professional development?

# Be able to evaluate own performance

Once you have understood the requirements of your role and started to reflect on your practice, you will need to consider what you have done and evaluate it against the relevant standards.

## Evaluate own knowledge, performance and understanding against relevant standards

You should be able to think about activities you have carried out with individuals or groups of children and evaluate how the sessions went. Even if you always work in a particular way which seems to go well, you should consider different ways of approaching work you do with children. Questions you can ask yourself at the end of a session could include the following.

- What went well?
- What did not go as well as anticipated? Why?
- Did the children achieve the learning objectives for the session?
- What would I change if I did the activity again?

In this way your evaluation will encourage you to develop and change what you are doing if needed, to ensure that you are working effectively with the children. It may be helpful, if you have not evaluated your work before, for your class teacher or line manager to observe you working with children. They may then go through the evaluation with you afterwards and be able to offer suggestions and help you work though ideas.

## Reflect

How often do you think about work you have done with children and evaluated it? How much do you think it would benefit you in practice? Make a point of thinking carefully about at least one activity you complete with children each week.

## Functional skills

**ICT: Developing, presenting and communicating information**

If you complete any planning on the computer for the work that you do with the children, it is always a good idea to add an additional column on to the plan for evaluation. By saving these documents, you can revisit them after the session and add your evaluation for future reference.

By going through different aspects of your work in school, you will start to identify areas in which you are not as successful as others. Your reflections will enable you to draw conclusions about your work which may not be easy. Remember that this is a process and that by working through and addressing areas of your performance, you will improve your practice in the long run.

## Link

See pages 118–21 for more on evaluating your practice.

## Portfolio activity

Gather together all the notes and evaluation forms you have on your performance and put them in date order. You can then put these in your portfolio as evidence.

# Use feedback to evaluate own performance and inform own development

You will also need to be able to show how feedback has helped your own development. It may be useful for you to use assessment forms from your assessor visits in order to show how you have progressed since the start of your qualification. You will then be able to think about how you would like to move on in the future.

## Portfolio activity

As part of your qualification, your assessor will need to come into school and observe your work with children. They will then give you feedback on what they have seen and your work with the children and relationships with adults, and give you areas for development.

When you have received your feedback, think about any areas in which development issues have been raised, or where you have been given particular credit. Answer the following questions fully and use them in your portfolio.

- Are these areas different from what you had expected?
- Did any issues come up as part of your observation that surprised you?
- Why is it important for everyone working with children to reflect on their practice?

# Be able to agree a personal development plan

## Sources of support for planning and reviewing own development

In your school, there will be a number of sources of support you should be able to draw on to help you to plan and review your own development. Sources of support may include formal and informal support, appraisal, and may be within or beyond the organisation. You may choose to speak to a member of the Senior Management Team informally about your development if you do not have a formal procedure in your school. Alternatively, your school may undertake formal appraisals with all members of support staff. If you are undertaking a college course, you should also have a mentor or tutor who is able to advise and support you as you consider your performance and professional development.

## Work with others to review own learning needs and agree own personal development plan

The appraisal system is designed to help members of staff to consider their own professional performance on a regular basis. This should ensure that they think about their performance and continuing professional development.

The main consideration is that the **appraisal** process is a positive and non-threatening one. Each member of staff, including head teachers, will be appraised by the person who has responsibility for managing them. In the case of the head teacher, this will usually be done by governors. With teaching staff, the process is an ongoing cycle which takes place annually. As an assistant, you may be appraised by your line manager or member of staff responsible for teaching assistants. In the case of individual support assistants, this may be done by the school's Special Educational Needs Co-ordinator (SENCO).

### Key term

**Appraisal** — a regular meeting to discuss your development progress

You may find that the appraisal process is a good opportunity to discuss issues which may not otherwise be approached. It is also useful for discussing with your line manager anything you have done which you feel has been more or less successful than you had anticipated. In a similar way, you should also discuss

---

**CASE STUDY:** Sources of support for planning and reviewing own development

Mark has come into education as a mature student following a career in social services. He has started working in Key Stage 2 and is currently in his first term at a primary school. At present he is unsure who his line manager is in school as nobody has told him, and there are several issues which he would like to discuss with a more experienced member of staff to support his practice. He is also aware that he should have continuing professional development and has seen some courses run by the local authority which he thinks would be helpful. However, he does not know whom to ask, as everyone always seems too busy in school.

- What should Mark do first?
- How could this situation be avoided? Think about it both from the school's and Mark's point of view.

any areas in which you would like to have further training due to your own professional needs or interests.

You will usually be able to find out through your school the different courses and development opportunities which may be available. You may find that the school invites people from different outside agencies to speak to staff about particular subject areas during staff meetings, and these may be optional for support staff. Your line manager or supervisor should be able to give you information about training and help you to decide on the best courses and meetings to attend. The SENCO may be able to give you details about specific special educational needs courses, such as those run by the Sensory Support Service, or the Behaviour Management Unit.

If you have difficulty finding help, the local authority should publish details of courses which are run for teachers and support staff. You may also be able to contact the local borough for information about professional training for assistants, as this is undergoing a period of national change. Most local authorities will offer the induction training for teaching assistants which has been devised by the DfE and is aimed at those who are completely new to the role. It is fairly comprehensive and covers areas such as behaviour, literacy and numeracy, and special educational needs (SEN). These courses should be free of charge to assistants in local schools. The borough's education department should have a member of staff responsible for support staff training who will also be able to advise you.

### Over to you!

What development opportunities are available in your local area for support staff? How do you find out about these and are there regular opportunities for you to attend additional courses?

### Functional skills

**ICT: Using ICT**
Completing this task is a great way of making time to look further into continuing professional development (CPD) opportunities. Your local education authority's website may be a good starting point. When you find a good website that provides you with the relevant information, bookmark the page so that you can locate it again easily in the future.

### BEST PRACTICE CHECKLIST: Areas for development

- Make sure you are aware of when and where courses are run for support staff.

- Look out for opportunities for development as they become available and ask about them.

- Read information boards and magazines in your school.

- Speak to your line manager or the class teacher about particular areas of interest.

- Join any local early years cluster groups or networks.

### How the appraisal system works

The general appraisal form on the next page gives some idea of how the initial discussion with your line manager might be structured. However, this is a basic outline and further ideas such as whether you would like a more formal observation of your work may be recorded. If this is the case, the focus and timing of the observation should be decided at the initial meeting. An observation may take place if you or your manager feel that you would benefit from some feedback concerning your work: for example, if you are not sure that your methods for giving children praise are as effective as you would like. You will then agree on any action to be taken and new targets for the coming year. Following the meeting, copies of the appraisal form will be given to you and to the head teacher for record keeping, but will be confidential.

### BEST PRACTICE CHECKLIST: Preparing for your appraisal

- Check through your job description before the meeting.

- Be prepared by having some ideas of strengths and successes.

- Think about areas you may wish to develop before going to the meeting.

# General self-appraisal

It would be useful if you could bring this information with you to your initial meeting, to help you to identify your needs as part of the appraisal process.

1. Do you feel that your job description is still appropriate? Do you feel that there are any changes that need to be made?

2. What targets were set at the last appraisal/when you started your job? Have you achieved your targets?

3. What are the reasons for not having achieved your targets?

4. What aspect of your job satisfies you the most?

5. What aspect of your job has not been as successful as you had anticipated?

6. Are there any areas of your work that you would like to improve?

7. What training have you received? Has it been successful?

8. What are your current training needs?

*If you have not been given one, suggest to your line manager that you complete a form such as this before your initial meeting.*

## DVD activity

### Video clip 5 – Professionalism

Errison, the teaching assistant who is featured in the DVD clip, is having his appraisal meeting with the Deputy Head. She asks him to think about different aspects of his role so that they can devise some new targets for him.

1. What evidence is there that Errison has prepared for the interview and reflected on his current role and personal effectiveness? Why is this important? Which of the techniques of reflective analysis do you think that he has used to assess his own current practice? As a result, how effective is the appraisal interview?

2. Reflect on your own role, if you have not done so already as part of your own professional development. Note down any areas which you feel satisfied with over the past year and see whether you are able to identify any areas for development. (Use the 'General self-appraisal' form above if you need to.)

3. Are there any parts of this process which you find difficult? Why?

If you use a copy of your appraisal, which has been signed by your line manager, this will count towards the assessment criteria of this unit. Speak to your assessor about how much it will cover, based on what it says.

## How to develop and set targets

When thinking about areas for development, it may help to divide your knowledge and experience into sections. As an example, these might be knowledge and experience of:

- the curriculum
- behaviour management
- ICT
- relevant or new legislation

- health and safety
- working with or managing others
- record keeping
- special educational needs.

You will then need to think about your level of confidence in each of these areas so that you can begin to see areas of strength and those which may need further development. You will need guidance in order to turn these into targets.

Your line manager should be able to work with you to set personal development targets which are SMART (see the following table).

| Specific | You must make sure your target says exactly what is required. |
|----------|----------------------------------------------------------------|
| Measurable | You should ensure that you will be able to measure whether the target has been achieved. |
| Achievable | The target should not be inaccessible or too difficult. |
| Realistic | You should ensure that you will have access to the training or resources which may be required. |
| Time-bound | There should be a limit to the time you have available to achieve your target. This is because otherwise you may continually put it off to a later date! |

Table 1: SMART targets.

When thinking about these targets, you should not usually set more than three or four, so that they will be achievable. You should also ensure that you check between appraisal meetings to make sure that you are on course to meet your targets. There is little point in setting them if you have the meeting and then put the paperwork away again until next year.

You may find that because of the school development plan there are already training programmes planned over the next 12 months, for example, on the use of the interactive whiteboard in the classroom (see below), and that you will be attending this anyway. This will therefore form one of your targets. You may also like to think about training courses which will be useful to attend.

# Be able to reflect on how learning opportunities contribute to personal development

You will constantly be coming across learning opportunities in school which will help you to develop professionally. Whether these are just through talking informally with others, your own experiences, or through more formal training or INSET, your learning will shape the way you manage future situations and contribute to your personal development as you think about and reflect on what has happened. It is therefore useful to take time to think about how these learning opportunities have affected your own practice.

New targets for professional development:

1. To attend whole-school training on developing interactive whiteboard skills

2. To attend course on Early Years Foundation Stage

3. To complete level 3 qualification in Supporting Teaching and Learning in schools.

Part of a completed appraisal form.

## How learning activities have affected practice and how reflective practice has improved ways of working

### Classroom management

You may pick up new information on classroom management in different ways. In the course of your work and through experience you may gather information which you can integrate into your practice. Alternatively you might have been on a course which suggests that you try a new approach. You can also be more proactive by asking to observe other teaching assistants who may have more experience than you, or who manage children in a particular way.

### Meetings

You will find that you pick up new information during whole-school meetings or those which are run for assistants. Sometimes, colleagues may pass on details of training which they have attended or give handouts if they have found something which may be useful to others. If you find something useful, it is always worth mentioning this to others for their benefit.

### INSET/training

It is likely that you will need to attend whole-school training and INSET, which usually takes place at the start of a new term. You may be required to implement new ways of working if the whole school is taking on a new initiative, for example. You may then be asked to evaluate how things are going and whether the changes have been beneficial to the children.

### Skills builder

Keep a list of all the INSET and training you attend each time you do it. This will be valuable to you when you are filling in job applications or looking at your own professional development.

### New legislation

New legislation is brought in from time to time which will affect the way we work in schools. It is likely that if there are legal implications, the school will be obliged to offer training so that the requirements can be explained in detail. You may find that this affects your practice on a daily basis, or that the changes to your work are very slight.

### Portfolio activity

How do the headings above support you in thinking about the way in which your learning has affected your practice? Give examples of the ways in which your practice has been enhanced as your own experiences have developed.

### Functional skills

**ICT: Developing, presenting and communicating information**
You could create a document on the computer that contains a table where you can track and record any learning opportunities that you take part in. Make sure that you save this document so that you can edit it again and add to it when necessary.

### Curriculum changes

During the course of your career, there will be regular changes to the way in which different subject areas are taught and in particular the way in which support staff are deployed to deal with them. You will be given information and training as the need arises and these will affect your practice as you will be required to implement them. It is likely that you will also form your own opinions about whether they have had a positive effect.

### Informal conversations with others

You might find that just through chatting to others, you pick up on new information which may affect your work with children. You should make the most of breaks and other times which give you the chance to catch up and discuss your practice with others.

### Working with a child who has specific needs

You will gain a great deal of experience through working with pupils who have specific educational needs. This may be from learning about dyslexia, for example, or how to support a pupil who has a hearing impairment. It is useful to keep information or helpful ideas for your own benefit, as you may need to refer to them again at a later date.

## How to record progress in relation to personal development

Make sure you keep any paperwork from your targets and personal development plans so that you can refer to them later. They will also be useful as they will show how you have progressed professionally during your time in school. You should also always keep a record of all courses, qualifications and other ways in which you develop professionally during the course of your career. Your school may be able to track those you have attended since starting, but it is worthwhile keeping your own record. This will be a good aide-memoire for you but will also be useful when applying for jobs or further qualifications. You should list courses in date order and keep a record of who was running it, and whether there were any qualifications or credits attached, in case you need this information later. The quickest and easiest way is to keep a file which you can add to and also a Word® document on your computer with a list such as the one opposite. Always keep handouts and other paperwork, certificates or letters of attendance, as you never know when these may be useful.

---

**CASE STUDY:** Improved ways of working

As part of her qualification in Supporting Teaching and Learning, Helen needs to have a professional review meeting with her line manager so that targets can be set for review. She has discussed this with her assessor and is keen to identify areas for development, as she has started to reflect on her practice. She asks her line manager whether this is possible, as at present, teachers in the school have professional development meetings but not teaching assistants. Her line manager is not enthusiastic about the idea as she says it will make more work for her, but says that she will speak to the Head Teacher. In case there is no comeback, Helen starts to talk to her assessor to find out whether there are other ways for her to gather this evidence.

Three weeks later, the Head Teacher asks Helen about the evidence she needs to gather. The Head says that it would be good practice for all the teaching assistants in the school to have performance management meetings and tells Helen it will be an item for discussion at the next staff meeting.

- How did Helen show sensitivity in her request for professional development?
- Should she have gone straight to the Head Teacher, in retrospect?
- How might the school benefit from Helen's request?

---

**Portfolio activity**

If your school does not usually carry out a professional appraisal for teaching assistants, you may like to use the example on page 130. You can then use this in your portfolio.

## Sally Robbins – Record of courses attended

**September – December 2003:** DfES Induction Training for teaching assistants (12 sessions on Monday afternoons)

**January 2004:** whole school INSET on managing behaviour

**April 2004:** Early Years numeracy course – twilight 4–6pm with local maths co-ordinator

**September 2005:** Interactive whiteboard training for teaching assistants – afternoon as part of INSET

**September 2006 – June 2007:** Level 2 NVQ for support staff in schools at Bromley College

**September 2007:** one day whole-school Science INSET with John Branston

**September 2007:** whole-school Ofsted preparation

**July 2008:** Early Years Foundation Stage training – two-day course at local authority

*You will need to keep your own record of professional development.*

# Professional Review Meeting

Name: .................................................... Date: ....................

Line manager: ..............................................

Areas discussed:




Review of last year's targets:

1. ................................................................................target met/not met

2. ................................................................................target met/not met

3. ................................................................................target met/not met



New targets for professional development:

1. ................................................................................

2. ................................................................................

3. ................................................................................



To be reviewed on: ..............................................................


Signed ....................................(TA)

....................................(Line manager)

*An example of a professional review meeting form.*

## Getting ready for assessment

The appraisal meeting as a whole should cover much of the learning outcomes and assessment criteria for this unit *if they are all discussed*, although you should check with your assessor to make sure that your awarding body will accept this. If your assessor can be present at your appraisal interview and witness it, this will be even better evidence for your portfolio, although this can be difficult to arrange.

### Target setting examples

1. Some candidates choose to have one of their targets as completion of their award by a set date.

2. Include any INSET training that your school will offer during the next 12 months, for example, whole-school training on the new curriculum in 2011. In this way, you are including something you will be doing anyway, rather than setting additional work for yourself.

3. Include any training you have requested specifically for yourself, for example, a sign language course or a qualification to upgrade your maths or English skills.

Remember that targets will all need to be SMART (specific, measurable, achievable, realistic and time-bound). If your line manager has written a target which is not clearly achievable within the timescale, or which is not clear, it is important that you point this out.

If you are having some difficulty in setting a meeting in your school, speak to your assessor. You may be able to set and review some targets of your own through your college course.

## Check your knowledge

1. Why is it important to have an up-to-date job description?

2. What kinds of strengths should a good teaching assistant have in addition to professional knowledge?

3. Which of the following might a member of support staff be asked to do?

    a) carry out a playground duty

    b) work with a child who has specific learning difficulties

    c) clean classrooms

    d) put up displays

    e) take assemblies

    f) work on speech and language targets with individuals

    g) carry out first aid.

4. Why is it important to keep track of your own professional development?

5. What kinds of things should you consider when setting targets for the following year?

6. How can you find out about professional opportunities which may be available to you?

### Websites

**www.education.gov.uk** – Department for Education
**www.learningsupport.co.uk** – *Learning Support* magazine (for teaching assistants in primary schools)
**www.napta.org.uk** – National Association of Professional Teaching Assistants (NAPTA)
**www.ofsted.gov.uk** – Office for Standards in Education, Children's Services and Skills (Ofsted)
**www.qcda.gov.uk** – Qualifications and Curriculum Development Agency
**www.teachernet.gov.uk/teachingassistants** – Teachernet: information about support staff
**www.education.gov.uk/publications/eOrderingDownload/nos_for_supporting_teaching_learning.pdf** – National Occupational Standards for Teaching Assistants
**www.tes.co.uk** – the *Times Educational Supplement* (TES) website

# School life

## My story Nicola

I am a new member of staff and came to my current school last term after six years at a small primary school. I really needed to change and move on as I had been unhappy in my previous role. But it took me a while to get the confidence to start applying for other things, even though I am quite experienced. I decided to go for it and started applying with the support of my friends and family. Now I have moved on and things are so different here. We have a large staff and regular meetings, and I really feel as though I am part of a big team. Everyone has been really welcoming and I am wondering what took me so long to make the change. I have also been able to take on a slightly different role from that in my previous school and am currently working on my level 3 in Supporting Teaching and Learning in Schools. If possible, after this I am hoping to go on to qualify as a higher learning teaching assistant. Things are great!

## Ask the expert

**Q** I am always asking to go on courses but never seem to be able to – what should I do?

**A** You should be entitled to some courses through your school, although head teachers can sometimes be reluctant to allow support staff out on a regular basis. Do not ask too often – if you can find one or perhaps two each year that are of particular interest to you or that are linked to your role, this is plenty as you should also be attending staff development days in your school.

### VIEWPOINT

How would you feel if your school sent you on courses you didn't want to go on but never let you choose them? This may happen if, as part of your role, your training needs updating – for example, if you are a first aider or you need to have EpiPen® training. Additional courses may be expensive or time-consuming and will need to be linked to your role – you will not be able to go on them just because they interest you.

# CYP 3.4 Support children & young people's health & safety

This unit requires you to know about procedures which exist in your school for keeping children safe in the learning environment. You may also be required to help in outdoor environments or on school visits or journeys. For your role and responsibilities with regard to child protection and safeguarding issues, see CYP 3.3.

## By the end of this unit you will:

1. understand how to plan and provide environments and services that support children and young people's health and safety

2. be able to recognise and manage risks to health, safety and security in a work setting or off-site visits

3. be able to support children and young people to assess and manage risk for themselves

4. understand appropriate responses to accidents, incidents emergencies and illness in work settings and off-site visits.

# Understand how to plan and provide environments and services that support children and young people's health and safety

Planning and providing environments means that you will need to be aware of how to take into account the health and safety requirements of pupils when setting up learning activities. Before starting any learning activity, you should always make sure that the environment is free of any **hazards** and that children will be able to work safely.

## Factors when planning healthy and safe indoor and outdoor environments

### The function and purpose of environments and services offered

Rooms should be organised safely and there should be adequate space so that the number of people who will be using them can move around comfortably. Everyone should be able to access materials and equipment as required without causing **risk** to others. You should consider the following aspects.

- **Light/noise:** there should be sufficient light for the children to work without discomfort. You should also be aware that harsh lighting (for example, from fluorescent bulbs) can sometimes be uncomfortable after a prolonged time and cause headaches for some people. You may also find that an area which you had thought was suitable in which to work with children is too noisy or too dark and therefore not suitable for use.

- **Specific risks to individuals:** you should take any specific risks to individuals into account. These may include pregnancy, or sensory impairments, and will impact on the way in which you plan the environment.

- **Organisation:** equipment should be stored safely so that it does not present a hazard. Drawers and storage should be clearly marked so that it is clear where different equipment is kept and pupils are able to find it easily.

- **Furniture:** this should be an appropriate size for the age of the children so that they are able to sit comfortably when working. Children should not be hunched over tables which are too small or have difficulty in sitting comfortably.

- **The individual needs, age and abilities of the children and young people:** you should take the specific needs of pupils into account when setting up the environment – for example, the age, abilities and needs of the children with whom you are working. You should in particular take note of any pupils who have special educational needs (SEN).

- **The duty of care:** as we have a duty of care towards pupils, we should ensure that they are comfortable and safe and that the environment is secure and conducive to learning. Equipment should be stored safely so that it does not present a hazard.

We should always ensure that we take desired outcomes into account when setting up the environment. For example, if the outdoor environment is more appropriate to what they are learning it should be used wherever possible. However, it should always be checked before use to ensure that it is safe.

### Outdoor spaces

Outside areas to be used by children should be secure and boundaries regularly inspected to ensure that they are safe. When children are going outside, the area should be checked first to ensure that it is tidy and any litter, broken glass or animal mess has been

> ### Key terms
>
> **Hazard** – something that is likely to cause harm
>
> **Risk** – the likelihood of a hazard's potential being realised

*You will need to be aware of safety issues in all learning environments.*

cleared up. If you are responsible for putting out toys and equipment, make sure that children are aware of how they are to be used; reinforce rules wherever possible to remind them how to behave. Ponds and sandpits should be covered when not in use, as sandpits left uncovered can attract foxes and dogs, and can also be hazardous if children are unattended. Any toys or equipment should always be appropriate to the space available and should be put away safely. Plants can also be dangerous — thorns or nettles should be kept back and any poisonous plants noted and/or removed.

## Lines of responsibility and accountability

Make sure you are aware of lines of responsibility for checking the learning environment for risks and hazards. You should always speak to your health and safety officer if you are unsure.

> **CASE STUDY:** Planning healthy and safe environments
>
> Leila is working with Year 5. Although she works hard at putting equipment away and making sure that the environment is safe for the children, she has found that the classroom is not as organised as it might be. In addition there is a pupil in the class who has reduced mobility and a visual impairment. Although she is sitting by the window, which is important as she needs as much light as possible, her seat is quite difficult to reach and this presents problems for her.
>
> * What could Leila do in this situation?
> * Have you experienced these kinds of issues? If so, how have you managed them?

## How health and safety is monitored and how people are made aware of risks and hazards

The person responsible for health and safety in your school should carry out safety checks routinely or make sure that these take place on a regular basis. There should be regular walk-rounds or other means of making sure that hazards are not being left unreported. Where hazards are discovered — for example, items stored on top of cupboards which could fall down when the cupboard is opened — these should be recorded and reported immediately. Safety checks should also be made on all equipment which could be hazardous if neglected. All electrical items which are used in school should have annual checks carried out by a qualified electrician. Equipment such as fire extinguishers should also be checked annually, and the date of each check should be recorded on the outside of the extinguisher. Health and safety should also be a regular discussion point at any meetings which you attend in the school, and staff should be regularly reminded about any issues. If a specific hazard has arisen and all staff need to be notified quickly, there should be a procedure for doing this.

## Sources of current guidance and how legislation, policies and procedures are implemented

The Health and Safety at Work etc Act (1974) was designed to protect everyone at work through **procedures** for preventing accidents. Although it applies to all environments, it is very relevant to school settings and all staff will need to be aware of its main points.

### Report any hazards

Everyone should be alert to any hazards which are likely to cause injury to themselves or others in the school. The school is required to carry out an annual risk assessment to determine which areas and activities of the school are most likely to be hazardous, the likelihood of specific hazards occurring, and those who are at risk. Children and staff need to be vigilant and immediately report any hazards which they notice to the appropriate person. This may be the school's health and safety representative, the head teacher or another member of staff. You should be aware of the designated person to whom you should report health and safety matters.

### Follow the school's safety policy

The school needs to have a safety policy, which should give information to all staff about procedures within the school to ensure that it is as safe as possible. All new staff joining the school should be given induction training in safety procedures and what to do in case of emergencies. Safety should be a regular topic at staff meetings and staff should sign the health and safety policy to state that they have read it.

*How many of these safety symbols do you recognise?*

## Make sure that their actions do not harm themselves or others

Staff also need to ensure that any actions which they take are not likely to harm or cause a danger to others in the school. This will include tidying up and putting things away after use. You also need to consider the effects of not taking action – for example, if you discover a potential danger, it is your responsibility not to ignore it but to report it as appropriate.

## Use any safety equipment provided

Staff will need to ensure that safety equipment which is provided for use when carrying out activities is always used. This will include safe use of tools which are used for subjects such as design and technology, or gloves when handling materials in science activities. There should be guidelines in the school's policy for the safe use and storage of equipment.

## Ensure equipment is safe and appropriate

All materials and equipment used in schools will need to fulfil recognised standards of safety. The most widely used safety symbol is the Kitemark, which shows that an item has been tested by the British Safety Institute. Products are not required legally to carry a Kitemark, but many do so in order to show that they meet these requirements. However, European regulations require that many items must also meet legal requirements before they can be offered for sale within the European Union. These items will carry a CE symbol (this stands for *Conformité Européenne*, 'European conformity') to show that they meet European rules.

Always make sure that equipment you are offering for use to children is age- and ability-appropriate. The guidelines given by manufacturers are intended to be a realistic means of checking that equipment is not misused. A child who is too young or too old may be unable to use the equipment, and may hurt themselves and others as a result.

All staff working within a school have a responsibility to ensure that children are cared for and safe. The Children Act 1989 and Children (Scotland) Act 1995 also require that we protect children as far as we can when they are in our care. This includes preventing any risks which may occur.

## Functional skills

**ICT: Finding and selecting information**
You could research these areas for the Portfolio activity on the Internet. Take care when using search engines that you only use information from suitable websites, to ensure that it is fit for purpose.

---

**BEST PRACTICE CHECKLIST:** Health, safety and security arrangements

- Always be vigilant.
- Use and store equipment safely.
- Check both the indoor and outdoor environment and equipment regularly, and report anything that is unsafe, following the correct procedures.
- Challenge unidentified persons.
- Check adult–child ratios in all situations.
- Ensure you are aware of procedures at the beginning and end of the day.
- Make sure you are thoroughly prepared when carrying out unusual activities or when going on trips.
- Use correct procedures for clearing up blood, vomit, urine or faeces.

---

# Be able to recognise and manage risks to health, safety and security in a work setting or off-site visits

You will need to be able to identify a number of hazards in all situations, both in your setting and when managing children off site. This means that you should be vigilant both when working with others and when planning school trips or off-site visits. It is also a legal requirement that schools complete a specific risk assessment form before carrying out some activities or taking pupils off site — for more on this, see page 141.

## Identify potential hazards to the health, safety and security of others

When supervising children, you should be aware of the kinds of risks to which they are exposed and how likely these are to happen, bearing in mind the age and/or needs of the child. Pre-school children, particularly those under 3 years, are more likely to have accidents as they will probably understand risk or danger less. If you are working with children who have learning difficulties, they may also be less likely

*Can you identify potential hazards in this learning environment?*

to have a fully developed awareness of danger. You will need to modify your supervision according to the needs of the children and their level of awareness.

## Identifying on-site hazards

- **Physical** — physical hazards will be varied and will range from objects being left lying around to more serious ones such as equipment not being checked. As you spend more time in school, you will get to know the kinds of hazards which you are likely to come across.

- **Security** — potential security hazards may be around unidentified persons on the premises and children being able to go off site. Make sure that you are always vigilant regarding security issues and do not be afraid of challenging any individuals if you do not recognise them (see also pages 143–44).

- **Fire** — ensure that you are aware of fire procedures, particularly if you are new to the school. Hazards may include the use of candles or safety issues while cooking, either with pupils or in the school canteen.

- **Food safety** — you should be a good role model for children and always follow good practice yourself with regard to hygiene. This will include washing of hands before any activity involving foodstuffs, such as at lunchtime or prior to cooking activities. You should also make sure that you do not leave children alone near items such as sharp knives, hotplates or ovens.

- **Personal safety** — you should have an awareness and be vigilant when alone with other adults, or if for any reason you are in an isolated part of the school and working alone.

## Identifying off-site hazards

You will need to be aware of safety issues when taking children out of the school. If you are taking a large number of children on an outing or residential trip, a member of staff should always go and look at the site, and undertake a risk assessment beforehand. This means that they will check what kinds of risks there might be and the likelihood of the risk occurring. The level of risk may be dependent on:

- the adult–child ratio

---

### CASE STUDY: Managing personal safety

Melissa works in a large 4-form entry school which has a number of portacabins for the Year 2 classes. It is Parents' Evening in February and Melissa always stays to support the class teacher in discussing the children's work. Tonight they are almost at the end of the evening and are talking to one last parent; the teacher wants to go and get something from another part of the school to show the parent. It is dark outside and Melissa feels uncomfortable about being left alone with him.

- What could Melissa do in this situation?
- What do you think the school could do to ensure that staff are not left in positions of vulnerability?

---

- where you are going
- how you will get there
- your planned activities on arrival.

You will need to look at the facilities and check that they are adequate for the needs of the children, for example, if you are taking a disabled child. As well as a risk assessment, preparation will need to include other considerations. You should always make sure your trip is thoroughly planned, so that you are prepared for whatever happens. You will need to:

- seek and gain parental consent
- ensure the responsible adult has completed a risk assessment
- arrange for suitable safe transport
- make sure you have a first aid kit and a first aider with you
- take appropriate clothing for the activity or weather
- make lists of adults and the children for whom they will be responsible
- give information sheets and hold briefings for all helpers, including timings and any additional safety information
- make sure that any children about whom you have concerns are in your group rather than with a parent or volunteer.

*How effective are you at directing children away from a hazard?*

## Skills builder

Think about the areas of risk for the following groups. How does the risk involved balance with the learning experience?

- Taking a group of pupils with learning difficulties to the park.
- Working with a Reception group in the outside classroom.
- Going on a maths walk to local shops with Year 1.
- Working with Year 2 on a design and technology activity, using hot glue guns and hacksaws.
- Doing a traffic survey with Year 4.
- Taking Year 6 swimming each week.

## Deal with hazards in the work setting or in off-site visits

If you come across a hazard whether you are in school or off site, you should act immediately to make sure that others are not put in danger. This includes making sure that any other individuals are warned and directed away from the area straight away. If you can, you should deal with the hazard but if this is not possible, you may need to direct others away from the area and/or send for another adult. Children in particular are naturally curious and if they see something happening they will want to have a look!

## Portfolio activity

Write a reflective account showing how you have dealt with a hazard, either in your school environment or on a school trip. You will need to describe the steps in the order you took them and how you ensure that the needs of all individuals were taken into account.

## Functional skills

**English: Writing**
When writing your reflective account above, it is important to consider the layout, content and audience of the text. Take particular care with your spellings, grammar and punctuation.

## Risk Assessment – Transport (Contract Vehicle)

| Hazard | Who may be affected? | Control measures | Further Action |
|---|---|---|---|
| Condition of vehicle/driver | All | If the condition of either the vehicle or the driver is considered to be dangerous the venture is not allowed to proceed. | Ask the company to confirm that vehicle to be used has appropriate documentation, is roadworthy and drivers hold relevant qualifications and experience prior to booking. |
| Unexpected movement/ braking of vehicle | All | Pupils sitting in seats with seat belts fastened at all times when the vehicle is in motion. Pupils must not distract the driver when the vehicle is in motion. All baggage stowed securely. | Staff supervision to ensure that this is complied with throughout the journey. |
| Road Accident | All | If the accident is not serious. On normal road keep pupils on the vehicle if it is safe to do so. If not the move the pupils to a safe location protected from traffic. When moving follow the highway code and use staff to supervise the pupils to avoid danger. **If the accident is serious** Move those able to walk away from the scene of the accident keeping them safe throughout. This will have to be assessed at the time. Deal with casualties as best as you can until emergency help arrives. | Control communication between pupils and parents/ carers. Contact school as soon as possible. Control communication between pupils and parents/ carers Contact school and Emergency Contact at the LEA as soon as possible. Co-operate with the emergency services and at least one member of staff accompanies an injured young person to hospital. They remain there until parents or guardians arrive. |
| Mechanical breakdown – motorway | All | Get the party behind the side crash barrier as soon as possible. | Keep the pupils in a safe position until either the problem is fixed or replacement transport arrives. |
| Breakdown of transport – normal roads | All | On normal road keep pupils safe by remaining on the vehicle if it is safe to do so. If not the move the pupils to a safe location protected from oncoming traffic. When moving follow the highway code and use staff to supervise the pupils to avoid danger. | Keep the pupils in a safe position until either the problem is fixed or replacement transport arrives. |
| Organised break on journey/ on Ferry – a pupil(s) gets lost | Pupils | Head count taken on a regular basis especially when pupils leave and re-board transport. Pupils supervised by staff. Set clear guidelines for behaviour while on board. Ensure pupils are aware of emergency procedures | Communicate guidelines to all pupils and staff |
| Medical Emergency | Pupils | Staff to be aware of any pupils with medical needs and be aware of procedure for dealing with an emergency, Access to appropriate medication | Communication between parent/carers |
| Child Protection | Pupils | Staff supervision to ensure that there is no time where the driver is alone with either individual or small groups, of pupils. Supervision of pupils at public toilets if used during the visit. The age and maturity of the pupils will have to be taken onto account. No parent helper to take children, other than their own, to toilets alone. | |

*A risk assessment form.*

# Undertake health and safety risk assessments and explain how they are monitored/reviewed

In the normal course of your practice, it is likely that you will be involved in risk assessment at some stage, whether this is because you have some responsibility for health and safety or because you are going on a school trip or visit. There will usually be a member of staff responsible for ensuring that all risk assessments are carried out and the paperwork is completed in good time before the trip or activity is carried out. This will then need to be checked and signed by the representative and by the head teacher to show that it has been completed correctly.

You may be involved in risk assessment activities, in particular if you are taking children off school premises. Always encourage children to talk and think about any risks when they are working with you, so that they develop their own consideration of danger.

## Skills builder

When it is appropriate, for example, when you are going on a school trip, carry out a risk assessment alongside the person in your school who would normally be responsible for completing it. Ensure that you follow the normal procedures and that all staff who are required to see the forms have done so and that the forms are signed. These will then need to be copied and stored correctly so that they can be found quickly if needed and are on file for future reference.

- How will the risk assessment reduce the risk in this instance?
- How are risk assessments monitored and reviewed in your school?

# Be able to support children and young people to assess and manage risk for themselves

## A balanced approach to risk management and the dilemma between the rights/choices of children and safety requirements

It is important for all children to have opportunities to take some risks and most activities will carry some element of danger. Many educationalists now believe that the current tendency for many parents to keep their children indoors and take them everywhere by car is detrimental and overprotective, as it does not allow children to explore and discover the world for themselves or assess elements of risk. If children's experiences are limited due to adults' anxieties, it is likely that they will find it difficult to assess and manage risk as an adult. When a more **balanced approach** is taken and children are given more independence, they are more likely to grow in confidence. They should be encouraged to think about risks which may arise and act accordingly.

In school, while it is important to be vigilant and not put children in direct danger. We can help them to

think about risks in the environment and what we can do to avoid these risks. Although you are making sure that learning environments in which pupils can work and play are safe places, you can also encourage them to think about why certain courses of action, such as playing football or using ride-on toys close to other pupils, may not be sensible. As pupils grow older, they should have more opportunities, both in school and through extra-curricular activities, to consider how their decisions will impact on themselves and others. They should also have opportunities to discuss potential risks and problems with one another and adults.

## CASE STUDY: Taking a balanced approach

You are considering taking Year 1 to the beach as a year group, as it ties in with their topic on water. Your school is about 90 minutes from the sea, but some of the children have never been. At the year group meeting, some of the assistants voice their concerns about health and safety with such a large group in a wide open space.

- What do you think about this situation?
- Why is it important to discuss this as a group before planning to take the children?

## Key term

**Balanced approach** — taking into account a child's age, needs and abilities, avoiding excessive risk taking, not being risk averse and recognising the importance of risk and challenge to a child's development

## Functional skills

**English: Speaking, listening and communicating**
Discussing the case study would lend itself well to developing your speaking, listening and communicating skills. Try adopting different roles within the discussion, in order to take everyone's views into consideration. Try to make sure that you respond appropriately and move the discussion along.

## Supporting children or young people to assess and manage risk

You will need to be able to give examples from your own practice of how you have supported children in assessing and managing risk to themselves. This will show that you have an awareness of the kinds of situations in which you should be vigilant, but also how you are able to pass this awareness on to children.

> **CASE STUDY:** Supporting children to assess and manage risk
>
> There is a nursery attached to Amira's Reception class and all the children in the Foundation Stage use the outside area together. Amira is outside with a group of children when there are some men clearing back trees and undergrowth on the other side of the wire fence, using chainsaws. One of them says hello to the group.
>
> - What could Amira do in this instance?
> - Do you think that she should take the children indoors? Why?

> **Portfolio activity**
>
> Give an example of a time when you have given pupils an opportunity to discuss and evaluate risk within your setting or on a school trip. Show how you have supported them in the activity and what you consider the benefits to have been.

## Understand appropriate responses to accidents, incidents, emergencies and illness in work settings and off-site visits

In any environment where children are being supervised, it is likely that there will be incidents or injuries at some time. You may find that you are first on the scene in the case of an accident or in an emergency and need to take action. If you are the only adult in the vicinity, you will need to make sure you follow the correct procedures until help arrives. It is vital to send for help as soon as possible. This should be the school's qualified first aider and an ambulance if necessary.

You will also need to support and reassure not only the casualty but also other children who may be present. Children may become quickly distressed and, depending on what they have witnessed, may be in shock themselves. You should also ensure that you and any others on the scene are not put at unnecessary risk.

You must remember that if you are not trained in first aid, and if you are at all unsure about what to do, you should only take action to avert any further danger to the casualty and others.

> **Over to you!**
>
> Find out who your school's first aiders are. Was it easy to find the information? Is it displayed around the school?

## Policies and procedures in response to accidents, incidents, emergencies and illness

All schools need to ensure that they take measures to protect all adults and pupils while they are on school premises and on off-site visits. This means that there will be procedures in place for a number of situations which may arise. These include the following.

- **Accidents and first aid** – there should be enough first aiders in the school or on the trip at any time to deal with accidents. First-aid boxes should be checked and refilled regularly, and there should be clear lines of reporting so that accidents are recorded correctly. If you are off site, you should know where the first aider is.

- **School security and strangers** – this includes making sure that all those who are in school have been signed in and identified. Schools may have different methods for doing this – for example, visitors may be issued with badges. If staff notice any unidentified people in the school, they should be challenged immediately. If you are on playground duty and notice anything suspicious, you should also send for help. Schools may also have secure entry and exit points which may make it more difficult for individuals to enter the premises.

● **General health and safety** — health and safety should be a regular topic at staff meetings and during assemblies, so that everyone's attention is drawn to the fact that it is a joint responsibility.

● **Control of Substances Hazardous to Health (COSHH)** — anything which may be harmful should be stored out of children's reach or locked in a cupboard, for example, cleaning materials or medicines. COSHH legislation gives a step-by-step list of precautions that need to be taken to prevent any risk or injury.

● **Procedures for fires** — schools may need to be evacuated for different reasons — for example, fire, bomb scare, or other emergencies. Your school is required to have a health and safety policy which should give guidelines for emergency procedures and you should be aware of these. The school should have regular fire drills — around once a term — at different times of the day (not just before playtime for convenience!) so that all adults and pupils are aware of what to do wherever they are

on the premises. Fire drills and building evacuation practices should be displayed and recorded, and all adults should know what they need to do and where to assemble the children. If you are on a school visit, you should have been briefed as to what to do in case of fire or evacuation of the building.

● **Missing children** — fortunately it is extremely rare for children to go missing, particularly if the school follows health and safety guidelines and procedures. On school trips you should periodically check the group for whom you are responsible, as well as keeping an eye on children who are being supervised by helpers. If for some reason a child does go missing, you should raise the alarm straight away and make sure that you follow school policy.

### Portfolio activity

Using a copy of your school's health and safety policy, highlight the procedures your school has in place for the areas above. If it is not documented in the policy, find out whether it is recorded elsewhere. If you are unable to find the information recorded anywhere, you will need to speak to your head teacher or health and safety representative in order to find out and then write a reflective account under each heading.

Fire notice image

**Fire Action**

**Any person discovering a fire**
1. Sound the alarm.
2. [          ] to call the fire brigade.
3. Attack the fire if possible using the appliances provided.

**On hearing the fire alarm**
4. Leave the building by [          ] route.
5. Close all doors behind you.
6. Report to assembly point.

[          ]

Do not take risks.
Do not return to the building for any reason until authorised to do so.

Do not use lifts.

*Is this fire notice similar to those in your setting?*

## Procedures for recording/reporting accidents, incidents, injuries, signs of illness and other emergencies

Even if you are not a first aider, you should know the correct procedures for recording and reporting injuries and accidents in your school, as you may be called upon to do this. Remember that following all injuries or emergencies, even minor accidents and near misses, a record should be made of what has happened and the steps taken by staff who were present. You should also report verbally to senior management as soon as possible.

### Knowledge into action

Investigate your setting's procedures for recording and reporting accidents, incidents, injuries and illness. Are all staff aware of the location of the appropriate paperwork when the need arises?

## Primary School
## Accident report form

Name of casualty ....................................................................................

Exact location of incident .........................................................................

Date of incident .....................................................................................

What was the injured person doing? ...........................................................

How did the accident happen? ...................................................................

What injuries occurred? ...........................................................................

Treatment given ....................................................................................

Medical aid sought .................................................................................

Name of person dealing with incident ........................................................

Name of witness ....................................................................................

If the causualty was a child, what time were the parents informed?....................

Was hospital attended? ...........................................................................

Was the accident investigated? ..................... By whom?................................

Signed ............................................... Position..............................

*Find out where accident forms are kept in your school and the procedures for completing them.*

In addition to recording accidents, your school also needs to monitor illnesses which are passed around the school, as in some cases these will need to be reported to the local education authority. It is likely that your school office or sick bay will have a Department of Health poster showing signs and symptoms of some common illnesses so that staff will know what to look for. All staff need to be alert to physical signs that children may be incubating illness. **Incubation periods** can vary between illnesses, from one day to three weeks in some cases. Remember that young children may not be able to communicate exactly what is wrong. General signs that children are 'off colour' may include:

- pale skin
- flushed cheeks
- rashes
- different behaviour (for example, quiet, clingy, irritable)
- rings around the eyes.

Children often develop symptoms of illness more quickly than adults, as they may have less resistance to infection. Most schools will call parents and carers straight away if their child is showing signs or symptoms of illnesses. If a child is on a course of antibiotics, most schools will recommend that they stay off school until they have completed the course.

### Key term

**Incubation period** — the length of time between initial contact with an infectious disease and the development of the first symptoms

| Illness and symptoms | Recommended time to keep off school and treatment | Comments |
|---|---|---|
| **Chickenpox** – patches of itchy red spots with white centres; nausea; high temperature; muscle aches | For five days from onset of rash. Treat with calomine lotion to relieve itching | It is not necessary to keep the child at home until all the spots have disappeared. Chickenpox may pose an extra risk for pregnant women |
| **German measles (rubella)** – pink rash on head, trunk and limbs; slight fever, sore throat | For six days from onset of rash. Treat by resting | After being infected it usually takes between 14 and 21 days for symptoms to appear. Keep the child away from pregnant women. This illness is prevented by the MMR injection |
| **Impetigo** – small red pimples on the skin, which break down and weep | Until lesions are crusted and healed or 48 hours after commencing antibiotic treatment. Treat with antibiotic cream or medicine | Antibiotic treatment may speed up healing. Wash hands well after touching the child's skin |
| **Ringworm** – contagious fungal infection of the skin. Shows as circular flaky patches | None. Treat with anti-fungal ointment; it may require antibiotics | It needs treatment by the GP |
| **Diarrhoea and vomiting** | Until diarrhoea and vomiting has settled and for 48 hours after. No specific diagnosis or treatment, although keep giving clear fluids | |
| **Conjunctivitis** – inflammation or irritation of the membranes lining the eyelids, red, watering or sore eyes; sticky coating on eyelashes | None (although schools may have different policies on this). Wash with warm water on cotton wool swab. Lubricant eye drops can be purchased over the counter. GP may prescribe antibiotics | |
| **Measles** – fever, watery eyes, sore throat, cough; red rash, which often starts from the head, spreading downwards | Four days from onset of rash. Give rest, plenty of fluids and paracetamol or ibuprofen for fever | This is now more likely with some parents refusing MMR inoculation |
| **Meningitis** – fever, headache, stiff neck and blotchy skin; dislike of light; symptoms may develop very quickly | Get urgent medical attention. It is treated with antibiotics | It can have severe complications and be fatal |
| **Tonsillitis** – inflammation of the tonsils by infection. Very sore throat, fever, earache, enlarged red tonsils, which may have white spots | Rest; ibuprofen or paracetamol may be taken to ease pain and fever; in some cases antibiotics can be taken. Ensure the child continues to eat and drinks plenty of fluid | It can also cause ear infection |

*Table 1: Childhood illnesses and their characteristics.*

## Getting ready for assessment

A good way of producing evidence for this unit is to go for a health and safety walkabout in your school with your assessor during one of your setting visits. You can point out any hazards and carry out your own safety check of facilities and equipment in all areas of your school. This could include fire extinguishers and exits, first aid kits, access to first aid, how the school routinely checks equipment and prepares for school visits including risk assessment, and how accidents are recorded. If you are a first aider or have dealt with any incidents or illnesses, you could show the evidence to your assessor. They may also ask witnesses in your school whether you follow health, safety and security procedures yourself, and how you encourage pupils to do the same.

### Websites

**www.barnardos.org.uk** – Barnardo's, a children's charity

**www.bbc.co.uk/health/treatments/first_aid** – first aid guide

**www.hse.gov.uk** – Health and Safety Executive

**www.kidscape.org.uk** – Kidscape, a charity to prevent bullying and child abuse

**www.actionforchildren.org.uk** – Action for Children, the Children's Charity

**www.nspcc.org.uk** – NSPCC: Helpline 0808 800 5000 or help@nspcc.org.uk

**www.redcross.org.uk** – British Red Cross

**www.sja.org.uk** – St John Ambulance

**www.teachernet.gov.uk** – TeacherNet, which also gives a list of charities that work together with schools

**www.unicef.org** – UNICEF

## Check your knowledge

1. Name three factors you might take into account when planning healthy and safe indoor and outdoor environments.

2. Where would you find guidance and procedures for health and safety in your school?

3. What are your responsibilities regarding hazards?

4. What kinds of situations are potentially hazardous?

5. List the types of risk you might encounter when taking children off site.

6. Give an example of when you might need to undertake a risk assessment.

7. Why do children need to learn to be able to manage risk themselves?

8. Should only first aiders record and report accidents?

# School life

## My story Jim

I work in a rural infant school and we often take the children on school trips and for walks in the local environment. Recently I had to accompany a Reception class on a trip to the local playground. Before we left, I had been asked to carry out a check on the number of adults who were accompanying our class, most of whom were parents, plus myself and the class teacher. At the last minute the class teacher was unwell and unable to accompany the group. The other teachers were all teaching so unable to come, and health and safety requirements state that trips off site should be taken by a qualified teacher. I checked with the deputy (the head was off site), who said that we would have to postpone the trip as it was important to comply with regulations. Several of the parents, one of whom had taken the morning off work to come with us, were quite annoyed and said that we had enough adults to meet the adult–child ratio so should be able to go. As it turned out, we postponed the trip to the following week. I think we did the right thing, as I would not like to have been in charge if there had been any accidents or incidents while we were off site.

## Ask the expert

**Q** What happens if a supervising adult is unwell before or during a planned visit?

**A** Your school's risk assessment should outline what to do in this situation, but if an adult is unwell before setting off, it would be best to have another on standby. If the adult is a teacher it is important that the replacement adult is also a teacher, as the group leader should be suitably qualified and know about the expectations of the trip. If the trip has already been paid for, there should be another member of staff who can be sent instead – in the situation above it was easy to postpone the visit as it was just a walk to the local park.

### VIEWPOINT

How does your school prepare for trips, visits and school journeys? What plans do they have in place in these kinds of situations?

# CYP 3.1 Understand child & young person development

This unit requires you to have knowledge and understanding of the different areas of development of children and young people from the ages of birth to 19 years. You will also need to be aware of the factors which have an impact on children and young people's development and how various theories of development will influence current practice.

## By the end of this unit you will:

1. understand the expected pattern of development for children and young people from birth to 19 years

2. understand the factors that influence children and young people's development and how these affect practice

3. understand how to monitor children and young people's development and interventions that should take place if this is not following the expected pattern

4. understand the importance of early intervention to support the speech, language and communication needs of children and young people

5. understand the potential effects of transitions on children and young people's development.

# Understand the expected pattern of development for children and young people from birth to 19 years

## Sequence and rate of each aspect of development from birth to 19 years

Although you may be looking at and discussing different aspects of child development separately, it is important to remember that development should be viewed in a **holistic** way, and that each child is unique and will develop in their own way. Many of the skills and areas of development overlap with one another. A child does not learn the skills needed to play football, for example, which may be considered a physical skill, without having social, communication and cognitive skills as well. Aspects of development include physical, communication and language, intellectual/cognitive, social, emotional and behavioural, and moral.

### Physical development

This is an important area of children's overall development and one which can often be assumed will take place automatically as they grow and mature. Although children do develop many skills naturally as they get older, it is imperative that they have the opportunity to develop them in a variety of ways and they will need support in order to do this.

- **0–3 years.** This is a period of fast physical development. When they are first born, babies have very little control over their bodies. Their movements are dependent on a series of reflexes (for example, sucking, grasping) which they need in order to survive. In their first year they gradually learn to have more control over their bodies so that by 12 months, most babies will have developed a degree of mobility such as crawling or rolling. In their second year, babies will continue

**Physical**
- fine motor skills (writing, threading, painting and drawing)
- gross motor skills (running, jumping, hopping, skipping, balance)
- general co-ordination
- hand–eye co-ordination

**Social, behavioural and moral**
- taking turns
- co-operating with others
- developing social skills

**Emotional**
- development of self-esteem and self-expression
- learning about the feelings of others

**Areas of development**

**Intellectual/cognitive**
- developing creative and imaginative skills
- using skills in different ways
- using language to explain reasoning
- problem solving
- decision making

**Communication**
- using language to explain reasoning
- expressing feelings
- describing events

*How do the different areas of development overlap?*

to grow and develop quickly and it is at this stage that most children will start to walk. Their ability to control their movements will mean that they start to use their hands for pointing, holding small objects and start to dress and feed themselves. They will also be able to play with a ball and will enjoy climbing, for example, on stairs or furniture. In their third year, children will start to have more control over pencils and crayons, and will enjoy looking at and turning pages in books. They should be able to use cups and feed themselves. They will be starting to walk and run with more confidence, and will be exploring using toys such as tricycles.

- **3–7 years.** At this stage, children will be able to carry out more co-ordinated movements and will be growing in confidence as a result. They will be refining the skills developed so far and will have more control over fine motor skills such as cutting, writing and drawing. They will also become more confident in activities such as running, hopping, kicking a ball and using larger equipment.

- **7–12 years.** Children will continue to grow and develop, and will now be refining many of their skills. They may start to have hobbies and interests which mean that they are more practised in some areas, for example, sport or dance. They may also be able to make very controlled finer movements such as those required for playing an instrument or sewing. Girls in particular will start to show some of the early signs of puberty from the age of 10 or 11. In boys, puberty usually starts later, when there will be another period of rapid physical growth.

- **12–16 years.** At this stage of development, young people will be growing stronger. Boys will be starting to go through puberty and many girls will have completed the process and have regular periods. As a result, between these ages there can be a great variety in height and strength. At the end of this stage, most boys will be taller than most girls, on average.

- **16–19 years.** This is the stage at which young people are adults, but although many girls may have reached physical maturity, boys will continue to grow and change until their mid-20s.

*What signs of physical development have you observed in babies and small children that you see in everyday life?*

### Functional skills

English: Reading
ICT: Developing, presenting and communicating information
You could summarise the main points of the stages of development and put the information into a booklet. This is a good way of developing your reading skills. If you produce your booklet on the computer you could also develop your ICT skills by inserting relevant images.

### Skills builder

Choose a pupil who you know and make some observations on their behaviour, physical skills and social and emotional aspects of their personality. Are they around the 'average' for children of that age?

## Communication and language development

- **0–3 years.** From the earliest stages, adults will usually try to communicate with babies even though they are not yet able to understand what is being said. This is because it is important for babies to be stimulated and have an interest shown in them. In cases where babies are neglected and do not spend time with adults, they will find it very difficult to learn the skills of effective communication later. At this age, babies will be listening to language from those around them and will enjoy songs and games. Most will start to try to speak at around 12 months, although pronunciation will not be clear and words will usually be used in isolation. Between 1 and 2 years they will start to put words together, and their vocabulary will start to increase fairly rapidly so that by 2 years, most children will have about 200 words. Between 2 and 3 years, children will be starting to use negatives and plurals in their speech. Although their vocabulary is increasing rapidly, they will still make errors in grammar when speaking — for example, 'I drawed it.'

- **3–7 years.** As children become more social and have wider experiences, they will start to use an increasing number of familiar phrases and expressions. They will also ask large numbers of questions and will be able to talk about things in the past and future tenses with greater confidence.

*How can you encourage children to develop their language abilities during discussions?*

- **7–12 years and upwards.** By this stage, most children will be fluent speakers of a language, and will be developing and refining their skills at reading and writing. Their language skills will enable them to think about and discuss their ideas and learning in more abstract terms.

## Intellectual and cognitive development

Children's intellectual development will depend to a wide extent on their own experiences and the opportunities they are given from the earliest stages. It is also important to understand that children will learn in a variety of ways and that some will find particular tasks more difficult than others due to their own strengths and abilities. There have been a number of theories which outline the way in which children learn and it is important to bear these in mind when thinking about stages of learning.

- **0–3 years.** Babies will be starting to look at the world around them and will enjoy repetitive activities in which they can predict the outcome. They will start to understand, for example, that objects are still here even when hidden. At this stage, babies and young children will be learning to identify different items and be able to point to them. They may start to recognise colours.

- **3–7 years.** This will be a period of development in which children are becoming skilled at aspects of number and writing, as well as continuing to learn about their world. They will still be looking for adult approval and will be starting to learn to read.

- **7–11 years.** Children will start to develop ideas about activities or subjects which they enjoy. They will still be influenced by adults and are becoming fluent in reading and writing skills. They will be developing their own thoughts and preferences, and will be able to transfer information and think in a more abstract way.

- **12–16 years.** Young people will usually now have a clear idea about their favourite subjects and activities, and will usually be motivated in these areas. They will be reflecting on their achievements and choosing their learning pathway. They may lack confidence or avoid situations in which they have to do less popular subjects, to the extent that they may truant. It is particularly important to teenagers that they feel good about themselves and want to belong.

- **16–19 years.** By the time they come to leave school, young people will be thinking about career and university choices based on the pathway and subjects they have selected. They will be able to focus on their areas of strength and look forward to continuing to develop these as they move on.

## Social, emotional, behavioural and moral development

This area of development is about how children and young people feel about themselves and relate to others. They need to learn how to have the confidence to become independent of adults as they grow older and start to make their way in the world.

- **0–3 years.** Very young children will be starting to find out about their own identities. They will need to form a strong attachment, the earliest of which will be with parents and carers. In nurseries, children are usually given a key worker who will be their main contact. At this stage of development, children may start to have tantrums through frustration, and will want and need to start doing things for themselves.

- **3–7 years.** Children will still be developing their identities and will be starting to play with their peers and socialise using imaginative play. This will help them to develop their concept of different roles in their lives. It is important that they are able to learn to understand the importance of boundaries and why they are necessary. They will also respond well to being given responsibility, for example, class helpers, and will need adult approval.

- **7–12 years.** Children's friendships will become more settled and they will have groups of friends. They will need to have the chance to solve problems and carry out activities which require more independence. They will continue to need praise and encouragement, and will be increasingly aware of what others may think of them.

- **12–16 years.** At this stage, the self-esteem of children and young people can be very vulnerable. Their bodies will be taking on the outer signs of adulthood but they will still need guidance

in many different ways. They will want to be independent of adults and spend more time with friends of their own age, but can continue to display childish behaviour. They can find that they are under the pressures of growing up and of increasing expectations, and may be unsure how to behave in different situations.

- **16–19 years.** Children enter adulthood but will still sometimes need advice and guidance from other adults. They will lack experience and individuals will vary in emotional maturity and the way in which they interact with others.

---

**BEST PRACTICE CHECKLIST:** Supporting social, emotional, behavioural and moral development

- Make sure you are approachable and give children and young people your time.

- Give fair but firm boundaries and explain the reasons for these.

- Ensure children and young people feel valued and are given praise and encouragement.

- Give children the chance to develop their independence.

- Be aware of each child's overall development.

- Be sensitive to their needs.

- Encourage them to think about the needs of others.

- Act as a good role model.

---

**Functional skills**

**English: Writing and Speaking and Listening**
Completing the tasks in the following portfolio activity will allow opportunity for you to develop your English skills. Take care with your spellings, punctuation and grammar in the reflective account. When having the discussion make sure you listen carefully to what is being said so that you can respond in an appropriate manner.

## The difference between sequence of development and rate of development

Each child is unique and will develop at their own rate. However, while children will usually follow the same **pattern of development**, the ages at which they reach them may vary depending on the individual. Milestones of development are given as a broad average of when children may be expected to reach a particular stage. You may notice in particular classes or year groups some children who may stand out because they may have reached milestones in advance of or later than other children.

Sometimes, if children's growth patterns are very different from those of their peers, this may have an effect on their behaviour. For example, children in the last two years of primary school may become taller and develop some of the first signs of puberty. Girls in particular can become much taller than boys and this can put pressure on them to behave differently. There may need to be additional provision made in this instance, for example, when getting changed for PE. There may also be pupils who are very tall or very small for their age, and this can sometimes affect how they are treated by their peers. It can also affect social and emotional development. The patterns of development discussed here should therefore be seen as a guide to help you to draw up an overall idea of these different stages.

**Physical development**
fine motor skills and hand–eye co-ordination

**Social, emotional and behavioural development**
sharing mealtimes with one another, taking turns

**Cooking**

**Communication and intellectual development**
measuring quantities, deciding on appropriate menus, using language to describe foods, learning how food and nutrition affect growth and health, sitting down to eat together and conversing with one another

*Can you think of another activity that would develop a range of skills?*

Although development is often divided into different areas, it is important to remember that they are interconnected and link with one another. For example, developing physically and refining these physical skills will also affect children's ability to become independent, socialise and grow in confidence.

When planning or thinking about activities which you are going to carry out with children and young people, you should try to think not only in terms of specific areas, but also in terms of the broader picture. Many activities will stimulate children's interest and encourage them to develop skills in different areas.

For example, an activity such as cooking (or food technology for older pupils) will develop a range of skills.

### Functional skills

ICT: Developing, presenting and communicating information
Thinking of an activity that you have done with the children you could create a PowerPoint® presentation that demonstrates all the different areas of development that the activity promoted. Delivering this presentation to your peers is a great way of sharing good practice and ideas.

# Understand the factors that influence children and young people's development and how these affect practice

## How development is influenced by personal and external factors

Children's development will be influenced by a wide range of factors. Their background, health and the environment in which they are growing up will all have an impact, as each will affect all areas of development. You will need to have an awareness of some of these, as you will need to know how pupils may be affected and encourage them to participate and develop as far as possible.

### Personal factors
#### Pupils' health

If pupils suffer from poor health or a physical disability or impairment, this may restrict their developmental opportunities. For example, a child who has a medical condition or impairment may be less able to participate in some activities than other children. This may initially affect physical development but may also restrict social activities, for example, on the playground. The child's emotional development may also be affected, depending on their awareness of their needs and the extent to which they are affected. It is important that adults in school are aware of how pupils may be affected by these kinds of conditions and circumstances, so that we can support them by ensuring that they are included as far as possible.

### Learning difficulties

A child who has learning difficulties should be encouraged to develop in all areas to the best of their ability and as much as they can. If you are supporting a child who has learning difficulties, it is likely that you will have advice and guidelines from other professionals as to how to manage their needs while encouraging their development.

### External factors
#### Pupils' background and family environment

Pupils will come from a range of different family environments, cultures and circumstances. Many families go through significant changes during the child's school years, which the schools are not always aware of. These may include family break-up or the introduction of a new partner, bereavement, illness, moving house or changing country. Any one of these may affect children's emotional and/or intellectual development, and you may notice a change in pupil behaviour and ability to learn as a result.

### Poverty and deprivation

Poverty and deprivation are likely to have a significant effect on pupil development. Statistics show that children who come from deprived backgrounds are less likely to thrive and achieve well in school, as parents will find it more difficult to manage their children's needs, which will in turn impact on all areas of their development. These will all affect the way in which pupils are able to respond in different situations.

## Personal choices

The personal choices of children will affect their development as they grow older, as they decide on friendship groups, extra-curricular activities, academic involvement and so on. They may need advice and support from adults to enable them to make the choices which are right for them.

## Looked after/care status

If a child is looked after or in care, this may affect their development in different ways. However, they will usually be monitored closely and there will be regular meetings with the school to ensure that they are making expected levels of progress. Where there are any issues, these will then be addressed straight away.

## Education

In some cases, children may come to school without any previous education — for example, if they are from another country where formal education may begin later. Alternatively they may come from a home schooling environment or a different method of schooling, so they may need to have some additional support until they become settled.

# Theories of development and frameworks to support development

There have been a number of theories of development and many of them will influence the way in which we approach our work with children. Many psychologists have different ideas about how children learn — some feel that a child's ability is innate and others that it depends on the opportunities that they are given. This is often called the 'nature versus nurture' debate.

## Cognitive/Constructivist

Piaget believed that the way children think and learn is governed by their age and stage of development, because learning is based on experiences which they build up as they become older. As children's experiences change, they adapt what they believe; for example, a child who only ever sees green apples will believe that all apples are green. Children need to extend their experiences in order to extend their learning, and will eventually take ownership of this

themselves so that they can think about experiences that they have not yet developed.

## Psychoanalytic

Freud stated that our personalities are made up of thee parts — the id, the ego and the superego. Each of these will develop with the child and each will develop in a subconscious way, driven by psychological needs.

- The id is the instinctive part of our personality; in other words, it is based on biological needs, such as hunger. A baby will cry if it is hungry and will not consider the needs of others around it.

- The ego starts to develop as the child realises that its behaviour may affect how its needs are met. For example, if it is hungry, it may decide not to cry for its food but to wait, as food will come anyway.

- The superego develops later on in childhood and is based on the development of the conscience. The superego may develop conflicting views to that of the ego, and may punish the individual through guilt. Alternatively, if the ego behaves well, the superego will promote pride.

## Operant conditioning

Operant conditioning theory states that our learning is based on a consequence which follows a particular behaviour. In other words, we will repeat those experiences which are enjoyable and avoid those that are not. This is as relevant for learning experiences as it is for behaviour. For example, a child who is praised for working well at a particular task will want to work at the task again. Skinner called this positive reinforcement. His work is closely linked to that of John Watson below, although it differs from Watson's in that individuals are more active in the process of learning and will make their own decisions based on the consequences of their behaviour.

## Behaviourist

Watson believed that we are all born with the same abilities and that anyone can be taught anything — it does not depend on innate ability but on watching others. His idea was that of 'classical conditioning' and was born out of Ivan Pavlov's

*Can you think of examples that you have seen of Skinner's theory of operant conditioning?*

research using dogs. Pavlov devised an experiment by ringing a bell when the dogs were about to be fed, which made them salivate, as they associated it with food appearing. The bell was then rung repeatedly with no food and gradually the dogs stopped salivating. Watson discounted emotions and feelings while learning, and based his theories purely on how individuals can be 'trained' to behave in a particular way.

## Social learning

Bandura's approach was also one of behaviourism; in other words, it accepts the principles of conditioning. However, Bandura stated that learning takes place through observing others rather than being taught or reinforced. Children will sometimes simply copy the behaviour or activities of adults or their peers without being told to do so, meaning their learning is spontaneous.

## Humanist

Maslow was originally interested in behaviourism and studied the work of Watson. He also acknowledged Freud's belief in the presence of the unconscious — however, he did not think that individuals were driven by it. He felt that a knowledge of ourselves and our own needs was far more important. Humanistic psychology is based on our own free will, although we have a hierarchy of needs without which we will be unable to continue to progress.

## Social pedagogy

Social pedagogy is a humanistic framework to support development. It refers to a holistic approach to the needs of the child through health, school, family and spiritual life, leisure activities and the community. Through social pedagogy the child is central through their involvement and interaction with the wider world. The framework is socially constructed and may vary between cultures, contexts and the time at which it takes place.

### Portfolio activity

Find out a little more about the learning theories of Freud, Maslow, Bandura, Skinner and Watson. Use the information to create a reflective account for your portfolio.

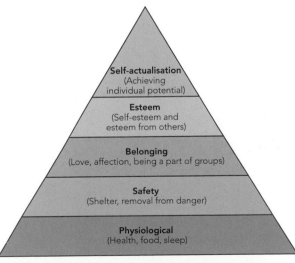

*Maslow's hierarchy of needs. Children will be unable to reach their potential without their needs being met.*

# Understand how to monitor children and young people's development and interventions that should take place if this is not following the expected pattern

## Monitor development using different methods

Different methods of monitoring include:

- assessment frameworks
- observation
- standard measurements
- information from carers and colleagues.

You will need to use different methods and opportunities to monitor the development of children and young people in the course of your work with them.

It is important to understand the purpose of observations as part of your role. This is because you will need to report back to the teacher, who will in turn report to parents and carers on pupil progress. Parents and teachers should share information about pupils to enable them to work together in the pupil's best interest. These observations may be carried out both formally and informally, and there are advantages and disadvantages to each.

Informal observations will be those which you carry out each day as you work with pupils. These may be small but over time will enable you to build up a picture of each pupil. You may notice, for example, that an individual is able to understand new concepts very easily, or that they are holding a pencil incorrectly. It is likely that you will discuss your observations with teachers as part of the feedback process after your work with pupils. A disadvantage of informal observations is that they may not be recorded and you might forget to pass on what you have seen to others.

You may also be asked to carry out formal observations on pupils to support the teacher in assessing pupils' levels of development (see TDA 3.3, Support learning activities, for more on formal observations).

Standard measurements are used to measure a child's physical development and to determine whether they are growing at the expected rate for their age. It is unlikely that you will be required to carry out this kind of check, as it will be done by health practitioners.

The Assessment Framework or Assessment Triangle is the term given to the way in which a child is assessed, to determine whether they are in need and what the nature of those needs is. In this way the child's best interests can be planned for with regard to their stage of development. It is looked at in more detail in CYP 3.3 on safeguarding children. Standard measurements and assessment frameworks will be useful in deciding on whether the child is reaching expected milestones of development in different areas. You should not be required to use these without the guidance and support of your class teacher or Special Educational Needs Co-ordinator (SENCO).

## Reasons why development may not follow the expected pattern

Children and young people's development may not follow the expected pattern for a number of reasons. You will need to consider personal and external factors (page 155) alongside developmental aspects of learning, and take advice from other professionals about how to proceed. If you have concerns about a child's development, you should always speak to the class teacher in the first instance.

## CASE STUDY: Concerns about a child's development

Hoi Ming is in Year 2 and is a very quiet child, although she has friends in her peer group. You do not know very much about her, but you are aware that she lives with her father, who has custody of Hoi Ming and her younger sister. You have noticed that recently she is increasingly withdrawn both in the classroom and when you are on duty at lunchtime. She has hardly anything in her packed lunch box. In addition to this, she does not seem to be making progress with her work or her reading, and she is falling behind others in the class.

- Would you say anything to Hoi Ming?
- Would you do anything else?
- Why is it important that you do something about what you have seen?

## How disability may affect development

Disability may affect development in a number of ways. Depending on the pupil's needs, it may cause a delay in a particular aspect of their development — for example, a physical disability may affect their social skills if they become more withdrawn or their behaviour if they become frustrated. Development may also be affected by the attitudes and expectations of others — if we assume that a disabled person will not be able to achieve and do not allow them the opportunity to take part, we are restricting their development in all areas.

When you are working with pupils who have special educational needs (SEN), you will find that many professionals and parents speak about the danger of 'labelling' pupils. This is because it is important that we look at the needs of the individual first, without focusing on the pupil's disability or impairment. In the past, the medical model of disability has been used more than the social model (see the following table) and this kind of language has promoted the attitude that people with disabilities are individuals who in some way need to be corrected or brought into line with everybody else. This has sometimes led to unhelpful labelling of individuals in terms of their disabilities rather than their potential.

| Medical model | Social model |
|---|---|
| Pupil is faulty | Pupil is valued |
| Diagnosis | Strengths and needs defined by self and others |
| Labelling | Identify barriers/ develop solutions |
| Impairment is focus of attention | Outcome-based programme designed |
| Segregation or alternative services | Training for parents and professionals |
| Ordinary needs put on hold | Relationships nurtured |
| Re-entry if 'normal' or permanent exclusion | Diversity is welcomed and pupil is included |
| Society remains unchanged | Society evolves |

Table 1: Medical and social models of disability (Source: Disability Discrimination in Education Course Book: Training for Inclusion and Disability Equality).

You should also be realistic about the expectations you have of pupils and consider their learning needs. For some, although not all, the curriculum will need to be modified and pupils may need support. However, it should not be assumed that SEN pupils will always require extra help and you need to encourage them to be as independent as possible.

## How different types of interventions can promote positive outcomes

As a teaching assistant, you are likely to be involved in intervention groups or other group work in order to support pupils who are not progressing at the same rate as others. This is likely to be advised by either the SENCO or another professional who will have links with the school. Any of the professionals below may come into school in order to discuss a child's progress or to advise teaching staff on next steps.

- **Social worker** — a social worker might be involved if a child has been a cause for concern in the home environment or if parents have asked for support. They will also liaise with the school regarding Looked After Children (LACs). Occasionally schools may contact social services directly if they have concerns about a child and their home environment.

- **Speech and language therapist** — see page 161 on supporting communication needs.

- **Psychologist** — see page 162 on supporting communication needs.

- **Psychiatrist** — a psychiatrist may be asked to assess a child if there are serious concerns about their emotional development. Children will usually have been referred through a series of assessments before this takes place.

- **Youth justice** — this form of intervention is a public body which aims to stop children and young people offending. The youth justice team may be involved in partnership with schools and the community where there are cases of offending behaviour. It also acts in a preventative way by running youth inclusion programmes, which are targeted towards those who may be at high risk of offending.

- **Physiotherapist** — a physiotherapist will advise and give targets for pupils to work on around the development of their **gross motor skills**. They may give exercises for school staff and parents to work on each day, depending on the needs of the child.

- **Nurse/health visitor** — these medical professionals may be involved in supporting the development of some children where they have physical or health needs. They will usually come into school to advise and speak to staff, generally with parents present.

- **Assistive technologies** — these are technologies which enable pupils who have specific needs to access the curriculum. They may range from computer programmes to specific items such as a speech recognition device or a hearing aid, and will give the individual an increased level of independence (for an example of an assistive technology, see clip 9 on the DVD).

In all of these cases, positive outcomes will be more likely to be achieved, since the child will be working with a specialist who will then advise teachers and support staff. Their progress will then be measured through setting and reviewing targets on a regular basis.

### Key term

**Gross motor skills** — control of the larger muscles, typically those in the arms or legs — for example, kicking a ball

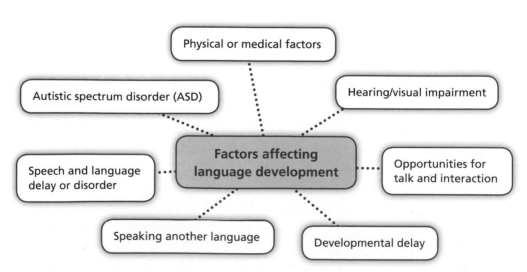

*Consider the impact one of these factors might have on a child's holistic development.*

# Understand the importance of early intervention to support the speech, language and communication needs of children and young people

## The importance of early identification and the potential risks of late recognition

Language is crucial to learning, as it is linked to our thoughts. It enables us to store information in an organised way. If children have difficulties in communicating with others due to a speech and language delay or disorder, they will be working at a disadvantage, as they will be less able to organise their thought processes and express themselves. As children become older and the curriculum becomes more demanding, the use of rational and abstract thought will become more important. The earlier the diagnosis of delayed language acquisition, the easier it will be for professionals and others to target the child's needs so that they are able to give support, and the more beneficial for the child, as the early years are a time of rapid learning and development.

---

**CASE STUDY:** Identifying speech and language delays and disorders

Mike is working in Year 1 as a teaching assistant and often supports a small group of children who are not making expected levels of progress. Anya in his group is a bright and enthusiastic child, but her understanding seems limited and she finds it difficult to express what she wants to say. He has noticed recently that she seems increasingly quiet even in the small group. Mike has registered his concern once with the class teacher and SENCO, but so far nothing seems to have happened, and he does not like to be pushy as he knows they are busy.

- What should Mike do?
- Can you think of any other ways in which he could support Anya?

---

Pupils with language delay may also find it harder to form relationships with others. As a result they may become frustrated, leading to possible behaviour problems, and isolated. Very young children in particular will not have the experience to recognise the reason for their feelings. If you are working with a child who has a communication delay or disorder, you should be sent on specific training or given additional support and strategies to help you in your work with them.

## How multi-agency teams work together to support speech, language and communication

There will be a number of other professionals with whom you may come into contact if you support a pupil with communication and interaction needs. They may also come together as a team in order to discuss and plan out how the child's needs can be best met. Those involved will depend on the specific needs of the child, but may include some of the following.

### Speech and language therapist

This therapist will sometimes be based in schools but is usually external. They will give a diagnosis of a particular communication delay or disorder and will also advise school and parents about ways in which they can support the child. Speech and language appointments will usually be delivered in blocks, followed by activities for pupils to work on before they are next reviewed. Parents and teachers will be closely involved in the monitoring and review of pupils' progress.

### SENCO

The SENCO will co-ordinate the work of the other professionals who work with the child and will ensure that paperwork and appointments are up to date. They will encourage communication between agencies which work with the child and may organise meetings at the school to discuss progress.

### Other support staff

You may work alongside other support staff to deliver learning programmes to a particular child. You will need to ensure that you have opportunities to meet with them regularly in order to discuss the child's progress.

### Sensory support teacher

This teacher from the local authority may come to school regularly to advise on how best to support pupils who have a visual or auditory impairment, which will also have an impact on their communication skills. They may also provide resources to support pupils with their learning.

### Autism advisory teacher

This support teacher may come into school to advise on how best to support a child who has a diagnosis of autism. Two aspects of autism are that individuals will have an impairment in the areas of social interaction and communication.

### Educational psychologist

The educational psychologist may become involved if, following intervention and action from speech and language therapists and teaching staff, the child is still not starting to make some progress. They will carry out an assessment and suggest the next steps.

You may be invited to contribute to a multi-agency meeting alongside other professionals to discuss the needs of the child and to draw up targets for them.

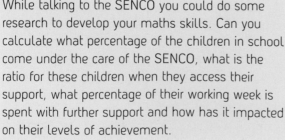

### Knowledge into action

Talk to your SENCO about which of the above professionals come into school on a regular basis and the children to whom they give advice and guidance.

### Functional skills

#### Maths: Analysing

While talking to the SENCO you could do some research to develop your maths skills. Can you calculate what percentage of the children in school come under the care of the SENCO, what is the ratio for these children when they access their support, what percentage of their working week is spent with further support and how has it impacted on their levels of achievement.

## How play/activities are used to support the development of speech, language and communication

You need to encourage children to develop language and communication skills as much as possible, as this is a key area of their development. Adults will need to give all children opportunities to take part in speaking and listening for different purposes and in different situations. It is important that children use language both in whole-class and small-group activities and that you encourage them by asking them to talk about their own ideas.

Play experiences can enhance all areas of development and can be directed specifically to address individual areas such as speaking and listening, or can be used more generally to support all. Through play, children will learn both about themselves and about others, and will be using their speech, language and communication skills in order to interact in a non-pressured environment.

As they grow older, children will still need to be given the chance to enjoy activities and equipment which support their play, creativity and learning across the curriculum. It is important that they are given opportunities to use their own initiative, work with others and develop in all areas. These can often be used to best effect when children are introduced to new ideas in practical, imaginative and stimulating ways. Giving children a project or getting them to decide in a group about how they are going to solve a problem can be very beneficial. An example of this might be asking them to design a house for a fictional character that they all know. They would then need to justify what features it might need and why, and present this to their class.

A great deal of our communication with others is expressed non-verbally. It is important for children that they are able to recognise and respond to non-verbal signals from others. Children who are autistic, for example, may well have difficulty in recognising and interpreting non-verbal signs. It is likely that, if you are working with a child who has communication and interaction needs, you will be using different non-verbal strategies to support them. Through using this form of communication, you will be giving children an additional aid to understanding. The kinds of strategies you could use might be:

- **using gestures** — this could be something as simple as a thumbs up or beckoning the child to come over

- **pointing to objects** — you can help children to understand by giving concrete examples of what you are discussing, and encouraging children to point to different objects in a similar way

- **through facial expressions** — a smile or nod can show approval, while you can also indicate excitement, disapproval, happiness and other emotions

- **through the use of body language** — you can show that you are giving the child your attention through the way in which you sit or stand.

You may also need to be specific and ask children what particular gestures or signals from others might mean if they are unable to interpret them.

A number of visual and auditory approaches can also be used to enhance communication and will give additional support to young children.

- **Puppets** are always popular with young children, as they are very appealing. They can be used to model language and will often hold a child's attention. Children may be invited to interact with the puppet and their responses will often be more relaxed than when speaking directly to an adult.

- **Pictures** can be used to initiate or supplement conversation, as they are a good starting point. The child can select a picture if they need to communicate something or show adults what they want to say.

- **Games** are often used successfully to initiate children's speech and involve them in social interactions with others.

- **Signs** are used to support pupils who are unable to communicate verbally. However, they should not be used exclusively by these pupils; other

children will enjoy learning different signs as well as teaching them to one another.

- **Technology** such as story tapes, CDs, computer programmes and interactive whiteboards is a useful means of stimulating children's communication skills.

**Functional skills**

**ICT: Using ICT**
It is important to remember when using tape recorders, CDs, DVDs, whiteboards and other electrical items, such as a roamer in your classroom, that they are all different forms of ICT. Maybe you could list all the different forms of ICT you use or take some pictures that you could share with your colleagues?

- **Modelling language** is important, as it gives children the chance to hear the correct use of language.

- **Songs and rhymes** are used in primary classrooms and are another excellent way of reinforcing language.

**CASE STUDY:** Support the development of speech, language and communication

Cassie in Reception has been in school for two terms but does not speak at all to adults. She interacts verbally with her peers, and both you and the class teacher will speak to her as to other children, but her only responses have been to nod or shake her head.

- What strategies might you use to encourage Cassie to communicate, both verbally and non-verbally?
- How could you work with others to support Cassie in school?

Communicating with others is an important aspect in the development of self-esteem. As we grow up, we interact with others, which in turn reinforces our understanding of who we are and how we fit into our own families and the wider community. It is important for children as they develop that they have opportunities to socialise and work with others, and to feel part of different situations. Pupils who have communication and interaction needs will require support and encouragement, and should be included in all activities alongside other children.

**Reflect**

How might you feel if you were unable to communicate effectively with others?

# Understand the potential effects of transitions on children and young people's development

Whatever age group you are supporting, at some stage you will be working with children or young people who are going through a transition phase. The term 'transition' is applied to different situations in which children and young people pass through a period of change. As well as the more obvious school-based transitions, such as starting school, changing classes or key stages, or passing on to secondary school, children will pass through other periods of transition which may be long or short term. These may include changes in personal circumstances or experiences, passing through puberty, or simply a change in activity in the classroom.

## How different types of transitions can affect development

**Link**

See page 155 for information on factors that influence development.

When it comes to times of change and transition, children should be given every opportunity to talk about what is going to happen so that they are prepared for it. In some cases, such as bereavement, this may not be possible. However, where they are given some warning or opportunity to ask questions about events, any negative or harmful effects on their development can be reduced.

Types of transitions may be:

- emotional — for example, bereavement, entering/leaving care

- physical — for example, moving to a new educational establishment, a new home/locality, from one activity to another

- physiological — for example, puberty, long-term medical conditions

- intellectual — for example, moving from pre-school to primary or post-primary.

### Emotional

Pupils' emotions will be affected by their personal experiences and their relationships with others. If these experiences or relationships are unsettled or traumatic, it is likely that children's emotional development will be affected. They may find it harder to form trusting relationships with adults. Alternatively they may be more immature than their peers or seek attention. In younger children, emotions may be affected for some time by incidents which are seemingly insignificant to adults, such as the loss of a favourite toy or the death of a small pet.

### Physical

This kind of change may mean simply that the child is being asked to move on to a different activity, which can be difficult for some children if they are absorbed in what they are doing. If this is a consistent problem with some children, their development may be affected if they are not then taking part in other activities or widening their experiences. Another example of a physical change can be changing schools or moving house; you should have advance notice about changes like these and be able to discuss and prepare for them with children.

### Physiological

Physiological transitions may be harder to manage for pupils, as they will be happening over a longer period of time. Children and young people may not be aware of the underlying effects of physiological transition and they may also be more sensitive to discussing them.

## Intellectual

This type of transition may be because children are moving between key stages or need to change settings, for example, from Nursery to school or primary to secondary. Transitions may also be between year groups within one school which, if not handled well, can be traumatic for some pupils.

As you get to know the pupils in the age range in which you work, you will find out about routines which schools use to familiarise children with new environments before moving to them. Examples of this may be home visits for children who are moving to Nursery, or opportunities to visit secondary schools and meet teachers and pupils before transferring to

### Primary/Secondary School Transition Policy

**Statement of Intent**

At Western View Secondary School we recognise that the transition from primary school to secondary is an important step in a child's school life and it is our intention to make this a positive experience for every child.

**Aims**

We endeavour to provide our children with a smooth transition from Year 6 (primary school) to Year 7 (secondary school). We ensure that the pace and quality of learning is sensitively maintained through the transition period so that children can continue to make good progress and develop the skills they will need to succeed in Key Stage 3.

**Procedures**

Transition to secondary school may be a stressful time for some children. We have built excellent relationships with local primary schools. The school also has procedures which will minimise difficulties or concerns and help children to settle into the new school environment as quickly as possible by:

- holding open days each October for Year 6 pupils and their parents.
- liaising with Year 6 primary teachers to discuss the strengths of individual children and any difficulties or specific needs they may have
- Year 7 teachers visiting primary schools in the spring term to speak to groups of pupils and answer any questions they may have
- the school holding one information evening and one information morning in May for parents with opportunities to speak to teachers and visit classrooms and specialist areas
- inviting Year 6 pupils in June to spend a day at the secondary school and take part in 'taster' sessions.

**Additional support**

We understand that some pupils may take longer to find their way around, feel part of their new school and come to terms with the new curriculum and learning and teaching methods. We aim to support pupils by:

- providing a buddy system – an older child is paired with each Year 7 child to give advice and support
- assigning a teaching assistant to each Year 7 classroom for each lesson during the first term, to provide support for the curriculum and pastoral support
- having a senior teacher with specific responsibility for transition who is available to answer children's or parents' concerns.

*An example of a transitions policy.*

Year 7. When managing the needs of older children, you should have opportunities to discuss with them the kinds of choices they will need to make. This may be the selection of GCSEs, A-levels or diplomas. They must also begin to consider their career options. Opportunities to take part in external activities such as work experience, voluntary work and enterprise can be very beneficial, as it will support young people to develop their confidence, decision-making skills and self-reliance.

## The effect of having positive relationships during periods of transition

It is important for children to have positive relationships during periods of transition, as they will need to feel secure in other areas of their lives. They may need to talk to someone about how they are feeling and you should make sure that there are opportunities for them to do this. If you have advance notice that a child or group of children will be going through a period of change, this will give you an opportunity to plan how you will support them.

### CASE STUDY: Supporting periods of transition

Year 6 started school as the first Reception class of a new one-form entry school in 2003 when it was first built. They are now reaching the end of their final year. As the teaching assistant supporting Year 6 for several hours a week, you have been asked to come to a meeting to discuss the needs of the class at transition.

- What kinds of issues do you think there will be as the pupils prepare for secondary transfer?
- Will these be any different from issues for a normal Year 6 class?

### BEST PRACTICE CHECKLIST: Supporting transitions

- Work to ensure positive relationships during periods of transition.
- Be sensitive to pupils' needs and think about how the transition may be affecting them.
- Ensure pupils are given opportunities to talk about and discuss what will be happening and to ask any questions.
- Give pupils the opportunity to visit new classes or schools.
- Liaise with pupils who are already in the year group in order to build relationships and encourage questions from the children who are moving on.

### Portfolio activity

Using examples from your own school, write a reflective account to show what provision the school makes for supporting pupils who are going through transitions. You may need to look at your own school's transitions policy.

### Functional skills

**English: Reading**
You could look at a range of different policies and then develop your reading skills further by comparing the content.

## Getting ready for assessment

For this unit you will need to show your awareness both of children's development and also of the kinds of monitoring which takes place to ensure that they are making expected levels of progress.

Carry out two case studies on different children in your school who have been the subject of intervention due to their developmental levels. You will need to change the children's names for reasons of confidentiality and also check with parents and teachers that they are happy for you to write about the pupils. Give a short account of their backgrounds and describe the kinds of factors which may have influenced their development. Write about the way in which the school has monitored their development and the different professionals who have been involved with each, including how this has made a difference to their progress.

### Websites and references

**www.makaton.org** – Makaton information
**www.autism.org.uk** – Natio utistic Society
**www.pecs.org.uk** – information on the Picture Exchange Communication System
**www.yjb.gov.uk** – Youth Justice Board

Donaldson, Margaret (1986) *Children's Minds*, HarperCollins
Hughes, Cathy and Pound, Linda (2005) *How Children Learn: From Montessori to Vygotsky – Educational Approaches and theories Made Easy*, Step Forward Publishing
Lindon, Jennie (2005) *Understanding Child Development Linking Theory and Practice*, Hodder Arnold
Tassoni, Penny (2003) *Supporting Special Needs – Understanding Inclusion in the Early Years*, Heinemann

## Check your knowledge

1. Explain the difference between sequence of development and rate of development. Why might children develop at different rates in different areas?

2. Explain how the emotional development of a child in Reception may be different from that of a child in Year 6.

3. What kinds of factors will influence a child's development?

4. Why is it important to have a basic understanding of some of the theories of child development? How will this help you in your practice?

5. What kinds of resources are available to support staff in schools when working with pupils who have developmental needs?

6. Which of the following are true? We monitor children's development by:

   a) observing them

   b) speaking to their peers

   c) carrying out assessments

   d) letting them choose learning activities

   e) speaking to parents.

7. What are the differences between the medical and social models of disability?

8. Why is it important to act early when monitoring children's speech and language development?

9. Give three different types of transition.

# School Life

## My Story Tamara

I have been working in the Reception class at my school for some time and am fully trained in the Foundation Stage, so know quite a bit about children of this age and stage of development. I became concerned about a particular child who came to us last year after she had been in school for a few weeks. Dalisha was a twin and was quite small for her age, but as far as we knew we had not been sent any information from her nursery to say that there had been any concerns up until now. She tended to play alongside other children – however, she very seldom spoke to anyone, although her sister seemed to be interacting with others and joining in with most activities. I observed that they did not spend much time together considering they were sisters. Dalisha also seemed to be in her own little world and did not seem to know what was going on in the class. When the teacher assessed her understanding of sounds and numbers, she did not seem to have any idea of these.

After the teacher had carried out the initial assessment, I was asked to check Dalisha's nursery records and found that these had not been sent on. I also found that several other children at the same nursery had no records in school and so we rang to check and they were then forwarded to us. As soon as Dalisha's records came through, it was clear that she had already been referred to Early Years Action due to concerns about her development – if we had known this beforehand, we might have been able to get help for her sooner. As it was, it took us almost a year to get some support. We have since made sure that we chase up all records from nurseries and visit them if possible before children start in our school so that we have a chance to speak to Nursery staff and if possible catch any special needs issues before children start in Reception.

## Ask the expert

**Q** There seems to be a lot of focus at my school on intellectual development but far less on the social and emotional – why is this?

**A** Schools should focus their attention on all areas of a child's development – it may seem that more emphasis is placed on the academic, but it is not usually true to say that it is all that children learn. There will, for example, be Personal, Social, Health and Economic education (PSHE) and Citizenship activities which are carried out on a regular basis and are part of the curriculum. Pupils will also learn how to behave through socialising with others and through finding out the expected norms of behaviour and school rules.

**VIEWPOINT**

Reflect on the development of different children. You may, for example, want to think about a child who is very able academically. Are they also mature in other areas of their development?

# CYP 3.3 Understand how to safeguard the well-being of children & young people

This unit is about the way in which you safeguard the well-being of children and young people. You will need to be aware of health and safety issues as well as those around e-safety and child protection. You will need to have a clear understanding of your role and what you should do in different situations, and of the roles and responsibilities of others both within and outside the school.

## By the end of this unit you will:

1. understand the main legislation, guidelines, policies and procedures for safeguarding children and young people

2. understand the importance of working in partnership with other organisations to safeguard children and young people

3. understand the importance of ensuring children and young people's safety and protection in the work setting

4. understand how to respond to evidence or concerns that a child or young person has been abused or harmed

5. understand how to respond to evidence or concerns that a child or young person has been bullied

6. understand how to work with children and young people to support their safety and well-being

7. understand the importance of e-safety for children and young people.

# Understand the main legislation, guidelines, policies and procedures for safeguarding children and young people

## Current legislation, guidelines, policies and procedures for safeguarding children and young people

The Children Act 1989 introduced comprehensive changes to legislation in England and Wales surrounding the welfare of children. As well as ensuring that the welfare of the child is paramount, the Act identified the responsibility of parents and of those who work with children to ensure the safety of the child. Its main aims were to:

- achieve a balance between protecting children and the rights of parents to challenge state intervention

- encourage partnership between statutory authorities and parents

- restructure the framework of the courts, in particular with regard to family proceedings

- redefine the concept of parental responsibility.

It remains an important piece of legislation due to its focus on safeguarding children and the duties of local authorities.

The Every Child Matters guidelines, which led to the Children Act 2004, came about as a direct result of the Laming Report following the death of Victoria Climbié. The report was highly critical of the way in which the Climbié case was handled and made 108 recommendations to overhaul child protection in the UK. The main points which emerged were that:

- there should be a much closer working relationship between agencies such as health professionals, schools and welfare services

- there should be a central database containing records of all children and whether they are known to different services

- there should be an independent children's commissioner for England to protect children and young people's rights (a children's commissioner for Scotland has been in post for several years)

- there should be a children and families board, chaired by a senior government minister

- Ofsted will set a framework which will monitor children's services.

The Children Act 2004 required that these recommendations became a legal requirement. As a result the Every Child Matters framework was introduced to implement the Act and the wider reform programme. In addition to this, the document 'Working together to Safeguard Children' set out how organisations and individuals should work together to safeguard children and local safeguarding children boards (LSCBs) were established through local authorities.

### Link

See also TDA 3.6 on promoting equality.

### The United Nations Convention on the Rights of the Child (1989) (UNCRC)

The UNCRC is an international human rights treaty which sets out the rights of all children to be treated equally. Under the treaty there is a list of rights to which every child under the age of 18 should be entitled. These include the full range of human rights — civil, cultural, economic, social and political — through articles such as:

- the right to services such as education and health care

- the right to grow up in an environment of happiness, love and understanding

- the right to develop their personalities, abilities and talents to their own potential

- the right to special protection measures and assistance.

The UK signed this legally binding act in 1990 and ratified it in 1991, which means that the UK is required to implement legislation to support each of the 54 articles. In 2008 the government attended a hearing in Geneva and reported on the progress that the UK has made since the implementation. The UK nations are continuing to work together and are also addressing the UN Committee's recommendations. For more on the UNCRC, see www.unicef.org/crc

The Common Assessment Framework, or CAF, is used across children's services in England and is a way of finding out about their additional needs and how these can be met. It aims to identify children's needs at an early stage and to provide a way of looking at a method of support which is appropriate for the child. A CAF should be used where practitioners feel that a child will not make progress towards the five outcomes of Every Child Matters (see page 24) without intervention. However, it should not be used in cases where you are worried that a child has been harmed or is at risk.

The Department for Education (DfE) also produces guidance and supporting documents for schools and local authorities regarding safeguarding and child protection. See www.education.gov.uk/publications

### Functional skills

**ICT: Finding and selecting information and Developing, presenting and communicating information**
There are a number of websites highlighted throughout this chapter. You could list them all in a document and produce a reference leaflet with a short summary of what each website provides information on.

### Portfolio activity

Go to the DfE website (http://publications. education.gov.uk) and search for the following document: Working Together to Safeguard Children: A guide to inter-agency working to safeguard and promote the welfare of children (March 2010). You may find a copy of it in your school.

What are the responsibilities of schools under this document? What reference does it make to the Children Acts of 1989 and 2004? Identify one chapter which is of interest to you and make a short presentation about it to your group.

### Functional skills

**English: Speaking, listening and communication**
It is important to remember when presenting to the group to speak clearly and use language appropriate for the audience.

## Child protection within the wider concept of safeguarding

The term 'child protection' is increasingly being replaced by that of 'safeguarding'. Safeguarding has been described as a broader definition of the range of ways in which adults and professionals working with the child need to act when managing child protection issues. These are designed to prevent risks of harm to the welfare of children and young people rather than react to them. The term child protection tends to be used for policies and procedures which should be followed in the event of suspected harm or abuse.

## How guidelines, policies and procedures for safeguarding affect day-to-day work

Day-to-day work involves, for example:

● childcare practice

● child protection

● risk assessment

● ensuring the voice of the child is heard (for example, providing **advocacy** services)

● supporting children and young people and others who may be expressing concerns.

### Key term

**Advocacy** – putting forward a person's views on their behalf and working for the outcome that the individual wishes to achieve

You will need to be aware of local and national guidelines for safeguarding in your work with children on a day-to-day basis. The kinds of issues which may arise in schools may vary — however, you should always be alert to any safeguarding concerns and ensure that you are acting appropriately and within the appropriate guidelines.

## Childcare practice

The term childcare practice applies to all those who work in schools, nurseries and other early years settings, childminders and children's homes. All professionals working with children will need to be fully trained and CRB (Criminal Records Bureau) checked. Those in childcare practice are required to ensure that they demonstrate the correct safeguarding procedures and follow the policy of the organisation when working with children and young people, and in reporting any concerns.

## Child protection

Child protection is the responsibility of all who work with children and you need to be aware of your school's policy for reporting and recording suspected abuse. As well as observing policies and ensuring that children are secure when on site, child protection records will need to be kept of what pupils have said, as well as notes, dates and times of any meetings that have taken place between the school and other agencies. If a pupil reports anything which is a cause for concern, the school needs to make sure that it is followed up. For child protection purposes, parents must be notified if any photographs of children are to be taken which are likely to be used or seen outside the school environment.

## Risk assessment

Individual risk assessments will need to be carried out prior to any activities where children or young people are undertaking an activity which has the potential to cause harm. This may be a school trip or visit but may also be in day-to-day practice where there are items of equipment or areas which carry potential risk. The school will have a procedure for risk assessment which it will need to carry out annually on the school buildings and grounds.

> **Link**
>
> For an example of a risk assessment form, see CYP 3.4, Support children and young people's health and safety, page 141.

> **Functional skills**
>
> **English: Writing**
> In order to expand your knowledge of writing for different purposes you could think of the last activity that you did with the children and write a risk assessment for it.

## Ensuring the voice of the child is heard

In cases of child protection, all agencies concerned will need to ensure that the voice of the child is considered. Advocacy services (for example, the National Youth Advocacy Service) should be provided in order to support the child or young person during a time which will be difficult and often traumatic for them.

## Supporting children and young people and others who may be expressing concerns

The initial response when considering child protection and safeguarding issues should always be to listen carefully to what the child says. After reassuring the child and clarifying what has happened, and explaining what action will be taken, it is important not to press for any further information or to tell them that what they say will remain confidential. This is important, as the child may need to talk to other adults about what has happened.

## LSCB (local safeguarding children board)

This body will have been set up by your local authority to ensure the safeguarding and welfare of children. If your school does have concerns about a child, the local authority will also act alongside to follow guidelines and ensure that all agencies work together.

## When and why inquiries/reviews are required and how the sharing of findings informs practice

According to the LSCB Regulations 2006, serious case reviews (SCRs) will be required in situations where a child has died due to known or suspected abuse or neglect. In some situations, reviews may also be carried out where a child has been seriously harmed or has suffered life-threatening injuries. The purpose of an SCR is for agencies to discuss the case together and to determine the lessons which are to be learned about the way in which professionals have worked and can work together in the future. A report will then be written which will be made public so that recommendations are known. The DCSF publication 'Working Together to Safeguard Children 2010' sets out the processes which should be followed when undertaking SCRs.

## How processes used comply with legislation covering data protection, information handling and sharing

The way in which the school handles information will be covered by the Data Protection Act 1998. Under this Act, information which is gathered by the school in the context of safeguarding and child protection must be used only for that purpose. If any individuals concerned (or their parents, which in a primary school is more likely) wish to know the information which is held about them, they have a right to access to it. They are also entitled to see their own educational record. There are only a few main exceptions to this, namely:

● information which may cause serious harm or risk of abuse to the health of the pupil or another individual

● information given to a court or in adoption or parental order records

● copies of examination scripts or marks prior to their release

● unstructured personal information, or information which is held manually and not in school records.

For more guidance on this and in particular how processes used by the school need to comply with legislation in different UK countries, see the website for the Information Commissioner's Office (www.ico.gov.uk), which deals with the Data Protection Act and Freedom of Information Act.

**Knowledge into action**

Find out and write a reflective account about how the processes used in your own school comply with data protection and information handling legislation.

**Functional skills**

ICT: Using ICT
You could complete this task by holding a discussion with someone involved in this role within the school. Maybe you could use ICT to record the conversation so that you could write up the response later or refer back to it at a later date.

# Understand the importance of working in partnership with other organisations to safeguard children and young people

## The importance of safeguarding children and young people

All adults, and in particular those who work with children, have a responsibility to safeguard children and young people from harm. As professionals, we have a duty to ensure that children and young people are protected while they are in our care and that where we have other concerns outside school, these are investigated fully. School policies and procedures need to be such that parents and governors are aware of them and that staff are fully trained with regard to safeguarding. Schools will need to consider and include in their policies:

- children's physical safety and security on the premises and on off-site visits
- children's safety when in the home environment
- e-safety and security when using the Internet
- staff awareness and training
- monitoring and record keeping
- partnership and involvement with other agencies.

It is also important that schools develop children's awareness of acceptable and unacceptable behaviour. This encompasses both in school and off site, and also when using the Internet (see also page 184). Children who are known to be on the 'at risk' register, or those who have been identified as being at greater risk, should be supported by the school and by outside agencies where appropriate.

## The importance of a child- or young person-centred approach

All agencies will need to consider the ways in which their approach is child centred, for example, involving the child in meetings and asking for their opinion when discussing matters relating to them as much as possible.

## The meaning of partnership working in the context of safeguarding

As there are a number of different agencies which may be involved when working in the context of safeguarding, it is important that they communicate and work in partnership to ensure the safety and protection of children. Each area of expertise may need to have an input in any one case and each should be considered when discussing issues around safeguarding. A working party or 'team around the child' meeting may be called involving a number of agencies in order to discuss how to move forward in the best interests of the child.

## Roles and responsibilities of different organisations involved when a child or young person has been abused or harmed

Different organisations involved in safeguarding are:

- social services
- the NSPCC
- health visitors
- GPs
- the probation service
- the police
- schools
- the psychology service.

### Social services

Social services will be concerned with the immediate care of the child and in ensuring that they are safe from harm. They will work in partnership with parents and other agencies in order to do this. In extreme cases, schools may need to contact social services directly where there are serious concerns about a parent or carer. Social services may then take the child into care.

### The NSPCC

The NSPCC (National Society for the Prevention of Cruelty to Children) is a charity which works to protect children from harm. However, it is the only charity which has a statutory power to take action where there are cases of child abuse. The NSPCC as a charity also provides services to support families and children through its helplines and draws attention and public awareness to the safety and protection of children.

### Health visitors and GPs

Health professionals may be involved in order to examine children to determine whether any injuries which may have been sustained are accidental. They will also always be alert during the course of their practice to any injuries which they may suspect are signs of child abuse and inform other agencies as appropriate.

### The police and probation service

The police work closely with other agencies in order to ensure that children are free from harm. All police forces have a Child Abuse Investigation Unit (CAIU); these units have been set up to gather information and to determine whether the police should begin a criminal investigation or take other immediate action.

### The psychology service

The psychology service may be called in to carry out an assessment of a child in cases of harm or abuse. They will make recommendations and suggest a course of action appropriate to the child's needs.

---

**Knowledge into action**

Speak to your SENCO or Safeguarding Officer about meetings your school has held with regard to safeguarding. Although you may not be able to discuss individual issues, what different agencies have been involved? How has their involvement and work as a team supported individual children?

---

# Understand the importance of ensuring children and young people's safety and protection in the work setting

**Link**

For more on health and safety issues and procedures, see CYP 3.4 Support children and young people's health and safety.

## The importance of ensuring that children and young people are protected from harm

As adults in positions of responsibility, we should all be aware of the importance of protecting children and young people from harm. While children are in school, we are acting 'in loco parentis', which means that we take over responsibility from their parents while they are in our care. This can be seen within all contexts, from health and safety issues to those around safeguarding, Internet safety and safety on school trips.

## Policies and procedures to protect children and young people and adults working with them

Policies and procedures for safe working include, for example:

- working in an open and transparent way
- listening to children and young people
- duty of care
- whistle-blowing
- power and positions of trust
- propriety and behaviour
- physical contact
- intimate personal care
- off-site visits

- photography and video
- sharing concerns and recording/reporting incidents.

Under the Health and Safety at Work Act, it is the responsibility of everyone in the school to ensure that safety is maintained and in particular that vulnerable groups such as children are safeguarded. Standards for safety are also set by the government department in each country responsible for education and are monitored by the body responsible for school inspections, for example, Ofsted in England and HMIE (Her Majesty's Inspectorate of Education) in Scotland. As well as having an awareness of safety issues, all routines should be planned carefully with safety in mind so that incidents are less likely to occur. Pupils should also be encouraged to think about safety in the learning environment so that they start to develop their own awareness. Your school will have health and safety policies as well as safeguarding policies, which will set out the procedures which you should follow as a member of staff.

It is likely that your safeguarding policy will give you guidelines about how you should work with children in a way which protects both them and you. This is important, as the school will need to be aware of and pass on to staff how they should best protect themselves against incidents of alleged abuse or inappropriate working practices.

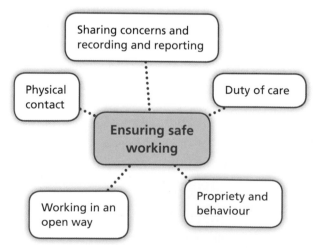

*How does your school ensure that staff and pupils are protected?*

## Physical contact

When working with young children, adults are often rightly concerned about having any physical contact with them because of issues around safeguarding. However, in some situations, it is appropriate to put an arm around a child, for example, if they are distressed or have hurt themselves. Young children are also demonstrative and will often hug adults affectionately. You should always act sensibly and behave reactively rather than initiating contact with children, and in particular ensure that you do not have any physical contact with children if there is nobody else around. There are some situations in which this cannot be helped, for example, if you are working with a child who has special educational needs and you need to attend to their personal care. You should make sure that you follow school policy at all times when you are doing this.

## Sharing concerns/recording and reporting

If you have any concerns about a safeguarding issue, due to what a child has said or because of your own observations, you should always share these concerns and ensure that you record exactly what has happened. In this way you will protect yourself if later on the child says that they have told you or that you knew previously. You should also inform managers if you have any concerns about other members of staff due to poor practice (see section below on whistle-blowing).

## Propriety and behaviour

In your capacity as a professional working in a school, you should ensure that you act in a professional way at all times. When working with children, we are required to behave appropriately and make sure that children and young people also understand what is expected of them. As adults we are role models and are required to set an example through our own behaviour and our interactions with others.

## Duty of care

Adults in schools have a duty of care towards children and young people, and should always act in a way which ensures their safety. We should remember that we are in a position of trust and always listen to children and reassure them about issues which concern them.

## Working in an open way

Your working practice should be such that you always work in an open way. This includes:

- ensuring that you are not left alone with pupils if at all possible. Try to keep doors open and ensure that there are other people around

- being clear about why you are acting in a particular way

- keeping other staff informed about any concerns.

# How to report concerns about poor practice

Staff in your school should all be aware of the way in which suspected poor practice, concerns or any illegality can be reported. It is important that those who are concerned about issues around safeguarding should be able to report them. This should be done confidentially and with no concerns for any repercussions towards the individual who reported the incident or those whose practice is being questioned; the process is known as whistle-blowing. All members of staff should feel that they are able to raise concerns without any fear of discrimination or victimisation as a result.

---

**BEST PRACTICE CHECKLIST:** Whistle-blowing

- Speak to your line manager or a senior manager about any concerns.

- If the concern is to do with your line manager, go to the next level. In the case of a head teacher, go to the chair of governors.

- Investigate your school or local authority's whistle-blowing policy.

- If you belong to a union, find out if they give any advice about whistle-blowing.

---

**Portfolio activity**

Find out about what your school would do in cases of whistle-blowing. Speak to others in your group about how their school or local authority's policy protects those who may be involved in whistle-blowing. Alternatively, there are a number of exemplar whistle-blowing policies available online which you may compare. Write your own account about how individuals can be best protected.

# How practitioners can take steps to protect themselves in the work setting and on off-site visits

**Link**

See Policies and procedures on pages 175–76.

# Understand how to respond to evidence or concerns that a child or young person has been abused or harmed

## Signs, symptoms, indicators and behaviours in the context of safeguarding

As an adult working with children, you need to have an understanding of the different signs that may indicate that a child is being abused. Although you will need to do your best to ensure a child's safety while they are in your care, you also need to look out for any signs that they are being mistreated while they are out of school. The signs may include both physical and behavioural changes. There are four main types of abuse:

- physical abuse
- sexual abuse
- emotional abuse
- neglect.

## Physical abuse

This involves being physically hurt or injured. Physical abuse may take a variety of forms and be either spasmodic or persistent. Injuries may come from children being hit, punched, shaken, kicked or beaten.

The signs of physical abuse are often quite straightforward to spot and can include bruises, cuts, burns and other injuries. However, you should be aware that such injuries can also be caused by genuine accidents. If you notice frequent signs of injury or if there appear to be other signs of abuse, it is important to take action. Less obvious signs of physical abuse may include fear of physical contact with others, reluctance to get changed for PE, wanting to stay covered up, even in hot weather, and aggression.

## Emotional abuse

This involves the child being continually 'put down' and criticised, or not given love or approval at a time when they need it the most. It includes bullying, discrimination and racism, which may also take place outside school. This could take the form of name-calling, humiliation or teasing. Increasingly, it can also take place through social networking sites and mobile phones (see page 180 for more on cyber-bullying).

The signs of emotional abuse are that the child is withdrawn and lacks confidence, shows **regression** or is 'clingy' towards adults, and has low self-esteem. Children who suffer from emotional abuse are likely to be anxious about new situations and may show extremes of behaviour or appear distracted and unable to concentrate.

### Key term

**Regression** – going backwards in terms of development to an earlier stage

## Sexual abuse

Sexual abuse involves an adult or young person using a child sexually, for example, by touching their bodies inappropriately or by forcing them to look at sexual images or have sex.

The signs of sexual abuse may include sexual behaviour which is inappropriate to the child's age, genital irritation, clinginess or changes in behaviour, regression and lack of trust of adults. Sexual abuse can be almost impossible to identify and its signs can be caused by other forms of abuse. It is therefore important that any signs are seen as possible, rather than probable, indicators.

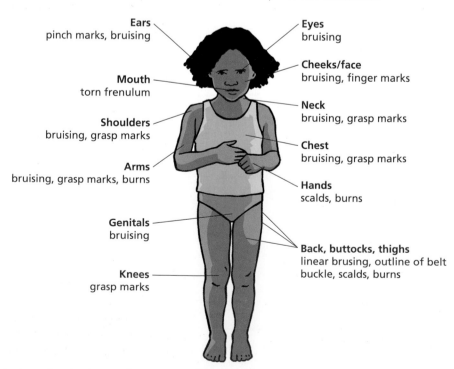

**Ears**
pinch marks, bruising

**Eyes**
bruising

**Cheeks/face**
bruising, finger marks

**Mouth**
torn frenulum

**Neck**
bruising, grasp marks

**Shoulders**
bruising, grasp marks

**Chest**
bruising, grasp marks

**Arms**
bruising, grasp marks, burns

**Hands**
scalds, burns

**Genitals**
bruising

**Back, buttocks, thighs**
linear brusing, outline of belt buckle, scalds, burns

**Knees**
grasp marks

*You will need to look out for the signs and symptoms of abuse.*

## Neglect

This means that the child is not being properly cared for and not having its basic needs met by parents or carers. Basic needs include shelter, food, love, general hygiene and medical care. The signs of neglect may include being dirty, tired, hungry, seeking attention and generally failing to thrive.

# Actions to take in line with policies and procedures of own setting

As a teaching assistant, you are in a good position to notice changes in pupils' behaviour which may be a possible sign of abuse. Children or young people may also confide in you or allege that abuse has taken place. If you have been told something by a child or you are at all concerned, speak to either your class teacher or the school's Child Protection or Safeguarding Officer. They will need to follow the school's safeguarding policy and, if necessary, local authority guidelines for informing social services. Always keep a note of exactly what happened and when, exactly how you reported it and whom you told.

---

**CASE STUDY:** Actions to take when a child alleges harm or abuse

Sanjit is working in a class which is split between years 3 and 4 in his school. He has, alongside other staff, been monitoring the behaviour and appearance of Ricky, a child who seems to be suffering from neglect. One morning when getting changed for PE, Sanjit notices that the child has a number of bruises on his back and the backs of his legs. He asks Ricky what has happened. Although usually Ricky does not say very much, he turns to Sanjit and says that his dad came round last night and hit him and his mum, and it made them both cry. He then says that his mum told him not to say anything.

- What should Sanjit do now?

- Discuss with others in your group the order in which things might happen and who else should be involved.

---

# The rights of children, young people and their carers

In situations where harm or abuse is suspected or alleged, it is important to remember that all individuals need to be treated with respect and have their own rights. In any case of harm or abuse to children all parties will have a right to be investigated through the correct channels and the outcome documented accordingly. They also have a right to confidentiality and those involved in any investigation should be reminded of this.

# Understand how to respond to evidence or concerns that a child or young person has been bullied

It is likely that at some stage you will need to deal with bullying in some form. This may be because you notice children picking on another child, or are asked to 'keep an eye' on a particular situation following concerns by parents or the class teacher. Alternatively, you may find that children confide in you if they feel that they are being bullied by others. You will need to know the course of action you should follow and the school's policy for dealing with bullying.

## Types of bullying and potential effects on children and young people

Children and young people may be victims of different types of bullying. There are a number of ways in which bullies can target children and the increasing use of cyber-bullying is of particular concern since this type of bullying is 'invisible'.

Bullying may be:

- **physical** (pushing, kicking, hitting, pinching, other forms of violence or threats)

- **verbal** (name-calling, insults, sarcasm, spreading rumours, persistent teasing)

- **emotional** (excluding, tormenting, ridiculing, humiliating)

- **cyber-bullying** (the use of Information and Communications Technology, particularly mobile phones and the Internet, deliberately to upset someone else)

- **specific bullying** which can relate to all of the above. This may be homophobic, gender-based, racist or relating to special educational needs or disabilities.

## Physical

This type of bullying is easiest to spot in school and in particular on the playground. You may need to speak to children about isolated incidents of violence; however, you should be alert to situations in which some children seem to be picked on more than others.

## Verbal

Children can bully one another through verbal insults, teasing and targeted comments towards a particular child. You will need to investigate all allegations of bullying as soon as they are made. However, be aware that younger children may sometimes say that they are being bullied without really understanding the term, when someone has been unkind to them, for example.

## Emotional

This kind of bullying can be particularly difficult to discover, and in particular if is carried out through cyber-bullying (below). Children may be subjected to ridicule or humiliation at the hands of others, which over a period of time will cause extreme emotional distress.

## Cyber-bullying

This type of bullying is relatively recent due to the increased use of mobile phones and the Internet

by children. The age at which children are able to have access to different technologies also seems to be falling, so that schools are having to draw up guidelines to support both children and parents for their safe use. Cyber-bullying can be very difficult to find out about and children should be reminded about the need to discuss any concerns with an adult.

### Functional skills

**ICT: Developing, presenting and communicating information**
You could create a poster for the children all about Internet safety that you could display in your computer room/area. Remember to think about the age of the children reading the poster. Try to use an appropriate layout and have a go at including images and a variety of different text.

## Specific bullying

This can relate to all or one of the above and may be based on, for example, racism, disability or gender. Children who are in a minority may be the object of this kind of bullying and they should be encouraged to report any incidents straight away.

# Policies and procedures in response to bullying and why they are in place

### Link

For more on policies and procedures on bullying, see also TDA 3.4.

Head Teachers are obliged to draw up procedures to prevent bullying in schools under the School Standards and Framework Act 1998. All staff, parents and pupils need to be aware of the procedures that should be followed and the consequences of bullying.

When dealing with any situations of bullying in your school, you will need to make sure that you follow your school's anti-bullying policy. Although you may need to deal with a single incident on your own, you should also ensure that you are not acting alone in dealing with any ongoing situation and have discussed your actions with a member of the school's Senior Management Team. It is likely that you will have to follow a series of steps, for example:

- deal immediately with any incidents of bullying
- record or report to the Head Teacher or a member of the Senior Management Team according to school policy
- inform the class teacher
- if bullying persists, parents will be informed
- measures will be introduced following discussion with all concerned.

---

**CASE STUDY:** Dealing with bullying

Ross is a teaching assistant working in a small village primary school. He is very experienced and has been at the school for several years. One day Ryan in Year 4 comes up to him and says that he is being bullied and needs to talk to him about it. He tells Ross that the boys in his class are picking on him because he finds school work difficult. Ryan is also very small for his age and unable to join in with some of the boys' more boisterous games. They regularly call him names and he is increasingly isolated on the playground. Ross speaks to the bullies briefly at lunchtime but does not take any further action. The following week, Ryan is not in school for a few days and Ross becomes worried, although he has not acted on his concerns.

- What should Ross do now?
- Why is it important to follow school policy?

---

## How to support a child or young person and/or their family

As part of the school's policy, there will be guidelines on how to support a child or young person and their family when bullying is suspected, and also what is available through the local authority. You will be working as part of a team and clearly each case will be different, although step-

by-step procedures will be the same. You should work with your school and follow school procedures to manage the situation and reassure the child and their parents. There are also a large number of websites and organisations available to support both the child and their family in coping with the distress which is caused by bullying (see the end of this unit).

# Understand how to work with children and young people to support their safety and well-being

## Support children and young people's self-confidence and self-esteem

Children's self-confidence and self-esteem are directly linked to the way in which they relate to others. Self-esteem can be high or low, positive or negative. It is how we feel about ourselves and leads to our self-image, or how we think about or perceive ourselves. Children develop positive self-esteem when they feel good about themselves and when they feel valued. They need to have the opportunities to develop positive relationships and participate in a range of activities, which will in turn impact on their social and emotional development. Where children do not have these opportunities, or are unable to find out about themselves and develop their communication skills through social activities, their confidence and self-esteem will be affected. This will also have an impact on their learning as they will be less likely to attempt tasks when they do not have confidence in their abilities.

In a safeguarding context, children need to be confident enough to be able to tell others if they are unhappy about something which is happening to them. This may be a situation in which they are being bullied, or forced into something which they do not agree with. A child who has a negative self-image or does not feel valued may not think that anyone will listen to them and may be reluctant to talk about something which is worrying them.

The way in which we treat children has a direct effect on this, so it is important that we:

- encourage and praise them
- allow them to feel independent
- value each child as an individual
- celebrate differences and similarities.

## The importance of supporting resilience in children and young people

Children who are going through a difficult period or who are lacking in confidence or self-esteem may need your support in order to help them to remain resilient in dealing with this. You may need to be sensitive when managing their emotions at times and in helping them when maintaining their confidence in difficult situations. You should do this by remaining approachable and facilitating opportunities for pupils to discuss any issues as they arise. You should also encourage them as much as possible and give them reassurance as they learn to manage their emotions.

## Why it is important to work with the child or young person to ensure they have strategies to protect themselves

All children have a right to be safe and feel protected. The UN Convention on the Rights of the Child, which was signed by the UK in 1990, sets out the rights of all children to be treated equally and fairly. These include the rights to:

- grow up in an atmosphere of happiness, love and understanding
- be as healthy as possible
- grow and develop to the best of their ability
- live in a safe environment.

Children and young people may also need your support in devising strategies to protect themselves and to maintain their own safety. Children will need to learn not to put themselves in a position of risk.

*Children's self-image will be based largely on adults' reactions to what they do.*

# Ways of empowering children and young people to make positive and informed choices

As well as encouraging their awareness of health and safety issues, you should also support their development by helping them to have a positive self-image. Children need to have plenty of opportunities and encouragement as they grow up in order to develop their independence and learn about their likes and dislikes. They should also be aware that they have a right to be safe and know what to do if they do not feel safe. If you are talking to pupils about their bodies, for example, using activities that you have planned with the teacher, be aware that people use different terms to describe body parts and functions, such as going to the toilet, when speaking to children. If pupils confide in you and tell you that something has happened to them, they may need time or additional help to use the right language or to draw what has happened. The curriculum should include giving pupils information about organisations that exist to protect them, such as the NSPCC, ChildLine and Kidscape.

**BEST PRACTICE CHECKLIST:** Supporting children and young people to empower themselves

- Ensure that pupils are taught to keep themselves safe.

- Encourage pupils to talk about their worries and speak to others.

- Use age-appropriate language when speaking to pupils.

- Never promise not to tell others if a pupil discloses that they have been abused.

- Set an example by encouraging co-operation and positive behaviour.

### Functional skills

**English: Writing**
You could plan a set of short activities that would promote keeping safe which you could deliver over a few weeks to the children. This will provide you with the opportunity to practice writing for a different purpose.

---

### Key Stage 2
### Pupil ICT Acceptable Use Agreement

➤ I will only use ICT in school for school purposes.
➤ I will only use my class email address in school.
➤ I will make sure that any ICT contact I have with adults and children is polite and friendly.
➤ I will not deliberately look for, save or send anything that could be unpleasant or nasty. If I accidentally find anything like this, I will turn off my monitor and tell my teacher immediately.
➤ If I see anything I am unhappy with or I receive a message I do not like, I will not respond to it but I will tell a teacher or a responsible adult.
➤ I will not open an attachment or download a file unless I have permission and I know and trust the person who has sent it.
➤ I will not give out my own details such as my phone number or home address.
➤ I will never arrange to meet someone I have only ever previously met on the Internet or by email unless this is part of a school project approved by my parent/carer and my teacher, and a responsible adult comes with me.
➤ I will be responsible for my behaviour when using ICT because I know that these rules are to keep me safe.
➤ I know that my use of ICT can be checked and that my parent/carer will be contacted if a member of school staff is concerned about my e-Safety.

My Name: _____

My Signature: _____

We have discussed these rules and _____ (child's name)
agrees to follow the e-Safety rules and to support the safe use of ICT at Unicorn Primary School.

Parent/Carer Signature: _____ Date: _____

*A Pupil Acceptable Use Agreement.*

# Understand the importance of e-safety for children and young people

As adults, we have a responsibility towards children and young people to make them aware of the dangers which they may face in the outside world. In school, this awareness has historically been around issues such as road safety, stranger danger and how to treat and respond to others. However, as well as being an additional resource, the emergence of the Internet has opened up a wide range of additional threats to children.

The Internet has brought with it a large number of benefits which outweigh the drawbacks. However, it is important to stress to children that anyone can set up a website, which means that there may be places on the Internet which represent extremist views or are disrespectful to others.

## Risks and possible consequences of being online and of using a mobile phone, and reducing risk

All adults working with children need to be aware of the increasing risks to children from being online and from the use of mobile phones. E-safety is gaining a higher profile as technology advances and schools are now required to have more policies and guidelines in place for staff, parents and children. Children and parents may also be required to sign an Internet safety agreement to show that they have discussed Internet safety and agree with the school's policy for safe Internet use. However, it is likely they will also use the Internet at home and they should be aware of the risks and possible consequences of using different technologies. This will also usually be discussed in school as part of children's ICT lessons.

### Social networking sites

The tragic case of Ashleigh Hall's murder in 2009 after befriending her attacker on a social networking site has led to a heightened public awareness of the dangers of the Internet and in particular social networking sites. Children should be reminded not to put personal information such as telephone numbers,

photographs or email addresses online. They should also limit other information such as school name, clubs they attend, where they meet up and so on, as this kind of information can easily be pieced together to gain an insight into their lives. Children may not have considered that by putting their personal information online it also becomes accessible to individuals other than their friends. Social networking sites can easily be accessed by others and parents should check that privacy settings are not open to all.

### Internet use

Children in school will be unable to access any material that is inappropriate due to filters which school computers are required to have. However, if home computers do not have filters or settings such as the Child Safety Online Kitemark to protect children, they may not be safe online. Schools are increasingly running information workshops for parents about the importance of ensuring that children are Internet-aware and protected as much as possible.

### Email

Children should be aware that they should only open emails and files sent from people that they know, as they will not know the contents. They could contain a virus or an inappropriate image. Children should also be told that if they are sent anything hurtful or unpleasant, they should tell an adult.

### Buying online

Children will need to be careful if they are using the Internet for purchases. It is possible that older children may have debit cards, but children of primary age may ask parents for their card information or use online vouchers in order to pay for items over the Internet. In this situation they should be warned about the possibilities of identity theft and of putting information online where others may see it.

### Using a mobile phone

If children are given mobile phones to use (this is often for safety reasons such as when walking home and so on), they should be warned about using them too often in public. Mobile phones can be the cause of muggings and theft, in particular if the equipment is very up to date. They can also be a means of bullying children, in the same way as email and social networking sites.

## Getting ready for assessment

For your assessment in this unit, you will need to show that you understand the purpose and process of safeguarding and child protection. If you have been involved in a safeguarding or bullying incident and have attended meetings to this effect, you should speak to your assessor about what happened. If you have not, find out about school policy and speak to staff about how such an incident would be managed in your school. While you should not record names or circumstances, you may be able to write a reflective account or have a professional discussion about the actions which were followed. Look carefully at the assessment criteria and include as many points as you can so that you can cover as much as possible, for example, procedures or policies that you followed and how the child and their family were supported.

## Check your knowledge

1. What are the main areas of legislation and guidelines in your home country which affect the safeguarding of children and young people?
2. Name some of the agencies which may help and support schools in cases of suspected child abuse. What are their roles?
3. Why should children and young people be given guidance about use of the Internet? What kinds of risks and consequences might there be of unfiltered Internet use in schools?
4. What should you do in cases where you suspect a child may be at risk of harm or abuse? How will you be protected against any repercussions?
5. Name some of the policies your school might have in place to deal with issues around child safety and safeguarding.
6. Name three ways in which adults in schools can empower children when supporting their safety and well-being.

## Websites

**www.abs-kids.co.uk** – information and support for children on bullying

**www.anti-bullyingalliancetoolkit.org.uk** – guidance and practical ideas to help tackle bullying

**www.antibullying.net** – established by the Scottish Executive for parents, teachers and young people

**www.beatbullying.org** – information on and support for bullying

**www.bullyfreezone.co.uk** – raises awareness of alternative ways of resolving conflict and of reducing incidences of bullying

**www.bullying.co.uk** – Bullying UK, the UK anti-bullying charity

**www.ceop.police.uk** – Child Exploitation and Online Protection Centre, an organisation which aims to provide information to parents, children and education professionals around safety online

**www.coastkid.org** – anti-bullying website with helpful advice and information

**www.education.gov.uk/publications** – guidance and supporting documents from the Department for Education (DfE)

**www.ico.gov.uk** – the Information Commissioner's Office

**www.keepingchildrensafe.org.uk** – the Keeping Children Safe (KCS) toolkit is available through their website to support those working in child protection and offers training materials as well as a CD-ROM to support agencies in putting child protection into practice

**www.kidscape.org.uk** – Kidscape, charity to prevent bullying and child abuse

**www.nspcc.org.uk** – the NSPCC is the UK's only free, online, specialised child protection resource for practitioners, researchers, trainers, policy-makers and other professionals working to protect children providing information on child abuse, child protection and safeguarding in the UK. NSPCC helpline: 0808 800 5000 or help@nspcc.org.uk

**www.nyas.net** – National Youth Advocacy Service: UK charity to provide children's rights and give children and young people a voice

**www.stoptextbully.com** – advice on what to do for anyone bullied by text, email, web and so on

**www.teachernet.gov.uk/wholeschool/behaviour/tacklingbullying** – Teachernet advice on tackling bullying

**www.unicef.org/crc** – the United Nations Convention on the Rights of the Child (1989) (UNCRC)

# School Life

## My story Nick

I work part-time as a general support assistant in a Year 4 class and am only in school Monday to Wednesday, as I spend two days a week in college. I had some concerns about a child who was in my class some time ago, as he often came to school with marks on his legs and back, and was very reluctant to speak about what had caused them. I spoke to my class teacher, who went to the Head about it; the teacher said that it may be nothing but we should always voice any concerns, particularly with safeguarding issues. It then emerged that the child had been beaten regularly by his father for some time and his mother was unable to report him, as she had been threatened with violence herself. Although it was awful at the time, I hope that we made some difference to the child's life – he left the school, but I have heard that he is now living with his mother in a different area.

## Ask the expert

**Q** There are quite a few children in my school that I think are neglected – do I report all of them?

**A** It may be that in some areas there is a higher proportion of children who suffer abuse or neglect – you should still say something even if there are several children as each case should be looked at individually. It will be the role of your Senior Management Team and those responsible for safeguarding in your school to follow these up.

### VIEWPOINT

Do you think it is better to speak up with concerns about a child even if they turn out to be unnecessary concerns? You should always say something, even if it turns out that you are wrong – if you have told someone else, you have passed on your concerns, which is the important thing.

# TDA 3.10 Plan & deliver learning activities under the direction of a teacher

This unit will support teaching assistants who work under the direction of a teacher to plan, support and assess individuals or groups of learners. You will need to reflect on how your own role complements the work of the teacher. All outcomes for this unit must be assessed in the workplace, so you will need to show evidence of ways that you use your own knowledge and expertise to support, extend and, where necessary, adapt activities for individuals and groups of children. You will also explore the role of assessment, considering the importance of observing and reviewing learners' response to the planned activities and their progress towards the learning objectives.

Information in this unit overlaps with other units, particularly TDA 3.3 and 3.7, so you may find that you are able to cross-reference some of your evidence.

## By the end of this unit you will:

1. be able to plan learning activities under the direction of the teacher
2. be able to deliver learning activities
3. be able to monitor and assess learning outcomes.

# Be able to plan learning activities under the direction of the teacher

## Objectives, content and intended outcomes of learning activities

It will benefit yourself, the teacher and the children if you are involved at the beginning of the planning stage. If you are not usually invited to planning meetings, you should ask when this takes place and if you can attend. Long-term planning will be in place well before the school year begins, with regular planning meetings throughout the term to agree on the detail of the content and delivery strategies. Before each lesson, you should receive a detailed plan of the learning objectives for the activities being undertaken.

Long-term planning outlines the scheme of work for each year group across the school year for each statutory and non-statutory curriculum area. It will show units of learning and how these will be sequenced.

Medium-term planning usually covers a term or half-term. It will include an overview of the subject and **learning outcomes**. There will be links to any cross-curricular learning, particularly if taught through a topic, and information on additional activities such as visits or visitors.

Short-term planning provides information on the week's lessons, broken down into the activities for each day. The planning will be detailed and include:

- **learning objectives**
- activities
- organisation, for example, timing, groupings
- inclusion/differentiation
- resources
- assessment opportunities
- role of other adults.

An example of an outcome may be that the majority of children in the class are 'able to use mental calculation strategies to solve number problems

by the end of the term'. The learning objective for an individual lesson (which will support children to achieve the outcome) is for them to be able to 'recall doubles in numbers to 20'.

## How the learning activities relate to statutory and non-statutory frameworks

The curriculum includes both statutory and non-statutory subjects. The National Curriculum provides the statutory part of the whole-school curriculum and applies to pupils at compulsory school age from 5 years to 16 years. With the exception of religious education, which is planned locally, each subject area sets out what must be taught in programmes of study.

| Statutory core subjects | Statutory foundation subjects |
|---|---|
| • Mathematics<br>• English<br>• Science | • History<br>• Geography<br>• Information and Communication Technology<br>• Art and Design<br>• Design and Technology<br>• Music<br>• Physical Education<br>• Religious Education |

*Table 1: National Curriculum Key Stages 1 and 2.*

The non-statutory framework is an essential element of the whole-school curriculum. It includes areas of learning which support children's overall development and improves their achievement in other areas of the curriculum.

## Key terms

**Learning outcomes** — broad statements of what children will know, understand and be able to do at the end of a topic or period of study

**Learning objectives** — statements of intentions, what pupils are expected to do and achieve by the end of the activity

Non-statutory subjects include:

- Personal, Social, Health and Economic education (PSHE) including sex and relationship education

- citizenship

- modern foreign languages (at Key Stage 2).

The programmes of study from both statutory and non-statutory framework provide the basis for lesson planning. Attainment targets describe the knowledge, understanding and skills expected of individual children when they reach the end of each key stage. As each key stage covers more than one year, this means that these expected targets or outcomes must be broken down into steps within the schemes of work.

- Key Stage 1: Years 1 and 2 (aged 5–6 years).

- Key Stage 2: Years 3, 4, 5 and 6 (aged 7–11 years).

The Numeracy and Literacy frameworks support whole-school planning. The frameworks provide guidance and support materials in relation to the National Curriculum mathematics and English programmes of study across Key Stages 1 and 2.

## Early Years Foundation Stage

If you are supporting children in Nursery or Reception class, activity planning will be based on the Early Years Foundation Stage (EYFS) framework. This framework sets out what babies and young children should know and be able to do from birth to 5 years. Areas of learning and development are set out in seven areas of learning and describe the outcomes or goals expected by the time children enter Key Stage 1. These are divided into prime and specific areas of learning. The prime areas are:

1. Communication and Language

2. Physical development

3. Personal, social and emotional development

The specific areas are designed to use skills which children have been developing in the prime areas:

4. Literacy

5. Mathematics

6. Understanding of the world

7. Expressive arts and design

### Portfolio activity

In geography the outcome for Year 5 pupils is to recognise how places compare with other places. They recently explored their local town. They then visited a national park where they explored the woods and riverside area. During each visit they studied maps and took a series of digital photographs. The teacher wants pupils to develop their literacy skills through their geography topic. She has asked you to plan and prepare the following.

1. An ICT activity for a group of pupils with above-average ability which will enable them to develop their writing skills.

2. An activity to support an individual pupil who is easily distracted to develop his speaking and listening skills.

Research the relevant curriculum framework and use this to plan two activities demonstrating how each activity supports the needs of children.

### Functional skills

**ICT: Using ICT**
You could create your plans on the computer and save them to a file or folder so that you can access them easily. You could also develop your ICT skills by emailing a copy of your plans to your assessor to check for you.

The curriculum for Scotland is non-statutory but provides a framework for schools. More information can be found at www.ltscotland.org.uk – Learning and Teaching Scotland (LTS).

Teachers must ensure that all aspects of the separate subjects or areas of learning are covered at each stage of learning. This is achieved through long-term planning. Schemes of work may be in relation to individual subject areas or cross curricular. In early years and the primary stage, the programmes of study are often taught through topics.

## Portfolio activity

At Tall Trees Primary School, the Year 1 classes have recently visited a city farm. The topic this term is linked to their visit. The teachers and the classroom assistants are planning a meeting to develop activities which will support children to meet the outcomes. The following diagram shows the planned outcomes in relation to the statutory curriculum, for each subject being taught through the topic.

- Select outcomes from at least two subjects and plan a learning activity for a group of six children.
- Identify the learning objectives.
- Describe how you could introduce the activity.
- Describe how you will develop the activity.
- Identify the learning resources you will use.

### Science

Learners will know:
- that animals need water and food to survive
- that animals are living things and that they grow and reproduce.

Learners will be able to:
- sort animals using simple features
- describe where different animals live.

### English

Learners will be able to:
- talk about their visit and listen and respond to other children
- use appropriate vocabulary to describe different animals
- read simple information about farm animals
- respond to stories and rhymes
- sequence a story
- spell common and topic words within their writing.

**The farm**

### ICT

Learners will be able to:
- use ICT to classify information about animals
- use ICT to produce text and images.

### Art and Design

Learners will be able to:
- explore different materials for their work
- design and make artefacts
- talk about their own and others' art work.

*Planned outcomes relating to the statutory curriculum for each subject.*

## Planning and preparing learning activities, as directed by the teacher

You may be asked to plan learning activities for a group or an individual child. If you have been involved in the long-term and medium-term planning, you will have an understanding of the outcomes and specific learning objectives which you need to consider. The activity you devise will need to take into account:

- the number of children
- previous learning
- the environment
- resources which are available to you
- time available.

If you work regularly within the class, you will know what children have learned previously and so be able to build on this knowledge.

### Personalised learning

A personalised approach requires teachers and teaching assistants to take into account not only different academic levels of achievement, but also children's individual needs and interests. Individual targets or learning objectives will support children to reach their full potential. Planning must take into consideration ways that children learn. Planning for the needs of each individual child may seem daunting, but children of similar abilities and interests can be grouped together and work towards the same targets.

## Using knowledge to contribute to planning partnership working with the teacher

Although your role is to work under the direction of the teacher, this should be viewed as a **partnership**. It is essential that you develop a rapport with the teacher you support. In order to make an effective contribution at the planning stage, it is important that you:

- become familiar with the programmes of study for the foundation or key stage you support
- understand the achievements, needs and interests of individual children in the class
- reflect on your own knowledge, expertise and interests.

As you become more experienced you will begin to contribute your own ideas at each stage of the planning process. If you are asked to plan and deliver activities, you will need a range of information about the individual learners from:

- records of learners' achievements
- individual learning plans
- information provided by the teacher
- your own observations.

You should consider the strengths you have that can enrich the learning experiences for children. You may have particular skills that you can bring to activities, for example, ICT skills, an interest in literacy or the ability to play an instrument. You should also reflect on areas where you lack confidence and take opportunities to seek advice or undertake training to develop these.

### Key term

**Partnership working** — working with the teacher to support teaching and learning towards shared goals, for example in whole-class plenary sessions

### Knowledge into action

Build up evidence of ways that you have contributed at each stage of planning. You could keep a diary or annotate meeting minutes or planning information to record your own contributions. For example, what suggestions have you put forward for activities? What ideas do you have for the resources or strategies you could use?

### CASE STUDY: Supporting mathematics to meet attainment targets

Margaret is working in Year 1 to support mathematics. The attainment target from the National Curriculum is for pupils to be able to use mathematical names for common 3D and 2D shapes, and describe their properties. She has been asked to support a group of four pupils to consolidate their understanding of 3D shapes. The teacher has informed her that the children have already investigated 2D shapes and are able to name and describe these. The children are of similar ability. Margaret knows the following information from her observations.

1. Jamie loses concentration easily and often distracts others. He works best when he is actively involved.

2. Pritpal is very quiet and withdrawn, and is often reluctant take part in group activities. She is very creative.

3. Chloe can articulate her findings but has difficulty in recording information on paper.

4. Paul enjoys working with others. He responds particularly well when he is challenged.

- How will the characteristics and needs of the individual children affect Margaret's planning?
- How can she use the children's previous experience and knowledge to support learning?
- What other information would help her to plan an activity?

# Be able to deliver learning activities

## The use of teaching and learning methods

Before you consider the teaching and learning method, you must know and understand the learning objectives for the group or individual. Whatever methods you use, it is essential that children are involved in their own learning. Young children learn best through play. Here they are able to explore their environment and learn through trial and error. As children get older they will develop a preferred learning style, although it is still important that they are allowed time to explore and talk about what they have learned. Children are more likely to understand and develop skills if they are allowed to discover things for themselves.

Your own role should be viewed as **facilitator**. Lev Vygotsky stressed the importance of the adult to provide activities which are both achievable and challenging. He called the stage when children had achieved their target by reaching a level of understanding or had mastered something the 'zone of actual development'. At this stage children are able to work independently. The stage when children are working toward their targets he called the 'zone of proximal development'. At this stage children are able to achieve with some help and support from an adult.

Jerome Bruner built on Vygotsky's theory. He used the term 'scaffolding' to describe the assistance given to children to support them to achieve the next level of learning. As children begin to understand a concept or master a new skill, the scaffolding or assistance can be gradually removed as they begin to work independently. At this stage there is a review of learning and children will begin to work toward a new set of targets.

**Key term**

**Facilitator** — someone who supports the process of learning

### Meeting agreed learning objectives and intended outcomes
Planning is not restricted to the content to be delivered and the activities to be carried out. For you to support learning effectively, you must know everything that will happen in the classroom so that you are able to

| | |
|---|---|
| **Zone of proximal development** | What children can do with the support of an adult |
| **Zone of actual development** | What children can do independently |

*Vygotsky's theory describes what children can do with and without help.*

give the same messages and work towards the same goals as the teacher. Before each lesson you should have agreed the strategies that will be used to:

- support children to meet their individual targets or learning objectives
- maintain children's interest
- challenge children's thinking
- observe individual pupils' progress and achievements.

### BEST PRACTICE CHECKLIST: Achieving learning objectives

- Share the learning objectives and individual targets with children.
- Build on what children already know and can do.
- Give children time to talk about the activity and what they have learned.
- Provide focused support to help children to move to the next level of learning.
- Encourage independence.
- Provide challenges.
- Have high expectations.

## Maintaining learners' motivation and interest

To maintain children's interest, it is critical that they are motivated, or enthusiastic, to learn. There may be a number of reasons why children want to take part in an activity and maintain their interest. Many children do so because they wish to please you by completing the task or because of a reward such as a sticker or house points they will receive. This is called **extrinsic** motivation. The children are likely to progress but are not taking part because they want to learn or realise 'what's in it for them'.

Learning which gives children personal satisfaction will be more enduring. This is referred to as **intrinsic** motivation. To support children to develop this 'inner' motivation, it is essential that you tap into their natural interest in the world about them. Children who are eager to learn will feel good about themselves and begin to recognise their own progress.

### Key terms

**Extrinsic** — outer or separate from

**Intrinsic** — something natural or belonging to

*How well do you maintain learners' motivation?*

Young children are naturally curious and want to find out about the world around them. When planning an activity, it is essential that you tap into this natural interest. As the activity develops, consider ways that you can maintain children's interest. Young children can easily lose concentration and become bored in a learning activity, so it is important that the learning objectives are realistic and achievable. Children need challenge but will soon lose interest where the learning activity is beyond their ability and skill. The converse is also true where children have already met their targets and are not 'stretched'.

## Supporting and challenging learners

Young children are only able to concentrate for short spells, so when planning an activity, you could think about ways that you can vary the tasks, such as keeping children moving, and varying the pace and groupings. **Passive learning** — sitting and listening to instructions or information — should be reduced to a minimum, as children can soon become bored and 'turn off'. Providing learning experiences which ensure that children are actively involved will help to support and challenge their thinking. **Active learning** does not necessarily mean that children are moving around the classroom or involved in free play, but interacting with new ideas and information. This could be through playing games or designing and producing something.

## Promoting independence

Sharing the learning objectives with children will support them to be in control of their own learning. This will have a direct impact on their self-esteem. The ways that you do this will depend upon the age and stage of development of the child. Strategies may include:

- involving children in identifying and reviewing their own learning targets

- giving children choices about their own learning

- storing and labelling resources and equipment so that children can access them easily

- teaching self-help strategies, for example, **mnemonics**, checking own work, how and where to find information

- pairing children with work buddies.

---

**CASE STUDY:** Meeting the needs and interests of a group of children

Pete works at his local primary school supporting children in Key Stage 2. He recently supported a group of Year 6 children investigating environmental issues in their local area. He is fully involved at each stage of planning, so when the teacher asked him to prepare an activity supporting children to plan and produce written information, he suggested making this an open-ended activity as the group he supports are mixed ability. One of the children has dyslexia and another has hearing loss.

Pete introduced the activity by showing the group information about a local town; the information was in different genres including brochures, leaflets, newspaper articles and a DVD. He then suggested that the learners identify their own audience and choose their own method to present information. All the learners met their learning objectives which related to knowledge and understanding of local history and literacy skills.

- In what ways will the activity meet the needs of all the learners?
- How will this activity help to maintain interest?
- How could Pete extend the activity for a pupil who is gifted and talented in English?

---

### Key terms

**Passive learning** — learners do not interact or engage in the learning process

**Active learning** — learners are involved and interact in the learning process

**Mnemonics** — systems for improving and aiding the memory

## Functional skills

**English: Speaking, listening and communication**
You could prepare a presentation to share with your colleagues or peers on how you have helped the children you care for promote their own independence. Presenting this information in a group is a good way of developing your confidence and sharing good practice.

## Functional skills

**English: Speaking, listening and communication**
This case study provides a good opportunity for discussion. When discussing the points, listen carefully to what others have to say so that you can respond in an appropriate way.

### Gather feedback on progress and achievements

As you support children it is important that you monitor not only whether they have achieved the learning objectives of the activity you are supporting, but also their level of interest and motivation so that at the end of the session you are able to feed back on each child's progress to the teacher. Ways to do this will be explored more fully on pages 110–112 and in TDA 3.7.

## Promoting and supporting the inclusion of all learners

Inclusion is concerned with ensuring that all children, whatever their background or ability, are given the opportunity to participate fully in the school curriculum. You will be aware of the children with special educational needs (SEN) or disabilities and the additional support they require. However, inclusion is not only concerned with children with SEN. There is a range of reasons why children may be more at risk of exclusion. Children who have particular problems such as health conditions or family problems, and those who have become disengaged or from minority ethnic groups are also more vulnerable.

Your own role is critical to support children to ensure that they are included and feel valued. When working with individual or small groups of children you will

**CASE STUDY:** Meeting children's needs in a history topic

Gemma supports a group of children in Year 4 with writing. Following a visit to a castle for their history topic, Gemma has been asked by the class teacher to plan an activity which requires children to produce information for visitors. The children are of mixed ability.

1. Liam is confident in writing and can structure his work well.

2. Amrit is of average ability. He moved to the UK last year and although he has made good progress in his spoken English, he continues to require some support.

3. Jessica is inconsistent with work. She is beginning to make good progress but lacks concentration.

4. Molly has dyslexia. She has a good imagination and is creative, but finds structuring her ideas difficult.

- How can Gemma ensure that her planned activity meets the children's needs across the different levels of ability interests and skills?
- How can she help to maintain each learner's interest and motivation?
- What opportunities are there for assessment?

be able to observe individual needs and any barriers, either long term or temporary, that children encounter and which prevent them from participating. For example, you might:

- provide physical help with tasks
- support communication by rephrasing the teacher's instruction or using picture aids
- break down the task into smaller chunks of learning
- provide additional or assistive technology or resources
- adapt resources or the activity to meet the individual needs of children.

## Over to you!

Obtain and familiarise yourself with policies and procedures which work to break down any barriers to participation within your school

## Functional skills

### English: Reading

Finding and reading the policies and procedures for your setting in this 'Over to you!' activity is a good way of expanding your knowledge of your setting. You could swap with a peer and then compare the similarities and differences between the different settings.

## CASE STUDY: Supporting children experiencing barriers to participation

A group of boys tend to dominate the large construction area in the Reception classroom. Two girls who are quiet and withdrawn would like to play there. They often watch the boys as they build but do not feel able to join in.

Mike is 8 years old. He has just started the school mid-term. He is from a traveller family and has already moved schools four times. He finds it difficult to make friends and other pupils tend to shun him and not invite him to join their games or choose him for their teams.

Sian is in Year 1 and has communication and language difficulties caused by hearing loss. She does have a hearing aid, but at times this does not appear to be working effectively. She often finds that she is unable to grasp the information when the teacher introduces the lesson. You have noticed that other children are reluctant to include her in the conversation during group activities.

- How might each child feel in these scenarios?
- How will it affect their academic progress and personal development?
- What strategies could you use to ensure that all children are included?

## Organising and managing learning activities to ensure the safety of learners

The health and safety of pupils is paramount. Although there will be someone with overall responsibility for health and safety, under the 1974 Heath and Safety Act, all those working in the school have a duty to ensure the health and safety of children in their care. You must also be mindful of your own health and safety, and that of colleagues and any visitors. When planning and supporting learning activities, you need to ensure that the classroom is prepared and maintained with health and safety in mind.

When planning an activity, you need to consider if the space is adequate and if you require access to particular facilities. As you prepare the area to carry out your activity, you need to check that the area is free from hazards such as bags or trailing wires. Children with mobility or visual problems are at particular risk, so you need to pay particular attention to lighting, sound levels and accessibility. You must also consider the age and stage of development of children; for example, the level of supervision for children in Key Stage 2 would not be appropriate for children in a Reception class.

As you supervise the children, you must continue to be vigilant so that you can deal with any safety issues as they arise – for example, mopping up spilt water or reminding children not to swing backwards on their chairs. The pupils should also be aware of risks and have an understanding of any dangers associated with the learning activities. You can support children by discussing the activity and ways they should work safely, using age-appropriate language.

### Functional skills

**ICT: Using ICT**

Before the children come in to your setting, you could use a video camera and do a walk around your setting videoing evidence of how you have considered the health and safety requirements and the needs of the children in your care. You could share the video with your assessor; it could be used to support the assessment of your knowledge and understanding of health and safety.

## Risk assessment

Risk assessments are carried out in schools to prevent accidents or ill health. Assessments must take into account any hazards, the likelihood of harm, who may be at risk and what form the risk may take. Hazards will be identified in relation to:

- the learning environment
- the activities which take place
- where there may be additional or particular risks to individual pupils, for example, children who are disabled.

Following any risk assessment, it will be decided what precautions will be taken to reduce any risks. You must be aware of the policies and procedures for the environments where the children learn. There will also be procedures for reducing risks in relation to the learning activities which take place. Some activities, such as design and technology, physical education or cooking activities, will have greater risk associated with them, particularly where equipment and tools are used. Some activities may be carried out off site. In this situation, the teacher responsible should have visited the site to assess any potential risks.

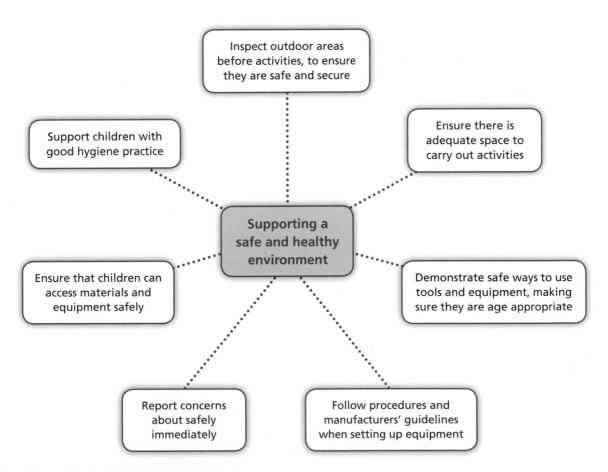

*Supporting a safe and healthy environment.*

*How experienced are you at working in partnership?*

## Working in partnership with the teacher to support learning activities

A report commissioned by the Training and Development Agency for Schools (www.tda.gov.uk) suggests that an increase in the number of teaching assistants is strongly associated with improved school attainment. School attainment relies upon effective teamwork where roles are understood. There is a range of strategies that teaching assistants can use when working alongside the teacher, as shown by the diagram on page 199.

## Be able to monitor and assess learning outcomes

Assessment should be integral to the day-to-day delivery of learning activities. You may hear the term **assessment for learning** used to describe this process. At the end of each topic or series of activities, the teacher may carry out a formal assessment of what children have learned. This is **assessment of learning** or summative assessment.

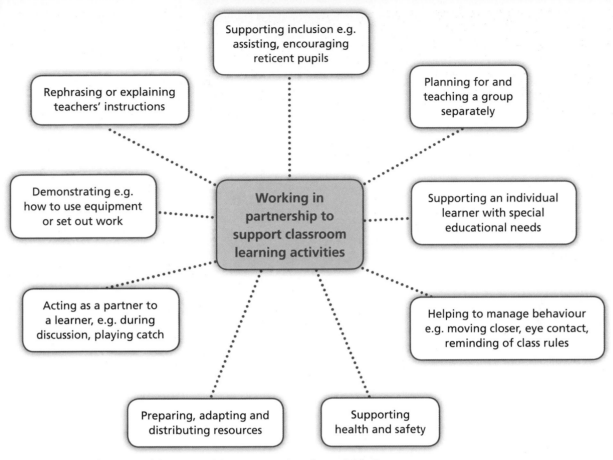

How many ways do you work in partnership to support learning activities?

## Key terms

**Assessment for learning** — using assessment as part of teaching and learning in ways which will raise learners' achievement

**Assessment of learning** — an evaluation of what learners know, understand and can do at a particular stage

## Link

See TDA 3.7, Support assessment for learning, for more on this area.

## Monitor learners' responses to activities

As learners undertake the activities, it is essential that their responses are monitored. Their responses will tell you whether the activity you have planned is appropriate and likely to support them to achieve their targets. This may be evident from their:

- **level of interest and engagement** — are they immediately interested, do they continue to stay on task and contribute their own ideas?

- **behaviour** — do they appear excited by the activity and immediately get involved, or are they distracted and even displaying inappropriate behaviour?

- **verbal responses** — do they ask pertinent questions and make interesting and appropriate suggestions or comments to yourself or peers?

- **level of independence** — how far are they relying on yourself or peers to support them as they work?

- **use of resources or equipment** — are they appropriate for the age and stage of development, and do they support the learning process?

## Ways of modifying activities to meet learners' needs

You may modify learning activities:

- before the activity, as you know the individual needs of pupils and have taken account of these during the planning stage

- during the activity, as when monitoring responses you observe that pupils are experiencing difficulty in some aspect of the activity.

Lesson plans should include **differentiated** activities for pupils who have special educational needs, disabilities or specific learning difficulties. You may be asked to support the teacher by modifying activities for a particular learner or group of learners. Modifications may be through providing additional support, changing the teaching and learning method or strategy, or adapting learning materials.

Materials may be adapted for a number of reasons. Children with reading difficulties may require information to be simplified and broken down into smaller steps. Adding illustrations or diagrams will also aid understanding. Children with visual impairment will require information to be produced using a larger font and children with dyslexia often benefit if coloured paper or overlays are used.

Some children with motor difficulties may require activities to be adapted through the use of technical aids or more appropriate resources. Consider the equipment and resources that you have chosen and decide if they are suitable for all the children. In PE, for example, children with motor difficulties may require a lighter bat and one with a different grip. A child with visual impairment may be able to take part if a brightly coloured ball is selected.

For some children a different approach may be required. Children learn by using all their senses. As children get older, planned activities are usually presented requiring children to rely on their sense of hearing and sight. Some children, particularly those with learning disabilities, dyslexia or **dyscalculia**, will benefit if a **multi-sensory approach** is used; others may work best when they are physically active.

### Key terms

**Differentiation** — planning teaching and learning activities so that pupils of different abilities will have access to them

**Dyscalculia** — a learning disability or difficulty involving innate difficulty in learning or comprehending mathematics

**Multi-sensory approach** — activities which require children to use a range of senses — auditory, visual and kinesthetic (touch) to receive and express information

### Reflect

In clip 6, Supporting ICT, the teaching assistant is supporting a group of mixed-ability children. Observe the way she supports individual children.

- How does she ensure that all children are motivated?

- In what way is the activity adapted for a child with dyslexia?

- What other strategies are used to support children who find ICT more difficult?

## Monitor learners' participation and progress

Before you deliver an activity, you will have agreed with the teacher the objectives for the activity and will know the learners' individual targets. You need to share these targets with learners at the start of the activity. As well as the academic achievement targets, learners should also understand exactly what they need to do and the expectations of behaviour.

**14th March**            **Design and Technology Y4**

Objectives:
- Research ideas for mask making
- Develop ideas on paper in preparation for mask making
- Discuss and reflect on own ideas

H.B.    Worked independently – researched ideas in books and used the internet. He was able to describe the process and materials he will use to produce the mask.

J.A.    Found difficulty in coming up with ideas initially and needed to be directed towards information. Has now planned the mask but was unsure of the materials she will use.

C.M.    Took a long time to settle down and had to be reminded of the objectives on two occasions. He has produced a plan for the mask. The sketch doesn't show his ideas clearly but during discussion C was able to describe his plans and what he will do to produce the mask.

*Handwritten notes are a useful reference for tracing pupils' progress.*

## Peer assessment

When planning an activity, it is good practice to allow some time, usually at the end of the session, for reviewing the learning and participation of individual pupils. This may be done individually or as a group review. For example, a group of Year 4 pupils may have been designing masks. At the end of the activity they could show their designs and discuss their plans for producing their masks. Discussing their progress in the group will help learners to assess whether they have met their targets and help them to develop ideas and focus on the next stage of development.

## Informal records

As learners work and you observe their progress, you will make a mental note of an individual's participation and progress. It is helpful also to jot down any specific information regarding progress or concerns which you need to feed back to the teacher. You may use a section on the activity planning sheet for this or have a small notebook with you. Remember, however, to observe confidentiality at all times and ensure that information written about children is stored securely.

In the example of peer assessment above, the teaching assistant also made notes on each pupil's progress.

It is important to feed back on individual children's progress to the class teacher.

## Skills builder

Negotiate a time when you can observe a small group or individual child as they take part in a learning activity. Before you start, prepare for the observation by identifying individuals you will observe and any special educational needs or specific needs they may have. Also identify the objectives of the lesson. Note what you see happening as the children take part, including their reactions. After the observation, take time to reflect and interpret what you saw. Identify what you have learned about each child and how this will help you in future planning.

## Providing learners with focused support and feedback

Assessment can only be effective where children receive specific information on their progress and their achievements. Feedback can be in relation to what has actually been achieved so far. It must be specific so that the child knows which target they have met or how they have improved. It is not constructive just to say, 'Well done, Adam you've worked hard today.' In contrast, saying 'Well done Adam, you have remembered to put in all the capital letters and full stops in your written work today' tells the learner what he has achieved and will help to motivate him.

Feedback should be continuous and constructive, focusing on the positives and ways to progress. For example, 'You have collected the information and have the correct labels for your graph, Charlotte, but remember to take more time when drawing your graph too so that the lines are drawn clearly.'

You should give feedback as children work or as soon as possible after the activity has taken place. If you are marking work, you may give written feedback, but it is only meaningful if you discuss this with children before they move on with work.

## Assessment techniques to support the evaluation of learners' progress

Earlier in this section you read about assessment for learning, which is ongoing, and assessment of learning, which takes place at the end of a period of learning. There is a range of ways to assess children's learning and development, but there will be a greater understanding of children's progress where several techniques are employed during each learning activity.

### Functional skills

**ICT: Developing, presenting and communicating information**
You could create a leaflet containing information on all the different methods of assessment. You could include a chart in your leaflet that shows a comparison of the different forms of assessment.

**Observation**

Observations will give you a great deal of information on pupils' knowledge, understanding, skills and attitudes towards their work. Observations may be informal or formal, targeted and used for a specific purpose.

**Questioning**

Open questions are a useful technique to help you to assess learners' understanding and thought processes as they work. Targeted questions may also be used to assess learners at the end of a stage of learning.

**Analysing written responses**

Work which learners produce in response to a learning activity is marked and graded. Grades can indicate knowledge and understanding but oral feedback and discussion is more effective and will help the teacher to understand and support learners' errors and misconceptions.

**Assessment techniques**

**Self-assessment**

Children may find assessing their own progress difficult. It is helpful to discuss individual learner's progress during each activity. It is also a useful strategy to find out what learners are finding difficult. Self-assessment helps to promote independent learning.

**Tests**

Formal, summative assessment such as statutory assessment tests (SATs) and end of key stage or topic tests developed and assessed internally.

Verbal or written tests may also be used periodically to check knowledge and understanding.

**Peer assessment**

It is helpful for learners to receive feedback from others. It will help them to understand what is expected and how it relates to the objectives. Peer assessment must be handled sensitively. Pupils must be clear on what the work is being assessed against.

*Assessment techniques.*

## DVD activity

Video clips 1 Classroom preparation, 6 Supporting ICT and 7 Planning

1. Watch clip 1, Classroom preparation. Reflect on the teaching assistant's role in this clip and consider how discussing the layout and resources will help to support the teacher, the TA and the children.

   Think about how you know how the environment is to be organised in your own school. Keep a record of discussions about the organisation of the classroom, including any written plans. You could annotate the plans to show your own contribution to the layout.

2. Watch clip 6. Note how the TA prepares the room to ensure health and safety. Reflect on your own role in setting up a learning area. Obtain guidance and procedures from your own school for preparing and maintaining the environment.

3. Watch clip 7 as the teaching assistant works in partnership with the teacher during a planning session. Consider the ways she contributes her own ideas. In the clip, the mechanism for planning in partnership is referred to.

   Identify the mechanisms which are in place in your own school. Keep a record of when you have taken part in planning and the contribution you have made.

## Getting ready for assessment

To achieve this unit you will need to demonstrate that you are able to support teachers in the classroom at each stage of the learning process, from planning and delivery to monitoring and assessing.

Your assessor is likely to observe you as you apply these skills but you should support this evidence by keeping a diary or log of any work you undertake under the direction of a teacher. As you gather evidence, you should take time each week to reflect on what went particularly well and things that did not go as well as you had hoped. Go on to consider the reasons why and what you might do differently in the future.

In addition to your diary or log, you should keep any other relevant evidence so that you can discuss it with your assessor. This evidence could include activity plans, resources you have produced or adapted, feedback from teachers or contributions you have made to the assessment process.

## Check your knowledge

1. What are the statutory subjects at Key Stage 1?

2. How does religious education differ from other subjects?

3. Vygotsky describes a stage where children can do something with help. What is this called?

4. Suggest three ways to promote independent learning.

5. Name the legislation which underpins health and safety in schools.

6. What is meant by risk assessment?

7. What is the difference between assessment of learning and assessment for learning?

8. What is meant by a multi-sensory approach?

### Websites

**www.education.gov.uk** – Department for Education
**www.dcsf.gov.uk/everychildmatters** – the five outcomes for Every Child Matters
**www.ltscotland.org.uk** – Learning and Teaching Scotland
**www.nicurriculum.org.uk** – National Curriculum, Northern Ireland
**www.scotland.gov.uk** – curriculum guidance for Scotland
**www.wales.gov.uk** – gives information on the National Curriculum in Wales

# TDA 3.11 Support literacy development

This unit is for those who support literacy development in schools. You may be working in a mainstream or special school and be supporting literacy as part of the main literacy lesson or as an intervention group. You will need to be able to use a variety of strategies to enable pupils to develop literacy skills.

## By the end of this unit you will:

1. understand current national and organisational policies and practices for literacy development

2. be able to support learners in developing reading and writing skills

3. be able to support learners in developing speaking/talking and listening skills.

# Understand current national and organisational policies and practices for literacy development

## The aims and importance of learning provision for literacy development

Learning provision for **literacy development** is important for pupils for several reasons. When pupils are developing their language skills, they are learning to communicate with others in a variety of ways: through speaking, reading and writing. The three areas of language interact with each other to promote the child's self-expression and imagination. Children need to be given opportunities to use and extend their language in all subject areas, so that they can develop higher-level thinking skills.

The aims of the literacy curriculum are that pupils explore the ways in which language works so that they can use this knowledge in a variety of situations. The Primary Framework for Literacy gives structure to the way in which pupils are taught in primary schools and suggested details for how this should be organised. In a typical literacy lesson, pupils will take part in a whole-class activity which may involve some discussion and a shared reading or writing activity. They may also work with a talk partner to discuss ideas before moving into groups or individual work to focus on specific areas. At the end of the session, they will then go back to a whole-class or large-group discussion to enable them to talk about what they have found out or worked on.

Literacy development is important for all children from an early age, and it is vital that these skills are accessible to all so that they can have access to the curriculum. You may be supporting pupils who have communication difficulties or other areas of special educational need which impact on their literacy skills, or children who speak English as an additional language.

### Over to you!

How is literacy taught in your school? Do all teachers plan their lessons in the same format? How is literacy made accessible to all pupils?

## The relevant policy and age-related expectations of learners relevant to literacy development

If you are supporting pupils' literacy development, you will need to be aware of your school's English or **literacy policy**. This will outline your school's approach to the teaching of reading, writing, speaking and listening and should follow local and national guidelines. In England and Wales, the National Primary Literacy Framework is a recommended structure for the teaching of literacy which can be found at http://nationalstrategies.standards.dcsf.gov.uk/primary. It includes 12 strands of learning across the entire primary phase, including the Foundation Stage. In Reception classes, teachers will follow both prime and specific areas of development related to literacy, which are Communication and Language, and Literacy. This means that children will be developing their language through using a range of activities and be supported in doing so. They will need to develop their skills in communicating with others and developing relationships, as well as starting to extend their thinking skills. They will also be learning to link the sounds that they hear with letters and starting to read and write regular and more complex words.

The Foundation Stage divides the subject area into:

● Listening and attention

● Understanding

● Speaking

(These are all prime areas of learning)

● Reading

● Writing

(These are specific areas of learning)

The expectations for the end of the Foundation Stage are known as the early learning goals.

### Key terms

**Literacy development** — the interrelated skills of reading, writing, speaking/talking and listening

**Literacy policy** — policy relevant to literacy development is the policy for English, Welsh and/or language as appropriate to the setting

For example, for Reading, they are currently as follows:

- children read and understand simple sentences
- they use phonic knowledge to decode regular words and read them aloud accurately
- they also read some common irregular words
- they demonstrate understanding when talking with others about what they have read.

As children move into Key Stage 1, learning objectives are then aligned with the 12 strands of the National Primary Literacy Framework.

## Speak and listen for a wide range of purposes in different contexts

1. Speaking
2. Listening and responding
3. Group discussion and interaction
4. Drama

## Read and write for a range of different purposes on paper and on screen

1. Word recognition: decoding (reading) and encoding (spelling)
2. Word structure and spelling
3. Understanding and interpreting texts
4. Engaging and responding to texts
5. Creating and shaping texts
6. Text structure and organisation
7. Sentence structure and punctuation
8. Presentation

Source: Primary Literacy Strategy, Standards site: http://nationalstrategies.standards.dcsf.gov.uk/eyfs/site/requirements/learning/goals.htm

The age-related expectations can currently be found in the document Primary Framework for Literacy and Mathematics (DFES 2006) or on the DfE website: http://nationalstrategies.standards.dcsf.gov.uk/eyfs/site/requirements/learning/goals.htm. This lists the core learning by year group and by strand.

In Scotland, there is no requirement to follow the Primary Framework. The curriculum provides all levels and strands for the three areas: listening and talking; reading; writing. In Northern Ireland, the literacy curriculum is again similar to that of England and is divided into talking and listening; reading; writing. You can find it at www.nicurriculum.org.uk

It is likely that your school policy will identify how literacy is taught throughout the school and how standards are monitored and assessed. You should make sure that you are also up to date with the latest national developments in your home country as these are now available online.

**Knowledge into action**

Write up a summary of your school's literacy policy and highlight how it relates to the work you do with pupils in the classroom.

**Functional skills**

**English: Reading**
Reading and summarising your school's literacy policy is a good way of developing your reading skills.

## The teacher's programme and plans for literacy development

If you are supporting children's learning in literacy, as in any other subject area, you should have some prior discussion or knowledge of the planned activities. In many schools, support staff will be given plans in advance or they may be on display in the classroom. You may also be involved in planning with the teacher and be able to give your own ideas as to how you might approach activities with pupils when you are at the planning stage. You may also have an input into planning for other subject areas which support the development of literacy skills.

You will also need to work with the teacher in order to monitor pupils' progress in all areas of literacy development. This will usually be through making sure that as you work on literacy activities, children are

## Year 4 LITERACY PLANNER – Unit: 2 Narrative – Term: Summer 1 – Week: 4
## Main focus for week: Imaginary worlds

**Main Learning objectives for Shared work:**

This week, children learn how to:

- Explain how writers use figurative and expressive language to create images and atmosphere
- Read extensively favourite authors/genres and experiment with other types of text
- Develop and refine ideas in writing using planning and problem-solving strategies
- Use settings and characterisation to engage readers' interest
- Show imagination through language used to create emphasis, humour, atmosphere or suspense.

| Main Learning Objectives for Phonics, Grammar, Vocabulary and Spelling for this week: | Main speaking and listening, drama and discussion opportunities for this week: |
|---|---|
| <ul><li>Organise texts into paragraphs to distinguish between different information, events or processes</li><li>Use adverbs and conjunctions to establish cohesion within paragraphs</li><li>Clarify meaning and point of view by using varied sentence structure (phrases, clauses and adverbials).</li></ul> | <ul><li>Tell stories effectively and convey detailed information coherently for listeners.</li></ul> |

| Opportunities for assessment: | Weekly evaluation: |
|---|---|
| By the end of this week, most children will:<br><ul><li>Be able to express opinions about an author's intended impact on a reader.</li></ul> | |

| Day | Phonics, spelling, vocab. & grammar VCOP | Shared reading or Writing | Activities | Assessment focus | Plenary |
|---|---|---|---|---|---|
| **Mon 09.5.11** | Set spellings – ambitious words. Identify meanings using dictionaries and use in sentences. | Remind pupils about the need to have settings which help create different atmospheres – look at example of work from previous week, peer assessment using 3 stars and a wish. | Children to look at boring description of a setting and up level it to make the place sound like an imaginary world. Encourage use of ambitious words, using thesaurus and dictionary. Focus on use of adjectives and adverbs to describe the setting and powerful verbs to describe the characters/movements. Children to copy out their piece of writing into their literacy books. CT with Red; TA to support Blue group, support and encourage use of more ambitious vocab. | I can develop and refine ideas for writing. | Children to select their golden sentence from their writing today and share with a partner. |
| **Tues 10.5.10** | Using adjectives to replace 'not' – use examples from page 23 in developing literacy, text level. | Read the description from page 23 of 'Peter Pan in scarlet' describing how the Lost Boys and Wendy became young again and flew back to Neverland. Discuss the idea that the adults became young by putting on other people's clothes. | Whose clothes would you like to put on? Children to write a description of whose clothes they would choose to put on and why. What do they think would happen? What would they do if they could spend the day living as someone else? CT to work with Yellow; TA with Green group. | I can create a character sketch based on what I have read. | Share their ideas with a partner – can children find anyone who wanted to become the same person? |
| **Wed 11.5.10** | Opposite of activity from Tuesday – identify they meaning of ambitious adjectives and use correctly in sentences. | Create a list of ideas from texts that have been read and then create a class setting to evoke a specific atmosphere. | Drama – what would it be like to put on someone else's clothes? Children to use notes from previous lesson to inform ideas for drama. Imagine searching for clothes belonging to that person, putting them on and becoming them. How would you change physically? What elements of your personality would change? How could you show these ideas through drama? CT with Green; TA to work with Purple group. | I can use roles and actions to show dramatic effect. | Peer assessment of drama – looking for character's emotions. Can children work out who they are becoming? |
| **Thurs 12.5.10** | Adjective flowers – pick noun as the stem, write associated adjectives on the leaves. | Discuss the idea that Neverland is a magical place created from dreams. Look at selected phrases which describe items in Neverland and give the reader the impression that this is a world which could only exist in a child's imagination. | What would your Neverland look like? Children to use setting's mind map to collect words and phrases to describe their Neverland. They may use similar ideas to those found in reading, or create a modern world with technology in it. They should imagine the sights, sounds, textures and items in their Neverland and use thesaurus. CT with Blue; TA with Yellow group. | I can develop settings to engage the reader's interest. | Share their plans with a partner – can they select one word or phrase their partner has used which they really like? |
| **Fri 13.5.10** | Input for Wicked Write: Connectives to link ideas and paragraphs. Use of ambitious words and phrases to create images. | | Children to write a postcard sent from their Neverland. They should include people they have met there, what they have seen around them, what they have done and anything else they have found. Encourage use of adjectives to create atmosphere (e.g. mystery, suspense, humour, etc.) CT and TA to circulate during lesson. | I can develop settings to engage the reader's interest. | |

*An example of a lesson plan, showing the role of the teaching assistant.*

focused and able to meet the learning objectives. You may need to encourage the participation of some pupils through the use of praise and feedback, and through clarifying any concerns or problems that they may have.

Careful monitoring of pupil progress also involves the communication of clear learning objectives and feeding back to the teacher at the end of sessions to ensure that everyone is aware how children have managed the task.

### Portfolio activity

You should obtain a copy of medium-term plans which you have worked on with the teacher and summarise how they fit in to the long-term programme for teaching and learning of literacy.

# Be able to support learners in developing reading and writing skills

All assessment criteria from here to the end of the unit must be assessed in the workplace.

## Strategies for supporting learners to develop reading and writing skills

Strategies for supporting learners to develop reading and writing skills include:

● use of targeted prompts and feedback to develop use of independent reading and writing strategies

● facilitating the participation of individuals or small groups in shared reading and writing activities

● using phonics to help learners understand the sound and spelling system and use this to read and spell accurately

● use of specific support strategies

● use of specific support programmes.

You will need to adopt different strategies to enable pupils to access the curriculum as much as possible. While some strategies may work for some children, not all strategies will work for every child, and you will need to be able to adapt what you are doing in consultation with teachers or the SENCO if children are not making expected progress.

## Use of targeted prompts and feedback to develop use of independent reading and writing strategies

Targeted prompts will enable children to develop their independence when reading and writing. Your school may use specific prompts, in particular when writing with children. However, if it does not, you should have a bank of these so that pupils start to learn to use them without asking you and can think of them without support.

Examples of the kinds of prompts they could use for reading could be as follows.

● Try sounding it out.

● Check the context – think about what the sentence is about – are there clues in the sentence around it?

● Does what you think the word says make sense?

● Are there any pictures in the book to give you a clue?

### Writing prompts

When planning, drafting and writing, many schools now use the following VCOP method to encourage pupils to remember to check their work as they go. They may have resources up in their classrooms or on tables to support this. The method has been pioneered by Ros Wilson and is designed to support children through giving them prompts in different areas.

● **V**ocabulary: Children should be encouraged to think of using ambitious vocabulary (sometimes called 'wow' words) in their writing, as much as possible. When they read through and check their work, they should think about whether there is a better word they could use.

● **C**onnectives: Rather than just using 'and', pupils should have a list of other connectives that they can use instead to make their writing more varied and interesting.

● **O**peners: Sentence openers should be varied. Rather than using 'the', 'my' and so on, children need to be encouraged to think about developing their ideas through more varied phrases such as 'later on', 'at last', 'finally', 'meanwhile' and so on.

● **P**unctuation: Children should be aware of a wide range of punctuation.

For more on Ros Wilson, the Big Write and VCOP methods, see the sites listed at the end of this unit.

Level 1
.
Level 2
. ?
Level 3
. ? , !
Level 4
. ? , ... ! ' " "
Level 5
- ? , ... ! ' " " : ; ( )

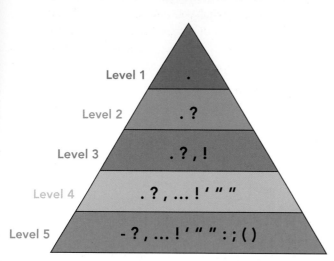

*The punctuation pyramid.*

**Reflect**

You should use feedback with children as much as possible when they are working on writing activities. Are you always positive and do you look for good points rather than focusing on any errors they have made? Do you question them if you think that there is something they may need to change?

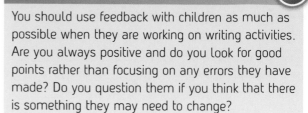

## Facilitating the participation of individuals or small groups in shared reading and writing activities

You may be asked to work with individual children or groups in order to support their participation in literacy activities. In shared reading and writing, this will take place in a whole-class situation, which means that you will need to sit close to targeted children so that they are able to take part while the teacher is taking whole-class activities. You may need to encourage the children to put forward ideas or support them in checking their understanding or working through what they need to do. Depending on how well you know

### CASE STUDY: Facilitating the participation of individuals

Graham works in Year 2 as a teaching assistant. He knows the children well and ensures that those with the greatest need sit close to him during whole-class teaching in case he needs to support them. Today the teacher is working on some shared writing with the class. There are several children in the class who might need support from Graham.

1. Natalie is immature for her age and unable to focus for very long.
2. Christopher is unable to recognise all of his sounds.
3. Marie has a speech impediment which affects her ability to hear her sounds.
4. Jamal speaks English as an additional language.
5. Sam is autistic and his behaviour can be unpredictable.

- Does Graham need to sit close to all of these pupils?
- What should he look out for?

| Reading method | Description |
|---|---|
| Shared reading | In the class, everyone looks at an enlarged text together. The teacher will usually go through the text, involving all the children, and practising basic skills. |
| Guided reading | This will take place in small groups using a set of books which are the same. Children will then read the books independently while the teacher or assistant supports them. |
| Individual reading | The child reads independently without help from an adult. |
| Paired reading | This will be two children reading together with one supporting the other. The children may be the same age, or sometimes infant children working with juniors for paired reading. |

*Table 1: Reading methods.*

the child or children, this may be harder for you to do and you will need to work with teachers in order to decide the best strategies to use with different pupils.

Different kinds of reading methods are employed to develop reading skills as well as individual reading and it is likely that you will be involved in group work using these.

The teacher may also use a range of questioning strategies which take into account the differing abilities of children within the class. You should remember, when you are dealing with groups of children, to use strategies to involve all children, particularly those who are quiet and reluctant to discuss what they are reading. Remember that it is very important for these children to have as much praise and encouragement as possible to build up their confidence.

Different resources may include:

● big books for sharing texts as a class

● a good variety of fiction and non-fiction texts

● reading schemes

● poetry and plays

● tapes of stories and rhymes

● sets of books for guided reading

● story sacks – these are sacks containing characters from books

● computer programs to develop reading skills – for example, to support a specific programme.

## Functional skills

### ICT: Developing, presenting and communicating information
You could produce a leaflet all about the different kinds of reading that the children do in your setting. This leaflet could be aimed at the parents to inform them how their child will be supported with their reading at school. You could also include some tips on how they could support reading at home. Think carefully about the layout of the leaflet and the language that you use.

It is likely that the school will teach writing according to the Primary Framework for Literacy, which is through shared and guided writing. You should understand the difference between the two, and your expected role during writing activities. You will need to clarify exactly what you have been asked to do with the class teacher, so that you are able to report back at the end of the session which children have achieved the learning objectives.

## Shared writing
Pupils will work as a class to compose pieces of work and discuss language, punctuation and grammar. Teachers will work through the different aspects of writing to enable children to structure and formulate their work while focusing on technical and phonic knowledge. They may then use this as a basis for the work they carry out independently. Shared writing may be carried out two or three times a week, and the teacher will usually act as scribe for the children's ideas. Assistants who are supporting individual children may need to sit with them at this stage to keep them focused on the activity, and help them to remain involved. Assistants who work in the classroom may be less involved at this stage, although if they are to work with a group, they will need to know what the focus of the session has been.

## Guided writing
For this, the children will be grouped and have more ownership of their work. It is designed to complement shared writing, and to act as a link between shared and independent work. Teachers or assistants may work with children of the same ability to support the development of specific targets or objectives. During guided writing, children will also have more specific support to help them to develop their own ideas. Assistants may need to help those children who are less confident about contributing to the group. They can do this by prompting and asking these children about their work. At the early stages of writing, it is not appropriate to correct all errors, since this will discourage the children in their writing. It is better to point out any errors related to the focus of the lesson – for example, if this has been on using capital letters and full stops, and these have been omitted.

## Individual writing
At the earliest stages of writing, support will focus on pencil grip and the formation of letters. If there is a problem with holding the pencil, children are sometimes provided with a grip or a wider pencil so that it is easier to hold. Staff should encourage pupils to

follow the correct letter formation so that they start to write more fluently. Children will start to use phonics to help them break words down and, eventually, start to write independently. As pupils become more confident and able writers, they will be able to concentrate more on the development of ideas. Through shared and guided writing, they will learn how to put these ideas into words and sentences. They may need support such as writing frames at this point, to structure their ideas. Pupils will need to have a clear idea of what they have been asked to do, and any support prompts which are available to help them. There may be class lists of words on the wall for children to refer to, or access to dictionaries or word banks. There may also be specific word prompts relating to the topic or book which is being studied during the week.

## Using phonics to help learners understand the sound and spelling system and use this to read and spell accurately

The use of phonics is the way in which children are taught the sound and spelling system from the earliest stages. Although schools may use different methods to do this through various commercial schemes, many of the ways in which they do this will be similar. Letter sounds are often taught through rhymes or songs and/or the use of cartoons or other characters in order to make the experience fun and memorable for children. There may be extended resource packs to support these. You should be familiar with the methods which your school uses so that you can support children in the most effective way though learning songs and so on. As well as letters of the alphabet, phonics schemes will also teach children additional sounds — for example, 'sh', 'ch' and 'th' separately — so that they are able to recognise the distinct sounds which they always make.

---

**CASE STUDY:** Using phonics to help learners

Holly has been working in Year 4 for the past three years and has just been told that she will be working in Reception next year. She has been sent on training for the Early Years Foundation Stage but is not familiar with the scheme which the school uses to teach phonics in Reception. However, there is no funding to send her on any other courses.

- What could Holly do in this situation?
- How could she ensure that she is able to deliver the best possible support to the children?

---

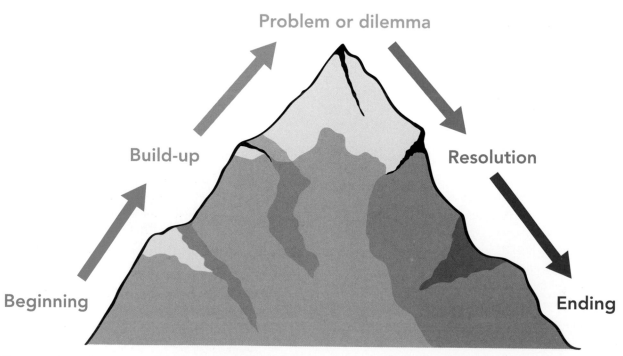

*The story mountain.*

## Use of specific support strategies

As well as the examples already listed, such as paired reading, you may be asked to use additional specific strategies which have been adopted by your school or requested by outside professionals when teaching literacy. This may be a strategy such as a story mountain or writing frame which will help children to structure what they want to say.

For more on the story mountain or writing frames, go to www.primaryresources.co.uk/ and click on 'English'.

## Use of specific support programmes

As a support assistant, you may not be involved in selecting specific support programmes, but it is very likely that you will be involved in their implementation. Government materials are often used in schools as they are easy to follow and do not require a large amount of planning. For example, at the time of writing, you may work on reading recovery or FLS (Further Literacy Support) programmes in school, both of which have a series of prescribed lesson plans which you should follow. In some cases you may find that you have too many activities to carry out with the group and you will need to go at their pace to ensure that pupils have the maximum benefit. You should ensure that you speak to teachers and give them feedback about how the sessions are going and ask for advice if necessary.

### Skills builder

What kinds of support programmes does your school have in place to support literacy? Make a list through speaking to your literacy coordinator. How many of these have you been involved with?

## Support strategies to meet the individual needs and learning targets of learners

If a child you are supporting has special educational needs (SEN), you will need to make sure that you understand what these needs are and have discussed them with the teacher or SENCO (Special Educational Needs Co-ordinator). Alternatively they may have literacy support needs and require additional help

in the literacy lesson. You should always agree the strategies which are to be used with children who need extra help or who have specific educational targets or an individual education plan (IEP). If the child has problems with reading or writing skills, these may be addressed in the form of more individual help to prompt the child to think about points which have been discussed in class. These may take the form of specific writing support programmes or small targets which are to be built up. The school may have additional resources to provide small group work for some of these children, so that they have more focused help.

### Portfolio activity

Make a copy of a learning plan for a pupil you are supporting who has additional literacy needs. Ensure this includes information about the kinds of resources you have used and how regularly the support is given. Alternatively, show it to and talk it through with your assessor when they observe you in school, and you will not need to include it in your portfolio.

### Functional skills

**ICT: Using ICT**

You could select a program on the computer that would allow you to create a list of what resources you have available to use in literacy, where they are stored and how many of them you have. A suitable programme to use may be Microsoft® Excel®.

### CASE STUDY: Meeting the individual needs of learners

David has dyslexia and has always found reading and writing challenging. He is in your class, Year 4, but does not have a support assistant, although you are often asked to work with him during literacy sessions. The class teacher has developed a learning plan for him alongside the SENCO but has not shown this to you.

- What can you do to meet David's individual needs in class?
- How should you approach the class teacher about sharing David's learning plan?

# Be able to support learners in developing speaking/talking and listening skills

## Strategies for supporting learners to develop speaking/talking and listening skills

You will need to develop children's speaking/talking and listening skills in a number of contexts, not just in literacy sessions. Although children will need to develop these skills in literacy, the context is vital for their general learning.

Speaking/talking and listening are now embedded in the Primary Framework as their importance is acknowledged as fundamental to the development of children's literacy skills. The curriculum specifies how this should be done and gives ideas for its implementation.

During the Early Years Foundation Stage, the prime areas of learning relating to communication and language are at the heart of children's learning experiences. Children will need to demonstrate their listening and attention skills as well as those of speaking and understanding. They should among other things be able to:

- listen attentively in a range of situations
- follow instructions involving several ideas or actions
- express themselves effectively, showing awareness of listeners' needs.

The National Curriculum for Speaking and Listening sets out the skills which are to be developed over Key Stages 1 and 2. During Key Stage 1, as children develop their use of language, they will learn to respond appropriately to different situations, and to listen carefully to others. By the end of Key Stage 2, children should be able to adapt what they say to the purpose and to their audience.

The school's English policy should outline the shared objectives for developing children's speaking and listening skills.

### Providing opportunities for learners to engage in conversation, discussion and questioning

You will need to ensure that all pupils have the chance to contribute to conversations and discussions with others, whether they are confident or not. Sometimes it will be necessary for you to support those who are less certain about what to say or who have limited understanding of what is being said. For those pupils, you should start by working in smaller groups if possible so that they are able to develop their confidence before asking them to contribute in larger group or class discussions. Many schools run additional groups for pupils with speech and language difficulties or to develop pupil confidence, and you may be asked to help with these.

### Using open-ended questions to encourage learners to contribute to conversations and discussions

Make sure you do not ask learners 'closed' questions which only prompt one-word answers but encourage them through asking those which are more open-ended, such as, 'Why do you think the boy could have been racing through the woods so fast?'

*What strategies do you use to involve quieter learners?*

## Prompting shy or reticent learners to contribute to conversations and discussions and to respond to questions

Although all classrooms will offer children opportunities for speaking and listening, staff will need to be aware of how they can make these beneficial for all children. It is important to observe and make a mental note of those children who are not comfortable in these situations and are reluctant to contribute, as well as children who are overenthusiastic about their own contributions but do not listen to others. Sometimes children may put forward negative comments about the contributions of others during discussions. Adults should always intervene to prevent this kind of intimidation, as it may stop children from speaking in front of others. If pupils speak with different accents or dialects from the majority of children in the class, they should feel comfortable speaking in front of others and should not be discouraged.

Some children may find it very difficult to speak in a class group, and will need to be encouraged to put their ideas forward. Table 2 lists some reasons for this.

| Reason | Ways to support children |
| --- | --- |
| Physical or emotional factors, such as a physical condition or speech difficulty which makes it hard for others to understand a child | Repeat back what they have said to the group after they have finished speaking. Do not interrupt the child or finish sentences for them. |
| Lack of self-esteem due to experiences at home and school | Give them opportunities to succeed, and praise their achievements. |
| Special needs – children with special needs may lack confidence or feel 'different' | Encourage them to talk through particular interests or experiences which they have had. |
| Speaking English or Welsh as an additional language | Reinforce language learning by giving pupils immediate verbal and non-verbal feedback and praise. Give them time to think about questions before they respond. Create more opportunities for speaking and listening, such as paired conversations with others. |

*Table 2: Why children may find it difficult to speak in a group, and how to overcome this.*

## CASE STUDY: Prompting shy or reticent learners

Lewis has a cleft palate which means that he has difficulty in pronouncing some sounds, particularly 's' and soft 'c'. He has been referred to the speech therapist but is still waiting for his first appointment. As time goes on, Lewis is becoming more reluctant to contribute to class discussions.

- Why do you think that Lewis becoming more reluctant to speak as he gets older?
- What could you do to encourage him to contribute?

## Using language and vocabulary which is appropriate to the learners' level of understanding and development

Make sure when you are working with children and young people that you take their age and needs into consideration. You should not use language or vocabulary that they will find difficult to understand. If you need to extend their vocabulary (see below), you should talk to them about the meaning of the word or phrase and then refresh this a few times so that they are able to remember. If you are not sure that they are clear on what you have said, it is worth asking, as children may not feel confident enough to ask you.

## CASE STUDY: Using appropriate language and vocabulary

Dan is working in Year 1 where they are carrying out a data-handling activity in maths. He tells his group to go and draw a table so that they will be able to fill in the data after they have collected it. When he returns to see how they are getting on, several of the children have drawn a kitchen table as they did not know what he meant.

- How could Dan have introduced this activity differently?
- What can he do now that he has discovered the problem, without damaging the pupils' self-esteem?

## Introducing learners to new words and language structures to help extend their vocabulary and structural command of language

You should wherever possible introduce children to new words and language structures and try to remind them of these so that you extend their vocabulary. It is important to do this on a regular basis, for example, when reading stories, using new equipment, introducing a new topic and so on. This may be a word which you think that they should know but which they ask you to explain, or perhaps a saying which they are not familiar with. You may decide as a group to display some of these words or phrases to help the children when they are working on writing activities.

## Opportunities to help learners understand the importance of attentive listening and taking turns to speak

Some children will find it very difficult to sit quietly and listen to others. At a very young age, children will often need to verbalise their thoughts immediately and will find it hard to wait. It may be difficult when children first come to school for them to get used to being part of a large group and having to wait for their turn. They may find activities such as 'circle time', where they need to spend a long time listening to others, quite difficult, or easier to manage in a smaller group. You should not persist in trying to get them to sit still for long periods straight away, but vary group sizes and change the experiences that they have in speaking and listening situations so that they learn why it is important. As children become older, they will need to understand the importance of actively listening to other people (see below) and showing good manners by not interrupting and by responding to others.

## Encouraging learners to contribute to discussions to enhance their self-confidence and self-esteem

Children who are not confident when speaking need to be aware that we value what they have to say. We can show them that we are interested by:

- making eye contact with them when they are talking to us
- smiling or encouraging them to continue while they are talking
- repeating back what they have told us: 'You enjoyed doing some cooking with Mrs Briggs this morning, did you?'
- asking them open-ended questions to encourage them to answer in more detail.

We should also make sure that all pupils are able to contribute and that the topic is within their realm of experience — for example, if the class are talking about snow and you have pupils who have never seen it, or if the majority of the class celebrate a particular festival but some of the children do not.

## Encouraging learners to respond constructively to others' contributions

You may find that you need to encourage some pupils to respond constructively to their peers during conversations and discussions. This means that they are listening to what others are saying and responding, rather than just taking it in turns to say what they want to. We can develop speaking and listening skills in many different situations, although it need not be a planned event. You may find that out of the classroom context, children are more relaxed about speaking, for example, on the playground or when they are working on a project together. Older children, however, may enjoy debates and discussions about set topics, and will be able to adapt their language and ideas accordingly.

## Respond to learners' use of home language and local accents and dialects

You will need to make sure that if you are working with bilingual pupils or children who are from another part of the country, you respond to them appropriately and in a way which values cultural diversity and reinforces positive self-images, and encourage other pupils to do the same. Your school will have a policy for equal opportunities which means that

you should support the positive self-image of each individual by embracing differences and regularly speaking to children about how we are all the same but all different. Make sure that if you hear of any children who are not respecting others by responding inappropriately, you speak to them straight away.

> **CASE STUDY:** Responding appropriately to the learners' local accents
>
> Shelley is working with a small group on an activity to support pupil understanding of specific vocabulary to do with the current topic. One of the children in the group, Adam, is from Yorkshire. He has a strong accent which is different from those of others in the school, which is based in Bristol. Kayleigh, who is also in the group, starts laughing quietly to her friend when Adam begins to speak to the rest of them.
>
> - What does Shelley need to do?
> - Why is it important not to ignore what Kayleigh is doing?

### Portfolio activity

During an assessment visit, speak to your assessor about the needs of pupils you support during literacy activities. You may wish to show them individual education plans (IEPs) and discuss the implications of the needs which the pupils have on their learning.

### Functional skills

**Maths: Representing**
You could calculate what fraction and percentage of the children you work with have an IEP. You could also look at the ratio of children to staff who are there to support them.

### Link

For more on this topic, see Unit TDA 3.17 Support bilingual learners.

## Getting ready for assessment

In order to gather evidence for the assessment criteria of this unit, you will need to show that you have a clear understanding of the pupils you are supporting, particularly any pupils who have special educational needs or who speak English or Welsh as an additional language. Your assessor should also have the opportunity to observe you in a literacy session and you should be able to go through the children's needs with them as part of this process, along with lesson plans, resources and any IEPs. You should also make sure that if you are doing this, you cover as many of the assessment criteria above as possible by reading through them carefully.

## Functional skills

**English: Speaking, listening and communication**
It is important to remember when supporting children's literacy that you are a role model to them. You could hold a discussion with your assessor or tutor that focuses on your literacy targets. Is there any area in which you feel you need support to develop your skills further? You could look at your continuing professional development (CPD) requirements to see if there are any courses available that you could attend to support you in your role.

## Websites and references

www.literacytrust.org.uk – National Literacy Trust
http://nationalstrategies.standards.dcsf.gov.uk/eyfs/site/requirements/learning/goals.htm – Primary Framework: Literacy
www.primaryresources.co.uk – Click on 'English' for more on writing frames and story mountains
www.education.gov.uk – Search for 'EYFS' for more information on the Early Years Foundation Stage

- Ros Wilson and VCOP: www.primaryresources.co.uk/english/pdfs/LiteracyResourceCard.pdf www.freewebs.com/miketemple/VCOP%201.doc
- *What works for pupils with literacy difficulties? The effectiveness of intervention schemes* (Department for Education and Skills, 2002, ref: 00688-2007BKT-EN, www.education.gov.uk/research/data/uploadfiles/RR380.pdf)

## Check your knowledge

1. Why is learning provision for literacy important?

2. What information should you have from the school before you start to deliver literacy intervention programmes?

3. Name four strategies which will support the teaching of reading.

4. How can you encourage pupils and support them in gaining confidence with their literacy skills?

5. Where would you find out about support strategies and individual programmes and targets for learners?

6. What kinds of strategies might you use to encourage pupils who are not confident about speaking in a large group?

7. Why is it so important to be mindful of a child's self-esteem when they are carrying out speaking and listening activities?

8. What kinds of activities might you try with older pupils to encourage them to speak?

# TDA 3.12 Support numeracy development

This unit is for those who support numeracy development in schools. You may be working in a mainstream or special school and be supporting numeracy as part of the main numeracy lesson or as an intervention group. You will need to be able to develop pupil's numeracy skills so that they are able to use and apply mathematics in different situations.

## By the end of this unit you will:

1. understand current local and organisational frameworks for mathematics

2. be able to support learners in developing numeracy skills

3. be able to support learners in using and applying mathematics.

# Understand current local and organisational frameworks for mathematics

## The aims and importance of learning provision for numeracy development

Learning provision for **numeracy** development is important for pupils as maths is a key part of our everyday lives. There can sometimes be too much emphasis on formal recording of 'sums' which, if introduced too early, can hinder pupils' progress in thinking mathematically. You should also be aware that maths may be taught very differently from your own experiences in school. This is because there is now a much greater emphasis, particularly in the early primary phase, on teaching children different methods of arriving at an answer, showing them different methods of working, and developing investigation skills.

The aim of the mathematics curriculum is to give children a solid grounding in all aspects of numeracy on which they will be able to base their working. A key aspect of developing skills in maths is that pupils understand its purpose and can learn to apply it to real-life situations. Mathematical skills are therefore developed in the earliest stages through practical work, which gives children a grounding in aspects of maths such as shape, pattern, counting, sorting and so on. As children progress, they build on these skills. You will need to have an awareness of the skills that children in your class will be working towards in order to support them fully and help them to access the curriculum.

### Key term

**Numeracy** — a proficiency which involves confidence and competence with numbers and measures

### Over to you!

In your own words, write a reflective account to outline why learning provision for numeracy development is important. How are numeracy skills made accessible to all pupils in your school?

### Functional skills

**English: Writing and reading**
When writing your account, it is important to think about your spelling, punctuation and grammar. You could also include a quote to support your work that you have found in a relevant article. This is a good way of developing your reading and writing skills.

## The national curriculum framework for mathematics including age-related expectations

In Reception classes, teachers will follow the Foundation Stage Curriculum for mathematics for children who are 40-60+ months old. Mathematics is one of the specific areas of learning and development:

- numbers
- shape, space and measures.

The expectations for the end of the Foundation Stage are expressed as early learning goals for each aspect of the subject area. For example, for number they are currently as follows:

- count reliably with numbers from 1 to 20, place them in order and say which number is one more or one less than a given number
- use quantities and objects to add and subtract two single digit numbers and count on or back to find the answer
- solve problems, including doubling, halving and sharing.

In England and Wales, the National Primary Numeracy Framework is a recommended structure for the teaching of numeracy which includes seven strands of learning across the entire primary phase, including the Foundation Stage. Learning objectives are then aligned to the seven strands so that progression can be seen in different areas. The seven strands are:

- using and applying mathematics
- counting and understanding number
- knowing and using number facts

- calculating
- understanding shape
- measuring
- handling data.

*(Source: Primary Numeracy Framework, Standards site: http://nationalstrategies.standards.dcsf.gov.uk/node/110240)*

The age-related expectations can currently be found in the document *Primary Framework for Literacy and Mathematics (DFES 2006)* or in the national archive website: http://webarchive.nationalarchives.gov.uk/20110202093118/http://nationalstrategies.standards.dcsf.gov.uk/node/18687.

This lists the core learning by year group or by strand.

In Scotland, there is no requirement to follow the Primary Framework, although numeracy is divided into three main areas:

- information handling
- number, money and measurement
- shape, position and movement.

In Northern Ireland the curriculum was reviewed in 2007 and was phased in over the following two years. Mathematics and numeracy are now divided into the following areas in Key Stages 1 and 2:

- processes in mathematics
- number
- measures
- shape and space
- handling data.

The Northern Ireland website gives up-to-date developments in the curriculum. Look under 'Curriculum and assessment' at www.deni.gov.uk

It is likely that your school policy will identify how numeracy is taught throughout the school and how standards are monitored and assessed. You should make sure that you are also up to date with latest national developments in your home country, as these are now available online.

### Skills builder

You will need to show that you know and understand the National Curriculum Framework for Mathematics which is relevant to your school, in this case the Foundation Stage and Primary National Framework. You can do this by writing a reflective account to outline the different stages.

### Functional skills

**ICT: Finding and selecting information**
When writing your reflective account, you may need to include information from the relevant site. Searching the site for the information you require is a good way of developing your ICT skills. It is important to take account of any copyright restrictions on the information.

## The organisation's policy and curriculum framework for mathematics

If you are supporting pupils' numeracy development, you will need to be aware of your responsibilities under your school's mathematics or numeracy policy. This will outline your school's approach to the teaching of different aspects of maths as defined by local and national guidelines. It is likely that your school policy will identify how numeracy is taught throughout the school and how standards are monitored and assessed. You should make sure that you are also up to date with latest national developments in your home country, as these are now available online.

### Portfolio activity

Either include a summary of your numeracy policy or outline its aims and objectives and key points, highlighting how it relates to what you do in the classroom.

## The teacher's programme and plans for mathematics teaching and learning

If you are supporting children's learning in numeracy, as in any other subject area, you should have some prior discussion or knowledge of the planned activities and how you are going to support them. In many schools, support staff will be given plans in advance or they may be on display in the classroom. You may also be involved in planning with the teacher and be able to give your own ideas as to how you might approach activities with pupils when you are at the planning stage. You may have an input into planning for other subject areas which support the development of numeracy skills – for example, in science activities. The Primary Framework for Mathematics gives a list of key objectives for each year group from Reception to Year 6. Examples of some of the skills needed in Reception are:

● find one more or one less than a number from one to ten

● use language such as 'circle' or 'bigger' to describe the shape and size of solids and flat shapes

● talk about, recognise and recreate simple patterns.

By Year 6, examples of the skills children are learning are:

● express one quantity as a percentage of another; find equivalent percentages, decimals and fractions

● visualise and draw on grids of different types where a shape will be after reflection, after translations, or after rotation through 90 degrees or 180 degrees about its centre or one of its vertices

● solve problems by collecting, selecting, processing, presenting and interpreting data, using ICT where appropriate; draw conclusions and identify further questions to ask.

*(Source: Primary Framework for Mathematics: Learning Objectives.)*

Your teacher will plan from the Primary Framework for Mathematics which sets out areas for learning by dividing them into blocks – for example, pupils will

study Handling Data and Measures during the year in three two-week units. Your school may allocate a set time each day for maths or this may be up to individual teachers – you will need to show how this is managed in your school.

### Knowledge into action

To cover this assessment criterion, include a copy of a weekly plan which you have annotated showing how you work with the teacher on a daily basis. How does the learning programme fit together?

# Be able to support learners in developing numeracy skills

## Strategies for supporting learners to develop numeracy skills

When planning mathematics, there are seven strands under the Primary National Strategy. These are then given objectives so that progression can be made within each strand. Children should have a range of opportunities to practise and to improve their competencies and to develop their **numeracy skills**. You will need to be able to show that you can support learners in developing these in each of the six strands listed here using the different strategies above. The seventh strand, using and applying mathematics, is explored in more detail on page 229.

### Key term

**Numeracy skills** – covers the skills needed to use and apply mathematics including: counting and understanding number; knowing and using number facts; calculating; understanding shape; measuring; handling data

You should check the Primary National Strategy for a detailed breakdown of the numeracy skills that pupils will need to develop during primary school.

| UNICORN PRIMARY SCHOOL – Maths Planning | | | |
|---|---|---|---|
| **NC YEAR:** 6 | **Teachers –** S Johnson | | **BLOCK/UNIT:** B2 <br> **BEGINNING:** 18th Jan 2010 |
| **DAY** | **ORAL/MENTAL** (highlighted LO means EOY expectation) | **Main Teaching** (highlighted LO means EOY expectation, key questions also highlighted) | **SUCCESS CRITERIA** |
| 1 | LO: I can add, subtract, multiply and divide whole numbers and decimals in my head <br><br> The answer is 12.6. what is the question? <br> Make up a question involving addition that has the answer 0.04. now try subtraction/x/÷ <br> How would you work out 25x9? And 96÷6? <br> What is 1.3÷4? How can you work out if your answer is correct? <br> Make sure all know what the inverse means. | LO: I can use my knowledge of multiplication facts to derive related facts <br> Intro – Give a variety of multiplication and division facts to solve, eg 0.6x4, 0.08x?=32, etc <br><br> Activity <br> AAR and AR: Working through missing number sums using multiplication, division and decimals <br> BAR: working on mainly multiplication an division using number facts, moving on if they complete quickly <br> Plenary: Review completed work <br> Resources: SP (teaching assistant to work with BAR group) <br><br> Extension: If chn finish, ask them to start from a 2 digit number with at least 6 factors (eg 72). How many diff multiplication and division facts can you make using what you know about 72? What facts involving decimals can you derive? What if you started with 7.2 or 0.72? | • Chn able to look at a sum and work out how to solve it using what they know about number <br> • Chn able to explain their method and reasoning <br><br> **Exceeding/ Not reaching** <br><br> All completed this but some errors from all children with those in set B. Jerry needed lots of help from SP and could not recognise the inverse, had to work out whole sum again. <br> All started extension – complete tomorrow. |

*Part of a maths plan.*

The learning objectives below are a progression of the skills pupils will be developing in each area throughout the primary phase.

## Counting and understanding number

Pupils will need to learn number names and to count with confidence from an early age. They will need to start to use vocabulary such as 'more' or 'less', compare numbers, count on and back, order numbers, round to the nearest 10, estimate, and recognise equivalents and positive and negative integers.

## Knowing and using number facts

Pupils will need to learn the relationships between numbers and will start to look out for patterns. They will look at the links between addition and subtraction, and division and multiplication. They will need to know number bonds to 10 and be able to transfer this knowledge to know and understand 20+80, 200+800, and so on.

## Calculating

Pupils will need to be able to calculate confidently using the four operations of addition, subtraction, multiplication and division. They will start with very practical addition and subtraction, and move on to recorded and mental methods. They will need to know and understand place value.

## Understanding shape

Pupils should have the opportunity to explore 2D and 3D shapes and to describe and classify them. They will make models, shapes and patterns, and talk about their features. They will learn to recognise and use reflective symmetry and translations in 2D shapes.

| Type of equipment/ resources | Where stored | Year group | Sign in/ out? |
|---|---|---|---|
| | | | |
| | | | |

Table 1: Listing mathematical equipment and resources.

## Measuring

Pupils will estimate, measure, weigh and compare objects using standard and non-standard units, use vocabulary such as 'greater', 'smaller', 'heavier'

### DVD activity

**Video clip 2 – Understanding shapes or measures**
As it covers such a wide range of topics and children will have varying abilities, mathematics can often be a challenging subject to support. In this clip, the teaching assistant is working with a lively group of Year 1 children. She has given them an opportunity to 'play' with the shapes first before giving them a task.

1. Why might this be an effective strategy? Looking at the list of strategies for supporting numeracy activities, how many more of these does the assistant use? Do you think that she could have used more? How does she use praise, commentary and assistance to promote pupils' learning?

2. Effective advance planning will also mean that you will have the opportunity to prepare mathematical resources (including ICT equipment) and familiarise yourself with them. Although the resources may be familiar to you, how do you know how to use them correctly? Draw up a table like the one below showing the location of mathematical equipment and resources in your school.

and 'lighter' to compare quantities. They will know and understand the relationships between different units of measure, for example, kilometres to metres, grams to kilograms. They will need to learn how to read different scales and interpret these on a range of measuring instruments. They should be able to calculate the perimeter and area of regular shapes, and estimate the area of an irregular shape.

## Handling data

Children will start by sorting familiar objects and identifying similarities and differences. They will need to learn to answer questions by collecting and recording data in different ways such as lists and tables, and start to use block graphs, pictograms and ICT to show their results. They will start to use Venn or Carroll diagrams to sort data and objects. Children will then start to construct different ways of recording to show the frequencies of events and changes over time, and later start to look at solving problems using data collection.

Strategies for supporting learners to develop numeracy skills and to use and apply mathematics include:

- helping learners to interpret and follow instructions
- reminding learners of teaching points made by the teacher
- questioning and prompting learners
- helping learners to select and use appropriate mathematical resources
- explaining and reinforcing correct use of mathematical vocabulary
- using praise, commentary and assistance to encourage learners to stay on task
- introducing follow-on tasks to reinforce and extend learning.

You will need to use these kinds of strategies when you are supporting pupils to develop their numeracy skills. It is likely that you will do this spontaneously as you get to know and respond to the pupils' needs and develop your working relationship with the teacher. You may always work with the same group during numeracy activities or move around the class on different days of the week – however you work, you should ensure that you are proactive in your support while gauging the needs of the children.

## Helping learners to interpret and follow instructions

Pupils with whom you are working on numeracy skills may find it hard to recall instructions or follow a series of points which the teacher has explained. You may need to be able to help them to follow what is required. You can do this by first questioning them to check their understanding or by asking them to repeat back to you what they think they need to do next.

## Reminding learners of teaching points made by the teacher

If pupils are finding a task challenging, you may need to remind them about specific teaching points to enable them to continue with the task. This may be because of their individual learning needs or their ability to focus on a task.

---

**CASE STUDY:** Helping learners to interpret instructions

Tom is working in Year 3 with a class who is focusing on partitioning of number in numeracy. After the main teaching activity they have been asked to look at a range of numbers and partition them into their component parts, then write a number sentence beneath. Tom tells the group he is working with to start the activity and see how they get on. As they do this, several of the children need the instructions to be clarified. Later on, Tom notices that two of the children in his group have started to do the partitioning activity but are finding this difficult. He also sees that they have not written anything underneath and are carrying on with the activity.

- How could Tom have approached the activity differently with his group?
- What might he do to support the learners now, so that they are able to gain the most from the activity?

---

## Questioning and prompting learners

It is likely that you will use this strategy regularly with all pupils, as children will often need to be refocused or to be asked specific questions to redirect their thinking. When questioning pupils, you should make sure that you ask in a way which does not 'lead' them to the answer.

For more on questioning learners, see the Using and applying mathematics section in learning outcome 3.

## Helping learners to select and use appropriate mathematical resources

You may need to prompt pupils or encourage them to think about resources available to them when working on numeracy activities. These resources may include number lines, measuring instruments, games, computer software and learning programmes. Pupils may need help if they have been asked to carry out an activity with unfamiliar resources. They may not have used some items before and younger children should be given the opportunity to look at and explore what they will be using before starting the activity. If pupils have sensory support needs, you may need to speak to specialist teachers to find out what additional resources are available.

## Explaining and reinforcing correct use of mathematical vocabulary

You should always reinforce vocabulary which is being used by the teacher and also extend pupil vocabulary and check their understanding of any terms used. Young children, or pupils who speak English as an additional language, for example, may need you to explain mathematical terms to them. The old numeracy strategy published an excellent booklet to support the development of mathematical vocabulary; maybe you can find a copy in your school (see end of unit). An example of the kind of vocabulary you might use by area is shown below.

---

### Year 3

#### Numbers, place value and ordering

Odd, even, every other, how many times?, multiple of, sequence, continue, predict, pattern, pair, rule, relationship, 'teens' number, the same number as, as many as, equal to, greatest, most, biggest, largest, less, fewest, smallest, one more/less, ten more/less, compare, order, size, first, second, third… tenth… twentieth, last, before, after, next, between, halfway between, above, below.

*(Source: The National Numeracy Strategy – Mathematical Vocabulary, ref. DfES 0313/2000.)*

---

## Using praise, commentary and assistance to encourage learners to stay on task

While learners are working on numeracy activities, you will need to support them through talking to them in different ways to encourage them to stay on task. You should always use praise wherever possible as it is an excellent motivator and gives children confidence. Commentary, or talking through with children what they are doing as they are doing it, enables them to become more familiar with the mathematical language they are using and also encourages them to think through the process as they are working. Children may also sometimes need a level of assistance in order to complete tasks, although you should be careful that you do not carry out tasks for them. If they are too challenging for the pupils, you will need to speak to the teacher.

---

### Functional skills

ICT: Using ICT

English: Speaking, listening and communication
You could ask for permission to use a voice recorder and record yourself supporting children with numeracy. You could then play it back and reflect on the different strategies that you use. This is a good way of developing your ICT skills and reflecting on your speaking, listening and communication skills.

---

### CASE STUDY: Using praise, commentary and assistance

Joel is in Year 2 and lacks confidence during numeracy activities. Today the class is working on a calculations task to use repeated subtraction. He has quickly become distressed as during the lesson opener the children are sitting in a circle and are going round taking away from a number in multiples of 2. You can see that he is trying to work out what number it will be when it reaches him.

- What could you do to reassure Joel in this instance?
- Could you suggest another way in which he might join in with the activity without feeling under pressure?

### Introducing follow-on tasks to reinforce and extend learning

The teacher may have given additional tasks (such as problem-solving tasks, mathematical games, puzzles) for pupils to work on if they have finished the initial activity. More able children may be asked to develop concepts and find their own objectives, but it is likely that you will still need to check through these with them. Follow-on or extension activities should be linked to the task and may take the form of more open-ended activities. (For more on this, see the section on using and applying mathematics on pages 229–31.)

## Support strategies to meet the individual needs and learning targets of learners

You will need to know and be able to use support strategies which will meet the individual needs and learning targets of learners. It is likely that all children in your class will have a specific maths target of which they will be aware, or which is easy for them to find. A pupil who has difficulty in remaining focused, for example, may need you to check that they have understood what they need to do when they start a task, whereas a child whose target is to know their number bonds to 10 may need you to check their knowledge of this and support them in finding ways to remember them at regular intervals.

Another support strategy you may be asked to work on with pupils are intervention groups which focus on different levels.

● Wave 1: inclusion of all pupils in high-quality lessons through differentiation.

● Wave 2: small group intervention, designed to supplement lessons for pupils working just below age-related expectations.

● Wave 3: one-to-one targeted intervention for pupils working well below age-related expectations.

*What support do your pupils need when using mathematical resources?*

At the time of writing, the main intervention programme in mathematics is known as Springboard maths, although schools may devise and run their own intervention programmes based on the needs of pupils. These sessions focus on key areas of number and are designed to be run in small groups outside the daily maths lesson and complement the structure of the Primary Framework. There are materials for pupils in Years 3 to 7.

You may also be working with children who have a statement of special educational needs, or are on School Action or Action Plus due to their mathematical understanding. Children who have special educational needs (SEN) may be working at a very different level from others in the class. You may find that you are supporting a child or group of children who need specific help with mathematical tasks. The special needs which you may experience in mainstream schools may cover a wide range of difficulties, and it is not possible to include them all here. The child may, for example, need specific help with vocabulary or speech and language, or have a visual impairment which makes it difficult to use some mathematical equipment. Your class teacher will need to seek advice from the school's Special Educational Needs Co-ordinator (SENCO) and other agencies outside the school for the best strategies to use with particular children.

### Link

See also Units TDA 3.19 and TDA 3.20 for supporting children with special needs.

You may also support pupils through the use of specific programmes such as Springboard maths. The DfES produced a particularly useful publication for supporting pupils with specific needs during the daily mathematics lesson which can be found on teachernet (see reference at end of unit). Pupils who speak English as an additional language may also need specific support during numeracy lessons in order to check their understanding and develop their learning. Many of the ideas and concepts explored in mathematics require children to have a good grasp of mathematical vocabulary as well as the cognitive and academic language required. The introduction

to the Framework for teaching mathematics gives guidelines for working with these pupils and places an emphasis on participation with other children, particularly in oral work such as counting aloud, number songs and so on, and the use of practical activities. You should also seek guidance from your local Ethnic Minority Achievement Service (EMAS) branch if possible about the particular needs of these children.

### CASE STUDY: Support strategies to meet the individual needs of learners

Alex is working in Year 3 and the group is learning to use addition and subtraction facts for all their numbers to 20. They are working on missing number sums on their tables. Alex can see that some of the pupils who are below average ability are finding the activity difficult. She knows that they need to learn the facts but sees that they are not doing this quickly. She therefore uses some cubes of different colours and asks them all to make towers of 10 starting with one, two, three or four blue cubes and then to make the towers up to 10 using a different colour.

- Why might the use of resources help in this instance?
- Can you think of other mathematical resources which may help the children in this situation?

# Be able to support learners in using and applying mathematics

## Strategies for supporting learners to use and apply mathematics to solve problems

As with developing numeracy skills, you will need to use a range of strategies such as those already discussed for supporting learners in **using and applying mathematics** to solve problems.

## Key term

**Using and applying mathematics** – problem solving or pursuing a line of enquiry that involves representing ideas using numbers, symbols or diagrams, reasoning and predicting and communicating results orally or in writing

The numeracy booklet *Mathematical Vocabulary* gives ideas and examples of different types of question. Examples of these are:

- recalling facts, for example, 'What is 5 add 6?'

- applying facts, for example, 'Tell me how you would find out how far it was from one side of the playground to the other'

- hypothesising or predicting, for example, 'Estimate how many there are'

- designing and comparing procedures, for example, 'How could you subtract 47 from 93?'

- interpreting results, for example, 'What can we see when we look at the graph?'

- applying reasoning, for example, 'How many different ways can three eggs go into an egg box?'

These different types of questions show the ways in which you can challenge pupils engaged in maths activities by giving them open as well as closed questions. You should always try to ask the pupil as much as possible by guiding them round the task rather than giving them direct instructions.

## Using and applying mathematics – examples of problems taken from the Primary National Strategy for Mathematics in Year 6 – Crown 2007

Solve multi-step problems, and problems involving fractions, decimals and percentages; choose and use appropriate calculation strategies at each stage, including calculator use.

1. Jemima thinks of a number. She says, 'Add 3 to my number and then multiply the result by 5. The answer is 35.' What is Jemima's number? Riaz thinks of a number. He says, 'Halve my number and then add 17. The answer is 23.' What is Riaz's number?

2. In a supermarket storeroom there are:

- 7 boxes of tomato soup

- 5 boxes of pea soup

- 4 boxes of chicken soup.

There are 24 tins in every box. How many tins of soup are there altogether?

3. Sapna and Robbie have some biscuits. Altogether they have 14 biscuits. Sapna has 2 more biscuits than Robbie. How many biscuits do Sapna and Robbie each have?

4. Parveen has the same number of 20p and 50p coins. She has £7.00. How many of each coin does she have?

## Functional skills

**English: Speaking, listening and communication**
You could choose one of the problems above and present it to your study group using the strategies that you would use with the children. Your study group could give you feedback on how you presented the information and this would help you to develop both your confidence and your speaking, listening and communication skills.

## CASE STUDY: Using and applying mathematics

Anneka is working in Reception with a group of children who have been asked to sort some different materials in any way they like. They have a selection of different-coloured plastic animals, vehicles, dinosaurs and insects.

- What kinds of questions do you think Anneka should use with the children?
- How could she ensure that each child has the opportunity to pursue their own ideas and methods?

## Support strategies to meet the individual needs and learning targets of learners

When using and applying mathematics in order to solve problems, pupils will often need to think about how they are going to organise their work and what is the best method to use. As this can be very language based, pupils who have learning difficulties or who speak English as an additional language may need to have the problem presented in a way which is more accessible to them – for example, you may need to reword the problem or activity for them. You may need to explain things to pupils in a different way or give them more time to think about how they will approach the problem, or give them more opportunities to ask you questions. Pupils who are more anxious about maths activities may need the reassurance of talking through what they are going to do or having adult support available if they need to ask questions while they are working. If pupils find a particular strand of numeracy difficult, you may need to focus on this aspect of the problem with them. (For more on targets and special educational needs, see page 263.)

(For more on targets and special educational needs, see page 263.)

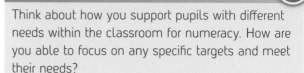

### Reflect

Think about how you support pupils with different needs within the classroom for numeracy. How are you able to focus on any specific targets and meet their needs?

### CASE STUDY: Supporting the individual needs of learners

Sohail has dyscalculia, which means that he finds it very difficult recognising and writing down numbers. He suffers from a lack of confidence during most mathematical tasks. He can lose track sometimes when organising his thoughts methodically, but has discovered that it helps him to draw diagrams when working through a problem.

- Apart from encouraging Sohail to draw his diagrams, what other strategies might you use to support him during problem-solving tasks?
- How else could you help Sohail with his confidence during problem-solving activities?

*How can you help pupils engage with learning?*

> **BEST PRACTICE CHECKLIST:** Working on using and applying activities
>
> - Look at the question together and ask pupils what they need to find out.
> - Identify with pupils the information or calculations needed to solve the problem.
> - Use questions to develop pupils' thought processes.
> - Encourage pupils to set out their working in a methodical way.
> - Explain reasoning using words, symbols or diagrams.
> - Encourage children to give explanations both orally and in writing.

## Encourage learners to pursue their own lines of enquiry and find their own solutions to mathematical problems

Pupils are often given more open-ended and problem-solving activities to carry out either independently or within whole-class and group activities. It is likely that you will be encouraged to support pupils as they work through their own lines of enquiry and find their own solutions to problems in a variety of ways (see also TDA 3.7, Support assessment for learning). Depending on their confidence, children will often enjoy the creativity which this affords them, although when they first start to develop their ideas they may need to have some guidance from adults to make sure that they stay on the right track and are following learning objectives. The more pupils are actively involved in their own learning, the greater their motivation and self-esteem. A key aspect of supporting pupils through this will be through questioning to develop their thought processes and encourage them to think about the consequences of each stage.

## Getting ready for assessment

In order to gather evidence for this unit, you will need to show that you have a clear understanding of the needs of the pupils whom you are supporting. Your assessor should have the opportunity to observe you in a numeracy session and you should be able to go through the children's needs with them as part of this process, along with lesson plans, resources, and any individual education plans (IEPs) or learning targets for pupils with additional needs. You should also make sure that if you are doing this, you cover as many of the assessment criteria as possible by reading through them carefully first.

### Websites and references

**www.education.gov.uk/publications/standard/ publicationDetail/Page1/DFE-00023-2012** – Statutory Framework for the Early Years Foundation Stage
**http://webarchive.nationalarchives.gov. uk/20110202093118/http://nationalstrategies. standards.dcsf.gov.uk/node/18687** – You can find the Primary Mathematics Framework here
**www.teachernet.gov.uk** – go to online publications and search by title: Guidance to support pupils with specific needs in the daily mathematics lesson (DfES reference 0545 2001)

- The National Numeracy Strategy – Mathematical Vocabulary (DfES reference 0313/2000)
- Primary National Strategy – Primary Framework for Literacy and Mathematics (reference 02011 – 2006BOK- EN)

## Check your knowledge

1. What are the national requirements for numeracy teaching in your home country?

2. Why is it important that you should have numeracy plans in advance?

3. How can you ensure that you use a range of different strategies when supporting mathematics with children?

4. How many different strands are there in the Primary National Strategy for maths?

5. Which of these strategies might you use with a pupil or group who need to develop their numeracy skills?

   - helping learners to interpret and follow instructions
   - reminding learners of teaching points made by the teacher
   - questioning and prompting learners
   - helping learners to select and use appropriate mathematical resources
   - explaining and reinforcing correct use of mathematical vocabulary
   - using praise, commentary and assistance to encourage learners to stay on task
   - introducing follow-on tasks to reinforce and extend learning.

6. What kinds of intervention programmes are available for pupils who are below average ability in numeracy?

7. Why is the strand of using and applying mathematics sometimes more challenging for children?

# TDA 3.17 Support bilingual learners

This unit is for staff who support bilingual learners. It is for teaching assistants who provide support for those who speak English, Welsh or Gaeilge as an additional language. You will need to support them both in developing skills in the target language and enabling them to access all areas of the curriculum.

## By the end of this unit you will:

1. be able to interact with bilingual learners
2. be able to support bilingual learners to develop skills in the target language
3. be able to support bilingual learners to access the curriculum.

# Be able to interact with bilingual learners

## Interact with bilingual learners in a way that demonstrates respect, shows sensitivity and reinforces positive self-image

You will need to show when you are interacting with **bilingual learners** that you take account of and respect each individual and their needs. This means that you should ensure that you are sensitive to their background, culture and beliefs. In order to do this you will need to find out about their home, language and educational backgrounds. Although there will be systems in place in your school for finding out some initial pupil information, you should also take time to get to know the children with whom you are working and their families, particularly when they first start at the school or when you first start working with them.

### Key term

**Bilingual learners** — pupils who have been exposed to two or more languages, both those newly arrived and new to the language used to deliver the curriculum, and those more advanced bilingual learners who can communicate confidently but need further support in academic contexts

The pupil's home background is important as this will have the greatest influence on the child. Children whose home backgrounds have been traumatic, such as refugees, may have had wide and varied educational experiences. The school needs to obtain as much information as possible and if possible seek the help of an interpreter so that discussions can take place directly with parents. The experiences a child has had may also affect their behaviour; for example, if they are non-responsive, this may be because they have suffered a trauma. Children who come from backgrounds with a different culture or religion from the majority of others in the school may feel isolated, and it is important for them that the school values cultural diversity in different ways.

Children's self-image will be directly affected by their perception of how others see them and in

their confidence when using language. Their self-esteem must stem from an acknowledgement and acceptance of themselves, whatever race, language, ethnicity or religion they may have. Children also need to experience a sense of belonging in their surroundings so that they are able to grow in confidence. If their parents do not speak English, this may be a child's first experience of having to communicate with others in a language other than their own. It is important for the child to be able to communicate in school and, although children will usually pick up language reasonably quickly, this can be a difficult time for them. If you notice that any children are finding it hard to make friends, it is important to discuss this with the class teacher. You may also be able to help them to socialise with others, if you are on duty in the playground, through the introduction of playground games.

### Reflect

How do you ensure that you find out about what is important, such as the preferred name which is used by pupils?

### Knowledge into action

What kind of information does your school gather when pupils start at the school? How do they obtain information from parents and what is the procedure for doing this if parents do not speak English themselves?

A child's language background and how much exposure they have had to the target language are also useful things to know. If staff know that the child has never been exposed to the target language before, this knowledge can help them to devise an educational or language plan. Each child will need an education plan that takes age, individual background and learning needs into account, including appropriate targets. Home visits may also be helpful at this stage for getting to know parents and valuing their input, and to involve them as much as possible in their child's learning from the start. Bilingual staff may also be involved so that the mother tongue can be used in the school where needed.

When interacting with bilingual pupils, it is also important that you support and encourage what they are saying through your communication skills.

## Link

For more on this see TDA 3.1, Communication and professional relationships with children, young people and adults.

## Use language and vocabulary which is appropriate to the learner's age, understanding and proficiency in the target language

As you get to know the bilingual and multilingual children pupils you support, you will need to think about the language that you use with them, to ensure that it is appropriate to the child's age and level of understanding. A pupil's age may make a difference to how they learn a **target language** — older pupils may be more self-conscious, and as a result less likely to speak, or be hindered by the higher demands of the curriculum. However, another view is that older children are more experienced at using language and this may make the process easier for them. A younger child may be more relaxed and less anxious about acquiring a new language — for children to attempt to initiate language, they need to feel relaxed and confident that their contributions will be valued. However, the process may take longer, particularly if they are learning two languages at the same time.

*How can you tell if a pupil really understands what has been said?*

If the teacher is talking to the class and has used language which is difficult to understand, you may need to clarify for pupils what has been said. You should also check regularly that they understand — in some cases, pupils may seem to know what is happening or what is being said when they have not really followed it.

### Key term

**Target language** — the additional or second language needed by bilingual learners, for example, English as an additional language (EAL), or Welsh or Gaeilge as a second language

## Be able to support bilingual learners to develop skills in the target language

### The organisation's policy and procedures for supporting bilingual learners

According to government statistics, 15.2 per cent of pupils at primary schools have a mother tongue other than English; over 200 languages are spoken by children who attend British schools. When supporting bilingual and multilingual pupils, all staff will need to think about how they can promote the development of the target language while valuing the child's home language and culture. This is particularly important if the child is an isolated learner in the target language. The school should therefore have its own policies and practices for how children with English as an additional language (EAL) are supported. The different types of strategies which the school has in place may therefore include:

- school policies to promote positive images and role models

- school policies and practices on inclusion, equal opportunities and multiculturalism

- identification of bilingual/multilingual children — for example, photos in staff room so that all staff are aware (if there is only a small group)

- providing opportunities for pupils to develop their language skills

- having established school and class routines
- finding opportunities to talk with parents of bilingual children and encourage links with the school
- celebrating linguistic and cultural diversity.

## Functional skills

### English: Writing
You could write a report that explains the different strategies that your school promotes for supporting EAL. You could do this in the style of a newspaper article so as to practise writing for a different purpose. Think carefully about the layout of your article and the spelling, punctuation and grammar.

Many schools also now have a governor and/or teacher in the school with overall responsibility for EAL pupils. The role of the teacher would be to advise other staff on the kinds of strategies which will be the most effective.

## Portfolio activity

Find out what policies your school has which may be relevant to children from bilingual or multilingual backgrounds. How are bilingual pupils and their families supported within your school community?

## Functional skills

### ICT: Developing, presenting and communicating information
You could produce a leaflet of different services available locally for bilingual learners. You may need to research this on the Internet or through contacting your local borough.

## Theories of first language acquisition and additional language acquisition and learning

There have been a number of theories put forward about how children learn or acquire language. Although there are many theories, there are still no definite answers about how language development takes place. However, most linguists agree that children will pass through two stages — the pre-linguistic and the linguistic stage.

The pre-linguistic stage is during the first 12 months, when babies begin to learn basic communication skills. During this time they will start to attract the attention of adults and repeat back the different sounds that they hear. This is true of any language, but although babies worldwide are born with the potential to make the same sounds, by the age of 12 months they can only repeat back the sounds that they can hear around them.

The linguistic stage is when babies start to use the words that they hear and learn how to make sentences. Children develop this stage gradually over the next few years so that by the age of about 5 years, they are fluent in their home language. Children who learn more than one language may learn to speak slightly more slowly as they absorb different language systems. This should not, however, affect their overall language development.

Table 1 below shows the stages of language development in children. Adults need to support children through all these stages in order to encourage and promote language development. At

| Age | Stage of development |
|---|---|
| 0–6 months | Babies try to communicate through crying, starting to smile and babbling. They start to establish eye contact with adults. |
| 6–18 months | Babies start to speak their first words. They begin to use gestures to indicate what they mean. At this stage, they are able to recognise and respond to pictures of familiar objects. |
| 18 months–3 years | Children start to develop their vocabulary rapidly and make up their own sentences. At this stage, children enjoy simple and repetitive rhymes and stories. |
| 3–8 years | Children start to use more and more vocabulary and the structure of their language becomes more complex. As they develop their language skills, they are able to use language in a variety of situations. |

*Table 1: Ages and stages of language development.*

each stage, the role of the adult may be different. For example, a baby needs positive recognition of their attempts to communicate through eye contact and speech. A 5- or 6-year-old child may need adults to help them to extend their vocabulary through the use of open-ended questions or 'what if?' strategies. Where children's language progresses more slowly through these stages, there may be other factors involved, such as:

● learning more than one language

● a communication difficulty, such as autism

● a speech difficulty, such as a stutter

● lack of stimulation from others

● a hearing impairment.

In the early part of the twentieth century, there were a number of theories with the same broad idea. This was that children acquire language by learning a word together with the thing it means or stands for. Through interacting with adults, they will begin to develop sounds which have meaning and which will gain a positive response. This is called the associationist theory.

Noam Chomsky, an American linguist working in the 1960s, claimed that we are all born with an innate knowledge of the system of language, or a 'Language Acquisition Device'. In this way, whatever language we need to learn and the accompanying grammar will be decoded by the child. This theory helps to explains how children will often apply grammatical rules which they have heard, sometimes wrongly, because they have not yet learned exceptions to these rules. An example of this might be, 'I bringed my drink.'

John Macnamara, working in the 1970s, proposed that children are able to learn language because they have an ability to make sense of situations. This means that they will understand the intention of a situation and respond accordingly. For example, if a child sees that an adult is beckoning towards them and holding out their hand, they will know that the adult's intention is for the child to come towards them. This will be the case even if the child does not understand the words that the adult is saying.

Additional research has taken place into the language acquisition of bilingual children. Patton O. Tabors, an American researcher, states that there is a particular sequence which children will pass through when learning an additional language.

1. At the first stage of learning a new language, children may continue to use their home language in the setting. It is likely that this stage will not last for long.

2. Children may then be silent for a while when they realise that their home language is not being used by others. They may take some time thinking about the new language and 'tuning in' to the new sounds. They may also start to rehearse the sounds to themselves as they build their confidence.

3. Children will start to experiment with individual words and phrases. They will often use lots of repetition or memorised sequences, or routine language and words used together, such as 'good morning' or 'happy birthday'.

4. Children will develop their use of the second language and start to use more complex constructions.

When learning a second language, some of the stages of language acquisition will be the same, and others different. For example, children will be starting the process again but will already have knowledge of a linguistic system. This will help them as they will be able to apply 'labels' to objects they already know. In addition, knowledge of many concepts and aspects will already have been instilled. Their first language will therefore help them in the acquisition of the second. If the first language knowledge is not fully developed, however, it can be difficult to add a second language successfully, and there may even be negative consequences.

Further research has shown that children who are bilingual or multilingual must be able to relate their home language to individuals when they are first learning language. For example, if a child speaks Arabic with their parents, it is important for the child to speak only Arabic with them and not to switch languages when first learning to talk. This is because for the child, it is important to develop a distinction between languages; this is easier for them if they relate to different people.

# Knowledge of language acquisition theories and the needs and interests of learners to support development of the target language

An awareness of language acquisition theories is helpful when supporting the learning and development of the target language. You will need to be aware of the different stages, in particular the silent stage, as children may need additional support during this time. Some strategies for use during this period are suggested by Priscilla Clarke in her book *English as a second language in Early Childhood* (1992).

1. Continued talking even when children do not respond.
2. Persistent inclusion in small groups with other children.
3. Use of varied questions.
4. Inclusion of other children as the focus in the conversation.
5. Use of the first language.
6. Acceptance of non-verbal responses.
7. Praising of minimal effort.
8. Expectations to respond with repeated words and/or counting.
9. Structuring of programme to encourage child to child interaction.
10. Providing activities which reinforce language practice through role play.

In addition, it will help you to develop pupils' skills in the target language if you are aware of their needs and interests, as you will be able to encourage them through the inclusion of specific issues which motivate them.

## Functional skills

### ICT: Using ICT

If you work with a child who has English as an additional language, you could ask for permission to voice-record one of your support sessions. You can then play it back and reflect on your own practice. This will help you to set targets that you need to work towards.

## CASE STUDY: Being aware of the needs and interests of learners

Sobiga is new to the school and speaks very little English. Although you do not work in her class, your daughter who is at the same school says that she has seen Sobiga at her dancing class in the town and that she is a very good dancer.

- How might this information be useful if you spoke to Sobiga's class teacher or teaching assistant?
- What could be done to encourage Sobiga to interact more with other children?

# Ways of introducing learners to new words and language structures to extend their vocabulary and structural command

Children from all backgrounds, whether they are learning one or more languages, need to be given opportunities to develop their language skills in a variety of different ways. However, bilingual learners will need additional support when learning new words and language structures in order to extend their vocabulary. You will need to encourage them and develop their vocabulary in a variety of ways, including through topic-based activities and the use of stories. In addition, if you are working with younger pupils or in intervention groups, you may be focusing on specific vocabulary at different times, for example, positional language (above, below, behind, between, next to and so on). You may need to work with pictures or other resources to help pupils to develop their understanding of these words.

It is also important to remember that there is a difference between the social language in which pupils may be starting to gain fluency and classroom language. This is because in social situations the meaning of what is being communicated is often backed up by visual cues. Classroom language is frequently more abstract and it can be difficult for pupils to tune in to the kinds of functional language required in some learning situations – for example, hypothesising, evaluating, predicting or inferring. It is likely that there will be less visual demonstration to support learning: if you have access to plans, this will be helpful as you may be able to provide support for this.

## BEST PRACTICE CHECKLIST: Working with bilingual learners

- Create a secure and happy environment where the children and their families feel valued and part of the class and school.

- Raise cultural awareness in school for all pupils.

- Involve parents of bilingual and multilingual pupils as much as possible.

- Use strategies that develop self-esteem and confidence.

- Reinforce language learning using resources such as dual-language texts.

- Reinforce language learning by giving children immediate verbal and non-verbal feedback and praise.

- Make sure that children are given time to think about questions before they respond.

- Create more opportunities for speaking and listening. These could include opportunities such as paired conversations with other children.

- Provide visual and physical supports to aid understanding.

# Be able to support bilingual learners to access the curriculum

## Develop learning resources to meet the needs of bilingual learners

If you are responsible for supporting EAL pupils in your school, you should have access to appropriate resources. Your school or Learning Authority (LA) will be able to put you in touch with sources of additional materials and you may have some already in school. The Internet is also an excellent resource, although you may need to have time to look for appropriate sites and programs to use with children (see the end of this unit for a list of websites). You may also be asked to produce resources, in particular if you are a bilingual assistant yourself, in order to support pupil learning. These might include development of displays or wordbanks for pupils, as well as dual-language texts and story sacks. If you find additional resources, you should always check with the teacher before using them with pupils.

## Skills builder

Complete the table below to show the kinds of resources you have used or produced with bilingual and multilingual pupils. An example has been given.

| Type of resource | Source |
|---|---|
| Bilingual reading program for computer | Local EAL advisory teacher |
| | |
| | |
| | |
| | |
| | |

## DVD activity

### Video clip 8 – Supporting EAL pupils

In this clip, the teaching assistant is carrying out a reading activity with a child who speaks English as an additional language. She is using a dual-language book and encourages the child to talk about the story.

1. After filling in the table above to show the kinds of resources available to you when supporting EAL children, think about where you might look for additional resources when required. As well as specific resources to support these children, what kinds of strategies do you use to ensure that teaching and learning experiences are engaging and purposeful for them?

2. As well as having language needs, children with English as a second or third language can sometimes come from backgrounds or circumstances which have had an impact on other areas of their development. How might you obtain and interpret this information? Give examples of the kinds of issues these children may have experienced and outline how these may affect their learning. How might you respond to these issues as part of your role?

# Teaching, learning and assessment methods to support learning and language development

You will need to be able to demonstrate that you use a variety of teaching and learning methods with bilingual pupils. This is because you will need to maximise the opportunities for them to use language in different contexts. You will also need to ensure that there is a mixture of speaking and listening, reading and writing, so that pupils are able to develop in all areas.

## Allowing time for learners to adjust and become familiar with structure and pace of lessons

When first arriving in school, bilingual and multilingual pupils will need to have additional time to adjust to the way in which lessons are structured. They will need additional time to absorb and become used to the way in which teaching and learning takes place — it is possible that they may not have been in school before, or their previous educational background may have been very different.

## Explaining learning objectives clearly through visual supports

You should always make sure that pupils are clear on learning objectives and this is particularly important for bilingual pupils. You may need to explain in more straightforward language or use visual representations, and check that pupils understand the purpose of what they are doing.

## Introducing, explaining and using key vocabulary related to subject content

A knowledge and understanding of key vocabulary is vital for all pupils but especially for those who are bilingual. Make sure you know the topic for the term or half-term, and have a list of key vocabulary so that you are prepared and able to explain specific language.

## Providing key visuals and displays

These are particularly helpful for bilingual pupils as you will be giving them a visual representation of the process they will need to go through and the steps they should take when working through tasks.

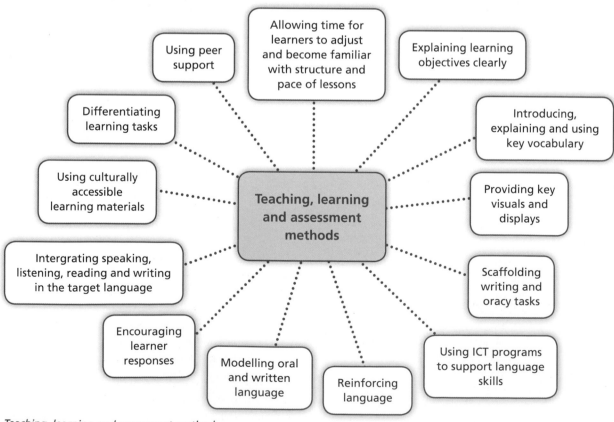

*Teaching, learning and assessment methods.*

## Scaffolding writing and oracy tasks

Scaffolding refers to the process of gradually building up what pupils need to do. For example, in a writing task this may be providing a model so that they have something to work on to support their written work.

## Modelling oral and written language

This refers to your role in demonstrating the correct form of written or spoken language to pupils. It is likely that you will do this subconsciously but you may need to work on specific vocabulary or text together.

## Using ICT programs to support language skills

You may find that there is a range of ICT programs which will support the specific language skills which you need to work on with pupils — for example, when working on comprehension activities. For ideas, you may need to ask your SENCO (Special Educational Needs Co-ordinator) or others in school who support bilingual pupils.

## Integrating speaking, listening, reading and writing in the target language

Bilingual pupils who are learning to speak English or Welsh as an additional language need to have opportunities to read, listen to and discuss a range of texts in the target language so that they can associate their developing verbal and written skills with the printed page. During literacy lessons they will be able to share texts with the whole class and smaller groups, although you may need to use additional strategies to maximise learning opportunities. Pupils may also need more support during guided reading sessions, but should benefit from these as they will be able to model good practice from other pupils. As with all pupils, they need to experience a wide variety of texts, both fiction and non-fiction, in order to maximise their vocabulary. If a pupil is able to read and understand more than has been expected, you should always continue to extend their vocabulary by discussing the text further.

## Reinforcing language

In most classroom situations, you will be reinforcing language as you are working and interacting with bilingual pupils. However, specific strategies to reinforce language include:

- repeating what the teacher is saying and in particular key vocabulary

- explaining what has been said
- highlighting key vocabulary
- rehearsing with pupils before they respond to a question
- acting as their talk partner
- encouraging them through smiles, nods, gestures and body language
- summarising and recording what has been learned
- revisiting key concepts through questioning.

### Over to you!

Consider the ways in which you reinforce spoken language with pupils when working with them. If you need support with this, ask a colleague to observe you and to note the ways down as you are working.

### Functional skills

**English: Speaking, listening and communication**
Once you have been observed, you may want to hold a discussion in order to get your feedback. Before you meet to discuss your observation, you could consider how you think the session went and what you would have done differently. Listen carefully to the feedback so that you can use it effectively to develop your own practice.

## Encouraging learner responses and promoting interaction using different forms of questioning

In order to encourage learner responses and interactions, you will need to think about the kind of questioning you use with pupils and how you use it. You should vary this according to the needs of the pupils and their level of confidence. For example, a pupil who does not understand what is being said may need you to model rather than persist with questioning, whereas a pupil whose second language skills are more developed will be more confident and able to answer more open questions.

Outline how you would promote interaction in the following cases.

1. A bilingual child is not speaking.

2. A bilingual child does not appear to understand your questioning.

3. A bilingual child does not socialise with others in the class.

4. A group of children from the same community are reluctant to mix with others.

## Using culturally accessible learning materials

Bilingual pupils need to be able to use learning materials which offer a broad cultural representation. You should work with others in school to ensure that pupils have access to resources and materials which do this.

## Differentiating learning tasks

It is important to remember that teaching and learning should be differentiated by ability and that bilingual pupils should not always be grouped with pupils of a lower ability or put together with each other. In order to develop their language, they will benefit from being in groups with pupils who are of the same or mixed ability and who are modelling the correct form of the target language. You should also ensure that learning tasks such as homework are set at a level which is manageable for bilingual pupils.

## Using peer support to promote thinking and talking in first language

Strategies such as using a partner who speaks their first language may help bilingual pupils to gain understanding and develop their ideas. This will in turn increase their confidence as they will have clarified what they need to say.

## Deal with the challenges of the language demands in ways that maintain confidence and self-esteem

The demands of the target language may cause challenges when supporting bilingual/multilingual pupils. If a group or pupil is finding a particular word or activity too challenging, you may need to modify or change what you are doing or saying to accommodate this. You can rephrase what is being asked, so that it is easier for the pupil to understand. If they are still finding an activity difficult as they do not understand what is being asked, you should move on to something different. You should also ensure that you do not spend a lot of time correcting pupils if their written or spoken target language contains errors — it is better to model the correct language or repeat back the correct word or phrase.

Some pupils may take a long time to become confident in a second language and it will be apparent that they understand much more than they are able to say. This is not unusual and staff must not push pupils into talking before they are ready. The most important thing to do is to encourage and

---

**CASE STUDY:** Supporting pupils of mixed ability

Gregory is working with a group of three Year 2 pupils, who all speak Gujarati. Although they have the language in common, their needs are all different.

1. Ahmed speaks very little English and has just come to this country.

2. Mahir has lived here all his life but has always spoken Gujarati at home and needs extra support with his English. He is of average ability.

3. Marian is bilingual and able in her written work, but is very anxious and reluctant to speak English, although she is able to.

- Would you approach the support you give these pupils differently even if you had to group them together?

- How could you balance the needs of the children while supporting them effectively?

praise pupils wherever possible, repeating the correct language structure or learning point back to them so that they develop a positive view of themselves.

It can take longer to detect a specific learning difficulty if a pupil is bilingual. This is because staff may feel that the pupil is finding school more difficult just because of their development of the target language. If you find that a particular child is not able to manage the tasks set as they are not making progress, you should always speak to the class teacher.

---

**CASE STUDY:** Dealing with the challenge of language demands

Cassie is working with Peheli, who is in Year 4. Although she speaks some English, Peheli is very quiet and lacks confidence, particularly in a larger group. Today while they are working on a guided reading activity alongside other pupils, Cassie directs a question at her which Peheli is unable to answer. Cassie repeats the question by rephrasing but then waits for a response.

- What should Cassie do next in order to maintain Peheli's confidence?
- What other strategies could she have used when seeking to find out if pupils understand the text?

---

## Encourage learners to become increasingly independent in their learning

You will need to show that you are encouraging pupils to manage their learning themselves as far as possible as they make progress in the target language. As you should be supporting them both individually and in groups, there should be a natural progression as they become more competent in the target language, although they may continue to need some individual language based support. You may need to use assessment for learning as they progress (see TDA 3.7) so that they can see for themselves how learning is assessed.

## Provide feedback to the teacher on the learner's participation and progress

When working with bilingual and multilingual pupils, you will need to provide frequent feedback to others on their progress in relation to:

- the learning activities
- language development
- subject knowledge, understanding and skills.

In a primary school, the other professionals you will need to report to will be the class teacher, and possibly the SENCO and EAL teachers who may visit the school. You should have opportunities to contribute to meetings and/or paperwork concerning the children with whom you are working, for example, IEPs (Individual Education Plans). It is important that there is a joined-up approach between all those who are working with bilingual pupils, so that their progress can be measured.

---

**CASE STUDY:** Providing feedback to the teacher

Chris is often asked to work with Hulya in Year 4, who has been in school since Reception and is a Turkish speaker. Although her English is good, there are some gaps in her understanding. Hulya does not have an IEP or any kind of learning plan as the teacher has said that she does not need one. Although Chris is asked to work with her, he does not have any specific areas to work on or guidance as to what to do with her. He feeds back to the teacher informally about Hulya when he has the time.

- Is there anything else that Chris could do to monitor Hulya's progress more effectively?
- What should he do if the class teacher were unwilling to help him plan specific activities to help Hulya?

---

## Getting ready for assessment

To gather evidence for this unit, you may wish to speak to your assessor about the pupil or pupils with whom you work and the kinds of strategies you have used to help support their listening, speaking, reading and writing in the target language, and how these relate to the teacher's plans. You can set up a professional discussion to do this, although be clear on the assessment criteria you are aiming to cover.

### Websites and references

The following websites are regularly updated with articles and information to support the inclusion of speakers of additional languages.

**www.britishcouncil.org** – the British Council is the UK's international culture relations body
**www.education.gov.uk** – the standards site has information under EAL learners
**www.mantrapublishing.com** – this company produces a range of books in different languages
**www.naldic.org.uk** – the National Association for Language Development in the Curriculum is an organisation which aims to raise attainment of EAL learners. The website contains a number of links and resources, as well as information on the latest research into bilingualism
**www.teachernet.gov.uk** – Teachernet – type in 'EAL' under 'search'

Bialystok, E. (2001) *Bilingualism in Development: Language, Literacy and Cognition*, Cambridge: Cambridge University Press

Clarke, P. (1992) *English as a Second Language in Early Childhood*, FKA Multicultural Resources Centre, Richmond: Victoria, Australia

## Check your knowledge

1.  Are the following true or false?

    a)  A 'silent period' is normal when children are learning a new language.

    b)  Pupils should be encouraged to talk in the target language as much as possible at every opportunity.

    c)  You should stop any bilingual support once pupils are able to speak in the target language.

    d)  We should correct pupils' mistakes when they are learning another language.

    e)  Bilingual pupils should always be grouped together in classrooms.

2.  What should you take into account when interacting with bilingual pupils?

3.  How might a pupil's age affect their ability to learn a second language?

4.  How can you ensure that you personalise language for individual learners when interacting with them?

5.  Why is it important that you always remember to consider the self-esteem of the pupil when working on language activities, and how can you do this?

6.  Give four examples of strategies you should use when working with bilingual learners.

7.  Where would you go to find resources to support bilingual learners?

# TDA 3.18 Provide bilingual support for teaching & learning

This unit is for those whose role is to provide support for pupils whose first language is different from that in which the curriculum is taught. If you speak another language, you may be asked to use this knowledge to help assess pupils' educational abilities and support needs and contribute to educational reviews. You may also be involved in providing support and liaising with families in order to promote pupil participation.

## By the end of this unit you will:

1. be able to contribute to assessment of bilingual learners
2. be able to provide bilingual support for learners
3. be able to support communication with families of bilingual learners
4. be able to contribute to reviews of communication with families of bilingual learners.

# Be able to contribute to assessment of bilingual learners

## Carry out an initial assessment of bilingual learners using learners' preferred language

An initial assessment provides the necessary information for the careful planning of learning activities needed of newly arrived learners including:

- first language and ethnic background
- fluency in English
- previous educational experience and achievements
- wider needs such as a learner's home situation.

As a bilingual assistant, you may be called upon to carry out an initial assessment of pupils in school. This will be important as it is the quickest and most effective way of finding out information about the pupil. The school will need to work promptly in order to gather as much information as possible about the pupil's background and previous educational experience. This is so that they will be able to consider and devise the most effective way of supporting the pupil from the start. It is also very important for **bilingual learners** and their families that their home language and heritage is recognised in school.

> **Key term**
>
> **Bilingual learners** – those who have been exposed to two or more languages

Bilingual pupils may have always lived in this country or may have recently arrived; they may be reasonably confident in two languages or proficient in their home language but not in the target language. Whatever their background, children will need to know that their culture and status is valued, as this helps them to feel settled and secure, factors which contribute to their being able to develop skills in a new language. Children need to want to learn; if they feel isolated or

| | |
|---|---|
| Name: | Adelina Haliti |
| Date: | 25/09/06 |
| Boy/girl: | Girl |
| Date of birth: | 28/08/2000 |
| Year group: | 2 |
| Date arrived in UK: | 30/06/2006 |
| Date admitted to school: | 06/07/2006 |
| Languages spoken: | Albanian |
| Languages pupil can read: | Albanian |
| Languages pupil can write: | Albanain |
| Previous school in UK: | – |
| Previous school elsewhere: | – |
| Community school: | – |

*Example of a pupil profile – preliminary statement. Source: Primary Induction Training for Teaching Assistants: Inclusion (TDA, 2006).*

anxious, they are more likely to find it difficult. Initial assessments should be carried out in a way which is not intimidating or daunting for them.

As well as seeking information from parents and other schools about pupil background and their home language, you will need to find out about the pupil's wider needs, such as their circumstances and whether there are any issues of which the school should be aware. You should receive guidance from teachers about the kinds of assessment they would like you to carry out and how to go about it. You may also be asked to assess and observe their level of English and to monitor their progress.

The QCA also produced guidance, *A language in common: assessing English as an additional language* on how to assess pupils who are in the early stages of learning English. This is so that there is some standardisation in how bilingual pupils are assessed, although individual local authorities may have produced their own versions. It enables teachers to track pupil progress in speaking and listening, reading and writing. The guidance comprises detailed descriptors for features of English language use up to level 1 of the National Curriculum (ref QCA/00/584).

Following assessment, staff can build up a profile of each pupil. This can then be amended as more information is gathered and pupil levels in speaking and listening, reading and writing can be added.

### Over to you!

What kinds of assessments have you carried out on bilingual pupils who are new to your school? How have you worked with pupils and their families to gain information about their backgrounds, both in their home and target language?

## Work with relevant people to assess the experience, capabilities and learning style of bilingual learners

**Relevant people** in this context may include:

- family members
- teachers responsible for the learner
- ethnic minority achievement co-ordinator

- bilingual language support teacher
- bilingual teaching assistants
- EAL (English as an additional language) specialist teacher
- language co-ordinator
- English/Welsh/Gaeilge language teacher
- relevant local authority advisory or **peripatetic** staff.

If you are working on initial assessments, you should have some additional guidance from teachers and others who are both internal and external to the school as to the work you are required to carry out. All of those who have been and will be involved with the pupil may need to contribute and support the assessment process.

### Functional skills

**Maths: Representing**
Have you carried out any initial assessment of the pupils you work with? If so, then you could calculate what percentage of your class are above, below or average for the level they are working at. You could also calculate the ratio of support to children underachieving in the assessment process.

- **Family members** should work closely with the school, in particular at the initial stages, in order to support them in assessing pupils' backgrounds and experiences.

- **Teachers responsible for the learner** will need to be closely involved as they will need to have a starting point for pupil learning. You should be guided by them as to the kinds of assessments you are required to carry out.

- The **ethnic minority achievement co-ordinator** may be based at the local authority and will co-ordinate the progress of pupils from ethnic

### Key terms

**Relevant people** – those with a need and right to provide and receive information about bilingual learners as relevant to the setting

**Peripatetic** – working in a succession of places, each for a short time

minorities. They may not come to the school but will need to be sent information about whole-school achievement and particularly initial competence in the target language.

- You may have a **bilingual language support teacher** in your school who is able to advise you and the class teacher about how to work on assessments with bilingual pupils who are new to the school.

- There may be **bilingual teaching assistants** in the school with the same role as yourself and with whom you may need to co-ordinate the assessment process.

- The **EAL (English as an additional language) specialist teacher** may come from the local authority in order to support pupils in school who speak English as an additional language. It is likely that they will come on a regular basis and work with staff and pupils in order to help raise achievement. They may also help with initial assessments.

- Your school may have a **language co-ordinator** who will work with you on initial assessments and suggest additional support strategies.

- Although the **English/Welsh/Gaeilge language teacher** will work on the target language, they will be able to advise on initial assessments.

- The local authority may provide other **relevant local authority advisory or peripatetic staff** who are able to give you support when working with bilingual pupils in the initial stages.

### Functional skills

**ICT: Developing, presenting and communicating information**

You could produce an information chart showing all the professionals listed above and how they can be contacted if you required their input. Your chart could be done on the computer and then printed numerous times so you could share this resource with other members of the team you work in.

### Reflect

Which of the professionals above have you been involved with when assessing bilingual learners? How have they supported you in doing this?

## Why a specialist assessment may be required and procedures for arranging this

Most pupils, over a period of time, will be able to understand and communicate in an additional language. It is quite common for pupils to pick up English or Welsh as an additional language quickly when they start school, as they have another language to relate it to. They may need support in order to develop their spoken and written English/Welsh language skills, but as these develop, the support should be required less.

However, in some cases, speaking English/Welsh as an additional language may hide additional language or other needs. As a bilingual teaching assistant, you

---

**CASE STUDY:** Referring pupils for specialist assessment

Nadia has been in school for half a term and started in Reception, and you have recently assessed her language needs. She has always spoken Lithuanian at home and you did not pick up any issues during your language assessment. However, on meeting her mother and discussing her home background, you feel that it would be appropriate to refer Nadia and possibly her family for more specialist assessment as to her care needs. Her mother

appears to be struggling to manage her situation as a single parent in this country and has asked you on several occasions whether you can bring Nadia home from school for her and do her shopping, even though you have explained to her that you are unable to do this. Nadia often appears to be dirty and her clothes and hair are untidy.

- What should you do first?
- How can you best support Nadia and her family?

will be able to tell if pupils are proficient in their own language or not; this can help to assess whether there is a language disorder or learning delay. In this situation, always speak to your class teacher and SENCO (Special Educational Needs Co-ordinator), who will need to refer the pupil for **specialist assessment**, either to an educational psychologist or a speech and language therapist.

## Key term

**Specialist assessment** – an assessment administered and interpreted by an appropriately qualified professional to explore specific needs, often in detail, for example, on proficiency in the first language, special educational needs, or a health or care assessment

Pupils may also have health or care needs which may not be apparent to others but which you pick up as part of your initial assessment or shortly afterwards. If you have any concerns about these issues, you should speak to your class teacher and SENCO in order to ensure that any necessary referral is made.

## Provide feedback to learners and others on the outcome of the assessment and the implications

As a bilingual assistant, it is likely that you will be involved in providing feedback to pupils and their families as well as other professionals about pupil progress, whether this concerns their learning, language development or well-being. Pupils should be involved in the procedure as much as possible, unless it is inappropriate due to the nature of the discussion.

---

**Language support plan:** Spring term 2012

**Name:** Jamilla Khan     **Year:** 1     **Date:** 15 January 2012

**Targets:**
1. To familiarise Jamilla with the school and routines, and start to learn school vocabulary
2. To know 10 initial sounds and 5 core words from the National Primary Strategy

**Support:** Daily during Literacy hour with Mrs Evans (assistant) Individual and group work

**Review:** End of Spring term 2011

**Signed:** _____  _____
       (teacher)                (parent)

*Example language support plan.*

The best way in which to do this is to set aside regular intervals with pupils to discuss their progress and to think about any additional support they might need.

The most commonly used method of tracking pupil progress is by target setting and monitoring. This will enable pupils, staff and parents to see the focus of the work that is being done in school and to assess how successfully it is being implemented. You may be invited to contribute to parents' evenings and other events in order to support teachers and other staff in passing on information to parents. If you are asked to speak to parents about pupil learning, you should have an opportunity to speak to teachers beforehand so that you know what information they need to have passed on and how they would like you to structure what you say.

## Provide information and support to relevant people

If you provide regular support to bilingual pupils, you need to give information and support to colleagues and other professionals, particularly if pupils speak very little English. Information about pupils' development in English and also their knowledge and use of their home language, which may reflect their confidence in using language generally, is very useful. A pupil who has a working knowledge of one language already understands the purpose of language and the process involved, and is more likely to be able to apply it to another language. The feedback you give to colleagues may be written or verbal depending on the school policy. You may also be required to attend meetings with others with or without the pupil and family present, in order to pass on and exchange information and to ensure that everyone involved with the pupil is aware of any specific needs they may have.

> **BEST PRACTICE CHECKLIST:** Providing information and support
>
> - Pass on information to colleagues about pupils' development in English and also their knowledge and use of their home language, which may reflect their confidence in using language generally.
>
> - Keep a record of the feedback you give to colleagues so that the information is available to others if required at a later date.
>
> - If required, attend meetings in order to pass on and exchange knowledge so that everyone is well informed.

## Be able to provide bilingual support for learners

### Use learners' preferred language to introduce and settle them into the learning environment

When you first meet bilingual pupils who are new to the school, whatever their age, you will need to introduce them to the learning environment in the most accessible way. As you are working as a bilingual assistant, you should use their preferred language in order to do this, whether this is their first or target language. You will need to speak to them about the rules and routines of the school and show them around different areas of the learning environment so that they are able to settle in more quickly. If they would prefer to do this in the target language, or if you have other pupils in school who speak their target language, you may decide to take other pupils with you to help and to point out things which an adult might not!

*You can ask students who speak the target language to help you when showing the school to new bilingual pupils.*

## Work with relevant people to identify learning activities that promote personalised learning

When you have settled the pupil into school and have spoken to others about how best to support their learning needs, it is likely that there will be some consensus from educational and other professionals about a focus for their language development. This may be documented in an individual plan in order to maintain a focus on their targets. Although **personalised learning** does not mean that the pupil will have one-to-one support separate from other pupils, it should ensure that their progress is monitored and has a focus.

You should have agreed with others the kinds of activities which will best promote the pupil's language development and which will help them in their classroom activities. It is likely that you will also be working with other children, as it will be important for bilingual pupils to be using their language in context. You may, for example, decide to focus on specific vocabulary which they will need as part of a topic or project within the class, or work on language activities which will also support what they are doing.

| Key term |
| --- |
| **Personalised learning** — maintaining a focus on individual progress, in order to maximise the capacity of all children and young people to learn, achieve and participate |

# Use bilingual support strategies to meet individual learner needs

A key part of your role will be using bilingual support strategies in order to meet learner needs. This will be in different circumstances, whether these are individual, group or whole-class sessions. You will need to ensure that you use a range of these so that you maximise the opportunities for developing pupils' language skills and the development of the target language.

## Interpreting oral and written information

Pupils may need you to interpret information for them in their first language, in particular when they are new to the school and there is a lot of information for them to take in.

## Using shared language or appropriate target language to explain information or instructions

In a similar way, pupils may need you to explain information or instructions which are being given to the class or group by the teacher. You may need to discuss with them how they will go about a particular task, on their own or alongside other pupils.

## Supporting the use of learners' first languages

Bilingual pupils may sometimes need you to support the use of their first language. If they are very young or their first language is not fully developed, they may need you to encourage its use in a learning context.

### Link

For more on this aspect, see TDA 3.17 Support bilingual learners.

## Developing bilingual learning resources

As a bilingual assistant, you will be well placed to develop a bank of bilingual learning resources. If you are working in a school where these already exist, you should still be on the lookout for additional resources which will be of benefit to pupils, and store them so that they are accessible to others.

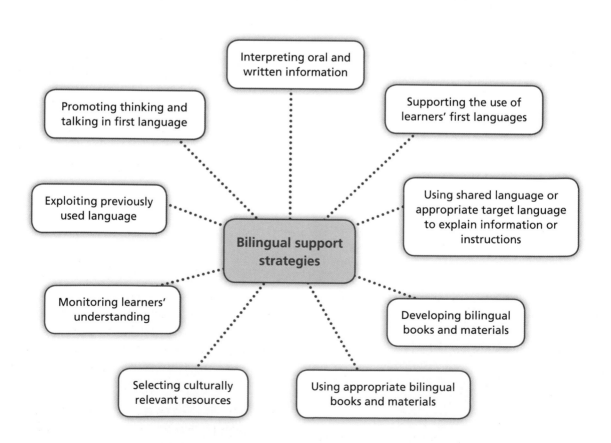

*Why is it important to use a range of bilingual support strategies?*

## Using appropriate bilingual books and materials

You may have resources such as bilingual books which are designed to show both the first and target language as the story or information is set out. These may be helpful to use in different contexts — for example, a bilingual child at the earlier stages will find it helpful to see the text in the target language, while a more competent linguist might try to guess how it has been translated.

## Selecting culturally relevant resources

In the same way that you have used bilingual learning resources, you should also select those which are culturally relevant to the child. In this way you will be able to motivate and involve them further in their learning, as they will be more able to identify with the context.

### Functional skills

ICT: Using ICT
English: Speaking, listening and communication
How many bilingual or culturally relevant resources do you have in your setting? You could photograph all the different resources you have and then use them in a discussion to show your peers how your setting supports bilingual and multicultural children.

## Monitoring learners' understanding

When checking that pupils have understood, make sure that you use both their target and home languages. In this way you will be able to monitor their understanding more closely.

## Exploiting previously used language

As you will be working with bilingual pupils regularly, you will be able to use prior knowledge of language they have used and remind them about the context and how it links to their experiences. This links with the next heading.

## Promoting thinking and talking in first language

Bilingual pupils who are in the earlier stages of learning a second language may need you to encourage them through talking about their learning in their first language. In this way they may be more likely to develop their thinking skills.

# Provide good role models of both the first and target language

While working with bilingual pupils, it is vital that you provide a good role model for both first and **target language**. You should ensure that you always use the correct form of language, as pupils will be taking this in when they are working with you. You should not correct any mistakes which they or others make, but repeat back in the correct form, using the right word or grammatical construction so that they hear it.

### Key term

**Target language** — the additional or second language needed by bilingual learners, i.e. English as an additional language (EAL) or Welsh/Gaeilge as a second language

# Use learners' first language to draw on previous knowledge and experience

Use of a pupil's first language will be important in the classroom context as through this you will be able to go back and revisit their previous learning or experience. They may be unable to explain or talk about what they have done in the target language, but their first language knowledge will enable you to talk to them about the extent of any prior knowledge. It can be frustrating for bilingual pupils who are only unable to carry out an activity or join in with a discussion because of the constraints of their knowledge of the target language.

### CASE STUDY: Using a first language to draw on knowledge and experience

Kayleigh is working with Rafael, who has recently started at the school in Reception. He speaks Spanish as his first language. The class are working on a topic about their holidays and beaches in particular, and talking about the kinds of activities they like to do. Rafael is able to talk about this in Spanish but not in English.

- How could Kayleigh support Rafael in this activity?
- Why is it important that he is able to join in with the discussion?

## Maintain and develop learners' first language in learning contexts

Despite keeping a focus on the target language and on pupils' skills in this, you should also ensure that pupils' first language skills are continuing to be developed. Although they will use this language at home, they may not have done so in a learning context; this may mean that they have more difficulty in applying what they are learning in the target language to their first language. This may be particularly true in the case of mathematical language or vocabulary which has a tendency to be more abstract, as pupils may find it more difficult to understand how the two languages relate to one another. Similarly, if pupils are learning a new topic such as a historical period, they may not have learned the vocabulary in their first language and this would be a good opportunity to introduce it.

---

**CASE STUDY: Developing learners' first language skills**

Chris is occasionally working in class with Sher, who is in Year 3 and has been in the country all his life but speaks Yoruba at home. He is able to speak English competently although he occasionally has some difficulty with more specialised vocabulary. Chris occasionally takes Sher out of class to focus on words which he may need as part of his topic.

- Is it important that Sher should have a bilingual speaker to help him with this vocabulary?
- Do you think that Chris and Sher should work together inside or outside the classroom?

---

## Be able to support communication with families of bilingual learners

### Interact with families in a way that demonstrates a non-judgemental attitude, values diversity and promotes trust

When communicating with bilingual learners and their families, you will need to be sensitive not only to language but also to different cultural needs. You will need to show that you are there to support them and that the process is one of inclusion. As you communicate with families, you should show that you respect them and that you value the contribution that they and their child make to the school community. This should also be evident through the ethos of the school which should value diversity and cultural differences. As a bilingual speaker, you may already be aware of these issues, which may be around dress or diet, but may also be to do with religious or cultural customs with which you may not be familiar. The school's policies will welcome pupils and families from all cultures and you need to make sure that you follow these policies.

If your communication methods are not effective for whatever reason and you find that some families are unable or reluctant to liaise with the school, you may need to adapt the support provided. As in all school practice, you need to identify any issues, evaluate how effective your methods are and think about whether any amendments or improvements may be necessary. Examples of adapting what you do may include:

- providing additional opportunities for parents to come into school. These may be through specific events and support networks for bilingual parents, particularly if they are reluctant or unsure about approaching the school. You may also invite parents into school to speak to pupils about cultural issues, such as different festivals

- being able to translate important letters that go home or provide alternative support so that families can access the information.

## Provide accessible information to families as agreed by the setting

If you are a bilingual teaching assistant working in a school with a high percentage of bilingual learners, it is likely that you will be involved in providing support and information to families. You should have opportunities to liaise with the named governor or teacher in the school who is responsible for advising teachers about EAL (English as an additional language) learners. There should also be systems in place to enable you to pass information to parents and carers and for them to pass information to the school. Where school documents need to be available for parents and families whose first language is not that used in school, you may need to provide help to ensure that the information is communicated.

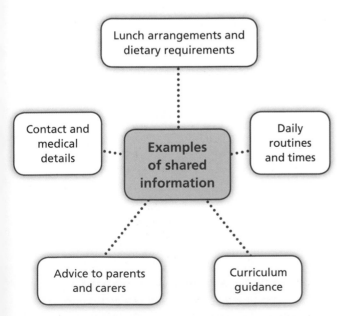

*What is shared information?*

## Encourage families to share information about their child to support the setting

Parents or carers of bilingual children may sometimes speak very little, if any, English themselves. In this situation the school needs to devise additional strategies to encourage their involvement and understanding (see also communicating with families on page 256). It is important that parents and carers feel able to approach the school and share information in order to maximise the opportunities to communicate. This may start informally or, in schools with a high percentage of EAL pupils, may be approached in a more structured way. Families of bilingual pupils may have complex needs themselves as well as communication issues and the school may be one of the first points of contact for them to access additional support and become established in local communities. Through school events, community projects and extended schools programmes, parents should be encouraged to be included in a variety of ways. However, remember that if you are passing information between school and families, this is all you should be doing. Be careful not to include your own opinions or ideas about what should be happening on either side without consulting with other staff first.

You may be communicating with pupils and families who are refugees or have come from situations where they have experienced difficult circumstances. In this case, seek outside support from your local authority to ensure that you are offering as much help, support and advice as possible. As a bilingual speaker, you will be well placed to offer the information. Pupils who have had unsettled backgrounds may take longer to settle into school, and communication and language development may be affected.

## Accurately record and pass on any information provided by families

You should make sure that any information which you gather from families is appropriately recorded and passed on to the relevant people as soon as possible. It will help you in this situation either to make notes or to record what is being said using a voice recorder, as it will be difficult for you to remember all aspects of the conversation, even if you have prepared specific questions in advance. Make sure you write minutes of the meeting which are clear and set out according to school policy. You will also need to ensure that you observe confidentiality when passing on information to others, particularly if you are given sensitive information.

### Knowledge into action

Keep any records which you have gathered yourself and use them for your portfolio, either by showing them to your assessor or removing names for confidentiality and copying the paperwork.

# Be able to contribute to reviews of communication with families of bilingual learners

## Consult relevant people about the effectiveness of communication with families of bilingual learners

Forms of communication may be:

- verbal or non-verbal
- informal or formal.

As the ability to communicate with families of bilingual learners is an important part of the overall process of pupil learning, it is likely that you will need to consult others regularly about how effective this is and whether you need to make any changes to your approach as a team. You should consider all aspects of communication and whether it is successful at different stages, for example:

- when the pupil first enters school
- when targets are being set

- the way in which targets are reviewed
- the day-to-day communication between school and families
- how much parents and families are involved with the school
- how easy it is to pass information to parents and vice versa.

At the same time as thinking about the different stages, you will also need to look at the following,

### Verbal and non-verbal methods of communication

It may be easier to tell if verbal methods of communication are effective, but you should also think about the effectiveness of non-verbal methods such as letters, emails and other ways in which information is passed between families and those professionals who are working with the pupil.

### Formal and informal methods of communication

Again, because parents should be involved in meetings and reviews, it will be easier to assess whether formal methods of communication are effective. However, you should also consider informal methods such as social events or after-school activities when you may be talking to parents.

### Skills builder

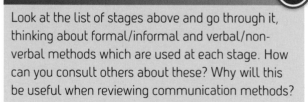

Look at the list of stages above and go through it, thinking about formal/informal and verbal/non-verbal methods which are used at each stage. How can you consult others about these? Why will this be useful when reviewing communication methods?

## Use knowledge of communication with families to contribute to reviews of communication methods

When reviewing communication methods with others, you will need to think about how effective your communication with families has been. As a bilingual speaker you will be well placed to consider the difference that your contribution makes to the overall process. You should think about the information you have been able to gather and how you think that this has supported the pupil and the difference that it has made. You will also be able to ask others how this has made a difference to their work and whether it has been effective.

## Identify any communication difficulties or issues due to differences

Communication differences between individuals may create barriers to effective communication between them, and can relate to:

- language
- sensory impairment
- speech, language or communication impairment
- cognitive abilities
- emotional state
- culture.

## Work with relevant people to resolve any communication difficulties or issues

There may be a number of difficulties which arise when communicating with pupils and their families which are a barrier to effective working, due to differences in communication methods. You may need to intervene and clarify any misunderstandings or difficulties as they arise — alternatively you may be asked to speak to parents if problems have arisen between families and other professionals during the course of their work with pupils.

### Language
Although you speak the pupil's first language, there may still be issues around their communication with other professionals. You may be asked to clarify or explain any points or issues which arise.

### Sensory impairment
Individuals with whom you are working may have a sensory impairment such as a visual or hearing impairment. You may need to adapt your communication methods or involve others to support your communication with them.

### Speech, language or communication impairment
If, over a period of time, parents or pupils find communication difficult, this may indicate that they have a speech, language or communication impairment. If it is clear that communication is being hindered, think about ways of changing your approach to meet the needs of pupils and their families, or find out whether they can be referred for specialist support.

### Cognitive abilities
You may find that parents are having difficulty in understanding the process despite your speaking their first language. It is possible that there are issues with their cognitive abilities and you may need to seek additional support for them.

### Emotional state
Communication methods may also be hindered due to the emotional state of parents or families. They may have had a difficult transition while moving to this country or have faced issues which make the situation very difficult for them. There may also be a reluctance on the part of the family to become involved in school life. This may be due to anxiety about what it involves and how the system differs from their previous experience.

### Cultural differences
Although you may speak the language, there may be cultural differences about which you are not aware but which mean that communication is hindered. You may need to work with your support or advisory teachers in order to ensure that any misunderstandings are dealt with as soon as possible.

## Getting ready for assessment

Write a reflective account to show the kinds of events and opportunities your school has to encourage communication with families of bilingual and multilingual pupils. Have there been measureable benefits? Why do you think these are important? If you have had to adapt the ways in which you communicate with families, outline how you have done this.

As with TDA 3.17, Support bilingual learners, rather than writing this down as a reflective account, you may wish to have a professional discussion with your assessor to show how you provide bilingual support for teaching and learning. Plan this so that you can decide which of the assessment criteria you want to cover. Your assessor may also wish to speak to the parents, teachers or other professionals with whom you work to support bilingual learners.

## Check your knowledge

1. Why should the initial assessment of a bilingual pupil be in their first language rather than in English?

2. What other professionals may be involved in assessments and decisions about the pupil?

3. What kinds of strategies might be effective when working with bilingual pupils in their first language?

4. Why is it important to maintain pupils' first language skills?

5. What should you do in order to be a good role model for language?

6. How can families be encouraged to share information with schools? Why is this important?

7. What kinds of communication issues might there be when working with parents and families?

## Functional skills

**English: Speaking, listening and communication**
When holding your discussion, plan your view before you sit down with your assessor and then listen carefully so that you can respond in an appropriate way.

### Websites

(See also those listed at the end of TDA 3.17 Support bilingual learners.)

**www.continyou.org.uk** – this is an organisation that supports inclusion and lifelong learning
**www.naldic.org.uk** – the National Association for Language Development in the Curriculum has a large amount of material, articles and suggestions on issues surrounding bilingual pupils
**www.teachernet.gov.uk** – visit this site for further ideas for supporting EAL pupils

# TDA 3.19 Support disabled children & young people & those with special educational needs

Working with children or young people who have special educational needs or disabilities will require you to have skills in a number of areas. You will need to be able to relate well to a variety of different people, including parents, carers and other professionals. You may have a high level of responsibility for working with these pupils and need to work in partnership both with the pupil and with those who support them, both at home and to provide educational provision.

## By the end of this unit you will:

1. understand the rights of disabled children and young people and those with special educational needs

2. understand the disabilities and/or special educational needs of children and young people in your care

3. be able to support the inclusion of disabled children and young people and those with special educational needs

4. be able to support disabled children and young people and those with special educational needs to participate in the full range of activities and experiences

5. be able to support others to respond to the needs of disabled children and young people and those with special educational needs.

# Understand the rights of disabled children and young people and those with special educational needs

## The legal entitlements of disabled children and young people and those with special educational needs

As a teaching assistant working at this level it is likely that you will be supporting intervention groups, individuals and groups of pupils who have **special educational needs** on a regular basis. You will need to know about the entitlements which these children have and the laws which affect the provision which your school makes for them. There have been a number of changes to legislation in the UK in recent years which have affected this and a gradual increase in the rights which these pupils have. Table 1 shows these in date order.

### Key terms

**Disabled** – the Disability Discrimination Act (DDA) defines a disabled person as someone who has a physical or mental impairment that has a substantial and long-term adverse effect on their ability to carry out normal day-to-day activities

**Special educational needs** – children or young people who learn differently from most children or young people of the same age, and who may need extra or different help from that given to others

| Legislation | Details |
|---|---|
| Education Act (Handicapped Children) 1970 | Transferred the responsibility of children's education from the health service to the local authority, and many special schools were built. |
| The Warnock Report (1978) | Study of the needs of SEN pupils which had an impact on subsequent Acts of Parliament. It introduced suggestions as to how these children should be supported – through access to the curriculum and changes to the curriculum/environment. Influenced the Special Educational Needs (SEN) Code of Practice 2001 through its focus on inclusion. |
| Education Act (1981) | Based on the findings of the Warnock Report, this gave additional legal responsibilities to local authorities as well as power to parents. |
| Education Reform Act (1988) | Introduced the National Curriculum into all schools in England and Wales. Allowed schools to change or modify what was taught for SEN pupils if the basic curriculum was not appropriate for them. |
| Children Act (1989) | Stated that the welfare of the child must at all times be considered and their rights and wishes should be taken into consideration. |
| Education Act (1993) | Required that a code of practice be introduced for guidance on identification and provision of special educational needs. Introduced the role of the Special Educational Needs Co-ordinator (SENCO) and parents were able to challenge local authorities about providing for pupils with SEN. |
| Disability Discrimination Act (1995) | Made it illegal for services such as shops and employers to discriminate against **disabled** people; extended in 2005 to education. Required better access to buildings and facilities for disabled people. |

| Legislation | Details |
|---|---|
| Special Educational Needs and Disability Act (SENDA)/Special Educational Needs (SEN) Code of Practice 2001 | Strengthens the rights of parents and children who have special educational needs to a mainstream education. |
| Children Act 2004 | Closely linked to Every Child Matters, which set out to change children's services and to improve multi-agency working. |
| Every Child Matters: Change for Children (2004) | This Green Paper aims to ensure that all organisations and agencies involved with children between birth and 19 years should work together to ensure that children have the support needed to stay safe, be healthy, enjoy and achieve, make a positive contribution, and achieve economic well-being. |

Table 1: Legislation relating to disabled children and young people and those with SEN.

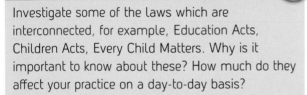

### Over to you!

Investigate some of the laws which are interconnected, for example, Education Acts, Children Acts, Every Child Matters. Why is it important to know about these? How much do they affect your practice on a day-to-day basis?

### Functional skills

**ICT: Developing, presenting and communicating information**
**English: Reading**
You could create a timeline of legislation that includes information from the chapter and further research. Your timeline will help you to see visually how legislation has changed and influenced the way we work today.

## The assessment and intervention frameworks

### SEN Code of Practice 2001

The Code of Practice 2001 changed the way in which assessment and intervention for children and young people was carried out in schools. Most importantly, the following came into effect.

- A child with SEN should have their needs identified which will normally be met in mainstream schools or early education settings.

- Those responsible for SEN provision must take into account the views and wishes of the child.

- Professionals and parents should work in partnership.

- Provision and progress should be monitored and reviewed regularly.

- Local Education Authorities (LEAs) should make assessments in accordance with prescribed time limits.

The Code of Practice also outlines the way in which assessments should be carried out in early years, primary and secondary settings, and gives a clear structure to the way in which assessments are carried out. Special educational needs legislation is due to be updated in 2013.

### Early Years Action/School Action

At this stage, the school or early years setting will put additional strategies in place if the pupil is finding it hard to keep up with their peers. This will usually take the form of additional targets on an Individual Education Plan (IEP).

### Early Years Action Plus/School Action Plus

If the pupil has been on Early Years or School Action for some time and is still behind their peers, they may be moved on to Early Years or School Action Plus. This means that the school will consult outside agencies for further assessments, advice or strategies for supporting the pupil's needs.

## Statement of Special Educational Need

This means that the pupil will be assessed as to whether they need a statement of SEN and additional support in school. The school will need to gather all the paperwork from professionals who have worked with the pupil, in addition to providing evidence of the strategies they have used. If the pupil has serious SEN or disabilities, they may have been assessed before entering school or nursery and issued with a statement then.

## The Common Assessment Framework (CAF)

This was introduced on a national scale in 2006 and is designed to be used across all children's services. Its purpose is to identify additional needs at an early stage through a holistic approach to children's needs and to encourage the working together of different agencies. It is not designed purely for those who have special educational needs and may be used where pupils are at risk from harm or you are concerned about an aspect of their behaviour. If you have concerns about a child, you should always speak to your school's SENCO.

## The importance of early recognition and intervention

The Special Educational Needs Code of Practice in 2001 introduced the identification and early intervention for young children before they start full-time primary education. The reason for this was that the sooner intervention can be put in place for pupils with these needs, the greater the benefits for their learning. Many early years workers had been able to identify children who would need extra support but there was no mechanism for starting to put provision in place before the child started school. This meant that the process was delayed when provision could have been put in place. Following the introduction of the Code of Practice, more children have entered school with a statement of special educational need or on Early Years Action or Early Years Action Plus. The benefits of this are:

- maximum information will be available to all professionals
- pupils will start to receive support sooner

- professionals in school are prepared for the arrival of children with specific needs and are able to put in provision sooner
- any adaptations can be made to the environment before the child starts to attend school.

---

**CASE STUDY:** The importance of early recognition

Jimmy has a disability and has always used a wheelchair. He has not been to nursery but has had his name down to start at the local primary school. Although his mother has filled in all the forms for the school and they have been notified, there has been no dialogue between them about preparing both Jimmy and the school for his arrival.

- How else can the school ensure that they find out in advance about pupils who have additional needs?
- What benefits would there have been for both sides if there had been more communication at these initial stages?

---

## The purpose of individual plans

Pupils who have special educational needs may need to have individual education plans to ensure that they have access to the curriculum. Although lesson plans should always include differentiated activities for pupils who have additional educational needs, these may need to be personalised further and individual education plans (IEPs) will give pupils specific targets to work on. If you plan alongside the teacher, you may be able to make suggestions at this stage for the pupils you support. You may also have had input from other professionals as to the kinds of strategies or equipment which you are able to use. Any additional training you have had around the needs of the individual may also give you ideas about the kinds of activities and resources which will be beneficial.

You may still need to adapt work, however, if the pupil is finding it challenging. You will need to monitor pupil participation and intervene if necessary so that they are able to achieve the learning intention.

# INDIVIDUAL EDUCATION PLAN

Name of pupil: _Peter Lim_

Date of birth: _31 Aug 03_                    T.A. _Arthur Comolli_

| Refer to Diagnostic summary sheet for background and assessment data |
| --- |

This IEP current from _Jul 2010_                    to _Oct 2010_

Goals to be reviewed after _____ months _____

| | |
| --- | --- |
| Summary of current level of performance | Peter demonstrates fairly good on-seat and on-task behaviour. He is a visual and experiential learner. However, he lacks focus and has short attention span.<br><br>He has no knowledge of alphabets and numbers and is unable to discriminate the alphabets and numeric digits (from 1 to 5). He does not discriminate or name objects when asked and does not attend to pictures or photographs. He also echoes the label of an object that is being said for the previous one.<br><br>He works better when given a work system and is able to carry out simple Take-Do-Finish (left to right) tasks. |
| Present educational needs | To introduce the numeral 1 and 2 by allowing him to feel and trace the numerals that are made from different materials and of different sizes. Encourage him to imitate the sound from teacher and say aloud the number when pointing to the numerals.<br><br>Teach him the recognition of the numerals through activities such as singing songs, matching games, reading of numerals in objects (e.g. numerals found in boxes, clock, books).<br><br>Teach him the concept of sequencing and associating the numerals to actual number objects. |

| Long term goals | Goal 1<br>Recognition of numerals 1 and 2 | Goal 2<br>Sequencing numerals 1 and 2 | Goal 3<br>Associating numerals 1 and 2 to quantity |
| --- | --- | --- | --- |

*Part of an individual education plan.*

## Portfolio activity

If you are working with an individual pupil as a learning support assistant, you should have a copy of their individual education plan. Remove the name of the pupil and highlight and annotate the plan to show how you support the pupil towards achieving their targets.

## The principles of working inclusively

Inclusion does not just refer to pupils with special educational or ASL (Additional Support for Learning) needs, but all pupils through the benefits of equal opportunities in schools. However, inclusion has come to be associated more closely with special educational needs as the term has been used widely since the introduction of the SEN Code of Practice in 2001. The theory is that with the right training, strategies and support, nearly all pupils with SEN can be successfully included in mainstream education. The benefits of inclusion should be clear — that all pupils are entitled to be educated together and are able to access the same education without any form of discrimination or barriers to participation.

When you are working with SEN pupils, you will find that many professionals and parents speak about the danger of 'labelling' children and young people. This is because it is important that we look at the needs of the individual first, rather than focusing on the pupil's disability or impairment. In the past, the medical model of disability has been used more frequently than the social model (see Table 2) and this kind of language has promoted the attitude that people with disabilities are individuals who in some way need to be corrected or brought into line with everybody else. This has sometimes led to unhelpful labelling of individuals in terms of their disabilities rather than their potential. You should be realistic about the expectations you have of the pupils you support and consider their learning needs. For some, although not all, the curriculum will need to be modified and pupils may need additional support. However, you should not assume that all SEN pupils will always need additional support and you should encourage them to be as independent as possible.

| Medical model | Social model |
|---|---|
| Pupil is faulty | Pupil is valued |
| Diagnosis | Strengths and needs defined by self and others |
| Labelling | Identify barriers/develop solutions |
| Impairment is focus of attention | Outcome-based programme designed |
| Segregation or alternative services | Training for parents and professionals |
| Ordinary needs put on hold | Relationships nurtured |
| Re-entry if 'normal' or permanent exclusion | Diversity is welcomed and pupil is included |
| Society remains unchanged | Society evolves |

*Table 2: Medical and social models of disability (Source: Disability Discrimination in Education Course Book: Training for Inclusion and Disability Equality).*

**BEST PRACTICE CHECKLIST:** Working inclusively with children with disabilities or SEN

- Have high expectations of all pupils.
- Celebrate and value diversity, rather than fear it.
- Be aware that all pupils have more in common than is different.
- Encourage the participation of all pupils in the curriculum and social life of the school.
- Work to include pupils in the main activities of the class wherever possible.
- Develop 'can do' attitudes in pupils through appropriate degrees of challenge and support.

# Understand the disabilities and/or special educational needs of children and young people in your care

## The relationship between disability and special educational needs

Pupils with special educational needs are defined on page 6 of the 2001 Code of Practice as having a learning difficulty if they have 'a significantly greater difficulty in learning than the majority of children of the same age' or 'a disability which prevents or hinders them from making use of educational facilities of a kind generally provided for children of the same age'. Disability is therefore considered a special educational need only if it hinders the pupil from participating in the day-to-day activities which are enjoyed by others. Having a disability may mean that a pupil has additional needs and therefore needs support. However, not all pupils who have a disability will have a statement of special educational needs, as many are independent and able to participate without support.

## CASE STUDY: Disability and special educational needs

Anisha is in Year 2 and has a disability which means that her mobility is affected and she is unable to walk very far or use stairs. She is able to move around the classroom with her frame if needed and her wheelchair is only used when she needs to leave the classroom. She is unable to participate in some PE activities with other pupils, although she has strength in her upper body and is able to participate in most lessons.

- Do you think that Anisha requires a statement of special educational needs and support from an assistant?

# Particular disabilities and/or SEN of children with whom you work and special provision required

For these assessment criteria you will need to identify specifically the details of particular disabilities or special educational needs of pupils with whom you work and discuss how you have managed them with the support that is available to you. You will need to show how you have worked with others in the school and local authority to provide a high-quality service to these pupils. For example, you should have information from within your school through teachers and the SENCO about the pupil's needs. You may also work with professionals such as occupational therapists or physiotherapists who may advise you on the kind of **special provision** and additional equipment or specialist aids which should be provided by the school and give suggestions as to how you can best support pupils.

### Key term

**Special provision** — provision which is additional to, or otherwise different from, the provision made generally for children of their age in mainstream schools in the area

### Over to you!

Talk to your assessor or write a reflective account to provide details of the pupil or pupils with whom you work and how you support them. Always remember to change names.

### Functional skills

**English: Writing**
When writing your reflective account, it is important that you plan your work through before you start. You need to make sure that your writing is clear and uses a range of sentence structures with good spelling, punctuation and grammar.

## The expected pattern of development

You will need to show how the pupil or pupils you are supporting differ from their peers in their expected pattern of development. If you work with pupils of a particular age range, it will be easier for you to identify whether they are fitting the normal pattern of development for their age, as you will be very familiar with what the rest of the class is able to do.

### Link

For all stages of physical, cognitive, communication and social/emotional development, see CYP 3.1 Understand child and young person development.

### Knowledge into action

Consider the needs of a pupil you support alongside the expected pattern of development for their age in the corresponding area (for example, physical, cognitive, social/emotional). You may wish to use the stages in CYP 3.1. Alongside the expected pattern, record the stage which the pupil has reached and how this has an impact on the pupil and their level of involvement in school activities.

### Functional skills

**ICT: Using ICT**
You could type up a report that shows the level the pupil has reached alongside the expected pattern and include some examples of work to support what you are saying. You could scan their work in, remove any names and then insert them into your report as evidence.

# Be able to support the inclusion of disabled children and young people and those with special educational needs

## Obtain information about the needs, capabilities and interests of the children with whom you work

You will be able to obtain information from:

- children and young people themselves
- family members
- colleagues within the setting
- external support agencies
- individual plans.

It is important that you get to know pupils and find out about their capabilities and interests as soon as you can, to best support them both through the curriculum and in additional ways. Before they start at the school you may be able to visit them at their previous setting or at home to speak to them and also parents about their needs and any specific information which is required. It is also likely that the SENCO will want to set up a meeting so that the school can discuss with parents or carers and the child themselves how they plan to work together. Many parents who have children with disabilities or special educational needs will have become experts on the need or condition. They will also be in a good position to offer support to others as they will be sympathetic to their situation and will have experienced the kinds of difficulties. Partnerships with parents and families is crucial to the process of working with pupils who have special educational needs. Schools will need to ensure that they are as supportive as possible through clear communication and discussion with parents.

Schools may wish to meet or talk to any other agencies or professionals who have worked with the pupil in the past. If these professionals are not available, they will be invited to send reports and recommendations in order to assist the school in making provision. If the pupil is not new to the

school, you should have the opportunity of meeting with colleagues to discuss their progress alongside the pupil where possible and to look at previous paperwork. On a more informal level, it is very important that you get to know that pupil's interests so that you can support them through a greater awareness of their personality.

---

**CASE STUDY:** Obtaining information about pupils' needs and interests

Yuvraj has been working at Red Hills Primary for some time as an individual support assistant. The school has recently confirmed that he will have some more hours, as there is a new pupil arriving at the school the following week who has Down's syndrome. He has been given some records by the SENCO about the pupil's needs and a meeting has been arranged with the parents to which he has also been invited before the pupil starts at the school.

- What else could Yuvraj do to obtain more information about the pupil?
- Why is this so important?

---

## Barriers to participation for disabled children and young people and those with special educational needs

All pupils, whatever their needs and abilities, have an equal right to education and learning, without **barriers to participation**. Equal opportunities should include not only access to provision but also to facilities within and outside the school setting. Schools and other organisations which offer educational provision must by law ensure that all pupils have access to a broad and balanced curriculum.

---

### Key term

**Barriers to participation** – anything that prevents the child or young person participating fully in activities and experiences offered by the setting or service

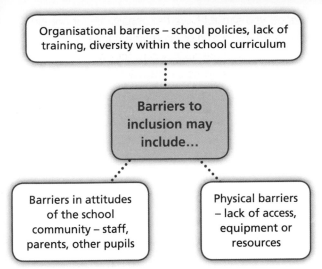

Organisational barriers – school policies, lack of training, diversity within the school curriculum

Barriers to inclusion may include...

Barriers in attitudes of the school community – staff, parents, other pupils

Physical barriers – lack of access, equipment or resources

*Barriers to participation in schools.*

## Physical barriers

Since the Special Educational Needs and Disability Act 2001 called for the amendment of the Disability Discrimination Act 1995, there should be no reason that a child or young person who has a disability or special educational need should not be able to gain access to an educational institution or to its facilities. If you are supporting a pupil who has additional needs, make sure that all staff are aware of the provision which needs to be made to ensure that they are able to participate. This may mean adaptations to the environment or the purchase of additional resources or equipment.

## Organisational barriers

Your school should have an up-to-date equal opportunities or inclusion policy which sets out its priorities for developing inclusion. It should also ensure that all staff who are working with pupils who have additional needs are fully trained and able to do so with the full support of the school.

## Barriers in the attitudes of the school community – staff, parents and other pupils

This barrier can be one of the more challenging to overcome, as it may be hard to change opinions and attitudes of others. You should always remember that the needs of the child or young person come first and to stand up for the rights of the pupils you support.

# How to remove barriers to participation

Provision in schools may be affected by any of the barriers described, if the school does not take active steps to ensure that they do not occur.

You will need to be able to show that in your work with children and young people, you actively remove any barriers to participation which exist as they arise. These may be straightforward, such as improved training opportunities or meetings set up to ensure that all staff are aware of the needs of the pupil. The most important aspect of this is continued communication between the school, home and outside agencies on a regular basis to ensure that the pupil's needs are being met in the most effective way. However, barriers may also be to do with attitudes of others which may be more difficult to challenge. While you should always remain professional, you may find it appropriate to refer those who hold particular views to your SENCO or Head Teacher.

> **CASE STUDY:** Removing barriers to participation
>
> Cheryl has been told that she is going to be working with David, a pupil who is in Year 5 and on the autistic spectrum, although he is not new to the school. She is an experienced assistant but has not supported an autistic pupil before.
>
> - How might Cheryl be a barrier to David's participation in teaching and learning activities?
> - What can she do to ensure that this does not happen?

**Functional skills**

ICT: Finding and selecting information
You could use search engines to search the Internet for any courses in your local area that you could attend to help develop your knowledge in particular areas. You may not need to attend the course at the moment, but you could bookmark the page so you know where to look in the future, in case you are ever in a similar situation to Cheryl.

# How to involve and consult children, young people and others at each stage to support participation and equality of access

You should ensure when working with pupils that they are involved at each stage in discussing and identifying steps or targets which need to be taken, to encourage their **participation**. Even at a young age, pupils should be able to work with you to talk about what they will be doing in school and why they need to have additional support, and how success will be measured. At these different stages a range of **others** may be present, but the constants should be their support assistant, their parents, the class teacher and the SENCO. At review meetings there may also be representatives from the local authority or other professionals who come into school to work with the pupil.

## Reflect

How often do you attend meetings where the pupil is being discussed but is not present? If they are not included, have you been told why? Why is it important that pupils should be part of the process?

## Ways of supporting inclusion and inclusive practices in your work

It is important to remember that the child or young person should be at the very heart of your practice, and that your role is to empower them to be able to achieve to the best of their ability. This will involve getting to know them, finding out about their strengths, dreams and needs, so that you can ensure that they are valued and given as much support as they need.

As well as your support for individuals, you can also show that you support whole-school **inclusion** and inclusive practices in a number of ways. You will need to speak to your assessor about your school's inclusion or equal opportunities policy and identify the way in which pupils who have special educational

needs and disabilities are included in all school activities. You should also be able to identify the measures which are taken in your school to promote inclusion and the kinds of attitudes and expectations which staff and parents may have towards pupils who have special educational needs. You should as part of your practice always ensure that you include all children and young people both in curricular activities and through the wider work of the school — for example, in school councils, sports days, and support for one another and the school.

## Key terms

**Participation** — asking children and young people what works, what does not work and what could work better, and involving them in the design, delivery and evaluation of services, on an ongoing basis

**Others** — according to own role, these may be family members, colleagues within the setting or professionals external to the setting

**Inclusion** — a process of identifying, understanding and breaking down barriers to participation and belonging

## Skills builder

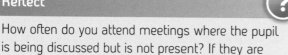

Consider the different ways in which your school supports inclusion and inclusive practices. How have you worked with others to ensure that pupils who have special educational needs are given a school experience which supports their wider learning?

## Functional skills

**English: Speaking, listening and communication** You could complete this Skills builder activity in the form of a discussion with your study group. You should listen carefully to what others say so that you can respond in an appropriate way and move the discussion forward. This is a good way of sharing practice.

# Be able to support disabled children and young people and those with special educational needs to participate in the full range of activities and experiences

## Identify and implement adaptations that can be made to support the participation of all pupils

When working with other staff to support pupil participation, you will need to consider the different adaptations you may have to make in relation to different aspects of what you are doing.

Adaptations can be made to support participation of disabled children and young people and those with special educational needs in relation to:

- **the learning environment** — for example, specialist equipment, a separate seating area, or where pupils sit in the classroom (such as a pupil with a hearing impairment who needs to sit near the front)

- **activities** — if tasks are too difficult or unsuitable, pupils may become frustrated or anxious, which will in turn make them reluctant to attempt further activities. You could find out exactly what pupils are able to do by asking others who work with them or have supported them in the past

- **working practice** — for example, the pupil you support may require adult supervision on the playground, which will mean that you will need to have your break at a different time from other staff

- **resources** — to make activities more accessible for the pupils you are supporting. Be on the look-out for additional resources which may benefit them in class.

**Portfolio activity**

Consider the kinds of adaptations you have needed to implement in order to support disabled pupils or those with special educational needs. How have these enabled them to participate more fully in the activities carried out by other children?

*Have you had to make adaptations to your activities for pupils with special educational needs?*

## Supporting pupils to use specialist aids and equipment as necessary

If you work with specialist equipment, you will need to be able to show this to your assessor and explain how it is used. For example, you may work with a pupil who needs to use mobility equipment such as a walking frame in order to access the curriculum fully. In this instance you should talk through its use and your role in setting it up and using it safely for the pupil. The increased use of technology in schools has meant that pupils will often have aids which require you to have specific training. If you are unable to show your assessor, you will need to have a professional discussion or write about what is involved.

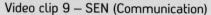
## DVD activity

**Video clip 9 – SEN (Communication)**

In this clip we can see Sara working with Kirk, who has complex needs. She is shown here reading with him and supporting his work using his communication equipment.

1. What kinds of strategies does Sara use to encourage Kirk to communicate? How effective do you think these strategies are?

2. What awareness does Sara have of Kirk's needs and how does this knowledge help her to encourage him? How will Kirk's learning be affected by his physical difficulties in communicating?

3. Sara communicates with Kirk here through signing and through the use of the communication aid shown. What kinds of specialist equipment have you used with pupils and how has this supported their learning?

4. Kirk has a range of needs which will have an impact on how he accesses the curriculum, both physically and emotionally. How can you best support a child to overcome or minimise the effects of these factors?

5. Kirk's needs are global, which means that all areas of his development are affected by his condition. How might this differ from, for example, a pupil who has dyslexia?

6. You may need to adapt or modify work regularly which is being done by the rest of the class, to make it more accessible to the child you support. How can you do this without doing the work for them? Why is it important that you recognise this?

## Ways of supporting participation and equality of access

As a teaching assistant, you should be working regularly with a wide range of people to support **equality of access** to teaching and learning of those with disabilities and special educational needs. Although you may be working with pupils as individuals and in groups during school activities, there will also be a support system to guide you

and ensure that you are given access to additional information. You should also talk to pupils on an ongoing basis about their own individual preferences and interests so that you can ensure that their wishes and needs are taken into account. Speaking to parents regularly is also important, as they may be able to pass on information which is helpful to you on a day-to-day basis.

Other professionals are also likely to come into school to speak to parents, the pupil and to the class teacher and SENCO about pupil progress and participation. They will provide advice and support, and may set targets for the pupil.

## Key term

**Equality of access** – ensuring that discriminatory barriers to access are removed and allowing for children and young people's individual needs

## Link

See also page 268 – How to involve and consult children, young people and others at each stage to support participation and equality of access.

# Be able to support others to respond to the needs of disabled children and young people and those with special educational needs

## Supporting others to observe the needs, capabilities and interests of pupils and to participate in activities with them

Although you may be the individual who knows the most about the pupil and is able to support them effectively, you will not be with them at all times. Your role may be shared or they may only have support for a few hours each week. Others in school should also know about the needs, capabilities and interests of the pupil so that they are able to respond to their needs if you are not present. If the school is small, it may be that all staff are aware of the needs of all pupils in the school. However, in a larger institution you may need to discuss pupils' needs both formally at staff meetings and informally to ensure that all information is passed between staff.

## Over to you!

How is this kind of information passed around in your school? Why is it important that as many staff as possible are aware of the needs of some pupils?

## Functional skills

**ICT: Developing, presenting and communicating information**
You could set up an email group where you send an email to a group of people that needs the relevant information. If you are going to send confidential information electronically, then the file that you send should be password protected so that it is not accessible to all.

## CASE STUDY: Supporting others to participate in activities with pupils

Finley is in Year 1 and has a stutter and a communication disorder. Although this means that he does have some difficulties, he is a very enthusiastic child. When excited and wanting to pass on information, he can become very frustrated. Today he is going on a school trip with your class to a local museum and is in a group with a teaching assistant from another class, Mareisa. He is particularly interested in fossils and is looking forward to seeing them as he has heard that the museum has some. Mareisa has not met Finley before as there are four Year 1 classes.

- What might be the issues in this situation?
- Why should you ensure that Mareisa knows something about Finley's needs?

# Work with others to review and improve activities and experiences provided

You should ensure that you work in a cycle in order to identify and improve the kinds of activities which are provided for pupils who have special educational needs and disabilities. As you should be doing this for all pupils, and those with disabilities and special educational needs are included in this, the review should take place as a matter of course. You will need to review:

- the curriculum you are using with pupils
- use of the learning environment
- the resources available
- the kinds of activities which have been successful and why, and those which have been less successful and why.

As well as discussing the provision, you should also ensure that you include the pupils in the same way or by giving them evaluative questions to consider. This can then feed into the provision the following year.

## Evaluation form for pupils

- What have you found most enjoyable this year and why?

- What have you found least enjoyable and why?

- Are there any subjects which you find particularly easy or challenging?

- Have you found any resources or equipment particularly helpful?

- What do you think the most successful part of the school year has been?

- If you had the opportunity to change anything, what would it be?

*An evaluation form for pupils.*

## Getting ready for assessment

The most useful way of gathering evidence for this unit is to have a professional discussion with your assessor. You should decide beforehand what you would like to cover so that you are ready to answer, but should be able to talk about the particular needs of the pupil or pupils you support and your role in relation to this. An example of a plan for discussion might be:

- look through and talk about the pupil's IEP and discuss their needs

- describe the relationship between the school and the child's parents, and specific support which is needed

- explain how you plan to support the pupil's individual needs and the use of any specialist terminology or equipment.

## Check your knowledge

1. What is the main piece of recent legislation which has affected the teaching and learning of children and young people with disabilities and special educational needs?

2. Why is it important for a pupil's needs to be recognised as early as possible?

3. Name four ways in which you can get to know the pupil you are supporting. Why is this so important?

4. What kinds of barriers to participation might exist when working with pupils?

5. Where might adaptations need to be made when working with pupils who have disabilities or special educational needs?

6. Should all pupils with disabilities or special educational needs have an IEP? If not, should they have anything else to support their learning?

7. How can you effectively review the kinds of activities and experiences which are provided in your school for pupils with disabilities and special educational needs?

## Functional skills

**English: Speaking, listening and communication**
This discussion is a good way of developing your English skills. It is important to be prepared and give clear and relevant information to your assessor using appropriate language.

**References and further reading**
There are a number of magazines and periodicals which are available for school staff who support pupils with special educational needs. You should also keep up to date by reading the *Times Educational Supplement* and checking websites such as those listed here.

- *Special Children*
- *Special Magazine*
- SEN Code of Practice (2001) – DFES publications. Ref: DfES 581/2001

**Support for families**
www.bbc.co.uk/health– this website has advice for a range of conditions and illnesses
www.cafamily.org.uk – this is a national charity for families of disabled children
www.direct.gov.uk – go to 'Disabled people' for advice and support
www.parentpartnership.org.uk – National Parent Partnership Network, a national organisation supporting parents and children
www.specialfamilies.org – this is a national charity for families of disabled children

- CAF (Common Assessment Framework) – for more information go to www.education.gov.uk; you can also download the publication at http://publications.education.gov.uk – ref: 0337-2006BKT-EN

# TDA 3.20 Support children & young people with behaviour, emotional & social development needs

You will explore these needs and their influence on development. You must demonstrate your skills to work with others to support behaviour management strategies and to support children and young people to build relationships and become confident and independent learners.

## By the end of this unit you will:

1. understand the influences impacting on the behaviour, emotional and social development of children and young people

2. understand the special educational needs of children and young people with behaviour, emotional and social development needs

3. be able to support the behaviour management of children and young people with behaviour, emotional and social development needs

4. be able to support children and young people with behaviour, emotional and social development needs to develop relationships with others

5. be able to support children and young people with behaviour, emotional and social development needs to develop self-reliance and self esteem.

# Understand the influences impacting on the behaviour, emotional and social development of children and young people

Behaviour, emotional and social development can be affected by a range of internal and external factors.

## How upbringing, home circumstances, and physical and emotional health could affect ability to relate to others

### Home circumstances and upbringing

For children to progress in all areas of their development they must experience consistency in care, a loving and supportive home, and the opportunity to interact with others. For some children their upbringing and home circumstances can fall short of these basic needs and this will impact on their development. From birth, children develop their behaviour and social skills from what they see and experience within the home. Children who experience lack of interest, lack of attention or even domestic violence or abuse are likely to develop behaviour, emotional and social difficulties.

Families will have different views on the expectations of children's behaviour although this will not necessarily have a negative impact. Problems arise where there are mixed messages. Children need to know boundaries and may become confused if these are applied inconsistently. Children also need attention from others but may learn that the only way to attract this is through unacceptable behaviour.

### Physical and emotional health

Children's physical and emotional health will have a direct bearing on their ability to interact with others. Children with serious ill health or disability will face particular difficulties in building new friendships. Children with a physical disability, for example, cannot join in as easily with play activities as their friends. This difficulty is exacerbated when children also have sensory impairment and/or communication difficulties.

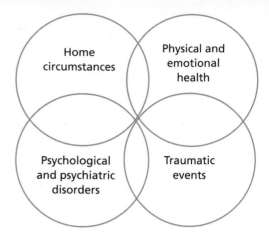

*Influences on children's ability to relate to others.*

When children have a delay in their emotional health they have less resilience to **transitions**. This will affect their ability to deal with difficult situations and to build friendships. Emotional health is critical to all other areas of a child's development.

> **Key term**
>
> **Transitions** – processes of change or events when children change from one stage or state to another

## The impact of negative or traumatic home experiences

Children may experience negative or traumatic events at some stage in their life. While some children appear to be able to bounce back from these difficult events, others will be seriously affected and unable to cope. Children who are refugees or asylum seekers may have experienced significant trauma in their lives. Even where children do not experience events first hand, such as terrorist attacks, natural disasters or accidents, they may have a significant impact on them.

## How psychological and psychiatric disorders may impact on relating to others

Behaviour, emotional and social difficulty (BESD) describes children with a range of behavioural problems which may delay learning and other areas of development. Where these difficulties impact on

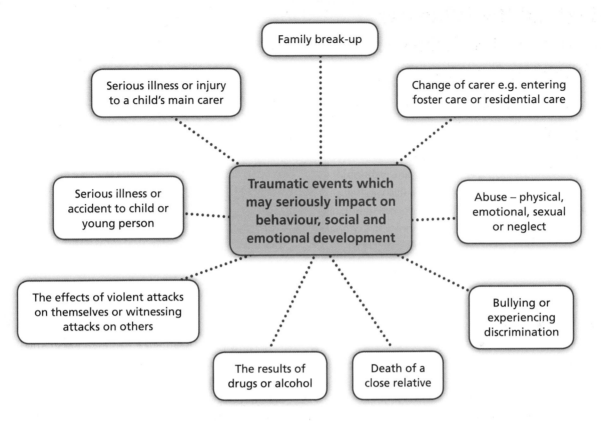

*Traumatic events which may seriously impact on behaviour, social and emotional development.*

| Disorder | Impact on behaviour, emotional and social development |
|---|---|
| Hyperkinetic disorders | Sometimes referred to as Attention Deficit Hyperactivity Disorder (ADHD) or Attention Deficit Disorder (ADD). Young children are often fidgety and like to be on the move, but children with hyperkinetic disorder are overactive and have problems in concentration compared to other children. This disorder is more common in boys. Children are distracted very easily, act without thinking and have difficulty in taking turns. This can lead to difficulties in making friends. Children often settle down in their mid-teens. |
| Emotional disorders | Includes disorders such as depression, eating disorders and post-traumatic stress disorders. These may be short term or reoccur at different times in a child's life. These disorders affect all aspects of their life as children often lose interest in their school work and outside interests. Their self-esteem is also affected. Children struggle to maintain friendships and make new friends. |
| Conduct disorders | Children with conduct disorder (CD) find difficulty in functioning in a school setting, as they deliberately display aggression towards others. Oppositional Defiant Disorder (ODD) causes children to have extreme tantrums and be rude, defiant and unco-operative. Conduct disorders seriously affect their ability to form relationships, as children find it difficult to understand the feelings of others. |
| Tourette's syndrome | Tourette's syndrome is a neurological disorder. It often appears between the ages of 7 and 10 years, but is more severe in early teens, improving as young people reach their 20s. Children display involuntary movements or sounds. It is sometimes associated with inattention and impulsive behaviour. It affects children's emotional and social development. Children may be teased or bullied and find difficulty in forming friendships. |

*Table 1: Disorders and their impacts on development.*

children's ability to function effectively in school, it will result in an assessment of a child's needs. This will enable the necessary support to be put into place. It is not always possible to identify the reasons for BESD. In recent years there has been more research in relation to disorders experienced by children and young people. There is also a greater understanding of mental health disorders and ways they may be triggered by traumatic events. Research suggests that at least one in ten children between 5 years and 16 have some form of mental disorder (source: Office for National Statistics).

## How medication may impact on abilities, behaviour and emotional responsiveness

Medication may be used for behaviour disorders. These treatments can have a positive effect and help children to function more positively. There is continued controversy around the success of medication. Children with ADHD, for example, may be treated with stimulant medication. This medication is not a cure but provides a calming effect and makes children less impulsive. Children with ADHD who take this medication may be inconsistent in their responses to learning activities. They may work well in the morning, but then become less focused as the medication wears off. Medication can have side effects such as reducing appetite or causing sleep problems, which will also impact on the child's physical development and self-esteem. Antidepressants are sometimes used by children with extreme anxiety disorders and depression. These may help to alleviate the worst symptoms, but the side effects may cause children to become agitated or withdraw.

Medication for behaviour disorders will affect children differently, so if you know a child is receiving medication, it is essential that their responses in school are monitored and any concerns reported.

# Understand the special educational needs of children and young people with behaviour, emotional and social development needs

## Particular behaviour, emotional and social development needs of children and young people

Every school will have a behaviour policy which outlines how the behaviour, social and emotional needs of all children and young people will be supported. When children display particular behaviour, emotional and social development needs they will require additional support. You may be aware of children who:

- experience emotional and social difficulties
- are withdrawn or isolated or display school phobic reactions
- are disruptive, hyperactive and lack concentration
- have immature social skills or personality disorders
- present challenging behaviours arising from complex needs.

## Portfolio activity

Obtain permission to carry out two observations of children with particular behaviour, emotional or social development needs.

**Observation 1:** A narrative observation of a child involved in a group learning activity (for a period of approximately 20 minutes). Focus on:

- ways the child relates to peers and adults
- their level of independence as they carry out activities
- their level of concentration and ability to stay on task.

**Observation 2:** A time sample – use a snapshot of the specific actions of a child with behaviour problems at set times during the day. This could be every 10 minutes for an hour or every 30 minutes during the morning. Focus on the child's behaviour.

Reflect on your observations to identify any particular difficulties in relation to the expected development norms for their age.

## Functional skills

**English: Writing**
When writing your observations, it is important that you think carefully about your spelling, punctuation and grammar, as if these are incorrect in an observation, it can have an impact on the overall meaning.

# Individual support plans of children and young people with behaviour, emotional and social development needs

Behaviour, emotional and social needs will be supported through **Early Years Action** or **School Action**, or Early Years Action Plus or **School Action Plus**. Where there is lack of progress at this stage, or complex needs are identified, children may undergo statutory assessment and a **statement of special**

**educational need** will be drawn up. Whatever level of support is required, an individual learning plan (ILP) or individual behaviour plan (IBP) will be put into place. Children with behaviour, emotional and social needs are found across all ability levels, including those with additional learning needs and those who are gifted and talented. Whatever the need, early intervention is critical to prevent the child falling behind with work and to reduce the need for exclusion.

Plans may be in relation to the child's:

- behaviour
- difficulty in building relationships with other children and/or adults
- lack of self-reliance and self-esteem.

Your role will be to work alongside teachers and other professionals to provide the additional support which is identified within the plan. Children may have low-level needs where support can be provided within the school. Where there are more complex needs, specialist support may be provided by outside agencies such as psychology services.

In Scotland there is a different process. Instead of statements, children's additional support for learning (ASL) needs are analysed and where necessary a coordinated support plan (CSP) is set up.

## Key terms

**School Action and School Action Plus (or Early Years Action for under 5s)** – a stepped approach which identifies the additional support requirements of the child or young person. School Action Plus is for when additional advice and guidance from outside services are required to meet children's needs

**Statement of special educational need** – a statement which contains details of a child's needs, following an assessment, and the provision which must be in place to support children with special educational needs

Individual behaviour plans will include goals, which support the needs of each child and are additional to the outcomes for other children of the same age. The plans should include:

- information about the child's previous achievement
- the long-term goals for the child's progress
- specific targets for the child to work toward
- what help will be given and how (the strategy, by whom and when)
- specific resource requirements
- how and when success will be measured.

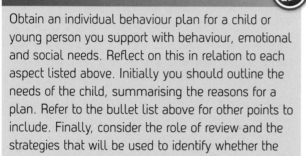

### Portfolio activity

Obtain an individual behaviour plan for a child or young person you support with behaviour, emotional and social needs. Reflect on this in relation to each aspect listed above. Initially you should outline the needs of the child, summarising the reasons for a plan. Refer to the bullet list above for other points to include. Finally, consider the role of review and the strategies that will be used to identify whether the child has achieved their goals.

When using information about children for your portfolio evidence, remember to remove all names and information which would allow the child to be recognised, to ensure confidentiality.

### Functional skills

**English**
Completing this Portfolio activity is great way of developing all three areas of your functional skills in English, as you will be required to read, write and possibly hold discussions with others to obtain all the relevant information.

# Be able to support the behaviour management of children and young people with behaviour, emotional and social development needs

## Identify and set behaviour goals and boundaries for children and young people with behaviour, emotional and social needs

Your role in setting goals and boundaries may be in a situation where a child has recently been identified as having behaviour, emotional and social development needs, and a new plan is being agreed. Alternatively you may take part in reviewing a pupil's progress and agreeing a new set of goals.

A number of people will be involved in setting goals including the teacher and other adults in the school who support the child. The child and their family should be central in this process. For children with complex needs, professionals such as an educational psychologist may also support and advise on appropriate goals and strategies.

Behaviour goals can only be effective where children are involved in setting them, rather than having goals imposed upon them. It is important that children see the reason for each goal and how it relates to them. Goals and boundaries should be clearly focused and appropriate for the individual child. Expecting a 5-year-old with behaviour problems to sit and concentrate for half an hour would be unattainable. This child is being set up to fail to meet the goal.

Goals should also be positive. Rather than setting a goal 'not to snatch toys from other children', an alternative could be to 'always ask other children if you can share their toys'.

## BEST PRACTICE CHECKLIST: Setting behaviour goals

- Start with the child's previous achievements — what they can do.

- Involve the child at all stages.

- Set a small number of goals. This will depend upon the child's stage of development and difficulty, but set no more than three or four.

- Use SMART targets — specific, measurable, achievable, realistic and time-bound.

- Ensure that the learner understand what the goals mean (using age-appropriate language) and what they need to do to achieve these.

- Use positive language.

## CASE STUDY: Setting goals for a child with ADHD

Fran supports 5-year-old James, who has ADHD. She contributes to developing behaviour goals and boundaries. Three goals have been planned. James will:

1. put away the toys at break time when asked by the teacher

2. sit and listen to a story

3. not throw sand at other children.

Fran suggests that one of the goals is negative and could be reworded, and that one of the goals is not SMART.

- Which goal did Fran identify as not being SMART?
- Rewrite the goal to make it SMART.
- Identify the goal which is negative and rewrite to make it a positive goal.

## How goals and boundaries support children and young people to develop and consolidate social and emotional skills

For children who lack understanding of accepted social behaviour, goals and boundaries provide a supportive framework. Children must want to change their behaviour. Goals and boundaries provide direction to enable children to make the right choices, supporting the development of their social and emotional skills. By being involved in setting goals, the children also take on some responsibility for their actions. Goals and boundaries must be relevant and children must be able to see what is in it for them.

### Functional skills

**ICT: Developing, presenting and communicating information**
You could use the computer to design a poster suitable for the age of child you work with that shows the goals and boundaries for their classroom. Your poster will give you the opportunity to try different layouts and editing techniques including text, colour and images.

## Support children, young people and others to understand and apply goals and boundaries

Supporting children with behaviour, emotional and social difficulties can be a challenging role, but also rewarding when you see children beginning to apply goals and boundaries. As you become more experienced and knowledgeable, you may find that others in the school look to you for support and advice. In your role you may also be required to liaise with parents to discuss how well strategies are working and any difficulties they are experiencing in applying the goals and boundaries within the home environment.

Children with BESD require a great deal of support from you in the form of positive reinforcement and encouragement. A smile, thumbs-up or a 'well done' can make the difference and provide a reminder of what they are working towards. You must also be aware with older children that overt praise, given in front of their peers, can have the opposite effect. It is helpful for some children to have a regular time — perhaps just before lunch or at the end of each session, when you can review each small step they

*Do children discuss their concerns about achieving goals with you?*

have taken toward the goal. This will give children the opportunity to discuss concerns and any barriers they perceive to achieving their goals and boundaries.

When a child is experiencing difficulty in meeting a goal, you could find ways to help them work towards it. For example, a goal for a Year 4 child was to raise her hand when she wanted to speak to the teacher, rather than calling out. The child was finding it difficult to wait for her name if she knew an answer or had an idea. The teacher and teaching assistant agreed that the TA would draw the teacher's attention as soon as the child raised her hand, to reduce the risk of her becoming frustrated by waiting. Gradually the child was able to wait for a longer period.

## Knowledge into action

What strategies might you use with the following children to support them to meet their goals?

1. Peter is in Year 6. One of his goals is to listen and respond to others when working in a small group.

2. Manveer is in Year 2. His goal is to work in class without disrupting other children.

3. Scarlet is in the Reception class. She finds playing cooperatively with other children difficult. Her goal is to ask to share toys rather than hitting other children or snatching toys from them.

# Work collaboratively with others to manage disaffection and challenging behaviour

Each school will have a behaviour policy in place which identifies the expectations of behaviour of all children and young people, and the rewards and sanctions which are in place which help to support the policy. Head teachers and governors must also develop a policy which supports children's holistic development and underpins the Every Child Matters framework. All staff must be aware of relevant policies so that there is a common approach to supporting behaviour and planning a curriculum which promotes behaviour, social and emotional development.

> ### Link
>
> You can find more information on the Every Child Matters framework in TDA 3.6, Promote equality, diversity and inclusion in work with children and young people.

When children are disaffected and/or display more challenging behaviour, there need to be personalised approaches to their behaviour management. It is important that all staff are aware of these and apply the agreed approaches in all aspects of the child's school life. Progress would be impeded if agreed approaches to behaviour management were used in some lessons but not others, or not supported at lunch or break times. The child and their family are central to this process. You may be invited to planning and review meetings which involve the child and their family to discuss and agree their role in implementing the agreed approaches.

# Contribute to the provision of safe and supportive opportunities to establish community-based rules and develop social interaction

## Establishing rules

Children with BESD have often experienced a disruptive home life and inconsistent expectations of their behaviour. They will frequently test out boundaries to see how far they can push them, so it is important that these are both clear and upheld consistently by staff.

Where there are too many rules for behaviour, it will be increasingly difficult for children to adhere to these, so fewer targets which are attainable are preferable. It is important that rules and boundaries for behaviour are agreed by all those working in the school and by the children themselves. In some schools, children contribute to this process through school councils. It is beneficial if all children are involved in discussion to agree the rules for their own class and for group work.

---

**CASE STUDY:** Supporting pupils with reading and writing difficulties

Madge has just begun her new role in her local primary school. As part of her role, she has been asked to provide additional support to a group of four children in Year 5 who have difficulty in reading and writing. Madge works with the children in a library area outside the classroom. One of the children is very fidgety and finds concentration difficult. Another child has an individual behaviour plan as he sometimes displays aggressive behaviour towards other children. The other two children concentrate well, although one child is quite withdrawn. During the first session Madge took time to get to know the children, then during the second session she suggested that they agree some rules for working together.

- Why is it important for Madge to involve the children?
- Why are rules important?
- What should Madge take into consideration when writing the rules?

## Developing social interaction

Social interaction can be particularly difficult for children with BESD. It is important that opportunities for social interaction are integrated within all areas of the curriculum, such as working together in pairs or small groups on class projects. Groupings should be flexible so that children are not always working with the same person, although this should be carefully managed so as to avoid clashes of personality. Even where children are working individually, you might look for opportunities to encourage positive interaction between children. For example, one teaching assistant observed that a child who had particular problems in relating to others had an interest and skills in ICT. She drew on this knowledge, asking the pupil to show another child how to copy and paste an illustration for his work. This strategy is also helps to promote a positive image of children with BESD to their peers.

Whole-school approaches such as Social and Emotional Aspects of Learning (SEAL) help to establish community rules and support children to develop their social interactions. It is also helpful if children are involved in lunch time or after-school activities, where they can socialise in a supportive and controlled environment. By getting to know children's personal interests, you will be able to guide them towards suitable activities.

# Promoting positive behaviour and managing inappropriate behaviour

Part of your role is to manage inappropriate behaviour. This happens when behaviour conflicts with the accepted values and beliefs of the setting or society. This can be difficult so you may need to refer to other professionals from time to time. Children with BESD often have trouble controlling their emotions and this may spill over into aggressive acts. Inappropriate behaviour may be displayed through:

- verbal abuse, for example, rudeness, swearing, racist or sexist remarks
- writing
- non-verbal behaviour
- physical abuse.

## Promoting positive behaviour

Although it is important to understand strategies to manage inappropriate behaviour, the focus should be on ways to promote wanted behaviour. Refer to pages 284 and 287 for more on strategies to promote and reward wanted behaviour

## Managing inappropriate behaviour

When inappropriate behaviour is displayed, it should be recognised and actions taken. You should help the child to understand that it is the behaviour of which you disapprove and not themselves. For low-level and attention-seeking behaviour, the appropriate action may be to ignore what has happened and give attention to others who are working effectively. For other behaviours, it is important that you know the sanctions that are available and how to apply these fairly and consistently. There will be a structure of sanctions that can be applied depending on level of behaviour — for example:

- use of orange/red cards
- losing part of break time
- withdrawal of privileges
- **restorative justice**
- referral to senior member of staff.

> ### Key term
>
> **Restorative justice** — making amends directly to the victim or community that has been harmed by an offence

In extreme situations, a child may be excluded or expelled. This will be used as a last resort and for children with special educational needs (SEN) or disability, not before all other approaches have been explored.

The use of sanctions should be used with care. Some sanctions may make children's difficulties worse. Missing break time for a child with hyperkinetic disorder will make them even more fidgety during the next lesson. Restorative justice is often more effective and appropriate for children with BESD. For example, if a child has intentionally knocked over the paint which another child was using, they are asked to wipe the table and fetch a new pot of paint.

## Bullying

Children with BESD may be the victims of bullying or become bullies themselves. Bullying can take the same forms as listed for inappropriate behaviour. There has also been an increase in cyber-bullying via the Internet and mobile phones. Whatever form it takes, bullying must always be taken seriously. The school must have a policy which supports and protects children from bullying.

### Over to you!

Check the sanctions which are available for you to use and for details of when to refer inappropriate behaviour to others.

# Be able to support children and young people with behaviour, emotional and social development needs to develop relationships with others

## Providing opportunities for children with behaviour, emotional and social development needs to establish social contacts

Schools must provide a wide range of opportunities for all children to establish social contacts in all aspects of school life. This could be through learning programmes such as Social and Emotional Aspects of Learning (SEAL). Opportunities for social contact should be integrated in all lessons. Extracurricular activities also provide excellent opportunities for children to establish social contacts.

The environment and organisation of the curriculum can influence the extent to which children establish social contacts as follows:

- the classroom — setting up learning areas will encourage children to sit and work in small groups
- teaching and learning through group activities

- vary groupings so that children have the opportunity to work with different children and in different groups
- lunch or after-school clubs which reflect children's interests.

## Encouraging co-operation between children and young people

Even where the organisation of the school facilitates social contact, you may need to provide additional encouragement for children with BESD. It is important to take into consideration the age of children and their stage of development, and have realistic expectations. You will also need to take into account children's language skills. Children with well-developed language skills find it easier to form relationships. If children have communication difficulties, you should help them to develop their skills to enable them to overcome barriers.

## Interacting with others to provide a positive and consistent example of effective interpersonal relationships

You should be aware of your own behaviour at all times, not only in class but around the school. Children will also notice your interactions with colleagues, so your behaviour should be professional and appropriate. Children will take their lead from your own actions and the way you speak to others. Speak with respect to children at all times, even when they may be displaying challenging behaviour and answering back. You should never use sarcasm.

## Responding to conflict and inappropriate behaviour with due consideration for own and others' safety

Your role is likely to involve dealing with extremes of behaviour. It is important that you remain calm so that the situation is not inflamed and you do not get into arguments. If you anticipate children becoming frustrated, you might defuse conflict by using humour. If conflict is unavoidable, it is helpful to give children time out to allow them to calm down before speaking to them about their actions. When

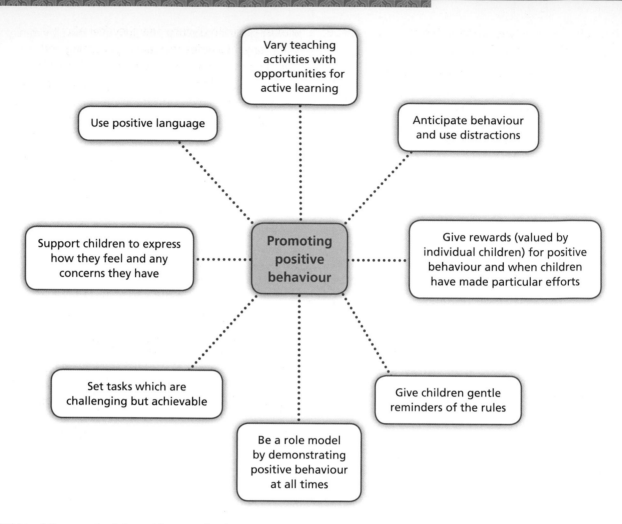

*Which of these methods is used in your school to promote positive behaviour?*

| Age group | Stage of development | Ways to encourage cooperation |
| --- | --- | --- |
| Reception | Children begin to have an awareness of how they fit into a group. They start to develop friendships with others but 'special friends' may change. | Free play opportunities help children to develop communication and negotiation skills. Support children to join in. |
| Key Stage 1 | Children establish friendships and become aware of acceptable levels of behaviour. They begin to take into account the feelings of others. | Plan activities which require cooperation or turn-taking. Use stories which help children to empathise. Teach children singing/activity group games at playtime. |
| Key Stage 2 | Children become more self-aware. They may be influenced by others and how others see them. They may start to have disagreements with others which they find traumatic. | Give opportunities for children to work together to produce an artefact. Help them to find ways to resolve arguments. Use role play to learn how to resolve differences, deal with conflict and to understand that there are choices. Encourage children to take part in lunchtime groups and clubs, or start one yourself. |

*Table 2: Encouraging cooperation for different ages and stages.*

the behaviour involves others in the class, you should separate children and speak to them individually.

If you feel uncomfortable when dealing with conflict or incidents are becoming more frequent, it is important to seek help. Information, advice and support will be available within the school from the SENCO or a teacher who has experience with the child. The school will also have contact with outside agencies such as behaviour units or psychological services.

In situations where you or other adults or children are put at risk, it is essential that you send for help. Physical restraint may be used when others are at risk from harm. It is essential that you are aware of the guidelines for dealing with violent pupils and the use of restraint within your own school. If you work with children who are likely to have violent outbursts, you may well receive training on ways to restrain children safely.

## Strategies for helping rebuild damaged emotional relationships

Whatever support strategies have been put into place, inevitably there are times when there is a breakdown in relationships between a child and their peer(s) or between a child and an adult. This may include yourself or another member of staff.

Initially it will be necessary to talk to each party to try to understand the underlying problem. This will also give you the opportunity to help children to recognise and come to terms with their own feelings. Wherever possible, encourage and support the child to resolve any conflict to rebuild a relationship. The way you approach this will depend upon a child's stage of development. Where the breakdown is more serious, it may be necessary to involve a senior teacher or outside agency.

## Supporting children to review their social and emotional skills and the impact of these on others

Children should be at the centre of the process of planning, support and review of progress. It is important that you identify a regular time to sit

with the child to discuss how they feel about their skills, any difficulties they are experiencing and how they think that other children might view their actions. These discussions will help children to take responsibility for their actions and to understand that there are alternative actions they could take. Support should involve:

● encouraging children and young people to think about the consequences of their actions

● supporting children to think about the way others feel about their actions

● providing opportunities for children to consider other choices available to them.

# Be able to support children and young people with behaviour, emotional and social development needs to develop self-reliance and self-esteem

## Encouraging and supporting children and young people to communicate their feelings, needs and ideas, make decisions and accept responsibility

All children need the opportunity to be self-reliant. This is particularly important for children with BESD who may lack self-esteem and confidence in their own ability. If your role is to support a child with BESD, you must ensure that you are not overprotective. Even when working with very young children, look for ways that you can support independence and not do things which children can do for themselves. You need to allow children to make mistakes in a controlled environment in order for them to be able to develop and grow.

Children's self-esteem directly relates to their behaviour, social and emotional development. Supporting children to develop a good self-image and self-reliance is essential to enable them to reach their full potential. Your own reactions to children will affect how they feel about themselves and their willingness to become independent learners, so it is important that you show children how you value their contribution.

## Encouraging and supporting children to communicate feelings, needs and ideas

Developing a good relationship with children is key to building sufficient trust so that children feel able to share their feelings, needs and ideas with you. You may agree a regular meeting time to talk through their needs. You can also support children within planned group activities such as circle time or through stories. Opportunities to express feelings through art work, music or drama can be particularly effective for children who find communication difficult.

As you get to know individuals, you will become more aware of when they need to talk or are worried. You can then encourage discussion – for example, 'I've noticed that you look a bit worried about your work today.' Your conversations should not always centre around problems. Find out about children's outside interests and school activities where they are making good progress to open a conversation – for example, 'I heard that you started dance class last night. What did you learn to do?'

### Reflect ?

Be aware that children may disclose sensitive information about themselves such as bullying or abuse. Do you understand how to respond and the procedures you should take?

### Skills builder

Plan and implement a small group activity which will support children to communicate feelings, needs or ideas. Reflect on the activity in relation to the response of children or young people.

## Encouraging and supporting children to make their own decisions

You cannot make children behave in a particular way. Children must make their own decisions on how they will behave. It is important therefore that children are given opportunities to make the right choices. This can be achieved by explaining the consequences of different actions. For example: 'Sanjay, if you get back to your task you will still have time to complete it by lunch, but if you continue to chatter you may have to stay behind to finish – it's your choice.'

## Encouraging and supporting children to accept responsibility for their actions

As well as rewarding achievement and effort, you should also observe when children have accepted responsibility for inappropriate actions. Show children you have recognised that, although the action was unacceptable, the way they have dealt with it is pleasing. For example: 'Snatching the glue from Peter wasn't a kind thing to do, but I was pleased to see that you returned it when he asked.'

Restorative justice can be particularly effective to support children to accept responsibility for their actions. If the sanction is proportionate to the action, it will be viewed as fair – not only by the child who has behaved inappropriately but also their peers. This form of justice helps children to see the link between their behaviour and the consequences.

# Supporting children to refocus when self-control has been lost

The progress which children make towards their goals is not always smooth. They may make great strides or appear not to progress for a while. Children may even take a step backwards and display inappropriate behaviour. When they lose control, children may also lose sight of their goals and agreed strategies. It is important that you support children and young people to understand the reasons for their outburst. This may be because events in the child's life are making their behaviour, social and emotional difficulties worse. You should remind children that everyone feels angry at some stage and that life sometimes appears unfair, but that they must remember how to deal with feelings in a positive way. You must give children time to reflect on and discuss events. You can then support children to refocus by:

- recognising that this is a blip and that they are still working towards their targets

- recognising why in this situation they were unable to use strategies to deal with their feelings

- reflecting on what happened and the alternative choices which were available to them

- reassuring children that learning to control anger is a skill and they need to practise it.

## Opportunities for children and young people to develop self-management skills

Supporting children involves providing a safe and secure environment which gives opportunities for them to develop self-management skills. The following skills reduce children's reliance on others and help them to feel more positive about their own abilities:

- problem-solving skills
- decision making
- exercising choice
- self-expression
- general life skills.

## Strategies for recognising and rewarding achievement and effort

You should give children regular feedback on their progress. This could be a word or a smile to show that you are approving and that they are making the right choices. You will also have rewards that you can use such as stickers, house points or certificates. Some schools use raffle tickets which are entered for a prize draw at the end of term. What works with some children may be totally inappropriate for others. As you get to know individuals, you will begin to find which they prefer.

### Functional skills

**English: Writing**
You could develop your writing skills by writing a letter to a parent/guardian of one of the children who you support, provided you have permission from the class teacher or Head Teacher. Your letter could include information on how they are doing in class and how they are developing their skills. Your letter would need to be formal and use a suitable layout. Take care with your punctuation, spelling and grammar in your letter, and make sure that you use appropriate language.

Rewards should only be used when there is real achievement or effort. Rather than saying, 'Well done, I'm pleased with your behaviour today', you must be specific about the progress: 'Well done Christopher, I noticed that you shared your car with Ben at playtime.' Rewards should also be given when children make small steps and not only when they meet their targets. A child may be expected to be able to work without distracting others for ten minutes. Giving him a favourite sticker after five minutes may spur him on to meet his target.

## Getting ready for assessment

For learning outcomes 1 and 2, you will have gathered evidence of your knowledge and understanding. As you move on to outcomes 3, 4 and 5 you will need to collect evidence of your own skills to provide support for children with behaviour, emotional and social needs. Share the learning criteria for the unit with the teacher and Special Educational Needs Co-ordinator (SENCO) and discuss the opportunities you will have to demonstrate your skills. You can then discuss your plans with your assessor.

### Websites

**www.angermanage.co.uk** – British Association of Anger Management

**www.nasen.org.uk** – aims to promote the education, training, advancement and development of all those with special and additional support needs

**www.rcpsych.ac.uk** – Royal College of Psychiatrists

**www.teachernet.gov.uk/teachingandlearning/ socialandpastoral/seal_learning** – Teachernet, Social and Emotional Aspects of Learning (SEAL)

## Check your knowledge

1. Identify three traumatic events which may affect children's behaviour, emotional and social development.

2. In what ways do kinetic disorders affect children's behaviour and how might this influence their emotional and social development?

3. Why are there concerns about medication to control behaviour disorders?

4. Why might children undergo a statutory assessment?

5. What is SEAL?

6. Identify five ways that you can promote positive behaviour.

7. What is meant by restorative justice?

8. Identify three ways to reward children's efforts or achievements.

# CYPOP 44 Facilitate the learning & development of children & young people through mentoring

Learning mentors are involved in helping to remove barriers to learning and raise pupil achievement in school. Working alongside the teacher, you will need to demonstrate how you mentor pupils in a formal or informal capacity, demonstrating how you take pupils' needs into account.

## By the end of this unit you will:

1. understand how to facilitate the learning and development needs of children and young people through mentoring

2. be able to support children and young people to address their individual learning and development needs

3. be able to promote the well-being, resilience and achievement of individual children and young people through mentoring

4. be able to review the effectiveness of the mentoring process.

# Understand how to facilitate the learning and development needs of children and young people through mentoring

## The interpersonal and communication skills required to facilitate learning and development needs

In order to work with children and young people as a mentor it is essential for you to have effective interpersonal and communication skills. It is important to be able to work with pupils to identify their learning and development needs, as well as offer pastoral support.

### Link

See also TDA 3.1, Communication and professional relationships with children, young people and adults, for strategies for effective communication.

Interpersonal and communication skills include:

- effective listening skills
- open questioning techniques
- use of appropriate body language
- giving constructive feedback
- empathising with children and young people while maintaining professional boundaries
- encouraging children and young people to participate and communicate effectively in the mentoring process.

## Effective listening skills

These are important communication skills and you should take the time to make sure that you are actively listening to pupils. Listening to what they tell you is vital as it values what they are saying, reinforces self-esteem and is a crucial part of building relationships.

### Reflect

How do you show that you are actively listening to pupils? For example, do you give eye contact? How do you react to what they are saying?

### Link

For more on active listening, see TDA 3.3, Support learning activities.

## Open questioning techniques

These will enable you to encourage pupils to speak about issues which concern them without trying to 'lead' their answers. For example, when asking them questions, you should not give them questions which will lead to a yes or no answer, but which will encourage them to talk in more depth, by using questioning words such as what, when, why or how.

## Use of appropriate body language

Make sure that you show your interest by the way in which you act when speaking to pupils. For example, with very young children, you will need to get down to their level so that you are not 'talking down' to them. You should also ensure that your body language is a positive reaction to what they are saying and that you are encouraging them to communicate with you.

## Giving constructive feedback

Constructive feedback is about how you offer verbal support to pupils when they are working. You should always ensure that the feedback you give them is shared in a way that is helpful rather than critical. The child should be left feeling that what they have said or done is worthwhile, even if they may still need to do more work on it.

## Empathising with children and young people while maintaining professional boundaries

The way in which you interact with pupils should always remain professional — you will need to ensure that you set boundaries with them and adhere to these. You should always maintain the relationship of professional carer to child. However, when mentoring, you will also need to show consideration and empathy with pupils. This should be possible in an environment in which you and the pupil are clear on ground rules.

## Encouraging children and young people to participate and communicate effectively in the mentoring process

Children and young people will need to be able to participate and communicate effectively with you and to engage in the mentoring process for it to work. You will need to develop trust and positive relationships with them and find out all about them so that effective communication is a natural progression. You should also use all of the strategies above to ensure that they are encouraged by the way in which you communicate with them.

### Skills builder

Ask a colleague to observe you working with your mentee for 15 minutes. Request that they note which of the interpersonal and communication skills listed here you have used when working with pupils.

### Functional skills

**ICT: Developing, presenting and communicating information**

You could transfer this list into a table on the computer and then add columns titled 'How I am going to maintain this' and 'How I am going to improve this'. This table will be a good way of identifying any targets for your professional development. You could share your completed table with your assessor.

## How different learning styles and methods impact on learning and development

Different learning styles and methods include the following.

The way in which work is presented and how they go about learning will affect how pupils learn, as they may all approach learning in a slightly different way.

Ideally all pupils should have a wide range of learning experiences and methods so that they can find out about the way in which they learn best.

## One-to-one learning

In situations where pupils are learning one-to-one, they will have the full attention of an adult and will be able to ask questions whenever needed. Often pupils with special educational needs will have one to one support to enable them to have full access to the curriculum. However, pupils who are learning in this way may also be restricted in their learning as they may find it easier to seek assistance than to try ideas out for themselves. This is why individual support assistants will often support a whole group which includes their named child, so that they are there to support the individual if needed.

## Working in pairs

Working in pairs gives pupils the opportunity to talk to another person during the learning process. This is useful both for sharing ideas and also for supporting pupils who may need additional confidence in order to speak out. Teachers will often ask pupils to discuss ideas with a talk partner, or work together, so that they are working together rather than through another adult.

## Group working

In a similar way, working in groups will enable pupils to share ideas, as well as giving them experience in listening to others and allocating responsibilities.

### CASE STUDY: Working in groups

Kerry is working with a Year 6 class who have been asked to work in groups to design and make a bridge to carry a model car. She notices that one of the groups seems to be taking a long time to make a decision on their design and there is some arguing. Kerry goes over to find that one very able member of the group is taking over and telling the group what to do; this is annoying the others as he is not listening to their ideas.

- What do you think is happening here?
- How could Kerry support the group?
- Why is this learning process important for all pupils but particularly for the one who is taking over with his ideas?

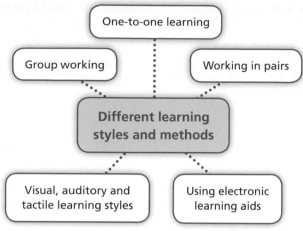

*Which of these methods are you most familiar with?*

## Using electronic learning aids

Electronic learning aids are a form of learning which is constantly changing due to the rapidly moving world of technology. An electronic aid can be any kind of electrical assistance or support for learning, so it may be computer based or through hand-held devices such as PDA's (personal digital assistants) which may be connected to a central workstation. Electronic learning aids may also be used by pupils with special educational needs to support their access to the curriculum and enhance their learning.

### Functional skills

Maths: Representing
ICT: Developing, presenting and communicating information
How many electronic learning aids have you got in your setting? How often are they used? What percentage of the child's week is spent using electronic resources to support their learning? You could log all the electronic resources you have in a database for everyone to access. This would be a good way of auditing the equipment you have in school.

## Visual, auditory and tactile learning styles

Visual, auditory and tactile learning styles were first developed by psychologists in the 1920s, who believed that most individuals have a dominant way of learning, or learning style. For example, visual learners may find it easier to learn by looking and reading, while tactile or kinaesthetic learners may prefer a more practical, hands-on approach. This method has been adopted in recent years by educationalists along with Howard Gardner's Multiple Intelligences, which refers to seven learning styles. Broadly speaking, pupils should have the opportunity to learn in different ways, and teaching and learning activities should be presented so that all pupils have equal opportunities whatever their learning style.

| Learning style | Description |
|---|---|
| Visual | Seeing and reading |
| Auditory | Listening and speaking |
| Tactile or kinaesthetic | Touching and doing |

*Table 1: Learning styles.*

### Over to you!

What is your learning style? Take a learning styles test at www.businessballs.com/vaklearningstylestest.htm

# Be able to support children and young people to address their individual learning and development needs

## Support children or young people to express their goals and aspirations

A key part of your work as a learning mentor will be to encourage and develop children's communication skills and self-esteem so that they are able to speak out and express themselves. This is because those children who need this kind of pastoral support are often those who are the most vulnerable and disadvantaged, and who need additional time with adults and other children. As well as communication skills, the level of children's self-esteem and how they feel about themselves and school will form a key part of their ability to learn and make the most of the school environment. You may need to encourage children who are reluctant to come to school or who have had limited social experiences to take part in a wider range of activities, so that they broaden their horizons. You will also need to give the child or children with whom you are working your time and positive attention through the activities you offer them on a regular basis.

Opportunities to support pupils may be varied but could include:

● giving pupils positions of responsibility such as helpers, captains, school council members

● encouraging them to take part in a variety of extracurricular activities, particularly if they have

| A learning mentor should... | A learning mentor should not... |
|---|---|
| • act as a role model<br>• be an active listener<br>• challenge the assumptions that others have of pupils and that they have of themselves<br>• observe pupils to assess their needs and devise supportive strategies<br>• be involved in running after-school activities<br>• work one to one with pupils<br>• be an 'encourager'<br>• form professional friendships with pupils<br>• give guidance<br>• negotiate targets<br>• be a reliable, approachable, non-judgemental and realistic supporter of pupils, families and staff<br>• run pupil drop-in sessions<br>• work with small groups on anger management, self-esteem and emotional literacy etc.<br>• support families<br>• develop pupils' self-esteem<br>• develop strategies to improve attendance and punctuality<br>• support KS2/3 transfer<br>• liaise with outside agencies to gain additional support for pupils and the school<br>• support mentees in class as part of a structured programme of mentoring support. | • be involved in *counselling* (involving properly qualified professionals, formal referrals and parental consent) sessions with pupils<br>• be a teaching assistant<br>• be the person to whom a pupil is sent when naughty and/or sent out of class<br>• be expected to support teachers in delivering Literacy and Numeracy lessons<br>• co-ordinate and administer whole-school attendance monitoring<br>• be child protection co-ordinator<br>• *teach* gifted and talented pupils. |

Table 2: Clarification of the learning mentor role, based on DfES Learning Mentor guidance (Source: Haringey Council's Learning Mentor Guidance document).

low self-esteem as a learner and have other skills or abilities they want to develop

● spending additional time with them both on a one-to-one level and with other pupils so that they have the input of both an adult and their peers

● being approachable and available to them if they need to speak to you at any time.

### Knowledge into action

Table 2 gives further examples of the kinds of skills you will need to have in your role as a learning mentor. Which of these do you use as part of your role? Can you think of any others which are not listed but which you do with pupils? Which of these do you think continue to develop their confidence and support them in developing goals and aspirations?

## Support children or young people to identify ways of removing barriers to achievement

Pupils you are mentoring on a regular basis may feel disempowered or unable to achieve due to a number of barriers. It is likely that they will need you to support them in identifying and removing these. Barriers may take a number of different forms and may come both from the learner themselves or from others.

Barriers to achievement may include:

● low levels of literacy/numeracy or communication skills

● bias and stereotyping in the learning process

● low learner motivation

● parental and/or peer influence.

### Low levels of literacy/numeracy or communication skills

Pupils may have low levels of literacy and/or numeracy or find it difficult to express themselves well. This may make it difficult for them to see ways of moving on with their learning. They may need to spend time talking with you about how they can overcome this, whether it is through additional learning support or through taking more time to plan their work with you or others.

### Bias and stereotyping in the learning process

You may find that you experience degrees of stereotyping from others when you are working with children. This could come from either children or adults, and you will need to handle it sensitively. Stereotyping means expecting particular characteristics of certain groups of people. For example, people might say that particular groups such as women, black people or gay people have particular characteristics. If you are working with a group of pupils, you may find that others in the group hold antisocial opinions or ideas. You should challenge biased opinions immediately so that children do not think that it is acceptable. The school environment should be one which welcomes all individuals equally and celebrates diversity.

### Low learner motivation

Low motivation is likely to come from a lack of interest in the activity but may also come from feelings of inadequacy or because pupils feel they are unable to participate in learning activities due to a lack of self-esteem. Pupils may need you to encourage them and give them plenty of praise. Children also need to be given plenty of opportunities to be in control of situations and to make decisions in a safe environment. As adults we can support this by making sure that activities give children opportunities to make choices in their learning and develop an awareness of risk.

### Parental and/or peer influence

Children will be influenced in a positive or negative way by the interactions and messages which they receive from adults and from their peers. If a child is continually told that they are no good or is given very little attention, or no positive attention, they will not develop a good self-image. This in turn can lead to a lack of confidence and reluctance to participate in learning activities. Your role will be to motivate pupils by giving them support and encouragement through the development of positive relationships, so that they feel confident enough to be able to work effectively.

## CASE STUDY: Removing barriers to achievement

Ronan is in Year 3 and has been working with Pete, his learning mentor, for two terms. He finds learning difficult and has low self-esteem, and his mother does not have time to work with him at home. She says that it is up to the school to manage his learning. Pete has been speaking to Ronan and his teacher about different ways in which he can try to support Ronan. They have worked with him to devise an action plan to support his learning (see below for more on these). However, Pete feels that it is also important to try to work alongside Ronan's mother and to try to raise his self-esteem.

- What could the team at school do and how could they involve Ronan?
- How might they work with Ronan's mother to support him?

## Action plans to address individual learning and development needs of children or young people

An action plan for learning:

- sets clear targets and outcomes appropriate for the individual learner
- sets clear timescales for achievement
- agrees the support that will be provided to help achievement of targets
- agrees clear review and revision processes and procedures.

When developing action plans to address individual development needs, you should make sure that you follow any agreed formats which are used by the school. In order to make them SMART you will need to be careful that you look closely at the targets you are formulating. You should work through these with the child and discuss them as they are being set, and ensure that they understand what the targets mean.

- **Specific** — you must make sure that the target states clearly what is required.

- **Measurable** — you should ensure that you will be able to measure whether the target has been achieved and what level of confidentiality is required.

- **Achievable** — the target should not be inaccessible or too difficult for the pupil.

- **Realistic** — you should ensure that the pupil will be able to attain what is being set in the time available and that any others involved have been consulted.

- **Time-bound** — there should be a time limit set to achieve the target. This gives an opportunity to look again at the action plan and discuss the pupil's progress.

It is not advisable to set more than three or four targets as they may then seem less achievable to the child. There should also be regular contact with the families or carers of the children receiving support, to encourage positive family involvement in the child's learning. Work with pupils should generally be regular, short and focused, and aimed at giving them the opportunity to discuss issues and to work on targets in their action plan.

You may wish to identify stages towards the goals being set. These will be helpful to the pupil as they will be able to see progress even within a short space of time. However, the targets themselves should not be too ambitious. Depending on the needs of your pupils, you should be able to set realistic timescales. If you are unsure about whether a pupil will be able to meet targets, perhaps because you do not know them well, it is advisable to start with less challenging targets or to work closely with the teacher.

### Portfolio activity

For your portfolio, include an annotated copy of an action plan which you have worked on with a pupil. Highlight each target and show how they relate to the pupil's prior learning and experiences. Show how you have made decisions about the rate of progress and the timescales selected.

---

### CASE STUDY: Developing an action plan to address individual needs

Frances is an experienced learning mentor who has just started to work with Andrew, who is in Year 2 and has some anger management issues. She has had an initial meeting with the SENCO to find out about what has been happening and what she needs to work on with Andrew. However, when Frances asks about an action plan, she is told not to worry, just to make sure she takes this term to get to know him.

- Should Frances say anything else?
- Can she do anything in this situation?

# Be able to promote the well-being, resilience and achievement of individual children and young people through mentoring

## The importance of promoting the well-being, resilience and achievement through mentoring

When mentoring individual pupils, you will need to be able to work with them to promote their **well-being**, **resilience** and achievement. In order to do this, you should get to know the pupils well so that you can find out their areas of strength and greater confidence as well as those of vulnerability. You should value their views and opinions, and show them that you are interested in what they have to say. In this way you will have a better starting point for the mentoring process.

Pupils who are more vulnerable will need to develop their confidence so that they are able to feel better about themselves and the learning process.

It is likely that you will be doing this anyway through mentoring although you may not have given a 'title' to what you are doing — for example, by:

- being upbeat and positive with pupils
- sharing jokes
- being able to remember details of things which are important to them.

You will need to nurture an atmosphere of positive acceptance when working with pupils. Children and young people who feel more confident and positive about themselves generally are more likely to achieve well in school and feel happy — you will need to promote this in your demeanour and the way in which you interact with pupils. Pupils must also learn to be resilient — that is, to be able to cope with upset and disappointments which will come their way. It may be that as a mentor you are more likely to be able to talk to them about these kinds of issues. We need to emphasise to pupils that these kinds of disappointments are part of life and that they will happen to everyone at different times.

## Key terms

**Well-being** — being in physical and mental good health, resulting in a positive outlook and feelings of happiness

**Resilience** — the ability to withstand normal everyday disappointments, hurts and assaults to one's confidence without it affecting self-esteem

## Over to you!

Think of the different ways in which you promote well-being, resilience and achievement of pupils you mentor. In particular, how can you promote physical and mental good health through the kinds of activities you carry out in school?

## Mentoring strategies and activities that support well-being and resilience

Feelings of well-being and resilience will develop naturally in children and young people in different ways both through their experiences and their relationships with others. However, with the pupils you support, extra help may be needed for them to continue to develop sufficiently in these areas. They will need to be exposed to a broad range of different situations in order to give them greater confidence.

### Working with others

Pupils' emotional well-being and resilience is directly related to their ability to relate to others. They may not be confident when working in a group and may need support in order to give input and express their ideas. You may need to question them in a way which is non-threatening in order to bring out their ideas, or encourage them to support one another — for example, by discussing with a partner first to build up their confidence.

### Looking at different scenarios/stories and thinking about and discussing how the child or young person is feeling

These kinds of discussions can be very helpful to pupils who are unsure about talking about their particular situation or emotions. They may not realise that others will be sympathetic to how they are feeling or that it is normal to behave or think in a particular way when faced with a particular scenario. In this way they will be talking about the individual in the story rather than themselves, which they may find less threatening.

### Using problem-solving techniques

Pupils need to learn to be able to develop problem-solving skills so that they have experiences in

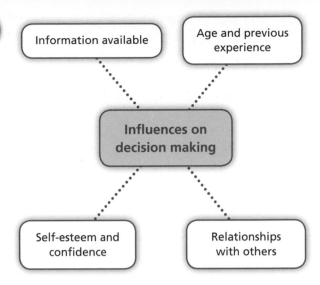

*Influences on a child's decision making.*

managing these kinds of situations for themselves. They will need to be able to approach tasks and problems in a structured way which enables them to develop logical thought. Some find it useful to draw thought diagrams and flow charts so that they can look at a problem in a more visual way, while others may prefer to talk things through. If you can support pupils in identifying their preferred learning style and way of working, they can find ways of approaching a problem which suits them.

### Using decision making

Where children are asked to make decisions about their learning or be responsible for decision making, their ability to do this will relate to their own experiences and ages. Very young children who have not had as much experience may not understand how a particular decision may impact on what they do. Even very basic decisions such as choosing where they going to sit or opportunities to explore new equipment will help them to feel more confident. If children are always told what to do without any explanation or involvement, they are more likely to challenge adults, which can cause a range of problems. However, by encouraging them to make choices, even at a very basic level, you will be supporting their confidence and emotional well-being. Older children who have been encouraged to make decisions and choices about matters which affect them will be more willing to accept boundaries.

## CASE STUDY: Supporting well-being and resilience

Howard works in Year 5 as a learning mentor for two pupils. He comes into school one morning to find that one of the girls he works with has been upset by an incident on the playground that day. She has become very quiet and is not focused on the activity which he had planned to do with her.

- What should Howard do?
- Why is it important that they talk about what has happened to her?

## BEST PRACTICE CHECKLIST: Supporting well-being and resilience

- Provide children with choices during activities and tasks, for example, giving more open-ended activities.

- Give them a variety of activities individually, pairs and in groups.

- Encourage and praise children through noticing their individual strengths and ideas.

- Discuss the effects of their decisions on others in the group if it is a shared activity.

- Use books and other resources to provoke discussion about different situations.

- Be positive and non-judgemental — comment on the behaviour or view rather than on the individual.

*How can you help a pupil to get the most out of a review of their progress?*

# Be able to review the effectiveness of the mentoring process

## Progress of individual children or young people against their action plans

At the end of the mentoring cycle, you will need to work with children and young people to consider how successful they have been at meeting the targets on their action plans. As their mentor, you will need to sit with pupils and their parents or carers to discuss their progress. When reviewing plans, you will need to make sure that pupils are able to think about the progress they have made so far and discuss any difficulties they have faced, so that they can apply this to setting future goals and suggest improvements. Similarly, where they have been successful, they should be able to look at factors that have influenced this.

Pupils should review their plans regularly with you to keep them motivated and also to check their progress. However, you should also remember that the plan is a working document and if circumstances change or it becomes apparent that the target is too ambitious, you should be able to amend it before the review date. Make sure that you note down any changes as soon as they happen and date them for information.

### Portfolio activity

Using an action plan which you have reviewed, annotate it to show how you have worked together to suggest changes at different times and have filled in the review column.

## Effectiveness of the mentoring process in facilitating learning and development

The mentoring programme in your school should be regularly evaluated to ensure that it is having an effective impact on the learning and development of pupils, and you may be involved in doing this. It may also be a requirement of your local education authority as it is essential that there are systems in place to monitor and evaluate the quality and impact of the learning mentor programme. The kinds of data and information which are useful might include:

- careful planning of work and mentoring sessions
- reviews of work with individual pupils
- pupil, teacher and parent evaluations
- review of targets and priorities in the action plan
- monitoring of cohorts (by ethnicity, gender, EAL (English as a foreign language and so on)
- monitoring of attendance, punctuality and exclusions
- performance appraisal for learning mentors
- line manager observations of learning mentor work.

It may be difficult for you to assess your own competence when mentoring pupils, as the process can be a slow one and any progress you make may well take considerable time. However, there should be opportunities for you to have an appraisal as part of your own professional development and this will enable you to consider, alongside your line manager, the effectiveness of your mentoring work with pupils.

The Every Child Matters initiative also highlights the importance of involving learners in the evaluation of work undertaken with them. This may take place through interviews or questionnaires, or through discussion following the process so that pupils have the chance to say what they think and mentors to act upon it.

## Getting ready for assessment

To gather evidence for this unit, it would be useful for your assessor to observe you carrying out a mentoring session with an individual or group of pupils. You should talk through the process from the beginning, discussing how you have formulated action plans bearing in mind the needs of pupils, how you have reviewed them and who was involved, and in particular how they have been evaluated.

### References and websites

DfES (2000) *Good Practice Guidelines for Learning Mentors* (ISBN 1 84185 616 9) – also available from the DfE website: an excellent and very helpful document containing a number of references, case studies and websites for further reference.

**www.cwdcouncil.org.uk/learning-mentors** – Children's Workforce Development Council offers information on learning mentors

**www.teachers.tv** – Teachers TV: enter 'Learning mentors' in the search for video and other links

## Check your knowledge

1. Give examples of four interpersonal and communication skills which you might need to facilitate the learning and development needs of children and young people.

2. How might the way in which a pupil learns impact on their learning and development?

3. Which of the following might you do to encourage a pupil to express their goals and aspirations? Why is it important that they should be able to do this?
   a) Spend time getting to know them.
   b) Ask them lots of questions.
   c) Give them opportunities to try a range of activities.
   d) Be approachable.

4. What barriers to achievement have you come up against when mentoring pupils? How have they been overcome?

5. How can you promote pupil resilience through the use of different strategies?

6. What kinds of systems might your school have in place for monitoring the effectiveness of the mentoring process?

7. How can you personally think about your own professional development as part of this?

# TDA 3.25 Lead an extracurricular activity

This unit is about supporting a range of activities which are held outside normal school hours. These may consist of setting up, checking health and safety aspects and ensuring that children and young people are motivated to carry out the activity. You will also need to make sure that you start and finish sessions correctly, and are able to review and improve the activities which are offered to pupils. All of the assessment criteria except for 1 and 5.3 need to be assessed in the workplace.

## By the end of this unit you will:

1. understand the aims and requirements of the extracurricular activity
2. be able to prepare for leading an extracurricular activity
3. be able to prepare children and young people for an extracurricular activity
4. be able to lead an extracurricular activity
5. be able to review and improve extracurricular activities.

# Understand the aims and requirements of the extracurricular activity

## The aims and content of the extracurricular activity

As can be seen from the list below, you may be leading **extracurricular activities** in a range of different situations and contexts. Extracurricular activities are of benefit to pupils as they enable them to try out or practise activities which they wish to work on in more depth or in which they have an additional interest. They provide enrichment to pupils' school experience through giving them a wider range of activities. You will need to be able to supervise a group of pupils and be clear on the aims and content of what you are doing.

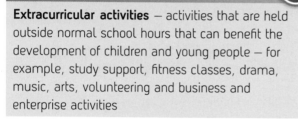

### Key term

**Extracurricular activities** — activities that are held outside normal school hours that can benefit the development of children and young people — for example, study support, fitness classes, drama, music, arts, volunteering and business and enterprise activities

The aims of the activity are the purpose of what you will be doing, or why you are doing it. The content of the activity is exactly what you are going to be doing for that session and for those which come next. For example, the aims of a fitness class are to encourage the participants to get fit, while the content is the kinds of exercise you will do to help them achieve it.

You may have been given lesson plans or outlines to help you, or you may have devised these yourself. Either way, you should be able to report back to others on what you are doing with the pupils and how you will be going about it.

### Skills builder

Write a reflective account about the extracurricular activity which you lead in school. If you have more information, use this and highlight the aims and content of what you will be doing.

### Functional skills

**English: Writing**

Writing your reflective account is a good way of developing your English skills. Make sure that you use appropriate language so that your report is suitable for the audience, with accurate spelling, punctuation and grammar.

## The values or codes of practice relevant to the activity

Values and codes of practice relate to belief systems and standards which need to be considered when carrying out the activity. They will usually take the form of guidelines, but you may decide to make them into rules so that pupils are clear on what they should and should not do. Although there may be some differences in the way in which people view them, they will usually include respect for self and others, and are related closely to Personal, Social, Health and Economic education (PSHE) and Citizenship education. They may also be tied in with the school rules. If the school is a church school, this will also be closely linked in with its values.

## The requirements for health and safety that are relevant to the activity

You will need to make sure, when leading extracurricular activities, that you are aware of the requirements for health and safety which are relevant to the activity. Check before each session, in particular if you are using different equipment or are working in a different environment from the usual one.

Requirements for health and safety include:

- health and safety policies and procedures of the setting
- duty of care
- the Health and Safety at Work Act
- requirements for activities in the scope of the national governing bodies for sports.

# Health and Safety Checklist

**ROUNDERS ENGLAND**

| Name: | | Date: | |
|---|---|---|---|
| Facility name and location: | | | |
| Location of nearest telephone: | | | |
| Location of first-aid kit: | | | |

| Emergency Contact Details | | | |
|---|---|---|---|
| Role | Name | Location | Telephone |
| Appointed first-aider | | | |
| | | | |
| | | | |
| | | | |

Emergency evacuation procedures:

Please tick ☑ to confirm that the following items have been checked:

- All equipment is safe and appropriate

- The playing area and facilities have been checked for actual or potential hazards

- The facility is suitable and appropriate for the planned activities

- A register of participants has been maintained

- Participants' previous experience established

- Participants' clothing, footwear, eyeglasses and jewellery checked as appropriate

Please tick ☑ to confirm that the following have been explained to participants:

- Health and safety procedures

- The rules of the facility/venue/session

- Any potential hazards

- The emergency procedures

*The health and safety checklist for Rounders England 2010.*

## Health and safety policies and procedures of the setting

Whatever the activity which you are leading with pupils, you will need to have an awareness of the relevant health and safety requirements. You should make sure through checking your health and safety policy and speaking to the school's health and safety representative that you have considered all aspects of the school's policies when carrying out that particular activity. You will need to be particularly careful when carrying out any activity which is off site or which requires a risk assessment.

## Duty of care

Anyone who is in a position of responsibility for children and young people will have a duty of care towards them — that is, they must look after their health, safety and welfare while they are in their care. You should also ensure that you encourage pupils to look out for one another and develop their awareness of safety.

### Functional skills

**Maths: Representing and analysing**
You could draw a plan of the area that you use for your extracurricular activity. On your plan you could label how you take health and safety into consideration, and how you consider your duty of care role. For example, if you are running a sports club, do you provide soft drinks or snacks?

## The Health and Safety at Work Act

This piece of legislation was brought in to protect everyone at work through procedures for preventing accidents. The kinds of procedures that everyone in the workplace will be expected to observe are:

● reporting any hazards

● making sure that their actions do not harm themselves or others

● using any safety equipment which is provided.

## Requirements for activities in the scope of the national governing bodies for sports

National governing bodies exist for each sport, and depending on your activity, you may need to check that you are meeting all health and

safety requirements for each organisation. An example from Rounders England is given on the previous page.

# Be able to prepare for leading an extracurricular activity

## Select and prepare equipment and resources for the extracurricular activity

You will need to obtain equipment and resources for the activity in advance so that the learning environment is ready for pupils when they arrive. Occasionally, when running after-school or lunchtime clubs, you may be limited in the amount of time you have to set up as the location or room you need is in use until the end of the previous session. In this situation you may also need to rely on pupils to help you (see also heading below). If you are going to be off site, you will need to carry out a risk assessment (see CYP 3.4 page 141 for more information on this) and should have the correct pupil–staff ratio. This is dependent on the age of pupils and your school will have its own policy on how many adults will be needed.

You should also ensure that you are prepared well before the activity takes place, so that you are not trying to find resources at the last minute. You must make sure that you have enough equipment for the needs of pupils — in particular if any have special educational needs — and that it is in working order. You should also check that you know how to operate any equipment in advance, so that you are not doing it when the children are present. Not only does late preparation make the activity more stressful, it is also much harder to do!

## Prepare the environment for the safe conduct of the activity

You should check the environment you will be working in as you are setting up, to ensure that it is safe for children and young people to work in. You will need to be aware of the needs of pupils to ensure that you are aware of any who may have special educational needs or issues with mobility. If you are getting out large apparatus or equipment, you will need to remember health and safety regulations and also make sure you leave enough time for safety checks. Take a look around the environment and:

- look at floor surfaces to ensure they are not wet or slippery
- check any wires are not likely to be tripped over during the activity
- check to make sure that equipment is not damaged or broken
- make sure fire exits are clear
- ensure pupils will have access to any equipment they need and will be able to move around safely
- always check with your health and safety officer that the environment is safe, if this is the first time you have run the activity, and that you are meeting health and safety requirements.

---

**CASE STUDY:** Preparing for an extracurricular activity

Arike is working as a basketball coach where he runs the group as a pre-school activity. He usually arrives at the school at 7.50 a.m. and gets the equipment out of his car before having a quick check of the hall before the children come at 8 a.m. However, due to traffic he has arrived late today and does not have time to check before the children start the activity. One of the basketball hoops is not secured properly and during the session it falls over, narrowly missing one of the children.

- What should Arike have done, even though he was going to be late?
- Could he have done anything else to improve safety for the children?

---

## Dress appropriately for the planned activity

You will need to make sure that you and the children have the correct clothing and footwear to carry out the activity safely. It is important that you set the correct example to pupils in the way that you dress, so that

they know what is expected when carrying out the activity. At primary school level, this will mainly relate to sports, although you may run an extracurricular activity which stipulates a particular uniform. If you are running an out-of-school activity or one which takes place over several days, pupils will need to have information and guidelines well in advance so that they are able to check that they have the correct clothing.

# Be able to prepare children and young people for an extracurricular activity

## Interact with children and young people in a way that makes them feel welcome and at ease

This may sound obvious, but if pupils are coming for an extracurricular activity, you will need to make them feel welcome. They may not have been involved in these kinds of activities before, or may be anxious about taking part, particularly if they are very young or have recently started at the school. You should always try to encourage pupils as much as possible through the way in which you communicate with them — body language, praise and showing that you are enjoying the activity yourself will all help with this.

---

**Link**

For more on this topic, see TDA 3.5, Develop professional relationships with children, young people and adults.

---

## Comply with organisational procedures for checking attendance and dress and equipment

You should always ensure that you comply with the school's regulations for checking attendance. You should have been provided with a list or register of names so that you know who is present and can sign pupils in at the start and out at the end. Even if you think that you know exactly who has arrived, it is very

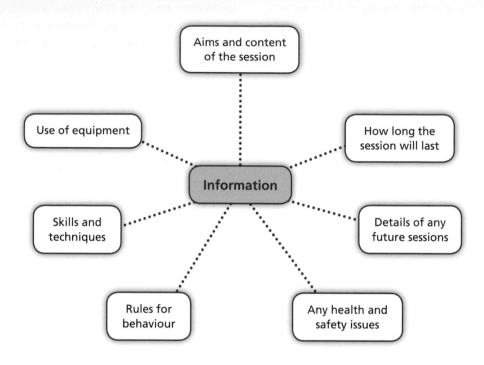

*Why is information about the activity essential for children and young people?*

easy for one person to be missed, and you will be accountable for each pupil who is present.

You will also need to make sure that pupils have brought the correct dress and/or equipment to carry out the activity as soon as you can, so that you know if there are any problems — it is important to ensure that everyone is able to work safely on activities. This includes checking to ensure that they are not wearing jewellery if this is not appropriate. If they do not have the correct equipment, they should be aware at the start of the activity that taking part will not be possible.

> ### Reflect ?
>
> How do you ensure that pupils have the correct equipment or dress at the start of each extra-curricular activity? What kinds of systems or rules are there in your organisation about this?

## Provide children and young people with information about the activity

At the start of the activity, you will need to give children and young people information about what will be happening — particularly if the activity is new to the school or if you have a lot of new participants.

- **Aims and content of the session:** The children should understand what you are going to be doing and why you will be doing it.

- **How long the session will last:** It should be clear that children know the length of the activity and what will happen at the end, and where parents or carers will come to meet them.

- **Details of any future sessions:** You should give the children details of future sessions so that they know when they will be continuing with the activity — for example, whether it will be at the same time each week or less often.

- **Any health and safety issues:** Make sure you point any issues out at the start, for example, if you are outside and there is something they need to watch out for, or if they are using equipment with which they need to take particular care.

- **Rules for behaviour:** Whatever session you are supervising, you should always make sure that you go through rules for behaviour with pupils at the start. In this way they will be clear on your expectations and what will happen if their behaviour is not appropriate.

- **Skills and techniques:** Pupils will need to know what skills and techniques will be covered in the session. The skills should be what you are aiming to do in the session and the techniques are the methods which you will be using to achieve them.

- **Use of equipment:** If pupils need to use any equipment, make sure that they know how to use it or are partnered with someone who can help them.

## Find out if the children and young people have any relevant experience and/or skills

Before starting a new activity with pupils, it is a good idea to ask if any of them have skills or experience which are relevant. You can do this at the beginning of the session when you are talking about what you will be doing that day. For example, if you are going to be carrying out a musical activity, you might ask them if anyone plays an instrument. This will help you to find out at the start how many of the group have some prior experience or skills which might help them.

## Ensuring the children and young people understand the activity and what they will be doing, and are prepared and motivated

In a similar way to your work when supporting learning activities, you will need to ensure that children and young people have a clear understanding of the activity and what they need to do, ensuring they are **mentally and physically prepared**. Before you start, and depending on the activity, you may need to discuss with them the importance of safety or check that they understand the nature of the activity.

> ### Key term
>
> **Mentally and physically prepared** — when participants are able to undertake the activity without unnecessary physical or emotional stress or risk of injury

> ### Link
>
> The rest of this unit is linked to TDA 3.3, Support learning activities, as you will be supporting pupils throughout the activity.

If the extracurricular activity requires you to teach the whole group something completely new that they have not done before, you will need to take them through step by step, allowing them to ask questions as you go. This may include learning new vocabulary, repeating instructions, and allowing plenty of time. If the activity requires them to use specific equipment which is new to them, you will again need to allow them time to explore it and become used to using it before you start. Although they may be keen to learn the skill, you should ensure that you take them through instructions slowly to ensure they carry out the activity safely.

While carrying out the activity, you should continue to engage and motivate pupils through providing them with opportunities to develop their skills and giving praise where appropriate. Always be aware that they have joined the group because they have an interest in the activity or subject, and so will want to learn or practise the activity, which may not always be the case when you are supporting their school work. You should be able to use this enthusiasm to encourage them to participate actively in the activity and aim to keep them motivated in an atmosphere which does not put pressure on them.

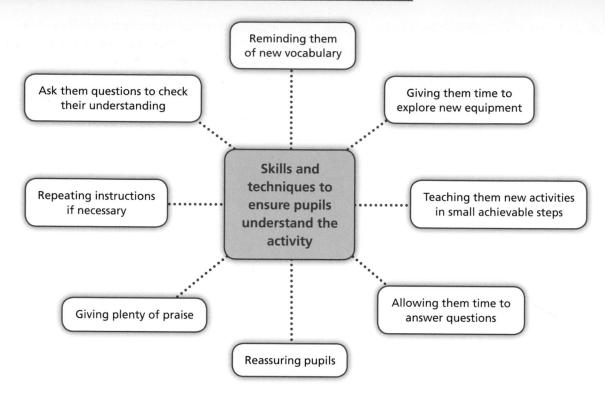

*How does each of these skills and techniques enhance the learning experience?*

# Be able to lead an extracurricular activity

## Develop the activity at a suitable pace and in a way that meets its aims

While you are running the activity, make sure that you take children through what they need to do at a pace which suits them and allows them to take on any new information or skills. You should consider:

- the age of the children and any special educational needs or disabilities
- the number in the group
- whether they have any experience of the activity
- the type of activity you are doing with them and any aspects which they might find challenging or for which they might need reassurance
- the aims of the activity
- whether it will be stimulating for the children
- the length of the session.

You will need to bear these points in mind when planning each session and its aims so that pupils

are able to focus on a different aspect of the activity each time, or develop their skills in a particular area. They should have adequate time to think about what they are doing and be able to acquire any new skills. As with any other type of learning, it is important for pupils not to do too much too soon, as this will put them off the activity and discourage them from learning.

---

**CASE STUDY:** Develop the activity at an appropriate pace

Marina is an experienced actor who is just starting a drama group with Key Stage 2, and has planned her first session. Her aims are to put the children into groups and to spend the session going through a reading of a play that they are going to put on at the end of term.

- What do you think of the way in which Marina has planned the session?
- How might you consider planning and developing this kind of drama session with children?

---

Print off and put into your portfolio some activity plans which demonstrate the way in which you have developed your extracurricular sessions with pupils. You can annotate them to show how you have taken some of the above points into consideration when running the activities.

**Functional skills**

**English: Writing**
**ICT: Using ICT**
Writing activity plans is a good way of developing your writing skills. You could organise your space on your computer and create folders to store your plans in. You should try to include a separate column on your plans where you can evaluate how the session went.

## Giving clear and supportive feedback at appropriate points

As the children are working on the activity, you should be able to give pupils clear feedback on their participation and progress at appropriate points. It is important for children and young people to have some idea of how well they are managing the activity and to know that you have noticed the effort which they are making. You can do this by giving verbal encouragement and praise while they are carrying out the task, and also by speaking to them and their parents at the end, if possible, to say how they have got on. If you end the activity on a positive note, pupils will feel more encouraged about returning for the next session and will be enthusiastic about what they have done.

## Providing additional explanations and demonstrations when necessary

However interested and engaged pupils are in the activity, there may be times when they need encouragement or help to continue. They may approach you and seek additional support, but it is possible that they will not always ask for it for a variety of reasons.

● They may not want their peers to see that they need help.

● They may not realise that they are approaching an activity incorrectly.

● They may wish to complete the activity themselves.

● They may not realise that they are losing concentration.

You should always be vigilant in case children or young people are showing signs that they are finding it difficult to continue. Look out for pupils who are lacking concentration, looking anxious or looking to others in the group to see what they should be doing. If a pupil looks as though they need help, you should ask them if they are all right or if they need you to explain something further. You may also need to model what to do for pupils who are finding the activity difficult and give additional explanations. If you find that a pupil is struggling but wants to complete the activity without support, you can provide encouragement through praise and recognising what they are doing.

---

**CASE STUDY: Providing additional explanations and demonstrations**

Ian runs a textiles club and is working with a group of Year 5 and 6 children to design and make appliqué features on T-shirts. He has about 15 children in the group, all of varying abilities. The activity is fairly challenging for the group, although most of them are working quietly in pairs and are getting on with it. However, Ian can see that two of the children are very quiet today and have not made very much progress since the previous week.

• What, if anything, should Ian say to the children?

• How could he support and encourage them without doing the work for them?

---

## Encouraging the children and young people to say how they feel about the activity

As they are carrying out extracurricular activities in their own time, you should encourage pupils to talk about how they feel about these, and respond to their feelings appropriately. You should make sure that you question them as you are carrying out the activity, so that you have a clear idea about their level of engagement in what they are doing. It is worthwhile to ask pupils what kinds of aspects of the activity they enjoy or what they find less appealing (see also page 313 on feedback). This will give you valuable feedback and help you in planning future sessions.

---

**CASE STUDY:** Encouraging children and young people to say how they feel about the activity

Nessa runs a cross-country club with Key Stage 2 pupils each week. She always follows the same format with children and goes on the same route around the school grounds, which are fairly large. The club lasts for just under an hour.

Nessa has decided that the club is in need of a few changes and has just implemented these — she tells the children that there will now be more warm-ups at the start of the activity, cool-downs at the end and she has changed the length of the route. Most of the group sound pleased about the changes, but one of the pupils says it was fine before.

- What should Nessa say to the pupil who is less enthusiastic about the changes? Should she have changed the format of the activity?
- Why is it important to tell the children first?
- How will it help Nessa by finding out how the children feel in advance?

---

## Vary the activity to meet new needs and opportunities

You may have to vary the activity or how it is run in order to meet new needs and opportunities which arise in the course of or outside the session. In other words, some things may come up before or during the activity which you have not planned for. For example, one of the children may have brought in a piece of equipment from home for the activity which will be interesting for the others to see, or a new participant may join the group and you need to go over aspects of what you have done already with the others. You should be adaptable as far as possible, in particular if it is something which will develop pupil learning.

---

**CASE STUDY:** Vary the activity to meet new opportunities

Kais is running a recorder group for Years 1 and 2. The group has been working together for two terms when Kais hears of an opportunity for them to join in with a borough-wide sponsored recorder day to raise money for charity.

- Why would it be a good idea for Kais' group to join in with the fundraiser?
- How might he need to vary his sessions to prepare for the day?

---

## Prepare children and young people to finish their activities

You should always make sure that you give children and young people adequate warning when it is nearly time for them to finish their activities. This is because they will then have some advance warning to finish what they are doing and bring it to an end. Very young children may not understand the timescale if you tell them that they have five minutes to go, for example, but most pupils will find it helpful to be told how long they have left to complete what they are doing. With older pupils, you may just need to remind them to look at the clock every so often, as some activities will require you to keep a close eye on the time. If you prepare pupils to finish their activities, they may be able to use up any resources or materials, or if they are carrying out a physical activity, they can start to cool down, or have some recreation time.

*What are the benefits of inviting pupils to feed back about an activity?*

## Knowledge into action

Copy and complete the table to show how pupils could use the last few minutes of their activity.

| Activity | Using the last few minutes |
|----------|----------------------------|
| Swimming club | |
| Art and craft club | |
| Chess club | |
| Pottery club | |
| School orchestra | |

*Table 1: Making use of the last few minutes of an activity.*

# Be able to review and improve extracurricular activities

## Work with children and young people to review the activity

Following your work on extracurricular activities, you may decide to review what you have done with pupils so that you can gauge their level of interest and motivation. You may wish to do this verbally at the end of each term. However, it is worth giving pupils a feedback sheet when you have completed a series of lessons, to see whether pupils have reacted to it as you expected. In this way you will also have a record of what pupils have said, as it can be hard to remember if you do this verbally. Pupils may also wish to be anonymous, particularly if they have not liked something, and may be more confident about saying what they think.

## Identifying what learning they can transfer to areas of their school curriculum and other areas of their life

While you are working on extracurricular activities it will be useful for children, particularly if they are very young, to think about how their new skills are relevant and why they might be useful and transferable to other areas of their life or the school curriculum.

All extracurricular activities are a form of enrichment of the school experience and will benefit pupils in different ways. As children become older, and particularly when they transfer to secondary school, the kinds of extracurricular activities which are offered may relate more to jobs and careers, or, in the case of activities such as the Duke of Edinburgh Scheme, be useful for their curriculum vitae (CV).

| | |
|---|---|
| 1. Why did you want to join this club? | |
| 2. Was it what you expected? Why? | |
| 3. What have you particularly enjoyed doing? | |
| 4. Is there anything you have not enjoyed about the club? | |
| 5. If you could change something about this club, what would it be? | |
| 6. Is there anything else you would like to tell us? | |

*Table 2: Example of an evaluation form for extracurricular activity.*

## Using feedback to reflect on and improve own contribution to extracurricular activities

You should always think about your own contribution to any extracurricular activities which you have led with pupils, so that you can evaluate it and consider any changes which you might like to make. If you have given them a feedback sheet, this may give you some ideas about how you could improve or change your own contribution to the way in which the activities have been run. You should also seek feedback from colleagues to see whether you can gather any additional useful information about the activity. For example, sometimes pupils may talk in class about activities they have carried out before or after school, and whether they have enjoyed them or not. Make sure that you take some time to think about the feedback and whether it has an impact on your future practice.

**BEST PRACTICE CHECKLIST:** Delivering extracurricular activities

- Always prepare equipment and resources well in advance.
- Make sure pupils have brought the correct clothes or equipment with them.
- Check health and safety issues before, during and after the activity.
- Make sure pupils know what to do in case of evacuation of the premises.
- Encourage pupils to take responsibilities during sessions.
- Develop positive relationships with children and young people.
- Keep an eye on pupils to see whether they may need additional help.
- Give them time after completing sessions to talk about the activity.
- Use a variety of methods to obtain feedback following the activities to inform and improve your practice.

## Getting ready for assessment

In order to be assessed for this unit, you should have information and other evidence about the kinds of extracurricular activities you have led and carried out with pupils, so that you can show them to your assessor. In addition, they will need to be able to observe you lead an extracurricular activity with a group of pupils, incorporating as many of the assessment criteria as you can, starting with the preparation of the environment and resources, and finishing with a review of what they have done together, identifying how they can transfer their learning to other areas.

### Websites

**www.bbc.co.uk/health/treatments/first_aid** – information from the BBC on first aid
**www.hse.gov.uk** – Health and Safety Executive

## Check your knowledge

1. Give examples of four different types of extracurricular activities which are run in your school.

2. What kinds of health and safety requirements might exist for extracurricular activities? How can you ensure that you are thoroughly prepared for these requirements?

3. What should you do in order to prepare for an extracurricular activity? How can you involve pupils in this?

4. When leading an extracurricular activity, which of the following methods can you use to keep children and young people motivated and on task?

   a) Giving supportive feedback
   b) Keeping routines the same
   c) Developing activities at an appropriate pace
   d) Keeping them informed about what is happening
   e) Checking they are doing everything correctly at regular intervals.

5. When might you need to give children additional explanations about what they are doing in order to support them?

6. Why is it important for you to be mindful of the pace of the activity?

7. How and why might you need to vary activities which you have planned to carry out with pupils?

8. Name two ways in which you can review extracurricular activities you have carried out with pupils.

# LLUK Engage parents in their children's early learning

Parental and family influences are the most significant on a child's well-being, learning and development. For this unit you will need to show how you work with parents to engage them in their child's learning in the early years. You should gather evidence to explain the importance of working in partnership with parents and communicating effectively with them to support their child's learning. The term 'parents' refers in this unit to parents and legal guardians or primary carers of looked-after children. This unit will all be assessed by portfolio activities and not by observations.

## By the end of this unit you will:

1. understand the policy context and research that underpins parental involvement in their children's early learning

2. understand how to work in partnership with parents to support their children's early learning

3. understand barriers to parents being involved in their children's early learning

4. understand how to use reflection to challenge and develop existing practice in working with parents to support their children's early learning.

# Understand the policy context and research that underpins parental involvement in their children's early learning

## Key research findings which show the importance of parental involvement in their children's learning

One of the four themes of the Early Years Foundation Stage (EYFS) is that of 'positive relationships', and this means that adults who work with children in early years environments should have positive relationships with parents and families. In 1994, the Start Right report (Ball, 1994) recognised the importance and nature of parental involvement in their children's learning. In it, it was suggested that early years professionals need to support parents through their practice and by giving them information about current research. In this way their own knowledge of children's development will be improved, which would then support their own self-esteem.

Some of the most important recent research has been the Effective Provision of Preschool Education (EPPE) project in 2004, which tracked the progress of 3,000 young children through different forms of pre-school provision and looked in particular at the impact of the home and family environment. In it, although other factors such as the quality of pre-school education, the socio-economic status of the family or the mother's level of education all play a role, the home learning environment is seen as of even greater importance. The research also showed that children achieve better in early years settings where educational aims are shared and discussed with parents, and the relationship is a partnership.

Ongoing research and legislation since the EPPE continues to reflect the importance of parental involvement. The Children's Plan, drawn up in 2007, set out targets to improve the outcomes for children through consultation with families and emphasised the importance of involving parents in policies which affect children. The consultation showed the belief of the DCSF that 'families are the bedrock of society and

the place for nurturing happy, capable and confident children'.

Pioneers of pre-school education such as Maria Montessori, Margaret McMillan and Loris Malaguzzi are well known to place a strong emphasis on working with parents. Reggio Emilia schools in fact started as a parent initiative — of ten key principles, two are relevant to the active involvement of parents.

Jillian Rodd (2006) cites the following values and beliefs as 'fundamental for the development of a partnership approach to parental involvement', as parents are:

- experts on their own children
- significant and effective teachers of their own children
- skilled in ways that complement those of practitioners
- different but have equal strengths and equivalent expertise
- able to make informed observations and impart vital information to practitioners
- inherently involved in the lives and well-being of their children
- able to contribute to and central in decision making
- responsible and share accountability with practitioners.

*(Source: Rudd, Jillian,* Leadership in Early Childhood – *OUP, 2006.)*

### Knowledge into action

See if you can find any other examples of where research into parental involvement shows its importance to a child's early learning.

### Functional skills

**ICT: Finding and selecting information**
**English: Reading**
You may use the Internet as a starting point for this information. Using a variety of search engines will help to increase your results, but ensure that you take account of any copyright restraints on information and check the validity of the source. This is also a good way of developing your reading skills.

## The concept of positive home learning environments and ways of promoting and supporting them

Part of the EPPE study looked at the effect of the home learning environment on a child's progress. They identified that a positive home environment is one in which children and parents visit the library together, sing and recite nursery rhymes, look at and explore numbers and shapes, and enjoy painting and drawing. In other words, the parents in these homes have made learning part of the child's day-to-day experiences from an early age. In this way, children become used to looking for learning experiences as part of their everyday lives. A positive home environment is important for children's early development as it will nurture their natural enthusiasm for learning in a safe and secure environment.

In order to promote positive home learning environments, parents will need to feel that they are able to contribute to their child's learning. Many parents do not feel confident that they are able to do this and may look to the school to support them. However, it is important that families do this at their own pace and in their own time, as there will be other pressures on them. Many Sure Start centres offer a range of services and provision for parents in areas such as health care, social support and links with local training, which help to act as support networks for communities, and these can help at a local level. Schools can encourage parents and help support their confidence in being educators in different ways. However, it is important to be led by the needs of the parent rather than by acting on a presumed need.

## Why it is important to work in partnerships with parents, including fathers

Jones and Pound (Open University Press, 2008) cite Charles Desforges (2003), who carried out a review of research studies which examined the effects of parental involvement in their children's education. He concludes that children themselves will be put under pressure when they first start school, as they are acting as a mediator between the two environments. He states that they are 'bridging the gap' between the home and school or early years setting, which can place unnecessary pressure and stress on them, particularly in situations in which the parents are not familiar with the system in this country.

When working in early years environments, you may need to encourage and support parents, and promote the importance of working together. It may be helpful to encourage the participation of parents by inviting them to help in school. However, although this may be a starting point in dispelling some of the mystery of what goes on in school, it should not be seen as the main way in which partnerships with parents are to be founded.

### Portfolio activity

Following some research and reading on parental involvement, carry out a professional discussion observed by your assessor in which you explain the importance of working in partnership with parents, and fathers in particular.

---

### CASE STUDY: Promoting positive home learning environments

Alia is working in a Nursery and Reception mixed class which is attached to a school. One of the children in the class, Zak, has some behaviour issues which are isolating him from other children. Zak's parents are also concerned and have asked to come in to discuss his behaviour, which is becoming more of a problem at both home and school. Along with Alia, who is Zak's key worker, they hold a meeting to talk about behaviour management strategies and some of the ways home and school could work together.

- Why is it important for parents and staff to communicate in this situation?
- How will this meeting help to promote a positive home learning environment for Zak?

It is important to work with parents from the earliest stages because the more comfortable parents feel with the school environment and staff, the more likely they will be to discuss and contribute their knowledge and information about the child. This will in turn enable staff to inform and involve parents in their child's education. Fathers in particular should be encouraged to develop a relationship with the school, as in many cases they can be excluded due to different circumstances. It is important, in particular for boys, to see their fathers in the school environment and working in partnership with educational staff. Barriers to this involvement can sometimes stem from the school themselves, which is not offering the type of support or opportunities that parents need. (For more on barriers, see page 323.)

> ### CASE STUDY: Working in partnership with parents
>
> John works in an infant school in which he is the only male member of staff. He has asked the Reception class teacher if they can set up a series of sessions for fathers in order to target their involvement in school, as he has seen a number of dads on the playground. They decide to run a reading group as two of the fathers in the class have asked about how they can support their children better with reading.
>
> * How might the school go about setting up and running the group?
> * How will this benefit the children?

## The importance of clear principles and policies to engage parents in their child's early learning

It is important that your school should have clear principles, values and policies to support the engagement of parents, and these should act as guidelines for staff and parents. Your school should have an early years policy which will explain how you start to work with parents from before the child starts school. There should be a policy and culture which welcomes parents and involves them through open days, involving them in their children's experiences

and valuing their contributions. All staff should know and understand the importance of this, of treating parents and carers with respect, and of remaining professional when communicating with them.

> ### Skills builder
>
> Look at your school's early years policy. Give examples of how it supports parental engagement and encourages the involvement of parents in their child's early learning. Do you think it covers all areas?

> ### Functional skills
>
> **English: Writing**
> You could complete this Skills builder in the form of a report. Plan your report through before you start, as this will help you to present your information in a clear manner. It is important to take care with spelling, punctuation and grammar, and to proofread your report once you have completed it.

# Understand how to work in partnership with parents to support their children's early learning

## How parents are engaged as partners in their children's early learning

From the earliest stages, it is important to start to engage parents as partners in their children's learning. Children will be part of a family and a community long before they become part of the school, and parents will know more about their child than the school can find out in a few weeks. The transition to school is one of the most important that the child will have made and parents, schools and nurseries will need to work together to ensure that it runs smoothly. Although parents and teaching staff are both experienced in the areas of children and families, their areas of knowledge are different and this should be recognised and co-ordinated so that the partnership is effective. Schools should communicate to parents the importance of working together and of what is meant by a partnership. As well as encouraging parents to help on a practical level, they can do this by seeking closer co-operation and shared goals for the benefit of the children. This can be done through offering training opportunities to parents, making time to support them in finding out about how children learn, and showing them how to carry out meaningful observations so that they can share information with teaching staff.

## Key relationship-building strategies and/or skills involved in working with parents in partnership

Before parents can become involved at a co-operative level, the school will need to have prepared some strategies to build relationships with them.

## Welcoming atmosphere for all communities

The school should feel welcoming to everyone who comes through the door. All schools should now have entry systems and visitor badges for added security, but this should not mean that parents feel that they are not welcome. The reception area should be tidy and there should be photographs, welcome notes and community notices, and other signs that visitors are welcome in school. Office staff should also be aware of the need to be friendly and open with all visitors.

## Recognising when parents need support

You may notice that there are parents in your school who need additional support which you are able to give. This may be in the form of advice or a referral, but it could also be simply that they are under pressure and need to talk to someone. Schools often have family support or liaison workers who are available to give additional advice where needed.

*Does your school make parents and children of all backgrounds feel welcome?*

### Over to you!

Find out who the family support worker is in your school. How do they find out about, make contact with and support parents who are in need of additional help?

### Functional skills

**ICT: Using ICT**
You could take some photographs around your school that show how you create a welcoming atmosphere for all communities. Sharing these with your study group is a good way of sharing ideas and good practice.

### Link

For more on this, see Unit TDA 3.1, Communication and professional relationships with children, young people and adults.

## Forming positive and respectful relationships

This means being professional and positive in your interactions with parents and respecting one another. This also shows good role models to children in their interactions with individuals from different cultures than their own.

## Involving parents as partners in their children's learning

Parents should be involved and encouraged to participate in all aspects of the school and in different ways, from help and support in classrooms to work at a governor level.

## Using formal and informal opportunities to build relationships

The school will run a variety of events throughout the year which will encourage the involvement of parents. However, parents may also run events through the school's Parent Teacher Association (PTA) or other means to involve the school, usually in fundraising activities and with the support of staff. These are all excellent ways of building relationships between the school and parents.

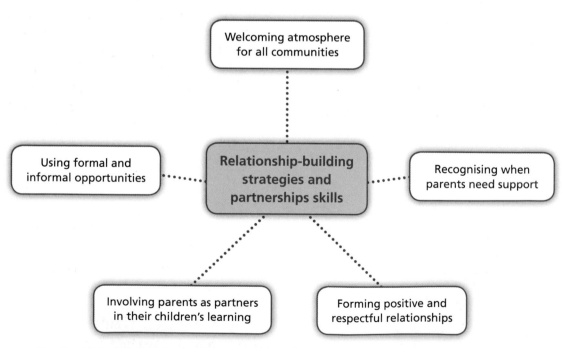

*Relationship-building strategies and partnership skills.*

> **CASE STUDY: Building relationships with parents**
>
> Alex has just started working at a new school as a learning support assistant in a Reception class. The school has asked him to come in for the evening the following week, as they always run a 'Welcome to school' social event for all new parents of children starting at the school. This is intended to encourage parents and staff to get to know one another.
>
> - How will this be supportive both to parents and staff?
> - Why is it important that Alex tries to attend the evening?

## Key communication strategies and/or skills involved in working with parents in partnership

Communication strategies for working with parents must stem from an open-door policy which welcomes communication. Whether it is the case or not, where parents perceive that the school or staff are not available or receptive to communicating with them, it is unlikely that they will be able to develop positive partnerships. These kinds of communication strategies will include the following.

### Open-door policy/welcoming atmosphere
A consistent open-door policy encourages a positive ethos of shared communication.

### Involvement of communities
Where possible, the school should try to involve and encourage community cohesion so that the school is part of the community. This may be through local events being held in the school or by developing links with local businesses or community groups. In this way, the school will feel part of the community rather than being set apart from it.

### Set times to discuss progress/staff availability
Schools will have one set opportunity each term to discuss pupil progress, but staff should also be available to parents by appointment to talk about any issues as

and when they arise. It is important that schools are able to be flexible, although staff will not always be available to speak to parents during school hours.

### Books to communicate with parents
Most secondary schools will have contact books, but for primary schools these are not always used, as parents will often speak to teaching staff at the beginning or end of the day. However, for children in younger year groups, they can be a useful way of communicating with teachers if children are being brought to school by a childminder or other adult. It may also be useful if teachers need to pass on messages. However, it will only be useful if it is checked by both sides!

### Translation services
These may be needed if there are parents with whom you need to communicate and there is no other means of doing so. You may need to work with the local authority if there is no support available in the local community.

### Being sensitive to the needs of parents
Parents of pupils who have special educational needs (SEN) are often more closely involved with the school due to the needs of their child. The **SEN Code of Practice 2001** emphasises the need for positive relationships and communication with parents, and lists a range of ways in which professionals can make communication with them more effective. Although it is more relevant to parents of children who have special educational needs, it is also worth considering from the perspective of all parents. It states that professionals should:

1. acknowledge and draw on parental knowledge and expertise in relation to their child
2. focus on the child's strengths as well as areas of additional need
3. recognise the personal and emotional investment of parents and be aware of their feelings

> **Key term**
>
> **SEN Code of Practice 2001** — document which sets out the requirements for the identification and monitoring of pupils with special educational needs

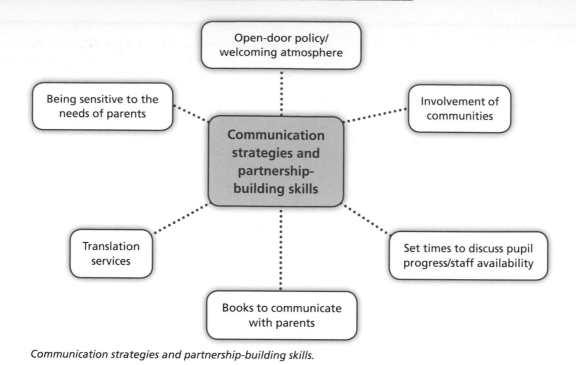

*Communication strategies and partnership-building skills.*

4. ensure that parents understand procedures, are aware of how to access support in preparing their contributions, and are given documents to be discussed well before meetings

5. respect the validity of differing perspectives and seek constructive ways of reconciling different viewpoints

6. respect the differing needs parents themselves may have, such as a disability, or communication and linguistic barriers

7. recognise the need for flexibility in the timing and structure of meetings.

*(Source: Special Educational Needs Code of Practice 2001.)*

### Functional skills

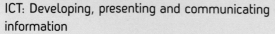

**ICT: Developing, presenting and communicating information**

You could design a booklet for parents to explain what services your school provides to include them in their child's learning. You could share this booklet with the Early Years co-ordinator, as it may be useful for prospective parents.

### CASE STUDY: Skills involved in working with parents in partnership

Diana is working in a Reception class in a small primary school. The teacher has decided to have a grandparents' afternoon in order to extend the school's positive relationships with parents and to involve grandparents, who often come to collect the children in this particular class. Diana is speaking to Ron, the grandfather of Rosanna, a pupil who does not speak to any adults in the class but who will speak to her peers. Although the teacher has tried several strategies to encourage Rosanna and has spoken to the SENCO, she is still reluctant to speak, which makes assessment of her abilities very challenging. Ron tells Diana during the conversation that Rosanna's mother was the same at this age and that she gradually improved as she grew older and gained confidence.

- Why is this information helpful to the school?
- What might Diana's next steps be?

# Strategies that can be used to build confidence in parents as their child's first educator

Some parents will lack confidence in their own abilities as their child's first educator. You may need to support and encourage them both through your own individual interactions with them and also through school-based support. Children who see parents and schools working together will feel more secure and confident about the learning process.

Parents may not have had positive experiences of school themselves, or may have found it difficult to engage with learning environments in the past. Just going towards a school building may bring back feelings of inadequacy, fear or mistrust. You may have to work with other staff to encourage and support them in their child's learning.

The kinds of strategies you might use could be:

- running education-based workshops for parents
- involving them in the settling-in process so that you are working with them right from the start
- inviting and supporting them in coming into the school to support children's learning
- building positive relationships with parents through an atmosphere of mutual support.

# Understand barriers to parents being involved in their children's early learning

## Personal, social and cultural barriers to parents being involved in their children's early learning

### Personal barriers

You may find that you come up against a range of barriers to parents being involved in their child's early learning. As already discussed, where there are issues in building relationships, this may be the case with some parents because they have not had good school experiences themselves. This can cause resentment to build up, in particular if the school does not attempt to overcome it.

### Social barriers

Social barriers may exist if a parent's own situation is difficult, stressful or means that they have very little time or opportunity to meet with early years workers to discuss their child's progress. Parents who work may not be able to come to the school themselves, or may be in a hurry if they are able to do so. They may also be single parents, refugees, travellers or others who come from minority groups within the community, or have alcohol- or drug-related issues or mental health difficulties.

### Cultural barriers

Cultural barriers may exist for various reasons. It may be that the family is from a different culture from that which is predominant in the setting or local community and that there are feelings of isolation or resentment. There may also be cultural barriers around communication — for example, the family may speak English as an additional language. They may also have different expectations about, for example, eye contact, touch, personal space, attitudes towards lateness and so on. These can cause barriers if they are not recognised by the school.

### Knowledge into action

What kinds of strategies are used in your school to build relationships with parents and to encourage them to become involved as partners?

### CASE STUDY: Barriers to parents being involved in their child's learning

Zuzana brings her daughter Laura to school each morning and leaves her at the door. She does not speak any English and although she will sometimes smile at staff, she has made no other attempt to communicate with anyone in the school or with the other parents.

- Why is it important to engage Zuzana in some way?
- Why might the barriers which Zuzana is experiencing have a detrimental effect on Laura?
- Read the strategies below. What do you think the school could do to support Zuzana and encourage her to participate in some way?

*How can you support and encourage parents in their child's learning?*

## Strategies to help overcome barriers to parental involvement in their child's early learning

When considering how to overcome barriers to parental involvement, it is important to think about the reasons for a parent's actions. These will usually be due to a breakdown or lack of communication. Misunderstandings and issues around communication will often cause resentment on the part of both parents and staff. It will be up to the school to attempt to involve parents as much as possible, and it is important to remember that any barriers will make the school experience more difficult for the child. The kinds of strategies the school might use could be:

- encouraging parents to communicate with staff in as many ways as possible and doing the same themselves

- working with parents to discuss the benefits of parent partnerships

- taking time to listen to parents as much as possible

- running workshops, open days and information mornings

- noticeboards providing information about local community groups, school documents in different languages if required, welcoming notices.

If after trying different strategies there are still some parents who are reluctant to become involved, you may need to try to talk to them individually about ways in which they can be more engaged with their child's learning and why this is important. This can be difficult if the parent does not see any need to do so. You should not do this without the involvement of other school staff, and remember to ensure that you are following school policy.

Look at the following two situations. How might you attempt to overcome the barriers and start to involve the parents in their child's early learning?

1. Steve is a single dad who cares for his twin daughters. He is in the middle of an acrimonious divorce but does not want to tell the school about it, as he feels it is a private matter. You are aware that there are some difficult issues to resolve as he always looks very stressed when he comes to school and is often on his mobile phone.

2. Charlie is a single mum who has one son who has just started in Reception. She left school at 16 and has not been in a school environment since. She does not feel comfortable coming into school and feels that her own educational background makes her very inadequate.

**Functional skills**

**English: Speaking, listening and communication**
You could complete this Portfolio activity in the form of group discussions. Plan your response to the situations so that you can present your ideas clearly and concisely to the group.

## How attitudes can be barriers to engaging parents in their children's early learning

Barriers to parental involvement may not be due just to the headings above. It is possible that parents do not see any particular reason why it is important to engage with the school. In some situations or belief systems, the child's learning is seen as the sole responsibility of the school and parents do not need to be involved. They may feel that they do not have anything further to offer their child and that the responsibility for their child's learning has now been passed to the school. Parents may say that they do not have time to hear their children read, talk to them about their day or work with them on their letter formation or sounds. In these situations it can

be difficult to engage parents and encourage them to support their child's learning.

**Reflect**

Can you think of a parent with whom you have had to work hard to engage them in their child's learning? What were the reasons for the initial barriers? How were these overcome?

## Understand how to use reflection to challenge and develop existing practice in working with parents to support their children's early learning

You should use reflection at all times when working in school, as you should be open to new ideas and suggestions from any source. This will help you to develop your practice and to continue to think of ways in which you can work more closely with parents. It is also worthwhile speaking to parents about ways in which they would like to be more involved in their child's learning and whether they feel that they are part of a partnership.

## Culturally sensitive ways of working with parents to help them provide appropriate support for their children's early learning

If, as in most schools, you are working with parents from different cultures and backgrounds, some of whom may speak English as an additional language, you will need to consider different ways of engaging with them. As already discussed, it is possible that there will be some cultural barriers to their involvement which you will need to work on with other staff or parents in order to overcome. Most schools are now multicultural and this in itself is very positive, as it is a clearer representation of society and encourages children to recognise and understand diversity. However, there may also be cultural issues around which you will need to show sensitivity. Some of these might be as follows.

## The need to communicate with parents in their home language

This may be an issue if there is a small number of parents from a particular community or who speak a different language from the majority. In these situations, it can be easy for parents and their children to become more isolated from others in the school. You may find that there are others in the community who are part of the school who speak both languages and who are able to help or that extended families can provide communication networks if needed. Whether there are small or large groups of parents from a particular community, it is important to be able to find ways to ask them about their needs and ways in which they feel they can work to benefit their children.

## Communication differences

Parents may not fit the school's ideal or expectation about the way in which they communicate with others, as already discussed. However, although cultural variations may mean that communication is different, this should not prevent schools from finding other ways to work with parents to support their children.

If there are cultural differences which make it difficult to engage parents, your school may need to seek advice or resources from local authority support teachers, such as those for traveller support or who speak English as an additional language.

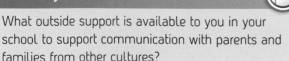

**Over to you!**

What outside support is available to you in your school to support communication with parents and families from other cultures?

## Ways of working with parents to help them provide appropriate support for their children's early learning

You will need to be able to work collaboratively with parents so that they are able to support their child's learning appropriately. Collaboration should start from the earliest stages, through home visits, information from school to home and vice versa, and clear communication about the expectations of each party. It should be easy for parents to send messages and communicate with the school, whether this is done through contact books, emails or telephone calls. The school should continue to reflect on what they are doing to involve parents, and should ask parents about their own needs so that the support offered by the school is appropriate. If parents are to be seen as members of the team and are to be involved in their children's learning through the school, the partnership between home and school should be reciprocal and there should be a balance to the relationship.

**BEST PRACTICE CHECKLIST:** Involving parents in children's learning

- Listen to parents with respect.
- Respect their views about children and their learning.
- Involve parents in their child's experiences.
- Use their areas of expertise and experience — for example, music, dance, cultural events.
- Ensure all interactions between adults and children are positive and consistent.
- Create opportunities to involve parents as partners in their child's learning in different ways.
- Demonstrate empathy and confidentiality when communicating with parents.
- Create both formal and informal opportunities to exchange information with parents.

## Support and changes needed to improve your skills and knowledge and build on your practice

You will need to consider any additional support you may need to improve your own skills and knowledge when working with parents, so that you can build on your practice. This may be through:

- carrying out further reading and reflection
- raising your profile in working with parents
- speaking to others both in your school and in other settings
- undertaking additional training.

Some of these activities may lead you to consider challenging existing practice in your school or in the way in which it develops relationships with parents. You should think about how you will manage any such situations which arise.

**CASE STUDY:** Challenging and developing existing practice

Sue has recently come to Terry's school from working in a private nursery and will be working in both the Nursery and Reception classes. She has completed her Early Years Professional (EYP) status, which means that she has been assessed against a set of standards showing her competence in early years practice. After she has been in post for two months, there is an early years meeting at which Sue starts to speak about some of the ways in which parents were engaged with children's learning at her nursery, and in particular how they worked with some of the 'hard-to-reach' parents. Some of her suggestions sound very helpful, but the early years manager does not seem to be interested.

- What could Terry do in this situation?
- Why is it important to consider the ideas of others?

## Getting ready for assessment

In order to present evidence for this unit, you will need to gather a range of material for your portfolio to show how you know and understand the importance of positive parental partnerships.

1.  Gather together any school documents, letters or emails, especially if you have written or received them yourself, to show how parents and the school communicate with one another in writing. Add to this by writing a reflective account to show how they are encouraged to communicate with the school verbally on both a formal and informal basis, and the opportunities for doing this.

2.  Show how your school encourages parents to volunteer in the school – for example, through hearing children read, helping on trips and supporting their children's learning in other ways.

3.  Consider whether there have been any difficulties in your own school's attempts to engage with parents. Why has this been the case? What else could your school do to support parents and families in engaging in their child's learning?

## Check your knowledge

1.  What are the key research findings into the importance of parental involvement in their children's learning?

2.  Why is the home environment so important in supporting early learning?

3.  What will be the benefits of engaging parents, and fathers in particular, in their child's learning?

4.  What kinds of strategies might you use to develop relationships with parents?

5.  How might you support the development of parents' confidence as their child's first educator?

6.  What kinds of barriers might exist to the involvement of parents? Give examples of how children may be affected.

7.  What sorts of cultural issues might exist when working with parents?

8.  How can you ensure that you continue to develop your practice when working with parents?

### Websites and references

www.education.gov.uk/everychildmatters/publication – search 'EPPE final report 1997–2004'
www.education.gov.uk/research/data/uploadfiles/DCSF-RR194.pdf – Parental Opinion survey 2009

*   *The Impact of Parental Involvement in Children's Education* (DCSF)
*   Parents' involvement in their children's learning and schools (Policy Discussion Paper, Jenny Reynolds)
*   Jones, C. and Pound, L. (2008), *Leadership and Management in the Early Years*, Open University Press
*   Rodd, Jillian (2006) *Leadership in Early Childhood*, Open University Press
*   Whalley, Mary (2008) *Leading Practice in Early Years Settings*, Learning Matters

# ASDAN TW3 Team working

Teams in primary schools comprise different groups of people who work together in order to achieve shared objectives for supporting individuals or groups of pupils, as well as the whole-school team. You will need to be able to contribute to the effectiveness of the team and work alongside others for the benefit of pupils. You will need to show that you can recognise and respond to issues impacting team effectiveness.

## By the end of this unit you will:

1. plan collaborative work with others
2. seek to develop co-operative ways of working and check progress towards agreed objectives
3. review work with others and agree ways of improving collaborative work in the future.

# Plan collaborative work with others

## What makes groups or teams effective in the workplace

You may belong to a number of different **teams** within your school. Whether these are year group, subject, class or school based, you will need to understand your role within that team and how it fits in with that of others.

> ### Key term
>
>
>
> **Team** — people with whom you work on a long-, medium-, or short-term basis, relating to the support provided for a specific pupil or group of pupils

To understand what makes a team effective in the workplace, it is important to look at a number of factors.

- **Communicate regularly** — a team cannot be effective unless there are regular opportunities for discussion, whether these are formal or informal. It is vital for teams to get together to ensure that they have all the information they need and that all members are able to contribute their ideas.

- **Share roles** — the roles of different team members should complement one another so that there is a balance of responsibilities.

- **Have a sense of common purpose** — the key part of working in a team is that you will be working with others towards a common objective. This means that in order to be effective, you will all need to have a shared vision about what you want to achieve.

- **Have equal levels of commitment** — all members of the team should be well motivated and have equal levels of commitment. They should also be open to change and never become complacent about what they are doing.

- **Members work for the team rather than for themselves** — the needs of the group should be more important than the needs of each individual. They will also be accountable for the outcomes as a team rather than as individuals.

- **Members are open about facing and resolving issues** — it is important that the team is able to discuss and debate any issues which arise in the course of the work of the team, so that different ideas can be aired.

- **All members of the team are valued and respected** — the team should be able to consider the ideas and opinions of all members and not gossip or show disrespect in other ways.

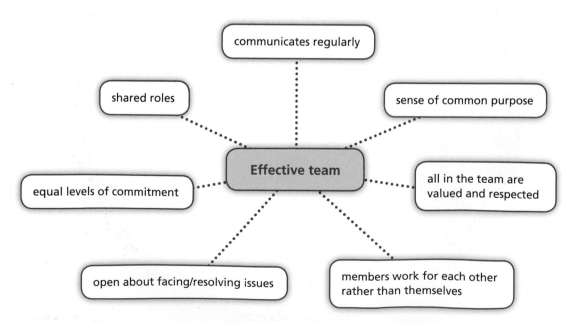

*Characteristics of an effective team.*

## Skills builder

Consider your team under each of the points above. Would you say that it is effective? Can you use this information?

## Functional skills

### ICT: Developing, presenting and communicating information

You could set up email groups with your team members in order to create another opportunity for communicating. This is especially effective if not all members of your team work the same hours.

## CASE STUDY: Team communication

Jan is a teaching assistant who works within a team of six other people in Year 3; the team includes teachers, assistants and other support staff. The team works well and has been together for some years, including going through a successful Ofsted inspection. The team members have always met regularly to plan together and discuss any issues. The year group leader has recently left and there is a new teacher leading the team who says that it is not necessary for them all to meet as there is not enough time in the school day, and it will be enough for the teachers to get together and then pass information on to others.

- What do you think about this arrangement?
- What might be a better idea?

*Members of teams should have regular opportunities to meet together and agree realistic objectives.*

# Realistic objectives for working together and what needs to be done to achieve them

Although there will be different members of your team with various responsibilities, as a team member you should be invited to contribute to the overall group process and may do this in different ways. Your class teacher or line manager should be the person to whom you report in order to agree your responsibilities, and these should be part of your job description. It is important that this job description is up to date, so that you can be sure that you are fulfilling your role and be clear where you fit in as part of your team.

As a team member, you will get to know those with whom you work quite well. You should make sure that you are able to strike a balance between being professional and also being open and friendly with other members of your team. You may work with different groups or teams in school on a short-, medium- or long-term basis. Although your role may be the same within each, these different teams will be focusing on different areas within the school. These may be:

- **supporting a named child** — assistants who work with individual children may work alongside others such as the SENCO, or other professionals who come into the school to support a child who has special educational needs (see TDA 3.1, Communication and professional relationships with children, young people and adults, for the types of professionals who may come in to schools)

- **within a specific class** — assistants will work with the class teacher but there may also be other adults or assistants within the class who work together. You should plan and discuss learning activities alongside teachers or at least have access to plans so that you have a clear understanding of what you are expected to do

within the class on a weekly and daily basis. Plans should show the roles of other adults as well as learning intentions and whether activities are whole class, group or individual (for more on planning with teachers, see page 191)

- **within a year group** — the school may be large and have three or four classes within a year group. Year groups may work very closely together and support one another in planning and moderating children's work

- **within the school** — all members of staff within a school are part of a team and will support one another. For example, the maths co-ordinator will be able to offer help and advice to any member of staff on any maths activities.

Sometimes you may find that you are part of a team which is only together for a short time — for example, if you are on a working party to organise a Christmas production or a summer fair. In this situation it is also important for someone to take charge and ensure that different members of the team are able to work efficiently and cohesively together.

# Share relevant information to help agree roles and responsibilities

In each of these situations, members of the team will need to understand their role and how it fits in with the roles of other members of the team. The most important part of any role within a team is communicating effectively with others. There should be clear and consistent methods of communication so that all members of the team feel that their opinions are valued. As part of this process you should attend regular meetings that give you a clear idea of how what you are doing fits in to the school or team as a whole. If you have a team leader, they should identify action points in any meetings you attend and give a timescale in which they will need to be carried out.

## Agree suitable working arrangements with other team members

Although you may be aware of one another's roles in your team and are able to work effectively together, it is also important to be flexible and able to support others in different ways. While you are in school you need to focus on your role, but there may be times when you need to come to an agreement about how your arrangements fit together as individuals in a broader context. This is because at any one time, members of the team may have issues of their own which may impact on their work. If you notice that a colleague is not their normal self, for example, it may be appropriate for you to offer them support in order to acknowledge this. Support staff may work in a range of school situations and you may not know what pressures they are under as part of their job. Many members of the team will have families and all will have another life outside school which at different times may have an impact on their ability to provide the same level of support for the school. You should be sensitive to any changes in behaviour or ability to juggle the demands of home and school, or to cope with what they have been asked to do at work.

### CASE STUDY: Supporting team members

Mandy is on playground duty, which is shared between all the assistants in the school on a rota system. As staff are not allowed on the playground with coffee for health and safety reasons, they are on duty for ten minutes and are then relieved by another member of staff for the second ten minutes. Mandy has just worked the whole playtime and has not had a coffee because Romena has not come out to take over. After looking for Romena, she goes straight to see the Deputy Head as she has had a long morning and this is the second time Romena has not been where she should that week. The Deputy tells Mandy that Romena's son has been in hospital and that she has been very worried about him and is preoccupied due to an operation which he is due to have that week.

- What might have been an alternative approach?
- How could the situation be resolved if Romena was unable to fulfil her duties for the time being?

## Seek to develop co-operative ways of working and check progress towards agreed objectives

### Organise and carry out tasks efficiently to meet responsibilities

As a team member in school, there may be very little time for you to carry out tasks, so it is important for you to be able to organise your time efficiently in order to meet the demands of your role. Different individuals will organise their time in different ways, but lists and reminders can help you to keep track of your responsibilities, or you can diarise deadlines and dates which are important so that you can prioritise your time. It may be that you also have individual professional targets to meet as part of your performance management (see page 125), but these should be tied in with what you are doing on a daily basis, rather than 'extra' tasks. As part of your team, you should always be supportive to others and try to balance responsibilities so that individuals do not have more to do than their colleagues.

*It is important to be sensitive to the needs and feelings of others in the team.*

### Knowledge into action

Consider the different ways in which you organise your time in order to carry out tasks efficiently as part of your role. How do you balance tasks as part of your individual role and those you carry out as part of a team?

## Seek effective ways to work co-operatively, including ways to resolve conflict

In order for individuals to work co-operatively, it is important for members to have good interpersonal skills. These are sometimes the most difficult skills to have, as within any team there will be a number of personalities. Individuals will need to have the skills to relate to one another well and be sympathetic, supportive and helpful. Members of the team should be sensitive to the needs and feelings

of others, and encourage those who they know are finding work challenging or difficult. This may be due to other issues which they have to deal with outside school.

There may be a combination of factors which makes it difficult for individuals to focus and tackle problems in the work environment. This may mean reading others' body language at times or realising that now may not be a good time to approach another member of the team with a problem. There may also be a member of the team who is much more of a speaker than a listener. This can be a problem if the person does not give others the chance to have their say.

### Valuing the expertise of team members

You should remember that all members of the team are equally important, and that your expertise and that of your colleagues is unique to each person's experience. If you are experienced or approachable, you may find that others come to you for help or advice. You should always think about your role and theirs within the team when doing this, while remaining supportive. Where you do not feel that it is appropriate for you to deal with a particular issue, you may need to refer to someone else within the team. You must remain non-judgemental about others and not allow your own opinions to intrude or cloud any decisions you may have to make. You may also find that you have an area of expertise which may be helpful to others, and in this situation you should offer it.

If you are working in a team, you should always respect the opinions and knowledge which others bring. In order to have a good working relationship with them you will need to show that you consider their opinions and experience. Bad feeling can quickly cause problems and unrest within teams.

---

**CASE STUDY:** Respecting others in the team

You are part of a large primary school which holds weekly or fortnightly meetings for all teaching assistants as required. This week, two of the teaching assistants who work in Year 5 are speaking to the group about some of the strategies they have been using with their classes to manage playground behaviour following a course they have attended. Some of the teaching assistants are speaking over what the two are saying, and are clearly not listening.

- Why is it important that schools give all staff opportunities to feed back to colleagues following development opportunities?
- Give two reasons why all staff should be attentive in this situation.

---

## Resolving conflict

However well your team works together, it is likely that at some stage there will be an **issue** or problem within it. This will need to be resolved before the team can move on and continue to progress.

---

**Key term**

**Issue** – situation or circumstance that hinders or prevents effective team performance

---

Examples of the type of issues that may arise when working with colleagues are:

- poor co-operation between members of the team
- interpersonal conflicts between members of the team.

There may be a number of reasons for this, among them:

- misinformation or incomplete information given to all team members
- resistance to change
- pressure to conform to a team decision which does not take account of individual preferences
- dominance of some team members, leading to inequality during decision making
- inability of individuals to accept feedback
- interpersonal conflict
- unproductive levels of competition.

As part of a team, you should remember that you will always get along with some personalities more than others, but this should not mean that you cannot relate in some way to all members of your team, as you will have a common purpose. Also in the course of your work you may find that work or home pressures may affect the way in which team members relate to one another. It is important to try to minimise conflict so that bad feeling and resentment do not build up over time. In order to do this, you should try to resolve any issues as soon as possible through the appropriate channels. Communication is the most important factor, as many conflicts arise due to either misunderstandings or lack of time to discuss what is happening. If you find that another member of your team appears to be making your work more difficult due to their attitude or opinions, you will need to either try to resolve the situation or refer the issue to a senior member of staff.

You should be familiar with your school's policy for dealing with difficulties in working relationships and practices. This is usually known as the grievance policy. The policy will give you information and details about how to approach any problems you may face when working with others. As an example, most policies will advise a set way of dealing with issues as they arise. There should be separate guidelines for individuals wishing to raise a grievance and for collective disputes.

# GRIEVANCE POLICY

**Informal procedure** (recommended course of action)

1) Speak directly and confidentially to the person or persons with whom you have a grievance. If agreement is not reached the issue should be taken directly to the Head Teacher. If the grievance is with the Head Teacher take the issue to the chair of governors.

2) The Head Teacher or chair of governors will act as mediator and encourage both parties to resolve the issue as soon as possible and to avoid using the more formal procedure. Parties may be represented by a trade union representative or colleague if required. If the issue is not resolved within seven days of the grievance being raised, it should progress to the next level, i.e. the formal stage.

3) A record of the mediation meeting and any agreed actions by both or either party should be kept on file so that it can be referred to if required.

**Formal procedure**

1) If the informal procedure does not resolve the issue or it has not been resolved to the satisfaction of both parties, a letter should be sent to the Clerk to the Governors outlining progress so far. This should then be addressed by the grievance sub-committee of the governing body.

2) A meeting will be called between all parties by the grievance sub-committee and each person given the opportunity to put forward their side. There will be opportunities for questioning and responses by all.

3) If there is still no resolution, the matter may be passed to the Director of Education of the local authority and/or the unions.

*A school's grievance policy.*

## BEST PRACTICE CHECKLIST: Working in teams

- Be considerate and respectful towards others within your team.
- Carry out your duties well and cheerfully.
- Do not gossip or talk about other people in your team.
- Make sure you discuss any problems as they arise.
- Speak to the appropriate team member if you need help.
- Prepare for and contribute to meetings.
- Acknowledge the support and ideas of other team members.

## Portfolio activity

Reflect on an issue or problem which you have encountered when working in a team. You may wish to have a professional discussion with your assessor about how you resolved the problem, so that they can record it for your portfolio. Alternatively you can write a reflective account to show how you have dealt with any issues which have arisen. If you write it up, be careful how you do this if your portfolio is likely to be seen by others in your team.

There will also be school policies relating to areas such as confidentiality and all members of teams should be aware of issues surrounding the exchange of information. You should be aware of whom you need to speak to on a professional level if you find that there are problems within your team or group which are affecting your work.

## Share accurate information on progress and agree changes to achieve objectives

As part of your role within your team, you will need to feed back in an accurate way on your progress to other team members. This may be done during a team meeting or more informally. You should be able to discuss progress frankly with other members of your team so that any concerns can be addressed and so that all members of the team are up to date with what is happening. It will also be helpful to have others' input and ideas to support your role, as you

may find that they are able to offer fresh ideas and insights. You may then need to amend your plans to integrate the ideas of other members of your team.

---

**CASE STUDY:** Developing timetables

Anna works as a higher level teaching assistant (HLTA) and support staff team leader in a special school. As part of her continuing professional development, she has been working on finding new ways of developing the timetables for individual support assistants so that the children are supported more effectively. Although she has started to do this, the task has been made increasingly difficult due to the variations in start time of the support staff in the mornings.

- What could Anna do in this situation?
- How could other members of her team support her in what she is doing?

*It is useful to discuss approaches you have used with others.*

# Review work with others and agree ways of improving collaborative work in the future

## Provide a detailed account of what went well and less well from own point of view

When you are working in a team, it is important to have opportunities to share and discuss in detail various approaches which you have used and also to listen to the ideas of others. It is likely that you will have opportunities to do this with other members of your team, both formally and informally, on a regular basis. This may be because the outcome has not gone as well as the team had expected, but it also may be that things have gone particularly well and you need to identify why so that it can be repeated in the future. There will be benefits to members of the team who are less experienced and also to those who may have more fixed ideas about how they approach things.

### Formal approach

This will usually be directly through meetings, INSET (In-Service Education and Training) or other training, when you may be invited to discuss strategies and ideas. This will be useful as it will enable you to ensure that you are following school policy in your own practice and will give you the opportunity to raise any concerns. You may also be able to listen to those who may have used similar approaches, so that you can discuss what has worked or been less effective.

### Informal approach

If you have good communication skills, it is also likely that you will be talking to other members of your team about how you approach your role on an informal basis. This is valuable as it gives you the opportunity to share different aspects of your role and may give you another perspective on issues or concerns as soon as they arise. Others may also be able to suggest alternative sources of information or help.

You may have opportunities to share ideas with others who are not directly involved in your own team but have similar experiences and are able to share these, for example, other support staff in school **cluster groups** or **collaboratives**.

> ### Key term
>
>
>
> **Cluster group/collaborative** — group of individuals from different schools who come together to share ideas and experiences

> ### CASE STUDY: Sharing strategies
>
> Davy has just spent his break talking to Pat, another assistant who works in the juniors, about a child she is supporting. She has just had a difficult session with him and over coffee talks about the kinds of problems which are coming up. Davy knows the child well as he worked in his class in Year 2. During the course of the discussion, Davy is able to talk to Pat about the kinds of strategies which he used with him which she may find useful.
>
> - In what ways will this informal chat be useful?
> - How else might Davy help Pat in the long term?

## Identify factors influencing the outcome of working with others, including own role

When considering the outcome of working with others, you will need to think first about the kinds of factors which will affect their work within the team.

### How information is given to them

Everyone in your team will work slightly differently and it may take some time for you to become used to different styles and preferences held by other people. You should be aware that their learning styles may be such that they find it easiest to absorb information in a particular way — for example, if you tell them something verbally, they may find it hard to remember. Others may ask for informal reminders, and some may complete what they need to do straight away if they are able to or if they are more methodical.

## Personalities within the team

Different personality types may find working in teams difficult and take some time to adapt. This may be because they are used to working on their own. They may be quieter personalities and feel uncomfortable speaking out in a group, or be returning to the workplace after a break and feel less confident. Individuals in any team will have a range of interactive styles. This means that they will have different personalities and may approach things in their own ways, which will usually be a strength but may sometimes cause problems!

There are a number of personality types which are referred to in the work of Isabel Myers and based on the theories of Carl Jung. These form the basis of the Myers-Briggs Type Indicator® (MBTI®) identity test, which is often referred to and used in business training to encourage managers to think about how they relate to their teams. These 16 personality types will all have their own strengths and areas to focus on, and none of these are 'right' or 'wrong'.

### Over to you!

Have a look at www.personalitypathways.com/type_inventory.html and see whether you can find out your personality type using the test. Although you are not working in this context, it is interesting to consider how your own personality will affect the way in which you relate to others and the success or challenges within your team.

### Reflect

Consider the different teams you belong to, whether at work or to do with leisure activities, family, college and so on. How do the different personalities in each context affect team dynamics?

## Stage in team development

Research surrounding the effectiveness of teams shows that they will pass through certain stages before they can operate effectively. One of the most succinct definitions has been reached by Tuckman (1965) and others, who believed that all groups need to go through a process of maturing before they are able to function efficiently, due to the different personalities within them. The process has been divided into four stages: forming, storming, norming and performing.

- At the **forming** stage, members of the team are just starting to get together and a leader emerges. Members of the group will need to have a clear sense of identity and purpose.

- When **storming**, members will start to view themselves as more of a team and will have reached an understanding of what is expected of them. There may be a challenge to the leader during this stage. Individuals will need to have clear roles and opportunities for participation within the group.

- **Norming** defines the stage at which the team organises itself into work groups and starts to develop different areas of activity. At this stage, the group will need to establish a culture around shared norms and values that they all agree on.

- **Performing** is the ideal state to which all teams aspire. The group is comfortable with one another and work effectively together.

These four stages may not have clear boundaries and teams may sometimes become 'stuck' at a particular stage, or go backwards and not develop fully. John O'Sullivan (2003) in his *Manager's Handbook*, describes a fifth phase of development, the 'transforming' stage, where the team continues to develop and improve. However, Harpley and Roberts (2006) describe the 'dorming' phase, when the team may fall into a state of complacency about its achievements and does not continue to move forward. This is usually avoided through consistent communication and planning.

## Level of support from other members of the team

As you get to know them, you may find out that others in your team have strengths or weaknesses in a particular area, or work better if particular support is given to them or if they are able to support others. This may need to be accommodated in different ways within the team.

### Level of experience

Different members of the team may or may not have experience of various situations in school. This may influence the outcome of their work with others.

### Clear purpose to what they are doing

Members of the team will need to be clear on the purpose of what they are doing. If they are motivated and enthusiastic about their targets, they are more likely to carry out their roles effectively.

## Identify ways of improving own work with others

In education, we are always encouraged to reflect on our work and to consider ways in which we can improve. Even if things are going well, it is useful to think about ways in which we can improve our approach or our methods. We can do this by:

- **asking others for feedback on our work.** Your school may or may not have performance management or appraisals for support staff. However, it is still worthwhile for you to ask your line manager periodically or those with whom you work for some feedback on your progress, particularly if you have limited experience

- **making sure we regularly reflect on what we are doing.** If you find that you have been working with others but it has not been successful, it will be useful for you to reflect on what happened and to consider ways in which you might have handled it differently if you were to approach it again. You may find it helpful to discuss what happened with a more experienced member of staff so that they can put forward ideas and suggestions of their own

- **attending regular training and keeping up to date with current practice.** You should have regular opportunities to attend training and INSET to keep you up to date. This will also give you the chance to discuss how you approach different situations in school and to find ways to improve

- **respecting and valuing the contribution of others.** When working with others, you will need to make sure you listen to them and take on board what they are saying. This is important – often people do not really hear others' views because they are too busy thinking about their own or are too eager to put their ideas across. You should remember that all contributions are important and valid.

### Knowledge into action

Consider the different ways in which you seek to find ways of improving your work with others. How does this make a difference to your practice?

## Getting ready for assessment

In order to gather evidence for this unit, you need to show how you support other members of your team and also how you deal with any issues that have arisen. Your assessor may be able to observe you in a team meeting. You will also need to have a professional discussion or write a reflective account to show how you have dealt with any issues that have arisen within your team. If you write an account, be careful how you do this if your portfolio is likely to be seen by others in your team.

### Websites and references

**www.humanmetrics.com** – this site enables you to take a test to discover your personality type

**www.myersbriggs.org/my-mbti-personality-type/mbti-basics** – more about Myers-Briggs test

**www.personalitypathways.com/type_inventory.html** – another site that allows you to take a test to discover your Myers-Briggs personality types

Harpley A. and Roberts A. (2006) *You Can Survive Your Early Years OFSTED Inspection*, Leamington Spa: Scholastic

O'Sullivan J. (2003) *Manager's Handbook*, Leamington Spa: Scholastic

## Check your knowledge

1. What different 'teams' might you belong to in a primary school?

2. How does being in a team support your work in school?

3. Give three examples of problems which may exist within a team.

4. Why is it important to be receptive to the views and ideas of others within your team?

5. Where in your school would you find information on how to deal with any difficulties you may have within your team?

6. What are the stages of team development sometimes known as?

7. How might you go about seeking to improve your work within your team?

# School life

## My story Jason

I work in Year 6, and am a learning mentor and basketball coach in my school. I work mainly with a group of boys who can find it hard to focus on school work – a lot of the time there are issues in their home lives and on the playground, which mean that they find some aspects of school irrelevant to them. The group was becoming quite disillusioned with school a year ago and behaviour was poor. I was quite concerned, so spoke to my line manager and other members of my team about how we could support pupils in other ways. I have worked closely with my team to set up the basketball team and coaching sessions, which have been really effective, and there has definitely been a renewed enthusiasm for school. My colleague also runs an ICT/music group with some of them, which has developed their collaboration skills in other ways and has developed their self-esteem – they are performing at the end-of-year leaving concert for Year 6. It has really helped them that they have a focus in school and having different interests has developed them in so many other ways.

## Ask the expert

**Q** Can I take the initiative if I have an idea?

**A** If you have an idea which you think will benefit the children and the school, you should definitely put it forward to your line manager or Head Teacher. It is likely that they will be keen to put your ideas into practice, particularly as you work closely with pupils and will know about their interests. Always make sure you ask before you start to arrange anything though, and remember that it may impact on other members of your team.

### VIEWPOINT

If there are no meetings for teaching assistants in your school, try suggesting to other members of your team that this might be a good idea. If it is not possible, this may be because there are very few times that everyone is available, as often support staff have so many different roles in school. Find out about other ways in which you could communicate – such as through email or through having access to staff meeting minutes – so that you are able to receive information which is important.

# Glossary

## A

**Active learning** — learners are involved and interact in the learning process

**Advocacy** — putting forward a person's views on their behalf and working for the outcome that the individual wishes to achieve

**Anti-discriminatory practice** — taking positive action to counter discrimination, which involves identifying and challenging discrimination, and being positive in your practice about differences and similarities between people

**Appraisal** — a regular meeting to discuss your development progress

**Assessment for learning** — using assessment as part of teaching and learning in ways which will raise learners' achievement

**Assessment of learning** — an evaluation of what learners know, understand and can do at a particular stage

**Assessment opportunities and strategies** — the occasions, approaches and techniques used for ongoing assessment during learning activities

**Autistic spectrum** — a spectrum of psychological conditions characterised by widespread abnormalities of social interactions and communication, as well as severely restricted interests and highly repetitive behaviour

**Autonomy** — doing things in a self-governed way

## B

**Balanced approach** — taking into account child's age, needs and abilities, avoiding excessive risk taking, not being risk averse and recognising the importance of risk and challenge to a child's development

**Barriers to participation** — anything that prevents the pupil participating fully in activities and experiences offered by the setting or service

**Behaviour support plan** — plan setting out arrangements for the education of children and young people with behaviour difficulties

**Bilingual learners** — pupils who have been exposed to two or more languages, both those newly arrived and new to the language used to deliver the curriculum, and those more advanced bilingual learners who can communicate confidently but need further support in academic contexts

## C

**Challenging behaviour** — behaviour which may involve verbal or physical abuse, or behaviour which is illegal or destructive

**Cluster group/collaborative** — group of individuals from different schools who come together to share ideas and experiences

**Code of conduct** — an agreed set of rules by which all children are expected to behave

**Community cohesion** — the togetherness and bonding shown by members of a community, the 'glue' that holds a community together

**Confidential information** — information that is provided only to those who are authorised to have it, for example, your teacher, your line manager or an external agency

## D

**Differentiation** — planning teaching and learning activities so that pupils of different abilities will have access to them

**Disabled** — the Disability Discrimination Act (DDA) defines a disabled person as someone who has a physical or mental impairment that has a substantial and long-term adverse effect on their ability to carry out normal day-to-day activities

**Dyscalculia** — a learning disability or difficulty involving innate difficulty in learning or comprehending mathematics

**Dyspraxia** — a brain condition causing co-ordination problems, poor concentration and poor memory

## E

**Early years education** — education for children up to the age of 5 in nurseries and reception classes

**Equality of access** — ensuring that discriminatory barriers to access are removed and allowing for children and young people's individual needs

**Evaluating** — assessing how well the teaching and learning activities achieved their objectives

**Extended school provision** — extra out-of-school activities, such as breakfast and after-school clubs

**Extracurricular activities** — activities that are held outside normal school hours that can benefit the development of children and young people — for example, study support, fitness classes, drama, music, arts, volunteering and business and enterprise activities

**Extrinsic** — outer or separate from

## F

**Facilitator** — someone who supports the process of learning

**Fine motor skills** — control of the smaller muscles, such as those in the fingers — for example, holding a pencil

**Format** — the way in which results of observations are recorded and presented

## G

**Global developmental delay** — a brain disorder where an individual may struggle with, for example, speech and fine/gross motor skills

**Gross motor skills** — control of the larger muscles, typically those in the arms or legs — for example, kicking a ball

## H

**Hazard** — something that is likely to cause harm

**Holistic** — emphasising the functional relation between parts and the whole

## I

**Inappropriate behaviour** — behaviour that conflicts with the accepted values and beliefs of the school and community

**Inclusion** — a process of identifying, understanding and breaking down barriers to participation and belonging and the right for all children to participate fully in the curriculum

**Incubation period** — the length of time between initial contact with an infectious disease and the development of the first symptoms

**Individual education plan (IEP)** — targets and planned implementation strategies for pupils with special educational needs

**Intrinsic** — something natural or belonging to

**Issue** — situation or circumstance that hinders or prevents effective team performance

## K

**Kinaesthetic learner** — someone who learns best through physical experience: touching, feeling and doing

## L

**Learning objectives** — statements of intentions, what pupils are expected to do and achieve by the end of the activity

**Learning outcomes** — statements of what children will know, understand and be able to do at the end of a topic or period of study

**Literacy development** — the interrelated skills of reading, writing, speaking/talking and listening

**Literary policy** — policy relevant to literacy development is the policy for English, Welsh and/or language as appropriate to the setting

## M

**Materials** — written materials and consumables needed for the learning activity, including general classroom items, written materials and curriculum-specific materials

**Mentally and physically prepared** — when participants are able to undertake the activity without unnecessary physical or emotional stress or risk of injury

**Milestones** — measureable points in development; the term is usually used to describe stages in children's development where progress can be measured

**Mnemonics** — systems for improving and aiding the memory

**Multi-sensory approach** — activities which require children to use a range of senses — auditory, visual and kinesthetic (touch) to receive and express information

## N

**Numeracy** — a proficiency which involves confidence and competence with numbers and measures

**Numeracy skills** — covers the skills needed to use and apply mathematics including: counting and understanding number; knowing and using number facts; calculating; understanding shape; measuring; handling data

## O

**Others** — according to own role, these may be family members, colleagues within the setting or professionals external to the setting

## P

**Participation** — asking children and young people what works, what does not work and what could work better, and involving them in the design, delivery and evaluation of services, on an ongoing basis

**Partnership working** — working with the teacher to support teaching and learning towards shared goals, for example in whole-class plenary sessions

**Passive learning** — learners do not interact or engage in the learning process

**Pattern of development** — usual rate of development (usual time frame in which development takes place) and sequence of development (usual order in which development occurs)

**Peripatetic** — working in a succession of places, each for a short time

**Personalised learning** — maintaining a focus on individual progress, in order to maximise the capacity of all children and young people to learn, achieve and participate

**Personalised learning goals** — goals which reflect the learning objectives of activities and take account of the past achievements and current learning needs of individual learners

**Planning** — deciding with the teacher what you will do, when, how and with which pupils, to ensure that planned teaching and learning activities are implemented effectively

**Positive relationships** — relationships that benefit children and young people, and their ability to participate in and benefit from the setting

**Procedures** — steps your setting says you must follow

**Professional development** — ongoing training and professional updating

## R

**Reflective practice** — the process of thinking about and critically analysing your actions with the goal of changing and improving occupational practice

**Regression** — going backwards in terms of development to an earlier stage

**Relevant people** — those with a need and right to provide and receive information about bilingual learners as relevant to the setting

**Resilience** — the ability to withstand normal everyday disappointments, hurts and assaults to one's confidence without it affecting self-esteem

**Resources** — furniture and equipment needed to support the learning activity, including classroom furniture and curriculum-specific equipment, such as computers for IT or apparatus for science

**Restorative justice** — programme in which pupils are encouraged to consider the impact of their actions or words on others

**Review of behaviour management** — opportunities to discuss and make recommendations about behaviour, including bullying, and the effectiveness or rewards and sanctions, including class, year and school councils, class or group behaviour reviews, and whole-school policy reviews

**Risk** — the likelihood of a hazard's potential being realised

## S

**Sanctions** — penalties for disobeying rules

**School Action and School Action Plus (or Early Years Action for under 5s)** — a stepped approach which identifies the additional support requirements of the child or young person. School Action Plus is for when additional advice and guidance from outside services are required to meet children's needs

**School community** — all personnel contributing to the work of the school including pupils, teachers, support staff, volunteer helpers, parents and carers, and other professional agencies

**School improvement plan** — document which sets out priorities for the school over a four- or five-year period

**School policy** — the agreed principles and procedures for the school

**School self-evaluation** — document which looks at and evaluates the school's progress

**SEN Code of Practice** — document which sets out the requirements for the identification and monitoring of pupils with special educational needs

**Special educational needs** — children or young people who learn differently from most children or young people of the same age, and who may need extra or different help from that given to others

**Special provision** — provision which is additional to, or otherwise different from, the provision made generally for children of their age in mainstream schools in the area

**Specialist assessment** — an assessment administered and interpreted by an appropriately qualified professional to explore specific needs, often in detail, for example, on proficiency in the first language, special educational needs, or a health or care assessment

**Standards** — statements about how tasks should be carried out and the minimum acceptable quality of practice that should be delivered

**Statement of special educational need** — a statement which contains details of a child's needs, following an assessment, and the provision which must be in place to support children with special educational needs

## T

**Target language** — the additional or second language needed by bilingual learners, for example, English as an additional language (EAL), or Welsh or Gaeilge as a second language

**Team** — people with whom you work on a long-, medium-, or short-term basis, relating to the support provided for a specific pupil or group of pupils

**Transitions** — processes of change or events when children change from one stage or state to another

## U

**Using and applying mathematics** — problem solving or pursuing a line of enquiry that involves representing ideas using numbers, symbols or diagrams, reasoning and predicting and communicating results orally or in writing

## W

**Well-being** — being in physical and mental good health, resulting in a positive outlook and feelings of happiness

# Index